Intellectual Property, Cul⸱ Property and Intangible C Heritage

Intellectual Property, Cultural Property and Intangible Cultural Heritage examines various notions of property, in particular cultural property and intellectual property, their relationship to intangible cultural heritage and how these notions of property are employed in rights discourses by governments and indigenous and local communities around the world.

There is a strong historical dimension to the book's exploration of the interconnection between intellectual and cultural property, intangible cultural heritage and indigenous rights discourses. UNESCO conventions, discussions in the World Intellectual Property Organization (WIPO), the Convention on Biological Diversity and the recent emphasis on intangible cultural heritage have provided various discourses and models. The volume explores these developments, as well as recent cases of conflicts and cross-border disputes about heritage. Case studies from Asia, as well as from Europe and Australia, examine the key issues surrounding the complex relationship between intellectual and cultural property and intangible cultural heritage.

Intellectual Property, Cultural Property and Intangible Cultural Heritage will be essential reading for scholars and students engaged in the study of heritage, history, law, anthropology and cultural studies.

Christoph Antons
University of Newcastle, New South Wales, Australia
Christoph Antons is Professor of Law at the Newcastle Law School, Faculty of Business and Law, University of Newcastle, Australia. He is an Affiliated Research Fellow at the Max Planck Institute for Innovation and Competition in Munich and Senior Fellow at the Center for Development Research, University of Bonn, Germany. His latest book publication is *The Routledge Handbook of Asian Law* (2017).

William Logan
Deakin University, Geelong, Australia
William Logan is Professor Emeritus at Deakin University and fellow of the Academy of Social Sciences in Australia. He was formerly UNESCO Chair of Heritage and Urbanism at Deakin, member of the Heritage Council of Victoria and president of Australia ICOMOS. He is co-editor of the Routledge Key Issues in Cultural Heritage book series and the *Blackwell Companion to Heritage Studies*.

Key Issues in Cultural Heritage

Series Editors:
William Logan and Laurajane Smith

For more information on the series, please visit www.routledge.com/Key-Issues-in-Cultural-Heritage/book-series/KICH

Intellectual Property, Cultural Property and Intangible Cultural Heritage

Edited by Christoph Antons
and William Logan

Routledge
Taylor & Francis Group

LONDON AND NEW YORK

First published 2018
by Routledge
2 Park Square, Milton Park, Abingdon, Oxon OX14 4RN

and by Routledge
711 Third Avenue, New York, NY 10017

Routledge is an imprint of the Taylor & Francis Group, an informa business

British Library Cataloguing-in-Publication Data

A catalogue record for this book is available from the British Library

Library of Congress Cataloging-in-Publication Data
A catalog record for this book has been requested

ISBN: 978-1-138-79361-3 (hbk)
ISBN: 978-1-138-79362-0 (pbk)
ISBN: 978-1-315-71428-8 (ebk)

Typeset in Times New Roman
by Apex CoVantage, LLC

Printed and bound by CPI Group (UK) Ltd, Croydon, CR0 4YY

Contents

Figures

Series general co-editors' foreword

The interdisciplinary field of heritage studies is now well established in many parts of the world. It differs from earlier scholarly and professional activities that focused narrowly on the architectural or archaeological preservation of monuments and sites. Such activities remain important, especially as modernisation and globalisation lead to new developments that threaten natural environments, archaeological sites, traditional buildings and arts and crafts. But they are subsumed within the new field that sees 'heritage' as a social and political construct encompassing all those places, artefacts and cultural expressions inherited from the past which, because they are seen to reflect and validate our identity as nations, communities, families and even individuals, are worthy of some form of respect and protection.

Heritage results from a selection process, often government initiated and supported by official regulation; it is not the same as history, although this, too, has its own elements of selectivity. Heritage can be used in positive ways to give a sense of community to disparate groups and individuals or to create jobs on the basis of cultural tourism. It can be actively used by governments and communities to foster respect for cultural and social diversity and to challenge prejudice and misrecognition. But it can also be used by governments in less benign ways, to reshape public attitudes in line with undemocratic political agendas or even to rally people against their neighbours in civil and international wars, ethnic cleansing and genocide. In this way there is a real connection between heritage and human rights.

This is the time for a new and unique series of books canvassing the key issues dealt with in the new heritage studies. The series seeks to address the deficiency facing the field identified by the Smithsonian in 2005 – that it is 'vastly under-theorized'. It is time to look again at the contestation that inevitably surrounds the identification and evaluation of heritage and to find new ways to elucidate the many layers of meaning that heritage places and intangible cultural expressions have acquired. Heritage conservation and safeguarding in such circumstances can only be understood as a form of cultural politics and that this needs to be reflected in heritage practice, be that in educational institutions or in the field.

It is time, too, to recognise more fully that heritage protection does not depend alone on top-down interventions by governments or the expert actions of heritage industry professionals but must involve local communities and communities of interest. It is imperative that the values and practices of communities, together with traditional management systems, are fully understood, respected, encouraged and accommodated in management plans and policy documents if heritage resources are to be sustained into the future. Communities need to have a sense of 'ownership' of their heritage; this reaffirms their worth as a community, their ways of going about things, their 'culture'.

This series of books aims then to identify interdisciplinary debates within heritage studies and to explore how they impact on the practices not only of heritage management and conservation but also the processes of production, consumption and engagement with heritage in its many and varied forms.

William S. Logan
Laurajane Smith

Contributors

Christoph Antons
University of Newcastle, New South Wales, Australia
Christoph Antons is Professor of Law at the Newcastle Law School, Faculty of Business and Law, University of Newcastle, Australia. He is an Affiliated Research Fellow at the Max Planck Institute for Innovation and Competition in Munich and Senior Fellow at the Center for Development Research, University of Bonn, Germany. His latest book publication is *The Routledge Handbook of Asian Law* (2017).

Miranda Risang Ayu Palar
Padjajaran University, Bandung, Indonesia
Dr Miranda Risang Ayu Palar completed her undergraduate degree in the Faculty of Law, Universitas Padjajaran, Bandung, Indonesia. Under the Australian Development Scholarships, she followed a Master of Laws (LLM) program in 2002 and a Doctor of Philosophy in Laws (PhD) Program in 2004–2008 at the University of Technology Sydney. She is a law lecturer and researcher in the Intellectual Property Postgraduate Program in cooperation with the WIPO Academy at the Department of Law on Information Technology and Intellectual Property and head of the Intellectual Property Center at Universitas Padjadjaran. She is Commissioner of the National Collective Management Organization for Authors and Related Rights of Indonesia and a member of the Intellectual Property Working Group *(Gugus HKI)*, Agency of Tourism and Culture of West Java Province *(Dinas Pariwisata dan Kebudayaan Provinsi Jawa Barat)*, Indonesia.

Kathy Bowrey
University of NSW, Sydney, Australia
Kathy Bowrey is Professor in the Faculty of Law at the University of New South Wales, Sydney, Australia. Her research explores laws and practices that inform knowledge creation and the production, distribution and reception of technology and culture. She is particularly interested in the thinking about western law through the lens of critical theory and colonial history, motivated by a concern for Indigenous rights and social justice.

Jianfu Chen
La Trobe University, Melbourne, Australia
Jianfu Chen is Professor at the Law School, La Trobe University, Melbourne, Australia. Professor Chen specialises in international and comparative law, international business and trade law, human rights law, globalisation and law and Chinese law. Professor Chen has published (authored, co-authored and co-edited) more than 20 books and over 80 book chapters and journal articles. Some of his publications have been translated into French and Chinese, and some have been collected in various collections of major works.

Alexandra Denes
Chiang Mai University, Thailand
Dr Alexandra Denes is a cultural anthropologist specialising in critical heritage studies in Southeast Asia. She has published numerous academic articles based on her field research in Thailand, including research on cultural rights at the Phnom Rung Historical Park in Buriram Province and on intangible heritage among the ethnic Khmer in Surin Province. She is presently a lecturer in the Media Arts and Design Program in the Faculty of Arts at Chiang Mai University and a certified UNESCO trainer for the Intangible Heritage Convention.

Leilene Marie C. Gallardo
National Commission on Indigenous Peoples, Manila, Philippines
Leilene Marie C. Gallardo is an Associate City Prosecutor at the Department of Justice, La Union, Philippines and formerly Bureau Director on Empowerment and Human Rights of the National Commission on Indigenous Peoples (NCIP) Philippines. She has worked with both non-government organizations and government for 30 years advocating for protection of indigenous peoples collective rights. Ms Gallardo belongs to the Ibaloi tribe of a city called Baguio. As former Director for the Government Commission on Indigenous Peoples, she pioneered implementation of the Indigenous Peoples Rights Act (IPRA) especially in its early years of operationalisation on the process of domain titling and sustainable ancestral domain planning including delivery of basic services. Ms Gallardo was a 2012 presenter in the World Intellectual Property Organization (WIPO) Intergovernmental Committee on Intellectual Property and Genetic Resources, Traditional Knowledge and Folklore (IGC) and as NCIP resource person for the DENR-PAWB in the identification of Globally Important Heritage Sites (GIAHS). She is also part of the University of the Philippines National Engineering Center (UPNEC) Trainors Pool on Environment and Social Sustainability.

Nicole Graham
University of Technology, Sydney, Australia
Dr Nicole Graham, Faculty of Law, University of Technology Sydney, researches the relationship between property and the environment in law, culture and land

use practices. She is particularly interested in the role of property rights in natural resources management and environmental planning policies.

Rajeswari Kanniah
University of Newcastle, New South Wales, Australia
Rajeswari Kanniah holds a doctorate in law and has previously served as the Dean of the School of Law at two private universities in Malaysia and as a part-time Lecturer in Law at Heriot Watt University, Malaysia. She has published on intellectual property rights and consumer protection law. She is currently Conjoint Senior Lecturer, Newcastle Law School at the University of Newcastle, Australia.

Dennis S. Karjala
Arizona State University, Arizona, USA
Dennis S. Karjala was the Jack E. Brown Professor of Law at Sandra Day O'Connor College of Law at Arizona State University, where he taught from 1978 until his untimely passing in April 2017. Dr. Karjala held a Ph.D. in electrical engineering from the University of Illinois and a J.D. from the University of California (Berkeley). As well as being a prolific author, he was well known for his opposition to copyright term extension in American law.

William Logan
Deakin University, Geelong, Australia
William Logan is Professor Emeritus at Deakin University and fellow of the Academy of Social Sciences in Australia. He was formerly UNESCO Chair of Heritage and Urbanism at Deakin, member of the Heritage Council of Victoria and president of Australia ICOMOS. He is co-editor of the Routledge Key Issues in Cultural Heritage book series and the *Blackwell Companion to Heritage Studies*.

Robert K. Paterson
University of British Columbia, Vancouver, Canada
Robert K. Paterson is a Professor Emeritus at the Peter A. Allard School of Law at the University of British Columbia in Vancouver, Canada. He is a member of the bars of New Zealand and British Columbia and the editorial board of the *International Journal of Cultural Property*. His research focuses on trade in cultural property and art law. He recently co-edited the *Handbook on the Law of Cultural Heritage and International Trade* (2014).

Matthew Rimmer
Queensland University of Technology, Queensland, Australia
Dr Matthew Rimmer is a Professor in Intellectual Property and Innovation Law at the Faculty of Law at the Queensland University of Technology (QUT). He is a leader of the QUT Intellectual Property and Innovation Law research program and a member of the QUT Digital Media Research Centre (QUT DMRC), the

QUT Australian Centre for Health Law Research (QUT ACHLR) and the QUT International Law and Global Governance Research Program.

Lisa Rogers
Deakin University, Geelong, Australia
Lisa Rogers is a Ph.D. student with Deakin University, researching the international legal framework for the safeguarding of intangible cultural heritage. Lisa is employed at Heritage Victoria, a cultural heritage agency of the State Government of Victoria, Australia. Lisa has a Masters in environmental law (University of Sydney), Bachelor of Arts in town planning (Victoria University) and Post-Graduate Certificate in heritage conservation (Victoria University).

Ana Filipa Vrdoljak
University of Technology, Sydney, Australia
Dr Ana Filipa Vrdoljak is Professor, Faculty of Law, University of Technology Sydney, and Visiting Professor, Dipartimento di Giurisprudenza, Università degli Studi di Parma. She is the author of *International Law, Museums and the Return of Cultural Objects* (2006 and 2008) and editor of the forthcoming *Oxford Handbook on International Cultural Heritage Law* with Francesco Francioni, *The Cultural Dimension of Human Rights* (2013) *and International Law for Common Goods: Normative Perspectives in Human Rights, Culture and Nature* with F. Lenzerini (2014). She is a general editor, with Francesco Francioni, of the new *Oxford Commentaries on International Cultural Heritage Law* and of a book series entitled *Cultural Heritage Law and Policy* and member of the Advisory Board, *International Journal of Cultural Property*. She is secretary of the International Cultural Property Society (U.S.). She has been Fernand Braudel Senior Fellow, Marie Curie Fellow and Jean Monnet Fellow, Law Department, European University Institute, Florence, and visiting scholar at the Lauterpacht Centre for International Law, University of Cambridge and Global Law School, New York University. She holds a Doctor of Philosophy (in Law) from the University of Sydney.

Gro B. Ween
Cultural History Museum, University of Oslo
Gro B. Ween (D.Phil. 2002) is Associate Professor in Social Anthropology at the Cultural History Museum, University of Oslo, and Keeper of the Arctic and the Australian collections. Her work involves indigenous peoples in Sápmi, Nunavut and Alaska on topics such as nature practices, cultural heritage and collaborative practices in the postcolonial.

Chapter 1

Intellectual and cultural property and the safeguarding of intangible cultural heritage

Christoph Antons and William Logan

The emergence of intangible cultural heritage

Intangible cultural heritage has recently become an area of great interest for a diverse group of 'stakeholders'. Among the chief reasons for this increasing interest are the embrace of culture in more recent development strategies and the emergence of cultural and heritage tourism. The interventions of UNESCO in the intangible cultural heritage field, most notably through its 2003 *Convention on the Safeguarding of the Intangible Cultural Heritage* (the 'Intangible Heritage Convention'), has done much to generate interest both globally and within the States Parties, that is, those UNESCO Member States that have ratified or acceded to the convention. UNESCO listings become important symbols and quality markers for tourist attractions connected with natural parks and parts of cities (see the contributions in Picard and Wood 1997). The attraction of the site is often augmented by intangible cultural heritage in the form of skills, knowledge, crafts and performances of local people.

The 'wisdom' of local people has further attracted attention in the context of the fundamental re-evaluation of concepts of wilderness. Very influential in this re-evaluation were the works of environmentalists such as Darrell Posey on the Kayapó Indians of the Brazilian Amazon (Posey 2008) and similar works by anthropologists (Fairhead and Leach 2008) and ecologists (Berkes 1999). Regarding wilderness as 'managed' or 'enriched' (Dove and Carpenter 2008), such works question the dichotomy between culture and nature. As Posey puts it:

> For indigenous people, *cultural expression* extends to 'nature' and the 'environment', since both are extensions (or manifestations) of society. For many groups, nature quite frankly *is* society; or, concomitantly, society is inextricable from nature.
>
> (Posey 1998: 43)

Along with the different perception of wilderness came greater respect for forest-dwelling people previously regarded as backward. In more recent natural resource management and nature conservation programs, they have morphed into the custodians of natural resources and the environment as well as of associated knowledge. The new approach is clearly visible in the strong role of 'knowledge, innovations and practices of indigenous and local communities embodying traditional lifestyles relevant for the conservation and sustainable use of biological diversity' in Article 8(j) of the United Nations *Convention on Biological Diversity* (CBD) of 1992.

Given the importance of genetic resources and associated 'traditional knowledge' for biotechnology industries, it is not surprising that intellectual property lawyers soon began to discuss the impact of traditional knowledge and the CBD on intellectual property rights in biotechnological products and processes. Almost simultaneously with the CBD, membership in the newly founded World Trade Organization (WTO) required signing of the Agreement on Trade-Related Intellectual Property Rights (TRIPS), which extended protection via patents or *sui generis* rights to 'plants and animals other than micro-organisms, and essentially biological processes for the production of plants and animals'. The relationship between the TRIPS Agreement and the CBD became a matter for heated debates between resource-rich but technology-poor developing countries and developed countries with a strong interest in biotechnology patenting. Specialized intellectual property agencies such as the World Intellectual Property Organization (WIPO) saw 'traditional knowledge' as part of a wider heritage concept. International lawyers frequently use the term 'cultural property' in this context (Boer 2008). Increasingly, environmentalists (Posey 1998) use the terms 'cultural property' and 'intellectual property' simultaneously and interchangeably, and legal academics advocating indigenous rights (e.g. Carpenter et al. 2008–2009; 2010; Tsosie 2012) believe that 'cultural property' should extend to forms of 'intellectual property'. This raises questions about the relationship of the two legal concepts and their position towards the broader notion of intangible cultural heritage. The contributions in this volume will throw some light on these questions, approaching the problem from a variety of angles and disciplines and in various geographical contexts.

Cultural and intellectual property concepts and intangible cultural heritage in international law

The understanding of the concepts of cultural heritage and cultural property has significantly changed since the end of World War II, when the concern to repatriate looted artwork and heritage led to the conclusion of the 1954 UNESCO *Convention for Protection of Cultural Property in the Event of Armed Conflict* (the 1954 'Hague Convention') (Hoffman 2006: 11). The 'cultural property' terminology was developed further in the 1970 UNESCO *Convention on the Means of Prohibiting and Preventing the Illicit Import, Export and Transfer of Ownership of Cultural Property* (Vrdoljak 2008: 209–11; Francioni 2008: 3; Merryman 2005: 22). Although UNESCO's 1972 World Heritage Convention has been celebrated as a watershed moment in heritage protection, because it brought the previously separate spheres of cultural and natural heritage into a single normative instrument, it continued the use of the proprietarian language. Ben Boer (2008: 85–7) noted that the terms 'cultural heritage' and 'cultural property' are used interchangeably, which certainly is the case in some of Asia's developing countries, as some of the chapters in this volume show (Antons and Rogers; Ayu Palar; Gallardo). Boer believes that '[t]his usage lends itself to the cultural and natural heritage being commodified to an extent, but serves also to emphasize one of the features of the Convention, namely that cultural and natural heritage is seen as being firmly under the control of sovereign states'. This was, of course, unavoidable given that UNESCO is an inter-governmental organization whose member states are jealous of their sovereignty and concerned to give primacy to national interests. Miranda Risang Ayu Palar's discussion of relevant constitutional provisions in Indonesia, shows that this is largely the case in that country, with important production sectors controlled by the state, which is also responsible for the enhancement of 'national culture' more generally. A new draft law for the protection of traditional knowledge and traditional cultural expressions also established priority rights of the state, where 'strategic resources' are concerned, a term to be determined further by relevant legislation.

In spite of wide definitions of the material and relevant communities in the 1989 UNESCO *Recommendation on the Safeguarding of Traditional Culture and Folklore*, the Recommendation was criticized by Blake as a document designed 'with the needs of scientific research and government officials in mind' and as not meeting the aspirations of indigenous peoples (Blake 2006: 33, as quoted in Smith 2006: 107). The UNESCO 2003 Intangible Heritage Convention recognized and gave a much stronger role to 'communities, in particular indigenous communities', but it also created overlaps between the elements of intangible cultural heritage that it covers and intellectual property rights (Kanniah, this volume). These overlaps will be discussed in greater detail in what follows.

WIPO's work related to intangible cultural heritage is as old as and in its normative aspects perhaps older than that of UNESCO (Antons 2015: 454, fn. 2). 'Folklore' protection was first included on the agenda of a conference on the revision of the Berne *Convention for the Protection of Literary and Artistic Works* in 1967 (Graber 2011: 240–42). This was followed by jointly rendered assistance with UNESCO to a Tunisian Governmental Expert Committee drafting a Model Law on Copyright for developing countries that included provisions on folklore (Weiner 1987) and by UNESCO/WIPO *Model Provisions for National Laws on the Protection of Expressions of Folklore Against Illicit Exploitation and other Prejudicial Actions* drafted in 1982 and published in 1985 (UNESCO/WIPO 1985). As discussed in the chapter by Kanniah, the UN Food and Agriculture Organization (FAO) was the first to recognise the traditional knowledge of farmers in developing the concept of farmers' rights in the International Undertaking on Plant Genetic Resources of 1989, a concept which was later transferred to the 2001 International Treaty on Plant Genetic Resources for Food and Agriculture. WIPO resumed its work in the broader field of traditional knowledge/traditional cultural expressions in the late 1990s and since 2001 in the Intergovernmental Committee on Intellectual Property and Genetic Resources, Traditional Knowledge and Folklore, which has meanwhile developed drafts for an international instrument or instruments in this field (Antons 2012; 2015: 466).

Shifting concepts and contested terminology

Global efforts to protect 'heritage' focused initially on the tangible heritage of artefact collections, monuments and sites. The International Council on Museums, a global NGO comprising museums and museum professionals, was founded in 1946. It has a formal relationship with UNESCO and was until 2014 housed in UNESCO's headquarters in Paris. The previously mentioned UNESCO Hague Convention of 1954 set out the international community's responsibilities towards cultural property in time of war and civil conflict. Cultural property was defined in Article 1 as monuments of architecture, art or history, whether religious or secular; archaeological sites; groups of buildings which, as a whole, are of historical or artistic interest; works of art; manuscripts, books and other objects of artistic, historical or archaeological interest; as well as scientific collections and important collections of books or archives or of reproductions of the property defined earlier.

It also included museums, large libraries and archive depositories and refuges intended to shelter the movable cultural property in the event of armed conflict and centres containing monuments. The convention has been unable to prevent massive loss and damage to artefact collections; indeed, war, civil unrest and severe lack of resources have seen problems grow worse. The particularly parlous state of archive collections led UNESCO to establish the Memory of the World program in 1992, which aims at improving the preservation of and access to significant documentary heritage. A UNESCO convention dealing with underwater heritage was adopted in 2001.

After 1972, much of the international discourse about heritage, its nature and how best to protect it shifted to the immovable, tangible heritage of places deemed to be of World Heritage significance and the implementation of the World Heritage Convention. Key debates have concerned the meaning of authenticity, one of the hurdle requirements for inscribing places on the World Heritage List. This concept, which has often been viewed as giving primacy to original physical fabric as chief signifier of heritage value, had its origins in European conservation history and was enshrined in the *International Charter for the Conservation and Restoration of Monuments and Sites* drafted at the Second International Congress of Architects and Technicians of Historic Monuments held in Venice in 1964. This so-called Venice Charter was increasingly criticized, most notably by the Japanese, who argued that while its use may be highly appropriate for the preservation of ancient stone structures in Europe, the charter was much less relevant in dealing with timber structures that require periodic renewal, the typical situation in much of Asia. A UNESCO-ICOMOS conference in Nara, Japan, in 1994 saw the adoption of the *Nara Document on Authenticity* (Larsen 1995), which put greater emphasis on showing reverence for the traditional symbolism and function of buildings by the renewal of their physical fabric using traditional craft skills. The Nara Document represents acceptance by the global organizations that the conservation approach taken by a nation or community should be appropriate to the cultural context in which that conservation is taking place.

The Nara Document also represents a major shift away from the Eurocentric way in which heritage was understood within the World Heritage system. The global organizations and the World Heritage Committee itself were aware of the need for such a shift; indeed, the Committee introduced a 'Global Strategy for a Representative, Balanced and Credible World Heritage List' in 1994. It had already approved a new World Heritage List category of cultural landscapes in 1993, which sought to deal with the criticism coming especially from indigenous peoples that seeing natural and cultural heritage as separate categories was a Western construct and inappropriate in many non-Western cultures. Again, this brought intangible forms of cultural heritage to the fore, another step in a reform process that eventually led to the Japanese Director-General of UNESCO, Koïchiro Matsuura, introducing first the 'Masterpieces of the Oral and Intangible Heritage of Humanity' program in 2001 and second the Intangible Heritage Convention in 2003.

In fact, the intangible element had not been totally absent from the conservation of places under the World Heritage convention and in national and local systems focused on places, but it was usually seen as merely supplementary, adding to the significance of a place judged to be heritage for other reasons. The Masterpieces program and 2003 convention focused on intangible heritage as a form of heritage in its own right and not necessarily tied to a specific place or location. Rather than seeking to preserve/conserve heritage as under the 1972 convention, the Intangible Heritage Convention aims at safeguarding heritage, and it sees significance as being dependent on intergenerational transmission rather than on the notion of authenticity. When implemented by the State Parties, some variation occurs in the way safeguarding processes are implemented. For instance, in chapter 13 in this volume, Jianfu Chen notes China's divergence from the 2003 convention in several important respects – the intention to limit safeguarding to the 'fine cultural traditions of the Chinese people' (PRC 2011: Article 1) and the insistence on maintaining the authenticity of these traditions (Article 4) rather than allowing for change as the tradition passes over time from generation to generation. In his chapter William Logan indicates that objections to aspects of the 2003 convention were so strong in a number of so-called settler states where indigenous peoples are now a minority that many – Australia, Canada, New Zealand and the United States – have so far refused to ratify the convention. Outside this category, however, other states such as South Africa and the United Kingdom have also not joined the convention.

In the international debates about intangible cultural heritage, various 'epistemic communities' approach the topic from different angles and have different concerns and terminologies (Antons 2015). The cultural property terminology, for instance, has largely been abandoned in more recent UNESCO Conventions aiming at international cooperation in the field. The term 'property' was used 28 times in the 1972 *Convention concerning the Protection of the World Cultural and Natural Heritage* (the 'World Heritage Convention') and sites listed on the World Heritage List, which was established under the Convention, are referred to as 'properties.' The *Operational Guidelines for the Implementation of the World Heritage Convention* (latest version October 2016) continue to reflect the mid-20th-century emphasis on the ownership aspects of heritage. By contrast the Intangible Heritage Convention uses the word 'property' only once, in Article 3, and in relation to intellectual property, where it is made clear that nothing in the convention affects the rights and obligations of States Parties deriving from any international instrument relating to intellectual property rights or to the use of biological and ecological resources to which they are parties.

The preamble to the 2005 UNESCO *Convention on the Protection and Promotion of the Diversity of Cultural Expressions* (the 'Cultural Expressions Convention 2005') recognizes 'the importance of intellectual property rights in sustaining those involved in cultural creativity'. This convention makes no other reference to property, although the protection of intellectual property is mentioned a number of times in the European Union's declaration that accompanied its accession to the convention.

Nevertheless, the cultural property emphasis has been strongly embraced by many academics, notably in law and some anthropology units such as Regina Bendix's Cultural Property research team at the University of Göttingen in Germany. NGOs and legal academics advocating a better recognition of the specific concerns of indigenous peoples have also continued to use the cultural property notion and term (Carpenter et al. 2008–2009, 2010). Their arguments are critically examined by Dennis S. Karjala and Robert K. Paterson in their chapter in this volume. They argue that the stewardship rights advocated in such writings require justification in view of their strong impact on the default position that information, including that contained in intangible cultural heritage, is freely available and shared. Different from the limited circumstances of intellectual property rights, the authors find this justification lacking in the case of indigenous intellectual/cultural property claims. They are particularly concerned with the details of implementation of a 'stewardship model' as discussed by Carpenter et al. (2008–2009), which they think are insufficiently thought through. They express similar concerns about the New Zealand Wai 262 Report with its recommendations of empowering a Commission to impact on existing intellectual property rights and its questionable distinction between Maori controlled treasures (*taonga* works) and works derived from such treasures as well as the problematic distinction between Maori and non-Maori use of knowledge.

Such legal problems notwithstanding, the notion of cultural property is frequently used in the all-too-common situation in which indigenous heritage interests are threatened by major development projects. In Australia, for example, conservation efforts have come into conflict with powerful mining interests at Kakadu and Cape York (Logan 2013). The first of these conflicts spilled over onto the World Heritage Committee stage and threatened to weaken the World Heritage in Danger mechanism – indeed, the credibility of the whole World Heritage system.

Intangible cultural heritage, nation building and the indigenous dimension

Who, if anyone, 'owns' the heritage is a subject that has the potential to generate much heat (Brown 2003). The state has many interests in claiming ownership to and regulating heritage found within its territory. Heritage is an economic asset: like mineral resources that lie in the ground, valueless until a marketable use is identified for them, the identification of a place, artefact or practice as heritage gives them cultural value but also economic value. Much state activity aimed at ensuring the profits from exploiting heritage – or at least the taxes on those profits – remain within the state (Kanniah, in this volume). The commodification of heritage occurs *inter alia* through cultural or heritage tourism; often considered negatively in the heritage discourse, the associated job and income generation can contribute to the improvement of community standards of living. Other examples of commercialization of heritage concern the use of traditional medicinal knowledge, as discussed by Kanniah in her chapter.

Heritage is also a political asset. By controlling what is to be regarded as significant heritage, the state controls the national narrative around which its nation-building strategies are based. The protection of cultural heritage is not therefore simply a technical matter, as some in the heritage conservation field have seen it, nor even merely about management technique: it is a form of cultural politics, linked to ideological ways of seeing the world, and nearly always complex and contested (Logan 2015). Heritage is thus a political asset that, on the one hand, may be used to weld disparate ethnic and social groups into more cohesive and tolerant national entities based on human rights. On the other hand, however, forcing minority groups to adopt the dominant narrative and cultural heritage may effectively wipe out their cultural identity. At worst, heritage can be used to generate support for aggression against minorities, neighbouring states or, indeed, in far-distant war zones.

Alexandra Denes argues in her chapter in this volume that international heritage instruments are always translated and implemented by state agencies within the context of existing heritage regimes. The original intent of an international heritage instrument and its interpretation is often distorted, as her case study of Thailand's current Intangible Cultural Heritage bill shows. Rather than empowering communities and culture bearers, the bill strengthens the hand of state actors to selectively promote and represent local difference and ethnic diversity within an established hierarchy of value. The difficulty of incorporating intangible aspects of traditional customs into modern state laws is an issue that arises in many parts of the world. In Africa the intangible heritage of rituals and belief systems is ignored by the modern legal heritage state systems in both their format and implementation. The state laws in Africa, which generally originated in colonial times, are mostly antagonistic towards the intangible aspects of traditional systems as, too, are both Islam and Christianity – indeed, this intangible heritage is seen by them as threatening both society and proper heritage conservation. In another volume in the Key Issues in Cultural Heritage series – *Managing Heritage in Africa. Who Cares?* (eds. Ndoro et al. 2018), case studies from sub-Saharan Africa are used to explore ways that state laws might better reflect the local communities' view of what heritage is significant and how it should be managed. Gro B. Ween's chapter in the current volume bears on the same issue but in relation to the Sámi, the indigenous peoples who inhabit Northern Scandinavia and the Russian Kola Peninsula. Here the key concern is that the Sámi intangible heritage cannot be adequately managed when culture and nature are governed separately in state bureaucracies and legislation.

Many states today are multicultural, a fact that state heritage laws should respect by defining heritage inclusively and, in particular, respecting the heritage of minority groups. This concern especially affects states where indigenous peoples live as a minority alongside newer arrivals, but it pertains wherever racial, ethnic and other minorities exist. The concept of indigeneity is a difficult one and is even rejected by some states in World Heritage Committee sessions (Logan 2013: 165). Others, such as Indonesia and India, are basically supportive but provide their own definitions (Antons 2009). A notable case of clear recognition of indigenous peoples in Asia is the Philippines (Eder and McKenna 2004). Leilene M. C. Gallardo in her chapter discusses case studies of free prior informed-consent processes in ancestral domain areas under the country's progressive Indigenous Peoples' Rights Act. Although it recognises community intellectual property rights, Gallardo finds that the struggle over resources in many cases continues. In Gallardo's view, not just intellectual property laws but also national heritage laws differ in their basic aims and concepts from the spiritual relationship indigenous peoples have with their heritage. At a practical level, there is an imbalance of technical know-how related to the value of heritage and a lack of practical complaints mechanisms and community control over violations of rights. Kanniah in her chapter also finds a lack of participatory mechanisms for indigenous peoples in Malaysia to be represented and for self-determination in loci relevant to them.

In some Asian countries, such as Vietnam, the indigenous people are the majority, and many of the ethnic minorities, notably those living in the mountainous regions, arrived in relatively recent times. But it is the indigenous minorities in settler states who have brought the matter to the foreground of discussions at UNESCO and other global forums, notably by adopting the language of rights (ibid: 169; Logan 2012).

Clearly cultural rights were being disregarded in many states and by UNESCO itself. In 2002 Sarah Titchen, then chief of the Policy and Statutory Implementation Unit of the UNESCO World Heritage Centre in Paris, reported publicly that UNESCO knew that

> Indigenous people are not always consulted when a site on their traditional lands is nominated for World Heritage listing . . . [and that] there are situations

when Indigenous peoples have been actually physically removed from protected areas as a way of justifying inscription of an area on the World Heritage list as a place of natural importance. . . . There are also examples of Indigenous peoples being restricted from practising traditional hunting, gathering, land use and trading practices as they are said to disturb the ecological balance particularly of natural World Heritage areas.

(Titchen 2002)

Gro B. Ween's chapter on the Sámi reinforces this, showing how their salmon fisheries have been continuously restricted by the Norwegian natural resource management authorities.

As previously noted, UNESCO and the World Heritage Committee have taken some steps to give a stronger voice to indigenous groups and local communities, including making changes to the Operational Guidelines. But the lack of meaningful engagement with indigenous and local communities continues to rankle. The Mirrar people, traditional owners of the section of the Kakadu national park that was excised for uranium mining, felt that their national government was not listening and took the exceptional step of going straight to the World Heritage Committee at its 2000 session in Cairns, Australia (Logan 2013; Meskell 2013). In the foyer outside the Committee meeting, delegates from indigenous peoples from around the world met to discuss strategies, including convincing the Committee to create a World Heritage Indigenous Peoples' Committee of Experts. When that attempt failed, the centre of action shifted to the United Nations Permanent Forum on Indigenous Issues, from which has emerged a campaign to ensure that indigenous people are given 'free, prior and informed consent' (Disko 2016). Ana F. Vrdoljak in her chapter shows that, although the protection of cultural heritage in international law remains dominated by states, the indigenous people have pushed for changes in the way the texts of the heritage treaties are negotiated and implemented after being adopted. She sees the impact of these indigenous initiatives as 'transformative' and continually moving the world's understanding of cultural heritage as holistic rather than a set of silos: tangible places, intangible cultural practices, historic documents and artefact collections.

Traditional knowledge systems, customary practice and the 'mapping' of culture

The definition of intangible cultural heritage in the 2003 UNESCO Convention extends to material that is also under consideration for protection in the context of intellectual property at international negotiations at the World Intellectual Property Organization in Geneva. The definition of intangible heritage includes 'knowledge' and 'skills' and, in a list of examples, 'oral traditions and expressions', 'performing arts', 'knowledge and practices concerning nature and the universe', and 'traditional craftsmanship'. In order to avoid potential conflicts with either a future WIPO treaty or with the CBD, Article 3 of the 2003 UNESCO

Convention clarified that the rights and obligations from these treaties were not affected by the Convention.

Whether there is an overlap in the discussion is seen differently by different commentators. Some international law experts have argued that intangible cultural heritage can be distinguished from intellectual property because it relates to the entire process of creating, while intellectual property is focused on the end product (Francioni, as quoted in Aikawa-Faure 2008, 29; Lixinski 2013: 8). Others are not so sure. Forrest (2012: 363–4) believes that '[f]orms of intangible cultural heritage fall within the scope of an overlapping and multifaceted international regime' and that the overlap between intellectual property (IP) rights and intangible cultural heritage requires 'close collaboration between the two regimes in order to ensure consistency'. The overlaps, according to Forrest, must be addressed 'in a way that does not undermine either one'. WIPO itself clearly regards the system as overlapping. In its 2001 report *Intellectual Property Needs and Expectations of Traditional Knowledge Holders* (WIPO 2001), it pictured the subject matter as overlapping circles with heritage as the widest circle containing the smaller circles of traditional/indigenous knowledge and expressions of folklore, all of which became subject to the international treaty negotiations in the Intergovernmental Committee on Intellectual Property and Genetic Resources, Traditional Knowledge and Folklore ever since (Antons 2012). Miranda Risang Ayu Palar in this book shows that there is an overlap in the understanding of the concepts in Indonesia, where the economic rights of intellectual property are seen as complementing the 'safeguarding' provisions of intangible cultural heritage. Similarly, in the Philippines, as described by Leilene M. C. Gallardo in her chapter, there is an approximation of the definition of community intellectual property rights under the Indigenous Peoples Rights Act and the definition of cultural property under the country's National Cultural Heritage Act. However, while the 'rights' are similarly defined, the objects of the laws are quite different.

Broude (2015: 475) sees the ICH convention as 'a de facto soft law instrument in formal hard law clothing' but regards the concept of ICH and the legalized mechanisms of the Convention also as 'assimilated to quasi-intellectual property instruments'. Rosemary Coombe found that 'multilateral institutions and NGOs . . . encourage people to adopt a possessive and entrepreneurial attitude toward their culture'. She points to anthropological studies that show that instrumental approaches by states to preserve cultural and biological diversity are often at odds with the needs and expectations of communities (Coombe 2009: 395, 406).

Studies of the implementation of different types of heritage protection legislation in developing countries confirm this impression. Social scientists and legal academics have pointed out how nationalist interpretations of copyright and other intellectual property laws combine with the concepts of cultural property to create serious frictions among neighbouring countries (Aragon and Leach 2008; Aragon 2012; Antons 2009; 2013; Chong 2012). The chapter by Antons and Rogers shows the merging and overlapping of the intellectual property and cultural property concepts in laws and the strong role of the state in heritage claims in countries like Indonesia, Laos and the Philippines. The chapter also discusses the recent interest in the link between commercialized representations of culture and geographical space. These become visible in debates about cultural tourism (Adams 1997), in the control of genetic resources (Flitner 1998) and in intellectual property laws like collective trademarks and geographical indications used for traditional crafts and agricultural products (Aylwin and Coombe 2011; 2014). Antons and Rogers show examples of considerable conflicts based on the commercialization of space that is not necessarily in accordance with national borders and of the interchangeable and overlapping use of the intellectual and cultural property concepts. Kanniah also points to potential challenges to heritage claims in culturally pluralist Malaysia that could come especially from China, India and Indonesia. A further development in this regard is visible from the chapter by Miranda Risang Ayu Palar and concerns the enactment of provincial intellectual property laws as in the Indonesian province of West Java that aim substantially at the protection of local culture.

If geographical and spatial representations of culture are used to commercialize and derive profits from them, then the obvious question arises of how precisely the geographical space is delineated and who will be allowed to operate in that space and in claiming a link to the culture. Kathy Bowrey and Nicole Graham add a further dimension to the relatively recent discussion in socio-legal scholarship about space (see e.g. Blomley et al. 2001; Benda-Beckmann et al. 2009). Their chapter focuses on 'place' and the absence of this concept in Australian law. 'Place', as distinct from 'space', is about 'human engagement with a specific physical location', and it synthesizes the realms of the 'natural' and the 'cultural' that law tends to separate. The chapter shows that this separation and dephysicalization is a fundamental feature of property law to facilitate exchange. The effects of this lack of recognition of place are discussed with regards to the Hindmarsh Island case in South Australia and the Uluru-Kata Tjuta National Park in the Northern Territory. Although the authors see similar limitations in cultural heritage laws, they express cautious optimism with regards to the concept of 'cultural landscape', which, if developed further in jurisprudence, has the potential to open the law to Aboriginal concepts of 'place'.

Regulation of 'biocultural heritage' through international and national law

Another issue that has occupied indigenous movements and the governments of developing countries for some time is what has become known as 'bio-piracy' – that is, the taking and patenting of plant material and related traditional knowledge originating in particular parts of the world by corporations in industrialized countries without compensation and/or acknowledgement (Robinson 2010). Exchange of plant material has of course happened since the early days of mankind. During the age of imperialism, it was common for the colonial powers to collect plant material in their dependencies, and these plants became the basis of diets, botanical gardens and much scientific research in Europe (Ellen and Harris 2000: 8–11; Schiebinger 2004; Brockway 1988). Transfers of plants had significant impact on the economies of countries and the history of industrialization. The most famous case to illustrate this is Henry Wickham's unauthorized taking of rubber seeds from Brazil that ended the rubber boom of the Amazonas and became the basis for the rubber boom in British colonial Malaya (Jackson 2008).

In legal academic discourse and in diplomatic efforts in treaty negotiations, the issue began to re-surface again with the development of the biotechnology industry and the attempts to protect their inventions via patents and other forms of intellectual property rights. Rajeswari Kanniah examines these developments for the agricultural sector in Malaysia and the attempts to protect local agricultural heritage under these circumstances. It becomes clear from the chapter that much of the protective legislation is either not relevant for indigenous and local communities or that there is little indication that it has been used, indicating that it is either not practicable or that there is too little knowledge about it and too little familiarity with it among the communities concerned.

As Matthew Rimmer shows in his chapter, intangible cultural heritage and traditional knowledge in the form of traditional calendars, weather forecasting and knowledge related to food production and storage also has potential in helping with climate change adaptation. Climate change poses a severe threat to the cultural heritage of small island nations in particular. Rimmer shows the ambiguous role of intellectual property in this context. On the one hand, it is potentially locking up technologies that could help with the effects of climate change. Networking between like-minded countries as in the Alliance of Small Island States (AOSIS) is important in that regard to promote access. On the other hand, broader notions of Indigenous intellectual property rights may result in better utilization of and greater respect for alternative forms of knowledge.

Conclusion

It cannot be denied that the discussion about cultural rights has triggered many positive developments in different parts of the world and a better understanding about the nature of intangible cultural heritage and the need for its safeguarding. Nevertheless, the simultaneous policy initiatives in different international organisations, such as WIPO, UNESCO, FAO and the UNEP, confusion about basic concepts and the boundaries of intellectual and cultural property in many countries as well as the increasing commercial interest in intangible cultural heritage have also brought new points for debate. There is a rise in 'heritage nationalism' and in exclusive claims by nation states that lead to international disputes rather than the collaboration envisaged by UNESCO. Also, regional intellectual property laws that base entitlements on ethnic ties or regional affiliation are emerging in some countries, and they are likely to create headaches for national governments interested in levelling the differences between different regions and population groups (Antons 2017). In this context, it is also interesting to note that studies of UNESCO World Heritage sites in Southeast Asia have found 'indifference or even antipathy' on the part of local villagers towards the sites in cases in which 'tourism-related businesses were owned by incomers' rather than locals (Cochrane 2016: 333).

From the viewpoint of such communities, both intellectual and cultural property approaches have shortcomings. While intellectual property rights are clearly defined and enforceable at national and international levels, they often require technical expertise, their administration can be cumbersome, and they focus on the commercial rather than spiritual and cultural benefits of heritage. Cultural property, on the other hand, as a concept derived from international law, shifts the discussion to the level of the nation state, which often attempts to monopolize the heritage and use it for its own purposes of nation building and its economic development plans. Most interesting are the attempts by first nations to shift the cultural property terminology away from the exclusive use by national governments and to make it available for indigenous peoples. The 2007 UN Declaration on the Rights of Indigenous Peoples is frequently cited in this context and provides fresh support for such positions.

William Logan in his chapter shows how UNESCO's language has absorbed the changing concepts to an extent, but since organizations are captive to the structures existing within them, the structural separation within UNESCO of tangible from intangible and natural from cultural still produces heritage-speak that confuses governments, NGOs, institutions, community groups and practitioners. He highlights the structural factor that UNESCO is an intergovernmental organization, meaning that it has limited legal power vis-à-vis the States Parties in heritage and other fields. It has therefore to rely on the powers of persuasion to influence State Party heritage attitudes and activities. He concludes by outlining the potentially highly significant November 2015 decision of the General Assembly of States Parties to the World Heritage Convention to adopt a sustainable development policy. The policy defines sustainable development as embracing human rights and social justice, environmental and social sustainability and peace and security and gives legally binding status to actions by States Parties to support these principles when nominating and managing World Heritage sites.

References

Adams, K.M. (1997) 'Touting Touristic "Primadonnas": Tourism, Ethnicity and National Integration in Sulawesi, Indonesia', in M. Picard and R.E. Wood (eds), *Tourism, Ethnicity and the State in Asian and Pacific Societies*, Honolulu: University of Hawai'i Press, 160–72.

Aikawa-Faure, N. (2008) 'From the Proclamation of Masterpieces to the Convention for the Safeguarding of Intangible Cultural Heritage', in L. Smith and N. Akagawa (eds), *Intangible Heritage*, Oxon: Routledge, 13–44.

Antons, C. (2009) 'What Is "Traditional Cultural Expression"? International Definitions and Their Application in Developing Asia', *The WIPO Journal*, 1(1), 103–116.

Antons, C. (2012) 'Intellectual Property Rights in Indigenous Cultural Heritage: Basic Concepts and Continuing Controversies', in C.B. Graber, K. Kuprecht and J.C. Lai (eds), *International Trade in Indigenous Cultural Heritage: Legal and Policy Issues*, Cheltenham and Northampton, MA: Edward Elgar, 144–74.

Antons, C. (2013) 'Asian Borderlands and the Legal Protection of Traditional Knowledge and Traditional Cultural Expressions', *Modern Asian Studies*, 47, 1403–1433.

Antons, C. (2015) 'Epistemic Communities and the "of Intellectual Property Law eople without History": The Contribution of Intellectual Property Law to the "Safeguarding" of Intangible Cultural Heritage', in I. Calboli and S. Ragavan (eds), *Diversity in Intellectual Property: Identities, Interests and Intersections*, Cambridge: Cambridge University Press, 453–471.

Antons, C. (2017) 'Geographical Indications, Heritage, and Decentralization Policies: The Case of Indonesia', in I. Calboli and W.L. Ng-Loy (eds), *Geographical Indications at the Crossroads of Trade, Development, and Culture: Focus on Asia-Pacific*, Cambridge: Cambridge University Press, 485–507. https://doi.org/10.1017/9781316711002.021.

Aragon, L.V. (2012) 'Copyright Culture for the Nation? Intangible Property Nationalism and the Regional Arts of Indonesia', *International Journal of Cultural Property*, 19, 269–312.

Aragon, L.V. and Leach, J. (2008) 'Arts and Owners: Intellectual Property Law and the Politics of Scale in Indonesian Arts', *American Ethnologist*, 35(4), 607–631.

Aylwin, N. and Coombe, R.J. (2011) 'Bordering Diversity and Desire: Using Intellectual Property to Mark Place-Based Products', *Environment and Planning A*, 43, 2027–2042.

Aylwin, N. and Coombe, R.J. (2014) 'Marks Indicating Conditions of Origin in Rights-Based Sustainable Development', in P. Zumbansen and R. Buchanan (eds), *Law in Transition: Human Rights, Development and Transnational Justice*, Oxford: Hart Publishing, 97–118.

Benda-Beckmann, F. von, Benda-Beckmann, K. von and Griffiths, A.M. (2009) *Spatializing Law: An Anthropological Geography of Law in Society*, Surrey: Ashgate.

Berkes, F. (1999) *Sacred Ecology: Traditional Ecological Knowledge and Resource Management*, Philadelphia: Taylor & Francis.

Blake, J. (2006) *Commentary on the UNESCO 2003 Convention on the Safeguarding of the Intangible Cultural Heritage*, London: Institute of Art and Law.

Blomley, N., Delaney, D. and Ford, R.T. (2001) *The Legal Geographies Reader*, Oxford and Malden, MA: Blackwell Publishers.

Boer, B. (2008) 'Article 3 Identification and Delineation of World Heritage Properties', in F. Francioni (ed.), *The 1972 World Heritage Convention: A Commentary*, New York: Oxford University Press, 85–102.

Brockway, L.H. (1988) 'Plant Science and Colonial Expansion: The Botanical Chess Game', in J.R. Kloppenburg (ed.), *Seeds and Sovereignty: The Use and Control of Plant Genetic Resources*, Durham, NC and London: Duke University Press, 49–66.

Broude, T. (2015) 'A Diet Too Far? Intangible Cultural Heritage, Cultural Diversity and Culinary Practices', in I. Calboli and S. Ragavan (eds), *Diversity in Intellectual Property: Identities, Interests and Intersections*, Cambridge: Cambridge University Press, 472–493.

Brown, M.F. (2003) *Who Owns Native Culture?*, Cambridge, MA and London: Harvard University Press.

Carpenter, K.A., Katyal, S.K. and Riley, A.R. (2008–2009) 'In Defense of Property', *Yale Law Journal*, 118, 1022–1125.

Carpenter, K.A., Katyal, S.K. and Riley, A.R. (2010) 'Clarifying Cultural Property', *International Journal of Cultural Property*, 17, 581–598.

Chong, J.W. (2012) ' "Mine, Yours or Ours?" The Indonesia-Malaysia Disputes Over Shared Cultural Heritage', *SOJOURN: Journal of Social Issues in Southeast Asia*, 27(1), 1–53.

Cochrane, J. (2016) 'It's a Jungle Out There: Contestation and Conflict at Indonesia's Natural World Heritage Sites', in V.T. King (ed.), *UNESCO in Southeast Asia: World Heritage Sites in Comparative Perspectives*, Copenhagen: NIAS Press, 313–346.

Coombe, R. (2009) 'The Expanding Purview of Cultural Properties and Their Politics', *Annual Review of Law and Social Science*, 5, 393–412.

Disko, S. (2016) 'Indigenous Peoples' Rights and the World Heritage Convention', in W. Logan, M. Nic Craith and U. Kockel (eds), *A Companion to Heritage Studies*, Chichester, UK and Malden, MA: Wiley Blackwell, 355–372.

Dove, M.R. and Carpenter, C. (2008) 'Introduction: Major Historical Currents in Environmental Anthropology', in M.R. Dove and C. Carpenter (eds), *Environmental Anthropology: A Historical Reader*, Malden, MA-Oxford-Carlton: Blackwell, 1–85.

Eder, J.F. and McKenna, T.M. (2004) 'Minorities in the Philippines: Ancestral Lands and Autonomy in Theory and Practice', in C.R. Duncan (ed.), *Civilizing the Margins: Southeast Asian Government Policies for the Development of Minorities*, Ithaca, NY and London: Cornell University Press, 56–85.

Ellen, R. and Harris, H. (2000) 'Introduction', in R. Ellen, P. Parkes and A. Bicker (eds), *Indigenous Environmental Knowledge and Its Transformations: Critical Anthropological Perspectives*, London and New York: Routledge, 1–33.

Fairhead, J. and Leach, M. (2008) 'False Forest History, Complicit Social Analysis: Rethinking Some West African Environmental Narratives', in M.R. Dove and C. Carpenter (eds), *Environmental Anthropology: A Historical Reader*, Malden, MA Oxford-Carlton: Blackwell Publishing, 102–117.

Flitner, M. (1998) 'Biodiversity: Of Local Commons and Global Commodities', in M. Goldman (ed.), *Privatizing Nature: Political Struggles for the Global Commons*, London: Pluto Press, 144–166.

Forrest, C. (2012) *International Law and the Protection of Cultural Heritage*, Oxon: Routledge.

Francioni, F. (2008) 'The 1972 World Heritage Convention: An Introduction', in F. Francioni (ed.), *The 1972 World Heritage Convention: A Commentary*, New York: Oxford University Press, 3–8.

Graber, C.B. (2011) 'Institutionalization of Creativity in Traditional Societies and in International Trade Law', in S. Ghosh and R.P. Malloy (eds), *Creativity, Law and Entrepreneurship*, Cheltenham, UK and Northampton, MA: Edward Elgar, 234–63.

Hoffman, B.T. (2006) 'Exploring and Establishing Links for a Balanced Art and Cultural Heritage Policy', in B.T. Hoffman (ed.), *Art and Cultural Heritage: Law, Policy and Practice*, Cambridge: Cambridge University Press, 1–18.

Jackson, J. (2008) *The Thief at the End of the World: Rubber, Power and the Seeds of Empire*, New York: Viking.

Larsen, H.E. (ed.) (1995) *Nara Convention on Authenticity in relation to the World Heritage Convention*, November 1–6, 1994, Nara Japan, Trondheim: Tapir Publishers.

Lixinski, L. (2013) *Intangible Cultural Heritage in International Law*, Oxford: Oxford University Press.

Logan, W. (2012) 'Cultural Diversity, Cultural Heritage and Human Rights: Towards Heritage Management as Human Rights-Based Cultural Practice', *International Journal of Heritage Studies*, 18(3), 231–44.

Logan, W. (2013) 'Australia, Indigenous Peoples and World Heritage from Kakadu to Cape York: State Party Behaviour Under the World Heritage Convention', *Journal of Social Archaeology*, 13(2), 153–176.

Logan, W. (2015) 'Whose Heritage? Conflicting Narratives and Top-Down and Bottom-Up Approaches to Heritage Management in Yangon, Myanmar', in S. Labadi and W. Logan (eds), *Urban Heritage, Development and Sustainability*, London: Routledge, 256–73.

Merryman, J.H. (2005) 'Cultural Property Internationalism', *International Journal of Cultural* Property, 12, 11–39.

Meskell, L. (2013) 'UNESCO and the Fate of the World Heritage Indigenous Peoples Council of Experts (WHIPCOE),' *International Journal of Cultural Property*, 20(2), 155–174.

Ndoro, W., Chirikure, S. and Deacon, J. (2018) *Managing Heritage in Africa. Who Cares?* London: Routledge.

People's Republic of China (PRC) (2011) *Intangible Cultural Heritage Law of the People's Republic of China*. Online. Available: http://english.gov.cn/archive/laws_regulations/2014/08/23/content_281474982987416.htm (accessed 12 May 2015).

Picard, M. and Wood, R.E. (eds) (1997) *Tourism, Ethnicity and the State in Asian and Pacific Societies*, Honolulu: University of Hawai'i Press.

Posey, D.A. (1998) 'Can Cultural Rights Protect Traditional Cultural Knowledge and Biodiversity?', in H. Nieć (ed.), *Cultural Rights and Wrongs: A Collection of Essays in Commemoration of the 50th Anniversary of the Universal Declaration of Human Rights*, Paris and Leicester: UNESCO/Institute of Art and Law, 42–56.

Posey, D.A. (2008) 'Indigenous Management of Tropical Forest Ecosystems: The Case of the Kayapó Indians of the Brazilian Amazon', in M.R. Dove and C. Carpenter (eds), *Environmental Anthropology: A Historical Reader*, Malden, MA-Oxford-Carlton, Victoria: Blackwell Publishing, 89–101.

Rachman, N.F. and Siscawati, M. (2017) 'Forestry Law, *masyarakat adat* and Struggles for Inclusive Citizenship in Indonesia', in C. Antons (ed.), *The Routledge Handbook of Asian Law*, London-New York: Routledge, 224–49.

Robinson, D.F. (2010) *Confronting Biopiracy: Challenges, Cases and International Debates*, London-Washington, DC: Earthscan.

Schiebinger, L. (2004) *Plants and Empire: Colonial Bioprospecting in the Atlantic World*, Cambridge, MA-London: Harvard University Press.

Smith, L. (2006) *The Uses of Heritage*, London: Routledge.

Titchen, S. (2002) *Cultural Heritage and Sacred Sites: World Heritage from an Indigenous Perspective, 15 May 2002 – New York University* (Online). Available: www.dialoguebetweennations.com/n2n/pfii/english/SarahTitchen.htm (accessed 12 May 2015).

Tsosie, R. (2012) 'International Trade in Indigenous Cultural Heritage: An Argument for Indigenous Governance of Cultural Property', in C.B. Graber, K. Kuprecht and J.C. Lai (eds), *International Trade in Indigenous Cultural Heritage: Legal and Policy Issues,* Cheltenham, UK-Northampton, MA: Edward Elgar, 221–45.

UNESCO (1954) *Convention for the Protection of Cultural Property in the Event of Armed Conflict with Regulations for the Execution of the Convention 1954* (Online). Available: http://portal.unesco.org/en/ev.php-URL_ID=13637&URL_DO=DO_TOPIC&URL_SECTION=201.html (accessed 11 May 2015).

UNESCO (1970) *Convention on the Means of Prohibiting and Preventing the Illicit Import, Export and Transfer of Ownership of Cultural Property (1970)* (Online). Available: http://portal.unesco.org/en/ev.php-URL_ID=13039&URL_DO=DO_TOPIC&URL_SECTION=201.html (accessed 11 May 2015).

UNESCO (1972) *Convention concerning the Protection of the World Cultural and Natural Heritage 1972.* (Online). Available: http://portal.unesco.org/en/ev.php-URL_ID=13055&URL_DO=DO_TOPIC&URL_SECTION=201.html (accessed 11 May 2015).

UNESCO (2001) *Convention on the Protection of the Underwater Cultural Heritage 2001.* (Online). Available: http://portal.unesco.org/en/ev.php-URL_ID=13520&URL_DO=DO_TOPIC&URL_SECTION=201.html (accessed 11 May 2015).

UNESCO (2003) *Convention for the Safeguarding of the Intangible Cultural Heritage 2003.* (Online). Available: http://portal.unesco.org/en/ev.php-URL_ID=17716&URL_DO=DO_TOPIC&URL_SECTION=201.html (accessed 11 May 2015).

UNESCO (2005) *Convention on the Protection and Promotion of the Diversity of Cultural Expressions 2005.* (Online). Available: http://portal.unesco.org/en/ev.php-URL_ID=31038&URL_DO=DO_TOPIC&URL_SECTION=201.html (accessed 11 May 2015).

UNESCO (2015) *Cultural Landscapes* (Online). Available: http://whc.unesco.org/en/culturallandscape/#2 (accessed 11 May 2015).

UNESCO (2016) *Operational Guidelines for the Implementation of the World Heritage Convention* (Online). Available: http://whc.unesco.org/en/guidelines/ (accessed 18 August 2017).

UNESCO/WIPO (1985) *Model Provisions for National Laws on the Protection of Expression of Folklore Against Illicit Exploitation and Other Prejudicial Actions*, Geneva: UNESCO/WIPO.

United Nations (1992) *Convention on Biological Diversity* (Online). Available: www.cbd.int/convention/text/ (accessed 11 May 2015).

Vrdoljak, A. (2008) *International Law, Museums and the Return of Cultural Objects*, Cambridge: Cambridge University Press.

Weiner, J.G. (1987) 'Protection of Folklore: A Political and Legal Challenge', *International Review of Industrial Property and Copyright Law*, 18, 56–92.

WIPO (2001) *Intellectual Property Needs and Expectations of Traditional Knowledge Holders: WIPO Report on Fact-finding Missions on Intellectual Property and Traditional Knowledge*, Geneva: WIPO.

Part I

Cultural heritage, cultural property, intellectual property

Shifting concepts and terminology

Chapter 2

UNESCO heritage-speak

Words, syntax and rhetoric

William Logan

This volume examines various property-related concepts, especially cultural property and intellectual property, and how they are employed in heritage, environment and rights discourses by indigenous, ethnic minority and local communities around the world. These concepts are fundamental in much of the work done by at least three sets of international organizations:

1 UNESCO, its World Heritage Committee and its Advisory Bodies – the International Council on Monuments and Sites (ICOMOS), International Union for the Conservation of Nature (IUCN) and International Centre for the Conservation and Restoration of Cultural Property (ICCROM) – and the Intergovernmental Committee for the Safeguarding of the Intangible Cultural Heritage, all of which operate under a cluster of conventions, declarations and charters relating to the management of tangible and intangible heritage;
2 World Intellectual Property Organization (WIPO), where the discourse focuses on traditional knowledge and traditional cultural expressions and deals mainly through legal regimes aimed at protecting intellectual property (IP);
3 United Nations Permanent Forum on Indigenous Issues (UNPFII), a newer global body established in July 2000, which has addressed aspects of heritage relating to indigenous peoples and their cultural rights.

Each of these organizational sets tends, however, to use the concepts in different ways, which leads to communication complexities and misunderstandings.

These global organizations are based in Paris, Geneva and New York respectively. In this age of easy international travel and electronic communication one would not expect geography to have led to the lack of coordination in the way key concepts are used. The disciplinary backgrounds of those responsible for the first formulation of these organizations' heritage, environment and rights programs seem to be implicated. Certainly there is a general divergence among university scholars according to discipline in the way they use the concepts and associated terminology. Archaeologists, historians, geographers and political scientists tend to refer to the most central concept in this volume as 'cultural heritage', whereas anthropologists, economists and law scholars see it as 'cultural property'.

This diversity is perhaps of no consequence in itself, merely part of the world's rich linguistic tapestry. There is a problem, however, when the concepts and terms making up the 'language of heritage' are differently understood and used from one institution to another, one discipline to another and one culture to another. Mis-understandings lead to inefficiencies in communication about heritage between those working in the field, in management teams and in policy-making bureaucracies. In trying to implement international models of best heritage conservation practice, national and municipal governments, community groups and heritage practitioners struggle to keep up with the international discourse and its confusing use of key concepts and terminology.

Reflecting this, my chapter explores the language used in the international discourse about what I call cultural heritage. The aim is to outline 'heritage-speak' as it has developed within the UNESCO network and especially in UNESCO's flagship World Heritage program under the World Heritage Convention (UNESCO 1972) and in UNESCO's more recent involvement in traditional culture, folklore and intangible heritage, which culminated in the Intangible Heritage Convention (UNESCO 2003). The chapter commences with a discussion of key terms and their meaning, showing important shifts in the conception of heritage across time. It moves then to consider the syntax of UNESCO heritage-speak, that is, how the language works through a set of structures and rules. Again this shows variation over time but also spatially as between national and more local communities.

Sociolinguistic studies have long recognized that there is also significant dialect variation within language communities, with a so-called prestige dialect being the one most respected and used by the most prestigious members of the community. Such people tend to be those with political, economic or social power. Transposing this observation into the heritage context, heritage bureaucrats and professionals within the UNESCO and national heritage systems have the power by dint of their official position or expertise to establish what Laurajane Smith (2006) termed the 'authorized heritage discourse'. Other 'dialects' – alternative views of heritage, what it comprises and how it should be protected – have lesser status. Heritage becomes therefore a focus of disagreements, rivalries and conflicts between and within world regions, states and local communities and often a context for social justice and human rights infringements.

The pragmatics of language – how to get the message across – is another critical aspect of UNESCO heritage-speak. A number of structural and legal factors both limit the organization's ability to act and determine the kind of statements it can make and their effectiveness. Some normative or standard-setting instruments are binding on UNESCO Member States; others are not. UNESCO heritage-speak therefore necessarily contains a good deal of rhetoric – not in the derogatory sense of insincerity and lack of meaningful content that is often given to the term but in the sense of using strategically conceived statements and persuasive speaking or writing aimed at motivating States Parties and other relevant audiences to act in particular ways in particular situations.

Yahaya Ahmed (2006) noted that early discrepancies in word usage between UNESCO and its Advisory Body, ICOMOS, were reconciled with the World

Heritage Convention in 1972. Even so, variations still exist within the UNESCO network and in nation states in their management of cultural heritage. The United States and the United Kingdom/Australia, for example, give opposite meanings to the two most fundamental of terms – preservation and conservation – while Australia insists on using 'places' rather than the standard UNESCO/ICOMOS terminology 'monuments, groups of buildings and sites'. Ahmed (2006: 299) called for UNESCO and ICOMOS to 'lead the intellectual discussions on common terms, scope and terminology'. This has not happened. Although a World Heritage glossary was approved in 1995 by the World Heritage Committee (UNESCO n.d.(c)) and a group of international experts drew up a glossary for the Intangible Heritage system in 2002 (Zanten 2002), these have not led to standardization of terminology either within UNESCO or in the States Parties to the two conventions.

Language: words and their meaning

Culture

There is a very long history of peoples, communities and regimes seeing the need to protect their 'culture'. Special aspects of cultures have been protected such as literature in universities, artworks in galleries and religious rituals in services and festivals. Even the protection of elements in the built environment is ancient, going back, in Europe, to the late Roman period at least (ICOMOS CIF 2005: 9), although such actions were focused on grand buildings, imposing monuments and archaeological sites; that is, monuments and sites narrowly defined. By the 1960s this view of what was worth protecting expanded to take in entire historic precincts, villages and town centres (Labadi and Logan 2016: 4).

In the 1970s and 1980s, the emphasis of UNESCO's work was increasingly concerned with the relationship between culture and development and the protection of mostly tangible cultural heritage. Following the 1982 World Conference on Cultural Policies in Mexico City, an important conceptual shift occurred in the way that UNESCO considered culture: its earlier definition focusing on traditional and high arts being replaced by a new, more anthropological definition that saw culture

> in its widest sense, [as] the whole complex of distinctive spiritual, material, intellectual and emotional features that characterize a society and social group. It includes not only the arts and letters, but also modes of life, the fundamental rights of the human being, value systems, traditions and beliefs.
> (UNESCO 1982)

While the anthropological definition has the effect of widening and democratizing the notion of culture in UNESCO's discourse, policies and practices, its breadth also creates difficulties, making it possible to claim almost all aspects of human behaviour as part of one's culture (Logan 2007b: 37–9). Where does 'culture' stop? How much should be protected? Clearly some elements conflict with the human rights of particular groups of people. Some religions, for instance, can be seen to limit the freedoms of their adherents, especially women. This leads to the proposition that some aspects of culture are best relegated to the history books.

Cultural property and heritage

The concept and term 'cultural property' came into use in the post-war years as a reflection of both time and place: war-torn Europe, destruction of historic places, continuing plunder of heritage items and calls for restitution to original owners. They were the focus of the first of UNESCO's heritage conventions, the *Convention for the Protection of Cultural Property in the Event of Armed Conflict* (the Hague Convention; UNESCO 1954), although 'cultural heritage' is also mentioned and defined as

> monuments of architecture, art or history, whether religious or secular; archaeological sites; groups of buildings which, as a whole, are of historical or artistic interest; works of art; manuscripts, books and other objects of artistic, historical or archaeological interest; as well as scientific collections and important collections of books or archives or of reproductions of the property defined above.
>
> (Art. 1)

UNESCO's second heritage convention took up the issue of looting and subsequent trafficking – the *Convention on the Means of Prohibiting and Preventing the Illicit Import, Export and Transfer of Ownership of Cultural Property* (UNESCO 1970). It, too, focuses on cultural property but also included a similar reference to cultural heritage (Art. 1). The end of colonialism in Asia and Africa reinforced the repatriation impetus, particularly in relation to items from scientific and art collections held in the museums of former colonial powers.

As Regina Bendix's Interdisciplinary Research Group on Cultural Property at the Georg August University in Göttingen, Germany, has claimed,

> Cultural property is a concept with far-reaching consequences. The interest in bringing cultural property to market (or to block it from reaching the marketplace) and thereby realize an economic, ideological, collective, or individual profit has proven difficult in light of the highly divergent circumstances that actors face in a post-colonial, late-modern world.
>
> (IRGCP n.d.)

The concept links directly with the powerful notion of 'rights to estate' that underlies capitalism and neoliberalism as well as much popular thinking, as manifested in expressions such as 'the Englishman's home is his castle'. The most obvious of such property rights is the right to inherit and bequeath, buy and sell, mortgage and develop one's own property.

The idea of cultural property is thus clearly based on the concept and practice of property ownership. Passing from generation to generation, the bequeathed property becomes inheritance or 'heritage'. UNESCO's founding Constitution of 1948 drew on the property inheritance concept, seeing one of the organization's purposes being to 'maintain, increase and diffuse knowledge by . . . assuring the conservation and protection of the world's inheritance of books, works of art and monuments of history and science' (UNESCO 1945: Article I.2(c)). The Constitution did not, however, use either the term 'heritage' or 'cultural property', nor did the *Athens Charter for the Restoration of Historic Monuments* (1931) which, along with the *International Charter for the Conservation and Restoration of Monuments and Sites* (better known as the Venice Charter; 2nd ICATHM 1964), set the principles for heritage conservation practice in the post–World War II period. The latter did, however, use the term 'heritage', if only twice and in reference to ancient monuments (Preamble) and architecture (Art. 2).

Of course, not all that we inherit is valued, the inheritors having a different sense of significance from those doing the bequeathing. This may simply reflect the passage of time and inter-generational differences. But it can also be the result of deliberate selection processes in which individuals, communities and states see certain features from the past as useful for a variety of economic, social and political purposes. In other words, the past is being exploited for the present and future, and the valuation we give to 'cultural property' or 'heritage' tells us as much about today's values as it does about the past. The concept links, too, with issues of power, advantage and disadvantage: who has the power to make the selection of what is significant? How and why are certain selections made, and for whose benefit? Conflicts arise between different groups struggling to control heritage, its definition, management and use, as well as between those who see heritage as an asset to be exploited for economic or political reasons and those for whom its significance lies in the way it underpins a group's or individual's sense of identity.

The notion of estate does not, however, always mean private ownership. In liberal-democratic Australia of the 1970s, for instance, the term 'National Estate' was given to the country's first register of heritage places (Logan 2007a: 208). Here ownership was symbolically held by the nation, the list was democratically constructed (anyone could nominate a place) and heritage was conceived inclusively (places could relate to Australian Indigenous or settler cultures and be natural, cultural or both). This *Register of the National Estate* was non-statutory and eventually replaced in 2007 by a new, narrower Australian Heritage Register that ensured government action to protect inscribed places.

The heritage of humanity

Moving away from individual property rights, the Athens Charter in 1931 raised the idea of a common world heritage. The 1964 Venice Charter went further, asserting that 'People are becoming more and more conscious of the unity of human values and regard ancient monuments as a common heritage'. The Venice

Charter took from this observation that there was a 'common responsibility to safeguard them for future generations' and that

> the principles guiding the preservation and restoration of ancient buildings should be agreed upon and be laid down on an international basis, with each country being responsible for applying the plan within the framework of its own culture and traditions (Preamble).

This proposition materialized in UNESCO's 1972 World Heritage Convention. Coming into force in 1975 after the required 20 ratifications by UNESCO Member States had been achieved, the Convention created a set of States Parties, an elected subset forming the World Heritage Committee, and, from 1978, a list of places deemed to be of world significance.

According to the Convention, inscription on the World Heritage List depends upon the nominated place meeting several key requirements, many of which are based on concepts that have proven difficult in both theoretical and processual terms. Nominating States Parties have to demonstrate that the places have Outstanding Universal Value in relation to at least one of ten criteria. From 2003 a Statement of Outstanding Universal Value (SOUV) has been required for all new nominations and a Retrospective SOUV for earlier inscriptions. A nominated place must also meet the conditions of integrity and authenticity and have adequate legislative protection and management in the home country. These requirements are elaborated in the frequently revised *Operational Guidelines for the Implementation of the World Heritage Convention* (UNESCO 2015a).

The notion of authenticity has been particularly troublesome and has undergone an important shift away from the early usage of the term, as in the 1964 Venice Charter. This foundational statement insists that 'It is our duty to hand them [monuments] on in the full richness of their authenticity' (Preamble). This may work as long as the emphasis is on the physical fabric of the place but not, as discussed later in this chapter, when the emphasis shifts to the intangible values of places. And what does OUV mean? Does the place have to be well known and valued universally; that is, by peoples all around the world? If this is the case, then most of the 1,031 places now on the List would not measure up. Rather than being universal in this sense the term OUV has moved towards regional significance and cultural particularism. Jukka Jokilehto (2006) explains this well:

> We can perceive cultural heritage of humanity to form its own universe, which is qualified by individual cultures and their products. As part of this human universe, a heritage resource will obtain 'universal value' so far as it is a true and authentic expression of a particular culture. In relation to World Heritage, 'outstanding' can be interpreted as: the best and/or most representative example or examples of a kind of heritage.

The 1972 Convention definitively entrenched the use of the terms 'heritage', 'cultural heritage' and 'natural heritage' within the UNESCO discourse. 'Cultural property' by contrast is only mentioned in the Convention as part of ICCROM's title, and while 'property' is used 28 times, it is largely used as a way of referring to the places that are either inscribed or in future might be inscribed on the World Heritage List. Only at two points does the Convention raise the ownership issue: in the preamble, where cultural and natural property is seen as belonging to people (rather than individuals), and in Article 6.1 where it acknowledges the primacy of the property rights provided by the national legislation existing in the States Parties to the Convention.

Syntax: structural constraints

A number of critical structural factors shape and constrain the kind of action UNESCO can take in pursuit of its mission. UNESCO is an intergovernmental organization (IGO) made up of Member States that jealously guard their independent sovereignty and protect their national interests. UNESCO relies heavily, therefore, on the good will and cooperation of its Member States. In the heritage arena, its mission is carried out by those Member States that have signed up to the various heritage conventions and have become States Parties to those conventions. In recent years the States Parties elected to the World Heritage Committee have been increasingly represented by diplomats and bureaucrats rather than heritage professionals. This is one of the factors leading to greater politicization of key Committee processes such as consideration of World Heritage List nominations. Indeed Lynn Meskell (2013a) claims to have identified outright 'pacting' between groups of Committee members on certain decisions. Organizational arrangements within UNESCO have also influenced decision making, as can be seen in relation to the creation of separate management regimes for tangible and intangible heritage. The Committee's reliance on three Advisory Bodies, which is required by the World Heritage Convention, acts as a brake on efforts to treat heritage in a holistic manner at both global and national levels. A clear case of this can be seen in the continuing natural/cultural divide.

Tangible and intangible

It is unfortunate in many ways that tangible and intangible forms of heritage are given largely separate treatment within UNESCO. Heritage professionals working in the field constantly see the overlap of tangible and intangible values, and the general public tends to see tangible and intangible heritage simply as heritage, whole and undivided. The system does recognize that the significance of the places protected under the World Heritage Convention can have intangible aspects. In fact, intangible elements had always been present in World Heritage criteria, notably in the associative values of Criterion (vi). Conversely the drafters of the Intangible Heritage Convention were forced to recognize that sometimes an intangible heritage element can only survive if the physical context in which it is played out – called 'cultural space' in the Intangible Convention (Art. 2.1) – is also conserved. If the desirability of treating heritage holistically was already being acknowledged in the 1990s, why was the Intangible Heritage system established separately from the World Heritage system? This bipartite structure was essentially determined by the strategic recognition that it would not be feasible to revise the World Heritage Convention because this would require all UNESCO Member States to reconsider and ratify it anew – a long, fraught and most likely unsuccessful process. The only realistic option was to establish a new convention, and this did allow, after all, some important philosophical and processual modifications to be made that better suited intangible heritage.

Moreover, structural arrangements and career paths within UNESCO cannot have helped bring the two heritage forms together. World Heritage came under UNESCO's Division of Cultural Heritage (DCH) initially but under the World Heritage Centre after it was created in 1992. The DCH had conducted what were known as International Campaigns for the Safeguarding of the Heritage of Humanity (e.g. the Nubian statues, Venice, Borobudur, etc.) until the campaigns were overtaken and replaced by the World Heritage List. The World Heritage Centre became the focal point and coordinator within UNESCO of all matters related to World Heritage and functions as secretariat for the World Heritage Committee. The World Heritage Convention has been approved by almost all UNESCO Member States, and World Heritage is often described as UNESCO's flagship program. There was little reason, therefore, to alter the World Heritage system to accommodate the intangible heritage, although attempts, such as the Yamato Declaration (UNESCO 2004a), were made to ensure that the two could work as smoothly as possible alongside each other.

Emergence of UNESCO's interest in intangible heritage had been a long process that had developed outside UNESCO's World Heritage organizational unit. Defined in the 2003 Convention as covering oral traditions, performing arts, rituals, festive events, knowledge and practices concerning nature and the universe or the knowledge and skills to produce traditional crafts, the term 'intangible' itself only came to prominence in the 1990s, replacing the earlier 'folklore'. In relation to the non–place-specific forms of intangible heritage, a UNESCO *Recommendation on the Safeguarding of Traditional Culture and Folklore* had been adopted in 1989 (UNESCO 1989). Ten years later, however, at a UNESCO conference hosted by the Smithsonian Institution in Washington, DC, to assess the Recommendation, serious reservations were expressed by various world regional representatives (Seitel 2001). Some Europeans saw infamous political abuses of folklore in Nazi Germany ('Volk'), and the Soviet Union (Kuutma 2016: 51) points out that in the title of the French official version of the Recommendation the term 'folklore' is replaced by 'popular culture', which she suggests shows the wish to avoid of the 'nationalist agendas and the term's pejorative political implications'. Meanwhile, delegates from Africa, the Pacific and Latin America saw the term having a strong link with European colonization and the looting of their heritage artefacts by Western anthropologists (Nic Craith 2007: 2).

The resulting stalemate was one of the factors leading UNESCO to take another tack: it shifted its efforts to the Masterpieces of the Oral and Intangible Heritage of Humanity program in 2001 and eventually to the 2003 Intangible Convention

(Aikawa-Faure 2009). But if 'folklore' had been a troublesome term, so too was 'intangible'. Difficulties arise in rendering the underlying concept even between English and French – the languages of Western European neighbours and the two official languages of ICOMOS. To French speakers 'intangible' means that one is not allowed to touch, and they use the term 'immatériel' instead, a word that in English translation usually signifies unimportance. Larger problems are the breadth of intangible/immaterial heritage if the anthropological definition of culture is used and, given that such heritage is embodied in people, the potential for safeguarding some forms of this heritage to collide with human rights principles (Logan 2007b: 37).

These difficulties notwithstanding, the intangible heritage system under the 2003 Convention is now fully developed alongside the 1972 World Heritage Convention, and while there is considerable 'conceptual traffic' between the two systems (Meskell and Brumann 2015: 29) there also are some important differences. A 'Representative List of the Intangible Cultural Heritage of Humanity' parallels the World Heritage List, and a set of *Operational Directives* equates with the *Operational Guidelines*. The Representative List inscribes intangible heritage elements that are not necessarily tied to a specific place (except in the sense that they might belong to a continent or a country) and is no longer limited by notions of outstanding universal value and authenticity. Instead of the latter, the key hurdle requirement for inscription on the Representative List is intergenerational transmission; in other words, an intangible element is deemed suitable for listing only if it has been passed on from previous generations. Intangible heritage is often referred to as 'living heritage' and as such may change. The World Heritage system in the last 20 years has moved to a 'values approach', which means that change is also permitted in inscribed places provided that the OUV is not negatively affected. In both systems how much change can be allowed before the essential heritage is lost becomes a critical question. An important difference between the operation of the two systems has been the greater control of the inscription process by the States Parties to the 2003 Convention than occurred in the World Heritage system, although the latter seems to be in a state of flux on this point in recent years (Meskell 2013a; Meskell et al. 2014; Meskell and Brumann 2015: 33).

Culture, nature and cultural landscapes

The separation of culture and nature is a major case in which institutional arrangements have not been helpful. To be fair, this way of understanding the world around us was well entrenched in global heritage thinking long before the adoption of the World Heritage Convention in 1972, as can be observed in earlier efforts such as the Athens Charter 1931 or the inter-American Roerich Pact 1935 (USCBS 2015) that only focused on protecting cultural sites. In the post–World War II period, the United States was strongly advocating protection of its wilderness areas, whereas Europeans, recovering from the devastation of war, were concerned with cultural heritage. An American White House conference in 1965 drew natural and scenic areas together with historic sites, proposing their protection for 'the entire world citizenry' (quoted in UNESCO 2012). This was to be achieved, however, by adding one to the other rather than through a true blending, as seen in the full title of the 1972 Convention – the *Convention concerning the Protection of the World Cultural and Natural Heritage*. Six criteria were established for Cultural sites and four for Natural. Sites that were inscribed for both cultural and natural values were termed Mixed.

As with tangible and intangible, it is unfortunate in retrospect that culture and nature were operationally separated. Although they cooperate where possible, the three advisory bodies named in the Convention reinforced the nature/culture divide, with the IUCN responsible for providing advice on the Natural and Mixed heritage categories and ICOMOS and ICCROM on cultural heritage. The nature/culture divide reflects Western philosophical tradition and is rejected by many non-Western societies as a separation that is at odds with reality as they understand it. Partly in response to this, the World Heritage Committee in 1992 recognized the 'Cultural Landscape', which is defined as the 'combined works of nature and humankind' that 'express a long and intimate relationship between peoples and their natural environment' (UNESCO n.d.(d)). There are three sub-categories: clearly defined landscape designed and created intentionally by man; organically evolved landscapes, both relict and continuing; and associative cultural landscapes whose significance lies in the 'powerful religious, artistic or cultural associations of the natural element rather than material cultural evidence'. Since resistance to the nature/culture divide was especially strong among indigenous communities, it was with them in mind that a key decision had been taken at a 1992 UNESCO experts meeting at La Petite Pierre in France to add the associative landscape category. It was hoped that the sub-category would enable underrepresented States Parties in Africa and the Pacific to nominate sites, and, indeed, the first places to be inscribed as cultural landscapes were Tongariro National Park in New Zealand (1993) and Uluru-Kata Tjuta in Australia (1994). However, the Europeans were quick to move on the other sub-categories so that this tactic has not been particularly successful. In the World Heritage List as a whole China, Mexico, India, Brazil, Japan and Iran are now rivalling European countries in the number of inscriptions, and their tentative lists indicate large ambitions, but Africa, the Pacific, South America and parts of Asia remain poorly represented (Aygen and Logan 2016: 410–11, 416).

Prestige dialect: whose heritage?

Cultural regionalism and particularism

By the late 1980s, heritage was increasingly seen as a common legacy belonging to all humanity. This trend towards broader concepts of heritage ownership had expanded through international efforts, most notably under the aegis of UNESCO, although it was also reflected in the Biodiversity Convention (UNEP 1992). States all over the world, both rich and poor, were intervening to protect national heritage, and heritage conservation legislation was established by many. The focus on ownership continued, however, with the moral campaigns and legal endeavours to achieve cultural property restitution and repatriation under the 1970 *Convention on the Means of Prohibiting and Preventing the Illicit Import, Export and Transfer of Ownership of Cultural Property*. Righting the wrongs inflicted on Jewish and colonized peoples was needed and was slowly being carried out, at least with regard to the former. The Native American Grave Protection and Repatriation Act in the United States, passed in 1990, showed that nation states could take effective measures to acknowledge the rights of descendant communities (Coombe 2009: 399). John Merryman (1986) nevertheless saw all this as part of a general resiling from 'culture of all humanity' to narrower ownership claims based on cultural particularism. This focus on ownership and particularism had been picked up in WIPO, which had been established by the United Nations in 1967 in relation to the protection of IP. As we shall see, it was also to be partly picked up by UNPFII, although the cultural particularism underlying its mission at least applies to *all* Indigenous peoples of the world.

Despite and perhaps partly because of the rapid development of the World Heritage program, criticism of the UNESCO heritage system was mounting on several grounds. Ironically, the optimistic universalism espoused by UNESCO and its Advisory Bodies was charged with aiding and abetting processes of globalization that threatened regional, national and local cultures (Turtinen 2000; Logan 2002a). Other critics, especially in East Asia, Australasia and sub-Saharan Africa, saw the UNESCO system as too biased in favour of a particular region – Europe. Indeed, following the 1990 World Heritage Committee deliberations in 1990 the List contained 336 inscriptions, of which 246 were Cultural properties. Of these, 106 or 43 per cent were located in Europe. Christina Cameron puts the blame largely on the fabric-focussed interpretation of authenticity that was being used: 'With four attributes of design, materials, workmanship and setting, the initial understanding of authenticity leaned towards tangible characteristics of properties, a reflection of European conservation philosophy at that time' (Cameron 2016: 324).

UNESCO and the World Heritage Committee were fully aware of the credibility issue raised by such Eurocentricity and were already taking steps to reduce it (UNESCO 1988). After considerable analysis and discussion the World Heritage Committee approved a 'Global Strategy for a Representative, Balanced and Credible World Heritage List' in 1994 (Labadi 2005; 2007: 39). This picked up the associative sub-category of Cultural Landscapes already adopted by the Committee in 1992 that was expected to cater to the less monument-based cultures of sub-Saharan Africa and the Pacific. As noted, this part of the strategy has largely failed because the European states have had the advantage of larger financial and human resources to prepare nomination dossiers, including in other Cultural Landscape sub-categories, thus perpetuating the North/South divide. Efforts have been made to discriminate positively in favour of under-represented States Parties, as at the Cairns World

Heritage session in 2000, where pressure was put on those already well represented to hold back their nominations. Again, this has largely failed; the World Heritage List statistics for 2015 now shows that of the total 1,031 inscriptions, 802 are Cultural, and of these, 380 or 47 per cent are in Europe (UNESCO 2016).

Nara, authenticity and intangible heritage

The most successful element in the effort to reduce Eurocentricity in the UNESCO heritage system, however, was the opening up for renewed discussion of the hurdle requirement for all World Heritage inscriptions – authenticity. Japanese heritage experts, such as Nobuo Ito (1995; 2000: 2), had long been uneasy trying to work within the Venice Charter, especially with the notion of authenticity. Ito pointed out that no word for authenticity exists in Japanese and 'probably many other Asian languages', and there are even major variations between English, French and German (Ito 1995: 35–6; see also Loulanski 2006: 219). For the Japanese, the physical fabric of places was less important than the continuing symbolism and use of the places and, when the physical fabric deteriorated, their renovation was carried out using traditional building practices. The arguments put forward by the Japanese were persuasive and led to a major UNESCO conference on authenticity in Nara, Japan, in 1994 and the adoption of the *Nara Document on Authenticity* (UNESCO 1994). The agreement reached at Nara changed global practice in at least three fundamental ways. First, it recognizes that different cultures understand concepts and terms like 'heritage' and 'authenticity' differently and that societies are entitled to go about conserving their heritage in ways that are appropriate to their culture (Article 11). Second, it shifted away from the fabric-based approach to understanding the authenticity of places and, instead, emphasized truthfulness as demonstrated by reliable information (Article 9). Third, the Nara Document strengthened the importance of intangible values in understanding the significance of places (Article 7).

Japan continued to play a major role in recasting the post-Nara heritage system (Akagawa 2014; Aygen and Logan 2016: 414). This extended to the negotiations leading to the appointment of Koïchiro Matsuura as UNESCO Director General in 1999 and, under his leadership, the introduction of a system for safeguarding intangible heritage, not only in the operations of the World Heritage system but also in its own right through the creation of the Masterpieces of the Oral and Intangible Heritage of Humanity program in 2000 (UNESCO 2001) and adoption of the Intangible Cultural Heritage Convention (UNESCO 2003). Japan's influence has promoted the development of a view that there is an 'Asian approach' to heritage conservation, a view that remains 'nebulous and elusive' (Fong et al. 2012: 41) and to an extent contested (Aygen and Logan 2016: 417).

Heritage from below: community engagement and benefit sharing

In universities in the 1990s a more critical approach began to develop in cultural heritage teaching and research programs, particularly in English-speaking countries and in humanities and social science faculties rather than architecture (Logan and Wijesuriya 2016). This approach saw the making of heritage as a cultural practice and, like other forms of cultural practice, only understandable in the broad context of economic, social and political factors (Logan 2012: 11). More intense and overt contestation and conflicts arose as cultural heritage became seen in the 1990s as an asset to be exploited like any other resource (Tunbridge and Ashworth 1996). With the revision of the notion of development by the World Bank and other development agencies, global and national, the traditional divide between heritage protection and economic development has gradually faded (Loulanski 2006: 224) and, rather than being seen as standing in the way of progress, cultural heritage was rebadged as a 'vector of development' (Logan 2002b: xxi; UN 2011). On the negative side, however, inequities often arise in the processes of heritage identification, inscription, management and monitoring, and the people living in and around a heritage site can feel aggrieved that their environment has been degraded and their existence exploited as the result of conservation projects imposed upon them by national agencies operating in the UNESCO heritage system. Rosemary Coombe (2009: 402) saw this as a consequence of 'development's cultural turn', a transition occurring under neoliberal governments in which culture is seen as 'a new basis for capital accumulation'. She notes that this change also provokes resistance.

Such inequitable impacts on the identification and conservation of heritage highlight another set of questions for heritage theoreticians and practitioners about what features of the environment should be regarded as significant, who should identify and manage this heritage, why and for whom. Issues are raised about the merits and demerits of top-down versus bottom-up management approaches and the need to recognize heritage not just of world or national significance but heritage that is important at the local level in providing community identity (Robertson 2008; Labadi and Logan 2016). Some scholars have argued that local communities need to have a 'sense of ownership' of their heritage: this reaffirms their worth as a community, their ways of going about things, their 'culture' (Logan 2008: 439). There are, of course, complexities in such an argument, as urban planning scholars have pointed out since the 1960s and more recently, in the heritage field, Laurajane Smith and Emma Waterton (2009). There has been a tendency to romanticize the notion of community (Joseph 2002; Brumann 2015) when in fact all communities have their own internal dynamics and tensions. Who speaks for the community, and how is that person chosen? What are the rights of the individual living in the community to not follow community rules? These are important concerns certainly, but they do not negate the frequent existence of hardship resulting from the imposition of heritage conservation projects upon local people. Indeed, in Africa and other parts of the developing world, these inequities have led some local communities to demand a share of the economic benefits of heritage tourism (Abungu 2016; Ndoro 2016).

Traditional knowledge systems and indigenous peoples

Traditional values, practices and management are part of another complex concept – traditional knowledge systems. Such systems have their own existence, are transmitted from generation to generation, evolve over time and have been highly successful in maintaining biological diversity and environmental balance. When UNESCO argues that 'it is imperative that the values and practices of local communities, together with traditional management systems, are fully understood, respected, encouraged and accommodated in management plans if heritage resources are to be sustained into the future' (de Merode et al. 2004: 9), it has been talking primarily about indigenous peoples and their traditional knowledge systems. Traditional knowledge, however, can also be associated with non-indigenous groups leading traditional lifestyles, such as the Amish in the United States and the Hutterites in Canada. The World Heritage system began to engage with traditional knowledge systems and indigenous peoples in the 1980s in the lead-up to the introduction of the associative Cultural Landscape concept in 1992 and the Global Strategy in 1994.

The use of the term 'indigenous' in relation to World Heritage has been problematic, partly due to the diversity among the 370 million indigenous peoples located in more than 70 countries (UNPFII: n.d.). In the case of New World states where colonial settlers moved into areas already populated by indigenous peoples, the term is relatively straight-forward, although calls for special treatment for indigenous people – whether negative or positive discrimination – run against notions of democracy and equality of all citizens before the law (Logan, Langfield and Nic Craith 2010: 13). Indeed, some settler states – Australia, Canada, New Zealand and the United States – have so far refused to ratify the Intangible Convention. Some indigenous heritage involves secrecy. This raises the difficult question of how claims that it is part of the common heritage of humanity and as such ought to be circulated widely sit alongside the indigenous owners' requirement that this traditional knowledge must remain confidential for spiritual or cultural reasons (Vrdoljak 2005: 21).

Use of the term can be problematic in other parts of the world, too. South Africa, and the United Kingdom, while not settler states, have so far refused to sign the Intangible Convention. Some Asian states, such as India, Thailand and, until 2008, Japan, have simply refused to accept that they have indigenous people at all (Logan 2013a: 166; Antons 2008: 291; Hasegawa 2010). In Vietnam, the most 'traditional' ethnic groups are the minorities in mountainous areas, most of which arrived in the area of today's Vietnam long after, rather than before, the dominant lowland Kinh Viet. To what extent is the notion of indigeneity meaningful in Europe? Clearly it is in relation to the Sámi of Fenno-Scandinavia (see Gro B. Ween's chapter in this volume), but where else?

Because of the diversity of indigenous peoples and their socio-political contexts, the UNPFII and other UN bodies have resisted adopting an official definition of 'indigeneity' and 'indigenous peoples'. They operate, however, according to an understanding of the terms based on self-identification as individuals and communities, historical continuity with pre-settler societies, strong links to their natural environment and resources, strong cultural, social, economic and political systems, minority status within today's so-called nation states, and resolve to remain distinct peoples and communities (UNPFII n.d.).

Intellectual property

Traditional knowledge systems are indigenous peoples' intellectual property. They have enabled indigenous people to achieve significant artistic creativity ('traditional cultural expression'). There is a long, complex and bitter history of struggles between the indigenous bearers of this heritage who want to maintain control over the traditional artistic ideas involved in this creativity and others who want to commercialize these ideas. WIPO and law scholars focus on the legal rights that result from intellectual activity in cultural, scientific and other fields and on the regulatory regimes, especially copyright and patents, needed to protect the rights of IP owners, both individual and community. This emphasis on intellectual property rights is made clear in Article 2 (viii) of the *Convention Establishing the World Intellectual Property Organization* (WIPO 1967), reinforcing the view that IP is cultural property (Shyllon 2016: 57). In UNESCO thinking this intellectual activity is the intangible heritage of people following traditional life and, like all intangible heritage, it is embodied in people in the form of knowledge, skills and practices and is part of their living culture.

Rosemary Coombe and Joseph Turcotte (2012: 31) ask whether UNESCO could not 'assume a proactive stance here, using its considerable powers as an international public authority to protect indigenous communities from unfair and misleading competition that would siphon profits away from community safeguarding efforts?' There is no sign of UNESCO taking on such a challenge. Indeed, there is not much focus at all on IP within UNESCO's organizational structure or program of activities at the present time. It comes within the relatively small Communication and Information Sector that seems mostly interested in the freedom of expression and the development of knowledge societies and the media rather than in legal ownership claims and issues of exclusive use. UNESCO prefers to think of intangible heritage as belonging to communities in a non-legal sense. This is perhaps naïve given the new set of conflicting claims that have arisen over intangible heritage both between and within states in the last decade. In Southeast Asia the commercial exploitation of traditional medicines has recently sparked diplomatic rows between Southeast Asian countries claiming ownership of such heritage. Disputes between Malaysia and Indonesia erupted over 'ownership' of a traditional song that Malaysia had used in tourism advertisements (*Jakarta Post* 2007). These two states as well as Cambodia and Thailand have also claimed ownership of the style of hand movements used in traditional dances, again a form of intangible heritage that features in these countries' tourism (*Asia Sentinel* 2009; Fitzpatrick 2009; Murdoch 2011). The existence of many ethnic minorities straddling Asian state boundaries gives further rise to rival ownership claims.

The relationship between UNESCO and WIPO seems to have always been rather uneasy, with a number of failed attempts to come together to formulate common policies and directives. Debora Halbert (2006) sees the poor relationship going back to the period after World War II. UNESCO had overseen the development of the 1951 *Universal Copyright Convention* which was largely in reaction to the much earlier Berne Convention (1888). According to Halbert, the supporters of the Berne Convention saw UNESCO as a threat and, not to be outdone, set in motion the creation of WIPO, which occurred in 1967 under the *Convention Establishing the World Intellectual Property Organization* (WIPO 1967). In the IP literature there seem to be only two cases in which UNESCO and WIPO came together to deal successfully with the legal requirements for protecting traditional knowledge – the Tunis Model Law on Copyright that was jointly prepared and adopted by UNESCO and WIPO in 1976 for developing countries wishing to safeguard 'works of national folklore' and in the UNESCO/WIPO *Model Provisions for National Laws on the Protection of Expressions of Folklore Against Illicit Exploitation and other Prejudicial Actions* of 1982 (UNESCO 1985). In the 1990s the two organizations again worked jointly on a *Draft Treaty for the Protection of Expressions of Folklore against Illicit Exploitation and other Prejudicial Actions*. The draft met strong opposition at a World Forum at Phuket in April 1997, however, from countries that had been benefitting from the free use of traditional expressions (Aikawa-Faure 2009: 15). The following year, WIPO decided to add genetic resources to the scope of its inquiry into a future IP rights protection treaty. This was clearly outside UNESCO's mandate, and cooperation between the two bodies on a treaty lapsed (Aikawa-Faure 2009: 15). Lack of a workable mechanism for settling IP ownership of traditional cultural expressions that can be found in more than one country was another of the reasons given by Christoph Antons (2012: 152) for the treaty being abandoned.

Not only does there appear to be something of a stand-off between UNESCO and WIPO in terms of cooperative activities but also a resistance to using the same language. WIPO still uses the term 'folklore', as in the title of its Intergovernmental Committee on Intellectual Property and Genetic Resources, Traditional Knowledge and Folklore, and in documents it prepared such as *The Protection of Traditional Cultural Expressions/Expressions of Folklore: Revised Objectives and Principles* (WIPO 2010). The document talks about the requirements of creativity and continuing 'authenticity', a term rejected by those establishing the UNESCO Intangible Convention, as noted earlier. On the other hand, the WIPO definition of traditional knowledge – 'knowledge, know how, skills and practices that are developed, sustained and passed on from generation to generation within a community, often forming part of its cultural or spiritual identity' (WIPO n.d.) – is much the same as the definition of intangible heritage in the 2003 Convention. Why then not cooperate at least to standardize terminology?

Rhetoric: persuasion and motivation

As previously observed, UNESCO is an IGO made up of sovereign states, and it is therefore unable simply to impose decisions on them. UN covenants and UNESCO conventions are legally binding on Member States that have ratified them and have thus become States Parties to them (UNESCO n.d.(a), (b)). Even so, there is not full or consistent compliance by States Parties. There has also been some extremely bitter division between States Parties over whether the wording of Article 6 of the World Heritage Convention permits the World Heritage Committee to put a property on the World Heritage in Danger list without the prior consent of the State Party in whose territory the property is located (Logan 2013a).

Other international normative instruments such as proclamations, declarations, documents and recommendations are not binding and merely have moral authority. This means that UNESCO has to engage in a very considerable diplomatic and promotional effort to persuade the States Parties to behave in particular ways towards the heritage located within their territory, to accept the heritage of humanity notion and, if necessary, to put national interest aside in order to acknowledge the higher obligation to protect World Heritage or intangible elements on the Representative List. Such exhortation helps set the tone of the heritage discourse and encourages positive activities at the national and local levels by policy makers and practitioners, teachers and scholars, the media and potential financial supporters, local communities and the general public.

UNESCO's desire to see meaningful engagement with local communities in the implementation of the World Heritage Convention demonstrates the organization's reliance on persuasion. The World Heritage Committee uses the rhetorical device of listing Cs to draw the attention of States Parties and other 'stakeholders' to its key goals, a fifth C for 'Community' being added at the Committee's 2007 session in Auckland, New Zealand, to the earlier Cs for 'Credibility', 'Conservation', 'Capacity-building' and 'Communication'. Article 5 of the Convention puts the community up front when it says that the overall aim of heritage conservation is 'to give the cultural and natural heritage a function in the life of the community', and community engagement is included in the Operational Guidelines. However, States Parties interpret this requirement in their own way, some paying it little more than lip service. I have given the example elsewhere of a joint World Heritage Centre/ICOMOS advisory mission to Lijiang, China, in 2008 (see Logan 2013a: 122). At a day-long 'Stakeholders Meeting' two community representatives sat silently in one corner of the room. It was not clear how they were selected and whether they were charged with reporting back to their community. The state's position seemed to be that government officials were there to represent the people. What can UNESCO do in such cases? UNESCO and the World Heritage Committee have to request the State Party to invite a mission, and the State Party decides the local participants. As Christoph Brumann (2015: 279) observes, site communities end up being side-lined. They are sometimes forced to take dramatic steps in order to be heard, as was the case with the Mirrar community living in the Kakadu World Heritage property (Logan 2013a).

The strategy of removing residents from World Heritage sites – as at Angkor, Hampi and Hue – is another example in which States Parties interpret the Convention and Operational Guidelines in their own way, although often letting it be believed that they are acting according to UNESCO's rules (Logan 2014: 163). Sometimes States Parties have the best intentions in managing their heritage but do not fully comprehend the concepts and terms used by UNESCO, the

World Heritage Committee, World Heritage Centre and experts on field missions. This is commonly the result of language barriers, and provision of key documents in translation is needed. Encouragement to take part in ICOMOS and other heritage networks will also help increase understanding and build up local confidence.

Heritage rights: individual and collective

Having a say in determining one's own life circumstances, including one's cultural and physical environment, is now commonly seen as a fundamental human right (Logan 2008: 439). I have argued in various places that it is essential to see cultural heritage – especially intangible heritage – within a human rights context and its protection as part of people's efforts to maintain their identity. Yet up until very recently – November 2015 – there has been a very slim legal basis for bringing human rights into the heritage field. The Intangible Heritage Convention acknowledges in the Preamble and at Article 2 the primacy of international human rights instruments, but there is no reference to human rights in the older World Heritage Convention. The single mention of human rights in the Operational Guidelines is in relation to the definition of partners and stakeholders at Paragraph 40 where a margin note is given to the United Nations *Declaration on the Rights of Indigenous Peoples* (UN 2007). Being a 'declaration', however, this is not a legally binding instrument in international law. Nor are the United Nations *Universal Declaration of Human Rights* (UNDHR) of 1948 and UNESCO's *Universal Declaration on Cultural Diversity* of 2001. Indeed, the only human rights instruments that are legally binding on UNESCO Member States in the heritage field are the United Nations *International Covenant on Economic, Social and Cultural Rights* (ICCPR) (UN 1966) and the UNESCO conventions (if ratified).

Today the position taken in the ICCPR is well accepted in international human rights discourse and the programs of global organisations; that is:

> In those States in which ethnic, religious or linguistic minorities exist persons belonging to such minorities shall not be denied the right, in community with other members of their group, to enjoy their own culture, to profess their own religion, or to use their own language.
>
> (ICCPR 1966, Article 27)

Despite this, some Member States do not abide by this in their domestic cultural and social policies. Efforts to protect and enhance human rights can only take place within states, and the record in Asian countries is very mixed (Logan 2016). First- and second-generation human rights, with their emphasis on the individual, are sometimes regarded as Western in origin and character, while third-generation collective cultural rights have been closely associated with Indigenous peoples, commonly living as minorities within European settler societies in the New

World. There are, however, different understandings of the 'collective' concept, which creates conflict between different regions of the world – Asia compared with Western Europe, for instance – but also within regions. Asian states tend to emphasize collective rather than individual human rights, but there are variations between and within them. In fact, upholding the collective rights of minorities within Asian states seems to face even less commitment than protecting individual rights.

None of the international normative statements relating to human rights refer specifically to heritage rights. Even the formulation of 'cultural rights', of which heritage rights is one element, have been relatively neglected (Stavenhagen 1998: 1). International law scholar Yvonne Donders (2010: 15) explains this lack of attention to cultural rights and consequently their less developed conceptual and legal status as being the result of the vagueness of the term 'culture'. Nevertheless, drawing on UNESCO's assertion that 'culture shapes all our thinking, imagining and behaviour' (UNESCO 1995: 11), Donders argues that 'culture may give individuals and communities a sense of belonging; it concerns their human dignity, which is where human rights come into play' (Donders 2010: 15). It was for reasons like these and with the legality provided by the ICCPR that UN Secretary-General Kofi Annan, in 1997, decided to make human rights a priority in every program and mission (Ekern et al. 2012: 217). His call was taken up by the United Nations Development Program (UNDP) and the United Nations Children's Fund (UNICEF) in 2003 when they adopted a 'Common Understanding' of a 'Human Rights Based Approach' in which the relationships between all the stakeholders in a project or a policy initiative would be clarified in terms of their rights and duties and ways would be sought to overcome the power differentials that might otherwise block the realization of rights (Boesen and Sano 2010).

Dragging their heels

It was in the area of indigenous heritage that the first moves towards the World Heritage Committee taking human rights seriously occurred. The Associative Cultural Landscape and Global Strategy of the early 1990s have already been mentioned. More recently indigenous peoples have pushed for direct representation in World Heritage processes, first through an attempt in the early 2000s to persuade the World Heritage Committee to establish a World Heritage Indigenous Peoples Council of Experts (WHIPCOE; Logan 2013a; Meskell 2013b). When that initiative was blocked, other means were found to influence Committee decision making, including the 'Linking Universal and Local Values' conference in Amsterdam in 2003. An outcome of the conference was adoption of the view that heritage protection should not depend only on top-down interventions by governments or the expert actions of heritage industry professionals but must also involve local communities. UNESCO now routinely argues that it is imperative that the values and practices of the local communities, together with traditional management systems, are fully understood, respected, encouraged and accommodated in management plans if the heritage resources are to be sustained into the future (de Merode et al. 2004: 9). Even though the human rights concept lay at the heart of the Amsterdam conference, the words 'human rights' were used only four times in the entire World Heritage Papers No. 13 (UNESCO 2004b), which is effectively the conference proceedings.

Their status as IGOs makes reform within UNESCO and the World Heritage Committee on matters touching on human rights enormously difficult. Raising human rights is like waving a red flag at a bull for many UNESCO Member States and State Parties to the World Heritage Convention – despite the fact that most are signatories to the UNDHR, ICCPR and other human rights instruments, that UNESCO is part of the 'UN family' and that the UNESCO General Assembly had said on several occasions that the organization would integrate a human rights–based approach into all it programs and activities (Disko 2016: 360). In fact the Advisory Bodies were already working doing just this, especially the IUCN, which had moved quickly and had largely reformed its approach to managing Natural and Mixed properties, the two categories for which it has prime advisory responsibility under the Convention (Oviedo and Puschkarsky 2012). ICOMOS has also been moving, if more slowly, and similar changes in its processes are afoot following important workshops organized by ICOMOS Norway and discussions with Farida Shaheed, Independent Expert and Special Rapporteur on cultural rights at the United Nations High Commission for Human Rights in Geneva (Ekern et al. 2012: 223–4).

Following the World Heritage Committee's rejection of the WHIPCOE initiative, the indigenous struggle to gain greater recognition in the nation-based UNESCO heritage system shifted to the United Nation Permanent Forum on Indigenous Issues (UNPFII). Here, after the UN's adoption of the *Declaration on the Rights of Indigenous Peoples* (UN 2007) campaigning began to persuade UNESCO to bring its World Heritage into line with the declaration and, in particular, to require free, prior and informed consent to be obtained from indigenous peoples before any UNESCO activity related to their heritage (UNPFII 2011; Disko 2016). However, this was again only a declaration, an aspirational rather than legally binding declaration. Stefan Disko (2016) outlines the pressure UNPFII had to put on the World Heritage Committee to put words into action. This eventually occurred at the Committee's 39th Session in Bonn, Germany, in mid-2015, where Decision 39COM11 reiterates its decision to re-examine recommendations of International Expert Workshop on the World Heritage Convention and Indigenous Peoples that took place in Copenhagen in 2012 and welcomed insertion of paragraphs in the Operational Guidelines that addressed issues relating to indigenous peoples. The 2015 revision of the Operational Guidelines picked this up in Paragraph 123:

> Participation in the nomination process of local communities, indigenous peoples, governmental, non-governmental and private organizations and other stakeholders is essential to enable them to have a shared responsibility with the State Party in the maintenance of the property. States Parties

are encouraged to prepare nominations with the widest possible participation of stakeholders and to demonstrate, as appropriate, that the free, prior and informed consent of indigenous peoples has been obtained, through, inter alia making the nominations publicly available in appropriate languages and public consultations and hearings.

(UNESCO 2015a: Paragraph 123)

Even though this is merely an encouragement to States Parties, it does at least recognize the cultural heritage of indigenous peoples to a far larger degree than has been afforded the cultural heritage of other groups within the 'local community,' such as women, children and youth or, in many parts of the world, ethnic and racial minorities that are not considered indigenous peoples (Logan 2013b). Respect for the rights of these groups to have access to and enjoy their heritage is still lacking in most parts of the world, and their heritage is still underrepresented in the global and national programs.

Sustainable development: from persuasion to policy

More significantly the 39th Session took the step of approving a draft policy relating to sustainable development that encompasses human rights and other related principles and that will be binding on all States Parties (Larsen and Logan in press). Concern about sustainable development had been building up in the heritage field over the past decade. This has been a two-headed concern that relates, first, to the sustainability of heritage places and practices and, second, to the contribution that heritage principles and practice can and should make to wider social, cultural and environmental sustainability. That is, on the one hand, more meaningful engagement of local communities and indigenous peoples in the identification and management of the places for which they have traditionally been custodians has been accepted as providing the best guarantee for the survival of traditional heritage sites. The World Heritage system has also generally moved to a 'values approach' to heritage management that is based on the view that provided the OUV is safeguarded, new development may be permitted within and around inscribed properties. On the other hand, with now more than 1,000 properties on the World Heritage List in 161 countries and setting the principles for national and local conservation, the World Heritage system has a responsibility to adhere to the wider United Nations sustainable development agenda, UNESCO sustainability principles, existing international humanitarian standards and other multilateral environmental agreements.

In meetings across 2014–2015 a UNESCO working group drafted a policy in 2015 for the integration of a sustainable development perspective into the processes of the World Heritage Convention. The draft policy went to the World Heritage Committee in Bonn, where it was endorsed and sent out for comment to all States Parties. The revised draft was then adopted by the General Assembly of States Parties to the World Heritage Convention in November 2015 (UNESCO

2015b), and the Operational Guidelines are now being revised. The policy is important in the way it conceptualizes the sustainability issue not only for World Heritage sites but more generally because the global discourse filters down to national and local heritage systems. It was based on the conceptual framework adopted at the wider UN level in the context of discussions leading to the UN's post-2015 development agenda. Drawing particularly on the UN Task Team Report *Realizing the Future We Want for All*, the draft policy saw the achievement of sustainable development as being dependent on four main sets of factors: environmental sustainability, inclusive social development, inclusive economic development and the fostering of peace and security. Each of these was broken down into sub-themes of relevance to the work of the Convention. The draft policy calls on States Parties not only to protect the OUV of World Heritage properties but also to 'recognise and promote the properties' inherent potential to contribute to all dimensions of sustainable development . . . [and to] ensure that their conservation and management strategies are aligned with broader sustainable development objectives', by which is meant the three overarching principles identified in the UN Task Team Report; that is, human rights, equality and long-term sustainability.

It should be noted that a parallel policy development has been occurring simultaneously under the Intangible Convention 2003, and some effort has been made to ensure consistency between the two policy statements. The draft of a new chapter to be inserted into the Operational Directives entitled 'Safeguarding intangible cultural heritage and sustainable development at the national level' (UNESCO 2014) was endorsed by the Intergovernmental Committee for the Safeguarding of the Intangible Cultural Heritage at its tenth session in December 2015 and will go before the General Assembly of States Parties to the Convention at its sixth session in June 2016. The World Heritage policy is important in that it is binding on all States Parties. It is not yet clear whether placing a chapter into the Operational Directives provides the same binding policy status, although perhaps a set of 'directives' has greater force than a set of 'guidelines'.

Conclusion: moving beyond rhetoric

Heritage philosophy and practice have come a long way since the 1960s. The world's cultural diversity has been better recognized, and new ways have been found to deal with it. Conserving the world's tangible heritage is no longer seen as merely a technical matter but as a process embedded within particular social, economic and political contexts and essentially linked with questions of community identity. Safeguarding intangible heritage has moved to centre stage and is seen as 'living', embodied in people and changing over time. Balancing heritage protection and new development is a challenge for governments everywhere and brings local communities' rights to the fore.

UNESCO's language has absorbed the changing concepts to an extent, but since organizations are captive to the structures existing within them, the structural separation within UNESCO of tangible from intangible and natural from cultural still produces heritage-speak that confuses governments, NGOs, institutions, community groups and practitioners. UNESCO needs to ensure it creates a language environment that enables effective collaboration between officers working under the various heritage conventions within UNESCO and its Advisory Bodies, and this entails at least standardizing glossaries and ensuring compatibility between the Operational Guidelines and the Operational Directives. A structural factor that cannot be changed is UNESCO's existence as an IGO with a constrained set of tools that are legally binding on States Parties. It must rely on its powers of persuasion to influence State Party heritage attitudes and activities. It has been and will remain necessary for senior UNESCO officers from the Director General down to constantly bring heritage concerns into the consciousness of States Parties and other stakeholders.

This is where the November 2015 decision of the General Assembly of States Parties to the World Heritage Convention to adopt a Sustainable Development policy is especially significant. It gives legally binding status within the World Heritage system to principles relating to human rights and social justice, environmental and social sustainability and peace and security. It greatly reduces UNESCO's reliance on rhetoric to persuade States Parties to behave ethically in relation to the management of their World Heritage sites. A positive decision by the General Assembly of States Parties to the Intangible Convention should have the same effect with regard to the safeguarding of intangible heritage. UNESCO heritage-speak is about to feel the impact of this move from rhetoric to policy, with new language needed to put the principles into practice.

References

2nd International Congress of Architects and Technicians of Historic Monuments (2nd ICATHM) (1964) *International Charter for the Conservation and Restoration of Monuments and Sites* (The Venice Charter) (online). Available: www.icomos.org/charters/ venice_e.pdf (accessed 23 August 2014).

Abungu, G.O. (2016) 'UNESCO, The World Heritage Convention, and Africa: The Practice and the Practitioners', in W. Logan, M. Nic Craith and U. Kockel (eds), *A Companion to Heritage Studies*, Chichester: Wiley Blackwell, 373–91.

Ahmed, Y. (2006) 'The Scope and Definitions of Heritage: From Tangible to Intangible', *International Journal of Heritage Studies*, 12, 292–300.

Aikawa-Faure, N. (2009) 'From the Proclamation of Masterpieces to the *Convention for the Safeguarding of Intangible Cultural Heritage*', in L. Smith and N. Akagawa (eds), *Intangible Heritage*, London: Routledge, 13–44.

Akagawa, N. (2014) *Heritage Conservation and Japan's Cultural Diplomacy: Heritage, National Identity and National Interest*, London: Routledge.

Antons, C. (2008) 'Traditional Cultural Expressions and Their Significance for Development in a Digital Environment: Examples from Australia and Southeast Asia', in C.B. Graber and M. Burri-Nenova (eds), *Intellectual Property and Traditional Expressions in a Digital Environment*, Cheltenham, UK: Edward Elgar, 287–301.

Antons, C. (2012) 'Intellectual Property Rights in Indigenous Cultural Heritage: Basic Concepts and Continuing Controversies', in C.B. Graber, K. Kuprecht and J.C. Lai (eds), *International Trade in Indigenous Cultural Heritage: Legal and Policy Issues*, Cheltenham, UK: Edward Elgar, 144–74.

Asia Sentinel (2009) 'Indonesian Outrage over a Dance', 25 August.

The Athens Charter for the Restoration of Historic Monuments (1931) (online). Available: www.icomos.org/en/charters-and-texts/179-articles-en-francais/ressources/charters-and-standards/167-the-athens-charter-for-the-restoration-of-historic-monuments (accessed 4 September 2015).

Aygen, Z. and Logan, W. (2016) 'Heritage in the "Asian Century": Responding to Geopolitical Change', in W. Logan, M. Nic Craith and U. Kockel (eds), *A Companion to Heritage Studies*, Chichester: Wiley Blackwell, 410–25.

Boesen, J.K. and Sano, H.O. (2010) 'The Implications and Value Added of a Human Rights-Based Approach', in B.A. Andreassen and S.P. Marks (eds), *Development as a Human Right: Legal, Political and Economic Dimensions*, Antwerp: Intersentia, pp. 45–68.

Brumann, C. (2015) 'Community as Myth and Reality in the UNESCO World Heritage Convention', in N. Adell et al. (eds), *Between Imagined Communities and Communities of Practice: Participation, Territory and the Making of Heritage*, Gottingen: Universitätsverlag Göttingen, 273–89.

Cameron, C. (2016) 'UNESCO and Cultural Heritage: Unexpected Consequences', in W. Logan, M. Nic Craith and U. Kockel (eds), *A Companion to Heritage Studies*, Chichester: Wiley Blackwell, 322–37.

Coombe, R.J. (2009) 'The Expanding Purview of Cultural Properties and Their Politics', *Annual Review of Law and Social Sciences*, 5, 393–412.

Coombe, R.J. and Turcotte, J.F. (2012) 'Indigenous Cultural Heritage in Development and Trade: Perspectives from the Dynamics of Cultural Heritage Law and Policy', in C.B. Graber, K. Kuprecht and J.C. Lai (eds), *International Trade in Indigenous Cultural Heritage: Legal and Policy Issues*, Cheltenham, UK: Edward Elgar, 1–35.

de Merode, E., Smeets, R. and Westrik, C. (eds) (2004) *Linking Universal and Local Values: Managing a Sustainable Future for World Heritage*, Paris: UNESCO World Heritage Centre, World Heritage Paper No. 13.

Disko, S. (2016) 'Indigenous Peoples' Rights and the World Heritage Convention', in W. Logan, M. Nic Craith and U. Kockel (eds), *A Companion to Heritage Studies*, Chichester: Wiley Blackwell, 355–72.

Donders, Y. (2010) 'Do Cultural Heritage and Human Rights Make a Good Match?' *International Social Science Journal* (online). Available: http://dare.uva.nl/document/225733 (accessed 3 April 2012).

Ekern, S., Logan, W., Sauge, B. and Sinding-Larsen, A. (2012) 'Human Rights and World Heritage: Preserving Our Common Dignity Through Rights-Based Approaches to Site Management', *International Journal of Heritage Studies*, 18(3), 213–225.

Fitzpatrick, S. (2009) 'Malaysia "Steals" Bali Dance', *The Australian*, 26 August.

Fong, K.L., Winter, T., Rii, H.U., Khanjanusthiti, P. and Tandon, A. (2012) "Same but different?": A Roundtable Discussion on the Philosophies, Methodologies, and Practicalities of Conserving Cultural Heritage in Asia', in P. Daly and T. Winter (eds), *Routledge Handbook of Heritage in Asia*, London: Routledge, 39–54.

Halbert, D.J. (2006) *The World Intellectual Property Organization: Changing Narratives on Intellectual Property* (online). Available: http://regulation.upf.edu/bath-06/1_Halbert.pdf (accessed 20 October 2015).

Hasegawa, Y. (2010) 'The Rights Movement and Cultural Revitalization: The Case of the Ainu in Japan', in M. Langfield, W. Logan and M. Nic Craith (eds), *Cultural Diversity, Heritage and Human Rights: Intersections in Theory and Practice*, London: Routledge, 208–25.

Interdisciplinary Research Group on Cultural Property (IRGCP) (n.d.) *The Constitution of Cultural Property* (online). Available: http://cultural-property.uni-goettingen.de/ (accessed 12 May 2015).

International Council on Monuments and Sites, Comité de Formation [Training Committee] (ICOMOS CIF) (2005) *Definition of Cultural Heritage. References to Documents in History* (online). Available: http://cif.icomos.org/pdf_docs/Documents%20on%20line/ Heritage%20definitions.pdf (accessed 30 October 2012).

Ito, N. (1995) ' "Authenticity" Inherent in Cultural Heritage in Asia and Japan', in *Nara Conference on Authenticity in Relation to the World Heritage Convention, Nara, Japan, 1–6 November 1994. Proceedings*, Paris: UNESCO/Tokyo: Agency for Cultural Affairs/ Rome: ICCROM/Paris: ICOMOS; 35–45.

Ito, N. (2000) *World Cultural Heritage and Self-Enlightenment of Conservation Experts*, Paper presented to the Consultative Meeting on Regional Cultural Heritage Co-Operation in Protection, Nara, 29 February–3 March.

Jakarta Post (2007) 'Malaysia Urges Indonesia to Drop Plan to Sue over Folk Song', 8 October.

Jokilehto, J. (2006) 'World Heritage: Defining the Outstanding Universal Value', *City & Time*, 2(2), 1–10 (online). Available: www.ct.ceci-br.org/novo/revista/docs2006/ CT-2006-45.pdf (accessed 7 September 2015).

Joseph, M. (2002) *Against the Romance of Community*, Minneapolis: University of Minnesota Press.

Kuutma, K. (2016) 'From Folklore to Intangible Heritage', in W. Logan, M. Nic Craith and U. Kockel (eds), *A Companion to Heritage Studies*, Chichester: Wiley Blackwell, 41–54.

Labadi, S. (2005) 'A Review of the Global Strategy for a Balanced, Representative and Credible World Heritage List, 1994–2004', *Conservation and Management of Archaeological Sites*, 7, 89–102.

Labadi, S. (ed.) (2007) *World Heritage: Challenges for the Millennium*, Paris: UNESCO World Heritage Centre.

Labadi, S. and Logan, W. (2016) 'Approaches to Urban Heritage, Development and Sustainability', in S. Labadi and W. Logan (eds), *Urban Heritage, Development and Sustainability: International Frameworks, National and Local Governance*, London: Routledge.

Larsen, P. B. and Logan, W. (eds) (in press) *World Heritage and Sustainable Development: New Directions in World Heritage Management*. London: Routledge.

Logan, W. (2002a) 'Globalizing Heritage: World Heritage as a Manifestation of Modernism, and Challenges from the Periphery', in D. Jones (ed.), *Twentieth Century Heritage: Our Recent Cultural Legacy: Proceedings of the Australia ICOMOS National Conference 2001*, Adelaide: University of Adelaide and Australia ICOMOS, 51–7.

Logan, W. (2002b) *The Disappearing 'Asian' City: Protecting Asia's Urban Heritage in a Globalizing World*. Hong Kong: Oxford University Press.

Logan, W. (2007a) 'Reshaping the "Sunburnt Country": Heritage and Cultural Politics in Contemporary Australia', in R. Jones and B.J. Shaw (eds), *Geographies of Australian Heritages*, Aldershot, UK: Ashgate, 207–23.

Logan, W. (2007b) 'Closing Pandora's Box: Human Rights Conundrums in Cultural Heritage Protection', in H. Silverman and D.R. Fairchild (eds), *Cultural Heritage and Human Rights*, New York: Springer, 33–52.

Logan, W. (2008) 'Cultural Diversity, Heritage and Human Rights', in B.J. Graham and P. Howard (eds), *Ashgate Research Companion to Heritage and Identity*, Aldershot, UK: Ashgate, 439–54.

Logan, W. (2012) 'Cultural Diversity, Cultural Heritage and Human Rights: Towards Heritage Management as Human Rights-Based Cultural Practice', *International Journal of Heritage Studies*, 18(3), 231–244.

Logan, W. (2013a) 'Australia, Indigenous Peoples and World Heritage from Kakadu to Cape York: State Party Behaviour Under the World Heritage Convention', *Journal of Social Archaeology*, 13(2), 153–176.

Logan, W. (2013b) 'Patrimonito Leads the Way: UNESCO, Cultural Heritage, Children and Youth', in K. Darian-Smith and C. Pascoe (eds), *Children, Childhood and Cultural Heritage*, London: Routledge, 21–39.

Logan, W. (2014) 'Heritage Rights: Avoidance and Reinforcement', *Heritage and Society*, 7(2), 156–169.

Logan, W. (2016) 'Collective Cultural Rights in Asia: Recognition and Enforcement', in A. Jakubowski (ed.), *Cultural Rights as Collective Rights: An International Law Perspective*, Leiden: Brill, 180–203.

Logan, W., Langfield, M. and Craith, M.N. (2010) 'Intersecting Concepts and Practices', in M. Langfield, W. Logan and M.N. Craith (eds), *Cultural Diversity, Heritage and Human Rights: Intersections in Theory and Practice*, London: Routledge, 3–20.

Logan, W. and Wijesuriya, G. (2016) 'The New Heritage Studies and Education, Training and Capacity-Building', in W. Logan, M. Nic Craith and U. Kockel (eds), *A Companion to Heritage Studies*, Chichester: Wiley Blackwell, 557–73.

Loulanski, T. (2006) 'Revising the Concept for Cultural Heritage: The Argument for a Functional Approach', *International Journal of Cultural Property*, 13, 207–233.

Merryman, J.H. (1986) 'Two Ways of Thinking About Cultural Property', *American Journal of International Law*, 80, 831–853.

Meskell, L. (2013a) 'UNESCO's World Heritage Convention at 40: Challenging the Economic and Political Order of International Heritage Conservation', *Current Anthropology*, 54, 483–494.

Meskell, L. (2013b) 'UNESCO and the Fate of the World Heritage Indigenous Peoples Council of Experts (WHIPCOE)', *International Journal of Cultural Property*, 20, 155–174.

Meskell, L., Liuzza, C., Bertacchini, E. and Saccone, D. (2014) 'Multilateralism and UNESCO World Heritage: decision-making, States Parties and political processes', *International Journal of Heritage Studies,* 21(5), 423–40.

Meskell, L. and Brumann, C. (2015) 'UNESCO and New World Orders', in L. Meskell (ed.), *Global Heritage: A Reader*, London: John Wiley & Sons, 22–42.

Murdoch, L. (2011) 'Thais Lay Claim to Lord of the Dance Gesture', *The Age*, 15 August, p. 11.

Ndoro, W. (2016) 'World Heritage Sites in Africa: What Are the Benefits of Nomination and Inscription?' in W. Logan, M. Nic Craith and U. Kockel (eds), *A Companion to Heritage Studies*, Chichester: Wiley Blackwell, 392–409.

Nic Craith, M. (2007) *Intangible Cultural Heritages: The Challenge for Europe*. Professorial Inaugural Address, University of Ulster, Londonderry, UK.

Oviedo, G. and Puschkarsky, T. (2012) 'World Heritage and Rights-Based Approaches to Nature Conservation', *International Journal of Heritage Studies*, 18(3), 285–296.

Robertson, I.J.M. (2008) 'Heritage from Below: Class, Social Protest and Resistance', in B.J. Graham and P. Howard (eds), *Ashgate Research Companion to Heritage and Identity*, Aldershot, UK: Ashgate, 143–158.

Seitel, P. (ed.) (2001) *Safeguarding Traditional Culture: A Global Assessment*, Washington, DC: Smithsonian Institution.

Shyllon, F. (2016) 'Cultural Heritage and Intellectual Property: Convergence, Divergence and Interface', in W. Logan, M. Nic Craith and U. Kockel (eds), *A Companion to Heritage Studies*, Chichester: Wiley Blackwell, 55–68.

Smith, L. (2006) *Uses of Heritage*, London: Routledge.

Smith, L. and Waterton, E. (2009) *Heritage, Communities and Archaeology*, London: Duckworth.

Stavenhagen, R. (1998) 'Cultural Rights: A Social Science Perspective', in H. Niec (ed.), *Cultural Rights and Wrongs*, Paris: UNESCO, 1–20.

Tunbridge, J.E. and Ashworth, G.J. (1996) *Dissonant Heritage: The Management of the Past as a Resource in Conflict*, London: John Wiley & Sons.

Turtinen, J. (2000) *Globalizing Heritage: On UNESCO and the Transnational Construction of a World Heritage*, Stockholm: SCORE [Stockholm Centre for Organizational Research] Report series No. 12.

United Nations (UN) (1948) *Universal Declaration of Human Rights,* New York: UN.

United Nations (UN) (1966) *International Covenant on Economic,* Social and Cultural Rights, New York: UN.

United Nations (UN) (2007) *Declaration on the Rights of Indigenous Peoples,* New York: UN.

United Nations (2011) *Culture and Development. Report of the Director-General of the United Nations Educational, Scientific and Cultural Organization.* General Assembly A/66/187 (online). Available: www.unesco.or.kr/eng/front/programmes/links/2_Noteby Secretary_General.pdf (accessed 5 February 2015).

United Nations Educational Scientific and Cultural Organization (UNESCO) (1945) *Constitution of the United Nations Educational, Scientific and Cultural Organization* (online). Available: http://portal.unesco.org/en/ev.php-URL_ID=15244&URL_DO= DO_TOPIC&URL_SECTION=201.html (accessed 31 October 2012).

United Nations Educational Scientific and Cultural Organization (UNESCO) (1954) *Convention for the Protection of Cultural Property in the Event of Armed Conflict*, Paris: UNESCO.

United Nations Educational Scientific and Cultural Organization (UNESCO) (1970) *Convention on the Means of Prohibiting and Preventing the Illicit Import, Export and Transfer of Ownership of Cultural Property*, Paris: UNESCO.

United Nations Educational Scientific and Cultural Organization (UNESCO) (1972) *Convention concerning the Protection of the World Cultural and Natural Heritage*, Paris: UNESCO.

United Nations Educational Scientific and Cultural Organization (UNESCO) (1982) *Mexico City Declaration on Cultural Policies* (online). Available: *http://portal.unesco.org/pv_ obj_cache/pv_obj_id_A274FC8367592F6CEEDB92E91A93C7AC61740000/filename/ mexico_en.pdf* (accessed 31 October 2012).

United Nations Educational Scientific and Cultural Organization (UNESCO) (1985) *Model Provisions for National Laws on the Protection of Expressions of Folklore against Illicit Exploitation and other Forms of Prejudicial Action, 1982* (online). Available: www. wipo.int/wipolex/en/details.jsp?id=6714 (accessed 8 February 2016).

United Nations Educational Scientific and Cultural Organization (UNESCO) (1988) *Progress Report: Synthesis and Action Plan on the Global Strategy for a Representative and Credible World Heritage List* (online). Available: http://whc.unesco.org/en/documents/1551 (accessed 30 October 2015).

United Nations Educational Scientific and Cultural Organization (UNESCO) (1989) *Recommendation on the Safeguarding of Traditional Culture and Folklore* (online). Available: http://portal.unesco.org/en/ev.php-URL_ID=13141&URL_DO=DO_TOPIC&URL_SECTION=201.html (accessed 31 October 2012).

United Nations Educational Scientific and Cultural Organization (UNESCO) (1994) *The Nara Document on Authenticity* (online). Available: http://whc.unesco.org/archive/nara94.htm (accessed 6 January 2016).

United Nations Educational Scientific and Cultural Organization (UNESCO) (1995) *Our Creative Diversity*, Paris: World Commission on Culture and Development (online). Available: http://unesdoc.unesco.org/images/0010/001016/101651e.pdf (accessed 6 January 2016).

United Nations Educational Scientific and Cultural Organization (UNESCO) (2001) *Universal Declaration on Cultural Diversity*, Paris: UNESCO.

United Nations Educational Scientific and Cultural Organization (UNESCO) (2003) *Convention for the Safeguarding of the Intangible Cultural Heritage*, Paris: UNESCO.

United Nations Educational Scientific and Cultural Organization (UNESCO) (2004a) *The Yamato Declaration on Integrated Approaches for Safeguarding Tangible and Intangible Cultural Heritage*, Paris: UNESCO (online). Available: http://portal.unesco.org/culture/en/files/23863/10988742599Yamato_Declaration.pdf/Yamato_Declaration.pdf (accessed 20 January 2016).

United Nations Educational Scientific and Cultural Organization (UNESCO) (2004b) *Linking Universal and Local Values: Managing a Sustainable Future for World Heritage*. World Heritage Papers No. 13, Paris: UNESCO (online). Available: http://whc.unesco.org/en/series/13/ (accessed 20 January 2016).

United Nations Educational Scientific and Cultural Organization (UNESCO) (2012) *The Director-General Pays Tribute to Leading US Conservationist and One of the Founding Fathers of the World Heritage Convention* (press release), Paris, UNESCOPRESS, 19 September (online). Available: www.unesco.org/new/en/media-services/single-view/news/the_director_general_pays_tribute_to_leading_us_conservationist_and_one_of_the_founding_fathers_of_the_world_heritage_convention/#.Veu_6Snsnrc (accessed 5 September 2015).

United Nations Educational Scientific and Cultural Organization (UNESCO) (2014) *Expert Meeting on Safeguarding Intangible Cultural Heritage and Sustainable Development* (online). Available: www.unesco.org/culture/ich/doc/src/ITH-14-9.COM-13.b-EN.doc (accessed 20 November 2014).

United Nations Educational Scientific and Cultural Organization (UNESCO) (2015a) *Operational Guidelines for the Implementation of the World Heritage Convention*, Paris: World Heritage Centre (online). Available: http://whc.unesco.org/en/guidelines/ (accessed 7 September 2015).

United Nations Educational Scientific and Cultural Organization (UNESCO) (2015b) *World Heritage and Sustainable Development* (online). Available: http://whc.unesco.org/archive/2015/whc15-20ga-13-en.pdf (accessed 5 January 2016).

United Nations Educational Scientific and Cultural Organization (UNESCO) (2016) *World Heritage List* (online). Available: http://whc.unesco.org/en/list/ (accessed 6 January 2016).

United Nations Educational Scientific and Cultural Organization (UNESCO) (n.d.(a)). *Legal instruments – Culture* (online). Available: http://portal.unesco.org/en/ev.php-URL_ID=13649&URL_DO=DO_TOPIC&URL_SECTION=-471.html (accessed 4 September 2015).

United Nations Educational Scientific and Cultural Organization (UNESCO) (n.d.(b)). *General Introduction to the Standard-Setting Instruments of UNESCO* (online). Available: http://portal.unesco.org/en/ev.php-URL_ID=23772&URL_DO=DO_TOPIC&URL_SECTION=201.html#name=1 (accessed 4 September 2015).

United Nations Educational Scientific and Cultural Organization (UNESCO) (n.d.(c)) *Glossary* (online). Available: http://whc.unesco.org/en/glossary (accessed 28 October 2012).

United Nations Educational Scientific and Cultural Organization (UNESCO) (n.d.(d)) *Cultural Landscapes* (online). Available: http://whc.unesco.org/en/culturallandscape/ (accessed 7 January 2016).

United Nations Environmental Program (UNEP) (1992) *Convention on Biological Diversity* (The Biodiversity Convention). Rio de Janeiro: UNEP.

United Nations Permanent Forum on Indigenous Issues (UNPFII) (2011) *Joint Statement on Continuous violations of the principle of free, prior and informed consent in the context of UNESCO's World Heritage Convention* (online). Available: www.aippnet.org/home/statement/489-joint-statement-on-continuous-violations-of-the-principle-of-free-prior-and-informed-consent-in-the-context-of-unescos-world-heritage-convention (accessed 4 April 2012).

United Nations Permanent Forum on Indigenous Issues (UNPFII) (n.d.) *Fact Sheet: Who Are Indigenous Peoples?* (online). Available: www.un.org/esa/socdev/unpfii/documents/5session_factsheet1.pdf (accessed 20 October 2015).

United States Committee of the Blue Shield (USCBS) (2015) *Treaty on the Protection of Artistic and Scientific Institutions and Historic Monuments* (Roerich Pact) (online). Available: http://uscbs.org/1935-roerich-pact.html (accessed 21 February 2016).

Vrdoljak, A.F. (2005) *Minorities, Cultural Rights and the Protection of Intangible Cultural Heritage* (online). Available: www.esil-sedi-eu/english/pdf/Vrdoljak 09–05.pdf (accessed 31 October 2012).

World Intellectual Property Organization (WIPO) (1967) *Convention Establishing the World Intellectual Property Organization* (online). Available: www.wipo.int/wipolex/en/details.jsp?id=12412 (accessed 8 February 2016).

World Intellectual Property Organization (WIPO) (2010) *The Protection of Traditional Cultural Expressions/Expressions of Folklore: Revised Objectives and Principles*, Geneva: WIPO (online). Available: www.wipo.int/edocs/mdocs/tk/en/wipo_grtkf_ic_17/wipo_grtkf_ic_17_4.pdf (accessed 2 March 2016).

World Intellectual Property Organization (WIPO) (n.d.) *Traditional Knowledge* (online). Available at: www.wipo.int/tk/en/tk/ (accessed 14 October 2015).

Zanten, W. van (2002) *Glossary Cultural Intangible Heritage/Glossaire Culturel Patrimoine Immatériel* (online). Available: www.unesco.org/culture/ich/doc/src/00265.pdf (accessed 12 December 2015).

Chapter 3

Indigenous peoples, intangible cultural heritage and participation in the United Nations

Ana Filipa Vrdoljak

While there is growing international and regional promotion of cultural diversity and acknowledgment of the importance of cultural heritage to the maintenance and development of individual and collective identities, the capacity of groups (and individuals) to effectively engage in its protection remains less well defined. This is because international law (and international society) remains dominated by the interests and concerns of states, particularly in the field of cultural heritage. This chapter focuses on indigenous peoples' efforts to participate in United Nations initiatives for the protection and promotion of intangible cultural heritage to explore the participation by non-state actors and the responses of key UN specialist agencies in the field: the UN Educational, Scientific and Cultural Organization (UNESCO), World Intellectual Property Organization (WIPO) and UN Environment Programme (UNEP).

Despite the dominance of the state in the protection of cultural heritage in international law, multilateral organizations have, in recent years, repeatedly reaffirmed the importance of cultural diversity – as 'all cultures form part of the common heritage of all mankind' (Art. I(3) 1966 UNESCO Principles). At the same time and within the same instruments, the international community has explicitly linked cultural diversity and human rights norms (Art. 1 Universal Declaration on Cultural Diversity). The links between human rights law and cultural heritage have been most overtly explored at the international level in respect of Article 15 of the International Covenant on Economic, Social and Cultural Rights (ICESCR, United Nations 1966a) and Article 27 of the International Covenant on Civil and Political Rights (ICCPR, United Nations 1966b). The jurisprudence of international and regional human rights bodies has acknowledged the importance of cultural heritage to group identity particularly for indigenous peoples.[1] Indigenous peoples have consistently maintained that the right to self-determination applies to them and that it incorporates the right to determine how their cultures are protected, promoted and presented (Arts. 3, 11–13 DRIP). This relationship between cultural diversity, the effective enjoyment of human rights relating to culture and access to cultural heritage has been emphasized by human rights bodies and through specialist cultural heritage instruments (UN 2011a: para. 58; and Art. 4, Universal Declaration on Cultural Diversity). The UN Special Rapporteur in the field of cultural rights has observed that individuals and groups have a positive right to contribute to identifying, interpreting and developing cultural heritage, the design and implementation of policies and programmes concerning its protection and effective participation in related decision-making processes (ibid.).

This chapter concentrates on the participation of indigenous peoples in multilateral initiatives to protect cultural heritage, with specific reference to intangible heritage. While an international instrument for the protection of intangible heritage was adopted more than a decade ago, the importance of intangible heritage for indigenous peoples is evident in their work in various UN fora. I examine indigenous peoples' interventions before UNESCO and bodies established to implement the Convention on the Safeguarding of Intangible Cultural Heritage; within WIPO in respect of ongoing moves to adopt specialist instruments on traditional knowledge and cultural expressions; and finally, within UNEP and the implementation of Article 8(j) of the Convention on Biological Diversity. They reflect indigenous peoples' determination to engage in the implementation of specialist instruments adopted by states and, more significantly, their growing push to effectively participate in the drafting and negotiation of multilateral instruments which directly impact their intangible heritage. It is these latter efforts which are yielding more comprehensive and potentially lasting avenues for their effective engagement in the protection of their intangible heritage.

UNESCO and intangible cultural heritage

UNESCO is the UN's specialist agency in the field of culture. Its purpose is defined as contributing to peace and security by promoting collaboration among nations through culture to facilitate respect for human rights, fundamental freedoms and non-discrimination (Art. I(1), Constitution of UNESCO). To achieve this, the organization is mandated to conserve and protect the world's 'inheritance of books, works of art and monuments of history and science' by recommending the adoption by Member States of 'necessary international conventions' (Art. I(2) (c)).[2] UNESCO is an intergovernmental organization. Membership is confined to states which are either members of the United Nations or have been admitted by recommendation of the Executive Board and two-thirds vote of the General Conference (Art. II(1),(2)). The final form of any international convention, like the Convention concerning the Protection of the World Cultural and Natural Heritage (World Heritage Convention) or the Convention for Safeguarding of the Intangible Cultural Heritage (Intangible Heritage Convention), is determined by the Member States at the annual General Conference. States that subsequently ratify a convention, that is, States Parties, govern its operation. This structure necessarily inhibits the participation of non-state actors without the consent of relevant states.[3]

Within the context of UNESCO, from time to time there appears to be a window that may open to allow non-state actors like indigenous peoples a role in the protection of their cultural heritage. However, experience shows that with respect to the World Heritage Convention and Intangible Heritage Convention these initiatives are often watered down in practice.

World Heritage Convention and WHIPCOE

Within UNESCO, the World Heritage Convention has become the focus of efforts to recognize and accommodate indigenous peoples' rights and interests to their cultural heritage. There appears to have been no overt indigenous participation during the drafting and negotiations prior to the Convention's adoption in 1972, and the final text does not explicitly refer to the participation of indigenous (and local) communities in respect of its implementation. Indigenous participation has been incorporated through the subsequent adoption and revision of Operational Guidelines by the World Heritage Committee. The revision of the Operational Guidelines to include 'cultural landscapes' and 'living traditions' in the selection criteria during the course of the 1990s served as an avenue by which the relationship between indigenous peoples and World Heritage sites could be acknowledged (WHC 1994: para. 35–42). These changes coincided with efforts by indigenous peoples within the United Nations to craft a dedicated human rights instrument (UNWGIP 1994).

These developments paved the way for the Mirrar people's challenge to the Australian federal government–approved expansion of a uranium mine in the World Heritage-listed Kakadu National Park, which laid bare the limitations of the World Heritage Convention in respect of consultation with and participation of indigenous (and local) communities. The World Heritage Committee accepted the findings of a report by its Chair and emphasized 'the fundamental importance of ensuring thorough and continuing participation, negotiation and communication with Aboriginal traditional owners, custodians and managers' in the conservation of the site (WHC 1998). The continued lack of consultation by the Australian government led the Mirrar community to directly request the World Heritage Committee to intervene and list the site as 'in danger' (Logan 2013: 57).

The Mirrar's push occurred as the World Heritage Indigenous Peoples' Forum was lobbying the World Heritage Committee to establish the World Heritage Indigenous Peoples' Council of Experts (WHIPCOE) as a new consultative body (Art. 10(3) WHC; WHC 2001a). The International Council for the Conservation of Nature and Natural Resources (IUCN) and International Council on Monuments and Sites (ICOMOS) had facilitated the Committee's efforts to better understand the Mirrar's objections (Australia ICOMOS 2001; 2000). However, these organizations are expert in the preservation and protection of the physical sites; the representation of indigenous and local communities is not their primary expertise or mandate. WHIPCOE was intended to 'add value rather than displace' these advisory bodies by providing a mechanism by which indigenous peoples could participate in the development and implementation of laws and policies for the protection of their intangible heritage which applied to ancestral lands designated on the World Heritage List (WHC 2001a: 2–5). It was to have been made up of representatives from World Heritage sites listed as 'cultural landscapes' or ' "mixed" cultural/natural properties' which 'hold indigenous values' (WHC 2001a: 7). The initiative was designed as a 'means of giving Indigenous people greater responsibility for their own affairs and an effective voice in decisions on matters which affect them' (WHC 2001a: Annex 1, 12). The proposal did not gain the support of the majority of States Parties to the Convention, particularly those in Africa and Asia (WHC 2001b). The UN Permanent Forum on Indigenous Issues has since taken up the question of indigenous peoples' effective participation in the World Heritage framework (Meskell 2013; Disko and Tugendhat 2014).

Intangible heritage convention and operational directives

Much academic discourse on the participation of non-state actors, particularly indigenous peoples, in UN processes involving cultural heritage has focussed on World Heritage. Yet multilateral initiatives for the protection of intangible cultural heritage have likewise seen indigenous peoples seek effective participation in these processes. Despite the failure of the WHIPCOE proposal in the World Heritage context, it had two lasting implications for the negotiation of the Intangible Heritage Convention. Indigenous representatives challenged States and intergovernmental organizations to understand heritage holistically by moving beyond the physical site to encompass its movable and intangible aspects and reinforced the rights of peoples to be consulted and involved in decision-making related to their heritage. These lessons are evident in the final text, despite its limitations.

UNESCO's normative work on intangible heritage started in 1973 with a Bolivian proposal for a protocol to protect folklore to be attached to the Universal Copyright Convention (1952). Folklore was viewed by developing countries, especially those with indigenous populations, as representing a significant component of their economies and cultural heritage. In 1978, UNESCO and WIPO formally agreed to divide their work in this field, with UNESCO examining the safeguarding of folklore from an interdisciplinary perspective and WIPO focussing on intellectual property relating to traditional knowledge (Blake 2002: 19). This led to the WIPO and UNESCO Model Provisions for National Laws on the Protection of Expressions of Folklore against Illicit and Other Prejudicial Actions of 1982 (Blake 2002: 20–22; WIPO 1998a); and UNESCO's Recommendation on the Safeguarding of Traditional Culture and Folklore of 1989. The Model Provisions refer obliquely to authorization by the 'competent authority' appointed by the relevant state and 'community' (sections 3 and 10(1); UNESCO and WIPO 1985). The 1989 UNESCO Recommendation, the first (non-binding) multilateral instrument to exclusively cover intangible cultural heritage, again refers to 'a cultural community' and their right to access their culture without fully articulating how they were to participate in the relevant decision-making processes concerning its preservation, protection and promotion (1989 Recommendation, paras. A and D(b)). Criticism was levelled at its failure to fully articulate a need to obtain free, prior and informed consent to the use or exploitation of intangible heritage (Weiner 1987; Posey and Dutfield 1996). Indigenous peoples were alluded to overtly or implicitly during the drafting of these instruments, but neither they nor their representatives were formally involved.

By 1999, when a joint UNESCO and Smithsonian Institute conference was held to work toward a binding instrument on intangible heritage, the international landscape had changed irrevocably. This shift was reflected in the contribution of indigenous participants and greater cognisance of indigenous concerns by delegates (UNESCO 1999). It was encapsulated in the 1992 Convention on Biological Diversity and its recognition of the interests of indigenous (and local) communities, discussed in what follows (Art. 8(j) CBD); the UN Working Group on Indigenous Populations' 1993 draft Declaration on the Rights of Indigenous Peoples prepared with substantial indigenous input (UNWGIP 1994); and its Principles and Guidelines on the Protection of the Heritage of Indigenous Peoples (Daes 1995; Yokota and Sami Council 2006). The draft Declaration and Principles and Guidelines made clear that effective protection of the cultural heritage of indigenous peoples must be based on the principle of self-determination (Principle 2, Principles and Guidelines). Specifically it stipulated that 'Indigenous peoples and their representatives should enjoy direct access to all intergovernmental negotiations in the field of intellectual property rights, to share their views on the measures needed to protect their heritage through international law' (Principle 56, Principles and Guidelines).

During the initial drafting phase of the Intangible Heritage Convention, UNESCO's General Conference adopted its Universal Declaration on Cultural Diversity, which made specific reference to the human rights of indigenous peoples (and minorities) and to their cultures (Art. 4 Universal Declaration). While the drafts did not specifically mention indigenous peoples, they made multiple references to the need for States Parties to the proposed instrument to ensure the participation of 'cultural communities' (UNESCO 2002: draft arts. 3, 5, 6). The Intangible Heritage Convention, adopted in 2003, references the participation of 'communities, groups and relevant non-governmental organizations' in respect of identifying and defining intangible heritage on its territory for safeguarding measures (Art. 11) and for States Parties to 'ensure [their] widest possible participation' in its management (Art. 15). The only specific reference to indigenous communities, their heritage and participation in its protection in the final text, occurs in the preamble. An internal evaluation of the Convention's operation defined Articles 11(b) and 15 as 'key to the implementation of the 2003 Convention'. It found that both States Parties and non-state actors found the Convention 'to be a highly relevant international legal instrument' (UNESCO 2013: iv and 40), because it encouraged 'bottom-up approaches that involve communities, groups and individuals as central actors' (UNESCO 2013: 9). However, it also observed that community participation was one of the 'most challenging aspects of its implementation' (UNESCO 2013: v). It found that States Parties' periodic reports showed ICH policy making was largely centralized, with NGOs usually providing the bridge between governments and communities. It recommended that the Intergovernmental Committee promote increased NGO and community involvement in the development and implementation of safeguarding initiatives (UNESCO 2013: 29).

The Operational Directives to the Convention, adopted and revised by the General Assembly of the States Parties, also refer to the need for consultation with and participation of communities, groups and individuals (UNESCO 2012). The 'widest possible participation' and 'free, prior and informed consent' are criteria for inscription on the In Need of Urgent Safeguarding List or the Representative List, for the purposes of awareness raising and requests for international assistance. Rather than simply 'sensitizing' communities, groups and individuals to the importance of intangible cultural heritage (UNESCO 2012: para. 81), the 2014 revised Operational Directives require States Parties to raise awareness so that the 'bearers of this heritage may benefit fully from this standard-setting instrument' (ibid.). The Subsidiary Body established by the IGC reminded States Parties that evidence of free, prior and informed consent from the relevant community, group or individuals must be obtained before nomination and could not be established afterwards. Further, it emphasized that 'utmost care' must be used in obtaining such consent in circumstances of violent conflict to encourage dialogue and mutual respect (UNESCO 2014a: 19).

The participation of communities, groups and individuals is subject to a proviso. The Intangible Heritage Convention, its Operational Directives and the reports of related committees have consistently reaffirmed the importance of ensuring that the implementation of the treaty conform with international human rights norms (including cultural rights), especially of vulnerable groups. The Consultative Body makes clear that because 'communities are not monolithic and homogeneous', States Parties must ensure 'women's voices' are 'fully represented among those providing consent' and 'the design and implementation of safeguarding measures' (UNESCO 2014a: 8). Also, the 2013 Evaluation Report referred to UNESCO's responsibility under the Global Priority Gender Equality compact (UNESCO 2013: 17). It found no conflict between safeguarding of intangible heritage and the requirement that traditional practices cannot violate human rights norms. Instead, it called for UNESCO and the IGC to facilitate through the participation of and negotiation with the relevant community that there is an 'evolution/adaption of traditional cultural practices in such a way that their core value to the community is retained while any seriously discriminatory aspects are removed or neutralised' (ibid.).

As with other specialist heritage instruments, the Intangible Heritage Convention envisages a role for civil society organizations. The Operational Directive covers the accreditation of NGOs and requires that they 'cooperate in a spirit of mutual respect' with relevant communities, groups or individuals. NGOs can be invited by the Committee to evaluate nomination files, requests for international assistance and safeguarding plans. The 2013 Evaluation Report observed that many NGOs felt that they were not being taken seriously by States Parties, largely because of lax accreditation criteria and the inactivity of many accredited organizations (UNESCO 2013: v). It recommended that the accreditation process be reviewed to ensure that they held the requisite experience and capacity to effectively advise the IGC (UNESCO 2013: 61).[4] The criteria for accreditation of NGOs under the Operational Directives require that they must have competence, expertise and experience in safeguarding intangible heritage, with local, national, regional or international exposure, objectives which, accorded with the Convention, cooperate 'in a spirit of mutual respect' with relevant communities, groups and, where appropriate, individuals, and operational capacity (including regular active membership, established legal personality under relevant domestic law, and been active for four years prior to initial accreditation) (UNESCO 2014b: para. 91).

Convention on the Protection and Promotion of the Diversity of Cultural Expressions

The Convention on the Protection and Promotion of the Diversity of Cultural Expressions adopted by the UNESCO General Conference in 2005 is viewed as complementary to the Intangible Heritage Convention. It originally was projected to be a vehicle for the codification of cultural rights but became a means of promoting cultural diversity through the protection of cultural expressions, replacing what had increasingly been viewed as the failure to achieve such protection for cultural goods through the World Trade Organization. This shift from a human rights instrument to one more attuned to trade-related concerns moved it away from the language of intangible heritage and towards WIPO's proposed instruments.

The Cultural Diversity Convention's preamble acknowledges the importance of indigenous traditional knowledge to sustainable development. Likewise, it flags that indigenous peoples should have the freedom to create and disseminate their traditional cultural expressions and access them and derive benefit from them for their development. One of its guiding principles is the 'equal dignity of and respect of all cultures' (Art. 2(3)). It calls on States Parties to create conditions on their territory that are conducive to this end, particularly for indigenous peoples, with 'due attention to the special circumstances and needs of women' (Art. 7(1) (a); UNESCO 2014c). While the Convention does not specifically provide for participation of indigenous peoples, its framework does enable the input of civil-society organizations generally (Art. 11; UNESCO 2009).

WIPO, traditional knowledge and cultural expressions

As noted earlier, the work of UNESCO and WIPO on the legal protection of folklore, now referred to as either 'intangible cultural heritage' (UNESCO) or 'traditional knowledge' or 'cultural expressions' (WIPO), has been inextricably tied together for decades. The 2013 Evaluation of the Intangible Heritage Convention recommended that UNESCO strengthen its cooperation with WIPO in the area to ensure 'an ongoing exchange and learning between the two organizations and their Member States', especially in the light of WIPO's efforts to finalize a multilateral instrument for the protection of the intellectual property rights of communities (UNESCO 2013: 59). Unlike the Intangible Heritage Convention and its related statutory bodies, WIPO and the Intergovernmental Committee (IGC) on Intellectual Property and Genetic Resources, Traditional Knowledge and Folklore, tasked with developing a treaty in this field, have specifically referenced and engaged indigenous peoples in their work. However, the draft treaty has not been finalized or adopted to date. The WIPO negotiations are important for understanding the participation of relevant communities including indigenous peoples in the development and implementation of the treaties at the supranational level and their participation at the national and local levels subsequent to their adoption.

The draft Articles on the Protection of Traditional Knowledge and the draft Articles on the Protection of Traditional Cultural Expressions prepared by the Secretariat and deliberated by the IGC in June 2014 go beyond the nebulous language of the Intangible Heritage Convention. The current drafts specifically refer to 'indigenous peoples and local communities' and the need for their 'prior informed consent' (WIPO 2014a; 2014b). This language borrows heavily from the Declaration on the Rights of Indigenous Peoples (DRIP) adopted by the UN General Assembly in 2007. Article 31 of the DRIP provides that indigenous peoples have the right to control their cultural heritage, traditional knowledge and traditional cultural expressions including intellectual property over it. It then calls on states in conjunction with indigenous peoples to take effective measures to recognize and protect such rights. The draft policy objectives of the proposed WIPO instrument on traditional knowledge requires that states provide indigenous peoples and local communities with means to encourage and protect its creation and innovation, control its use, promote equitable benefit sharing arising from its use with prior informed consent and prevent its misuse (WIPO 2014a: Annex, 4). Similar draft objectives have been prepared in respect of the instrument on cultural expression with an additional provision covering third party rights and the public domain (ibid.).

The then Chair of the UN Permanent Forum on Indigenous Issues (UNPFII), Dalee Sambo Dorough presciently observed that international trade law and intellectual property law are not properly able to fully and effectively protect indigenous peoples' human rights and cultures (Sambo Dorough 2014: 5–8). She noted that it was unlikely that the final text of the WIPO instruments covering traditional knowledge or cultural expressions would properly achieve this aim unless the drafting process complied with Article 18 DRIP, concerning indigenous peoples' right to participation in decision making in matters which affect their rights (ibid.). Another indigenous representative pointed out that the nature of treaty law meant that any instruments were dependent on states ratifying and effectively implementing the obligations arising under them (WIPO 2014c: 25). The IGC has called on states to use all means to facilitate indigenous participation including indigenous representatives as part of their delegations (WIPO 2003: 77). However, this occurs rarely (WIPO 2013: 3).

WIPO's Member States have emphasized the need to facilitate and strengthen the participation of observers in the IGC's work (WIPO 2011). The organization's General Rules of Procedure permit observers to take part in debates and submit proposals, amendments or motions at the invitation of the Chair (Rule 24, WIPO 1998b). From its first session, the IGC have accommodated NGOs and other organizations which do not have permanent observer status with WIPO as *ad hoc* observers (WIPO 2001). However, it does not go as far as initiatives by Economic and Social Council (ECOSOC) and the Human Rights Council which funds indigenous and local communities experts meetings, with representatives from each of the seven socio-cultural regions, prior to their sessions (WIPO 2013: 3). The organization recognizes that indigenous peoples do not necessarily organize themselves as NGOs, which has been a precondition for consultative status at the United Nations (WIPO 2013: 4; UN OHCHR 1996b). WIPO has also made a distinction between organizations representative of and accountable to indigenous peoples and local communities and NGOs working with or for indigenous communities and seeking to make the procedure for accreditation for the former more transparent and easily identifiable and thereby being able to access funding and invitations to present to meetings (WIPO 2013: 4).

The IGC has undertaken a number of initiatives to maximize the ability of indigenous and local communities to participate effectively and in person in deliberations of these instruments. For example, a panel of representatives of indigenous and local communities of the geo-cultural regions and chaired by a representative of an indigenous or local community who meet prior to the IGC sessions, and a summary report of these presentations is included in the IGC reports on their proceedings (WIPO 2013: 10). Furthermore, WIPO finances administrative support for these meetings and indigenous representatives through the Indigenous Peoples' Centre for Documentation, Research and Information (WIPO 2013: 11). To financially assist accredited indigenous and local communities' representatives to attend and participate at the IGC, a voluntary fund was established in 2005 (WIPO 2006). The Secretariat initially provided briefings to indigenous and local community representatives concerning the IGC's work, with this information now provided online (WIPO 2013: 11–13).

These initiatives within WIPO reflect the practices being utilized within another UN agency dealing with environmental protection, UNEP, which through an instrument adopted two decades ago has been an important site for indigenous engagement at the international level for the protection of their cultural heritage.

UNEP and Article 8(j) of the Convention on Biological Diversity

The Convention on Biological Diversity (CBD) adopted under the auspices of UNEP predates the Intangible Heritage Convention and the current WIPO initiatives. Yet it is an important example of a multilateral environmental law instrument, which also covers intangible heritage, providing a means of participation by non-state actors including indigenous and local communities within the text itself and its subsequent elaboration through its operationalization. This is explained by the fact that the CBD was finalized in the early 1990s when the Rio Declaration on the Environment and Development was adopted, and the UN Working Group on Indigenous Populations was finalizing the draft Declaration on the Rights of Indigenous Peoples. The Rio Declaration covers the participation of 'all concerned citizens', access to information, opportunity to participate in decision-making processes and access to justice (Principle 10). It recognizes that indigenous peoples have a 'vital role' in environmental management and requires that states recognize and support indigenous 'identity, culture and interests' and enable their effective participation in achieving sustainable development (Principle 22).

The CBD preamble acknowledges 'the close and traditional dependence of many indigenous and local communities embodying traditional lifestyles on biological resources' (UNEP 2003: 63). The States Parties to the CBD have established a number of mechanisms for the effective participation of indigenous and local communities in the meetings and operation of the treaty including an *ad hoc* open-ended Working Group on Article 8(j) and Related Provisions, which is viewed as 'a forum for dialogue between indigenous and local communities and [States] Parties, and other stakeholders' (UNEP 2013), a Voluntary Fund for Facilitating the Participation of Indigenous and Local Communities in the Convention Process (VB Trust Fund), providing financial assistance to attend and participate in meeting and related logistical support, and a dedicated Traditional Knowledge Information Portal and other non-electronic modes of information dissemination (UNEP 2010a). This is augmented through the work of the International Indigenous Forum of Biodiversity, the indigenous caucus.

The participation of indigenous and local communities in the conservation and sustainable use of biological diversity is covered by Article 8(j) CBD. The work programme for Article 8(j) requires '*just* implementation' from the local to the international level and ensures full and effective participation of indigenous and local communities (including women) throughout its implementation (UNEP 2000).[5] To this end, and at the behest of the Conference of States Parties in the early 2000s and UNPFII, the *ad hoc* Working Group prepared guidelines for conducting cultural impact assessment for development proposals (UNEP 2002: Recommendation D). The Akwé: Kon Voluntary Guidelines, adopted in 2004, cover effective participation of indigenous and local communities (especially women) in respect of development applications to identify and implement measures to prevent or mitigate any negative impact. Cultural, environmental and social impact assessment is integrated into a single process to recognize 'the unique relationship' indigenous peoples have with their land (UNEP 2004: 19). Cultural impact assessment is defined as:

[A] process of evaluating the likely impacts of proposed development on the way of life of a particular group or community of people, with full involvement of this group or community of people and possibly undertaken by this group or community of people: a cultural impact assessment will generally address the impacts, both beneficial and adverse, of a proposed development that may affect, for example, the values, belief systems, customary law, language(s), customs, economy, relationships with the local environment and particular species, social organization and traditions of the affected community (UNEP 2004: 14).

General considerations across all forms of impact assessment include prior informed consent from the affected indigenous and local communities, participation of women and youth (especially from indigenous and local communities), formulation of community development plans by indigenous and local communities, ownership and control of traditional knowledge, need for transparency and review and dispute-resolution procedures (UNEP 2004: 25–27).[6] However, the guidelines do provide for notification and public consultation by the development proponent, the identification of indigenous and local communities and other stakeholders, the establishment of mechanisms for their participation, agreed process of recording their concerns, sufficient resources for their participation, an environmental management plan and identification of persons responsible for liability and redress and the establishment of a review process.

Mechanisms for consultation and participation of indigenous peoples are further elaborated in respect of genetic resources under the Nagoya Protocol on Access to Genetic Resources and Fair and Equitable Sharing of Benefits Arising from their Utilization to the Convention on Biological Diversity, adopted in 2010.[7] Not only does it acknowledge the DRIP in its preamble, it also recognizes the diverse ways traditional knowledge associated with genetic resources is 'held or owned by indigenous and local communities' and their right to identify the rightful holders of this knowledge within their communities and affirms that the Protocol does not diminish or extinguish any of their existing rights. It requires that States Parties set out the criteria and processes for obtaining prior informed consent and the participation of indigenous and local communities in accessing genetic resources and associated traditional knowledge (Arts. 6(1)(f) and 7). Consistent with DRIP, it requires that they take into consideration indigenous and local communities' customary law, protocols and procedures in respect of same (including an Access and Benefit-sharing Clearing-House) and develop in conjunction with these communities' mechanisms to inform potential users of their obligations (Art. 12). To facilitate effective indigenous and local community participation they are required to implement awareness-raising measures (e.g. regular meetings, helpdesk, dissemination of information, promotion of voluntary code in consultation with the communities, their involvement in implementation processes (Art. 21)), capacity-building measures and financial mechanisms and resources for implementation should prioritize the needs of these communities, especially those of women.

Following concerns raised by UNPFII, the CBD Conference of Parties also adopted a code of ethical conduct concerning the cultural heritage of indigenous peoples in 2010 (UNPFII 2003: paras. 46, 55–57). Viewed as a sister instrument to the Akwé: Kon Guidelines, the Tkarihwaié:ri Code was designed in consultation with the UNPFII and is proposed to establish a 'new paradigm' by promoting capacity building for indigenous and local communities and equal partnerships with researchers and others working with them (Secretariat CBD 2011: 2). It is viewed as a collaborative framework for facilitating effective indigenous participation and obtaining prior informed consent in respect of research arising from their knowledge, territories and related resources (ibid.). It reaffirms and elaborates fundamental principles contained in DRIP. It also expands upon the 'methods' which speak to the participation of indigenous communities, including the need to negotiate in good faith, the need to respect indigenous peoples' decision-making structures and timelines, promotion of partnerships and cooperation, recognition of the special role of women, respect for restriction on access and confidentiality and sharing of information obtaining from interactions with the communities (Secretariat CBD 2011: paras. 26–32).

Conclusion

This chapter has concentrated on how indigenous peoples' participation is being engaged in respect of the negotiation of the text of treaties for the protection of cultural heritage and their implementation after their adoption. Although reference is made at key junctures to the work of indigenous communities, representatives and leaders to these ends, this has not been the focus.[8] Nonetheless, despite this lack of elaboration, it must be made clear that it is very much indigenous peoples that are pushing for these changes at the international, national and local levels. More recently, at the international level, this is driven through the work of UNPFII, the Expert Mechanism and the Special Rapporteur on the Rights of Indigenous Peoples, all of whom have made it clear that cultural heritage and indigenous peoples' effective participation in its protection is a priority.[9]

Indigenous peoples' efforts to participate in multilateral initiatives concerning intangible heritage before various UN agencies over the last two decades have had a transformative impact on how the obligations under these instruments are defined and implemented by states. As noted earlier, the protection of cultural heritage in international law continues to be defined and dominated by states. The push by indigenous peoples to participate effectively in decision making concerning their cultural heritage continues to fundamentally alter how cultures and cultural heritage are defined, going beyond a siloing of tangible, intangible, movable and immovable heritage to a holistic interpretation. Recent developments in respect of the Article 8(j) CBD, including the Akwé: Kon Guidelines, exemplify this approach. It is why indigenous peoples' focus is not just confined to specialist cultural heritage instruments. Equally, their work in redefining and providing greater clarity to what constitutes effective participation of non-state actors and how it can be realized in practice builds on environmental law initiatives around participation and access to justice. It is important to reiterate that these twin elements of a holistic understanding of culture and heritage and the deeper and broader interpretation of participation in decision-making accord with and reinforce indigenous peoples' steadfast emphasis on their centrality to the full and effective enjoyment of their human rights, including their cultural rights.

Notes

1   See for example, *Lubicon Lake Band (Bernard Ominayak) v. Canada*, No. 167/1984, UN Doc. A/45/40, Pt. 2, p. 1 (1990), para. 32.1; Case of the *Mayagna (Sumo) Awas Tigni Community v. Nicaragua*, (Judgment) (2001) 79 I/A. Ct H.R. (ser. C); and *Social and Economic Rights Action Center/Center for Economic and Social Rights v. Nigeria*, Communication No. 155/96, ACtHPR, 27 May 2002, UN Doc. ACHPR/COMM/A044/1.
2   There is the proviso that 'to preserv[e] the independence, integrity and fruitful diversity of the cultures . . . of States Members' UNESCO is 'prohibited from intervening in the matters within their domestic jurisdiction' (Art. I(3), UNESCO Constitution).
3   United Nations Secretary General (1996a: para. 28).
4   The IGC adopted the recommendation that the General Assembly of States Parties amend the Operational Directives to adopt this recommendation: Decision 8.COM 5.c.1, para. 6, 23 September 2013, UNESCO Doc.ITH/13/8.COM/Decisions, p. 6. The General Assembly failed to adopt it: General Assembly of the States Parties to the Convention, Fifth Session, Resolutions, 4 June 2014, UNESCO Doc.ITH/14/5.GA/Resolutions.
5   It referenced the Declaration of the World Conference of Indigenous Peoples on Territory, Environment and Development, Kari-Oca, 30 May 1992; and Declaration on Cultural and Intellectual Property Rights of Indigenous Peoples, Mataatua, 18 June 1993, and the need to make the CBD mutually supportive with international agreements on intellectual property. See also UNEP 2010b, 2011.
6   Unlike the environmental and social impact assessment components, there is no guidance in respect of baseline studies for cultural impact assessments.
7   29 October 2010, entered into force 12 October 2014, UNEP/CBD/COP/DEC/X/1.
8   See UN 2011b and Vrdoljak (forthcoming).
9   See in respect of UNPFII 2003: paras. 95–105; United Nations Expert Mechanism on the Rights of Indigenous Peoples 2015; and UN 2002: paras. 59–71, 113(d).

International instruments

UNEP. (1992). Convention on Biological Diversity (CBD), 5 June 1992, entered into force 29 December 1993, 1760 UNTS 79
UNEP. (2010). Nagoya Protocol on Access to Genetic Resources and Fair and Equitable Sharing of Benefits Arising from their Utilization to the Convention on Biological Diversity (Nagoya Protocol). 29 October 2010, entered into force 12 October 2014, UNEP/CBD/COP/DEC/X/1
UNESCO. (1945). Constitution of UNESCO, signed on 16 November 1945, into force 4 November 1946
UNESCO. (1952). Universal Copyright Convention. 6 September 1952, entered into force 16 September 1955, 216 UNTS 132
UNESCO. (1966). Declaration of Principles of International Cultural Cooperation, (1966 UNESCO Principles), resolution adopted by at the UNESCO General Conference, 4 November 1966

UNESCO. (1972). Convention concerning the Protection of the World Cultural and Natural Heritage (World Heritage Convention), 16 November 1972, in force 17 December 1975, 1037 UNTS 151

UNESCO. (1989). Recommendation on the Safeguarding of Traditional Culture and Folklore (1989 UNESCO Recommendation). Adopted by the General Conference at its 25th session, 15 November 1989

United Nations. (1992). Rio Declaration on the Environment and Development (Rio Declaration). Adopted by the United Nations Conference on Environment, 13 June 1992, UN Doc.A/CONF.151/26, vol.1

United Nations. (1966a). International Covenant on Economic, Social and Cultural Rights (ICESCR). GA Res.2200A(XXI), 16 December 1966, in force 3 January 1976

United Nations. (1966b). International Covenant on Civil and Political Rights (ICCPR), GA Res.2200A(XXI), 16 December 1966, in force 23 March 1976

UNESCO. (2001). Universal Declaration on Cultural Diversity, adopted by the UNESCO General Conference, 2 November 2001

UNESCO. (2003). Convention for Safeguarding of the Intangible Cultural Heritage (Intangible Heritage Convention), 17 October 2003, in force 20 April 2006, 2368 UNTS 1

UNESCO. (2005). Convention on the Protection and Promotion of the Diversity of Cultural Expressions (2005 UNESCO Convention). 20 October 2005, entered into force 18 March 2007, 2440 UNTS 311

United Nations. (2007). Declaration on the Rights of Indigenous Peoples (DRIP), GA Res. 61/295 of 13 September 2007

References

Australia ICOMOS. (2000) *Comments on the Australian Government Progress Report to the Bureau of the World Heritage Committee, 15 April 2000*, Burwood: Australia ICOMOS.

Australia ICOMOS. (2001) *Australia ICOMOS Statement on Indigenous Cultural Heritage*, Burwood: Australia ICOMOS.

Blake, J. (2002) Developing a New Standard-Setting Instrument for the Safeguarding of Intangible Cultural Heritage: Elements for Consideration, UNESCO Doc.CLT-2001/WS/8.Rev

Daes, E.-I. (1995) Revised Text of the Principles and Guidelines for the Protection of the Heritage of Indigenous Peoples, 21 June 1995, UN Doc.E/CN.4/Sub.2/1995/26, Annex

Disko, S. and Tugendhat, H. (eds). (2014) *World Heritage Sites and Indigenous Peoples' Rights*, Copenhagen: IWGIA Document 129.

Logan, W. (2013) 'Australia, Indigenous Peoples and World Heritage from Kakadu to Cape York: State Party Behavior Under the World Heritage Convention', *Journal of Social Anthropology*, 3(2), 53.

Meskell, L. (2013) 'UNESCO and the Fate of the World Heritage Indigenous Peoples' Council of Experts (WHIPCOE)', *International Journal of Cultural Property*, 20, 155–174.

Posey, D. and Dutfield, G. (1996) *Beyond Intellectual Property: Toward Traditional Resource Rights for Indigenous Peoples and Local Communities*, London: International Development Research Centre.

Sambo Dorough, D. (2014) Presentation by D. Sambo Dorough (Indigenous Panel), WIPO/GRTKF/IC/28/INDIGENOUS PANEL/MS.DALEE SAMBO DOROUGH, 9 July 2014, pp. 5–8. Available: www.wipo.int/meetings/en/details.jsp?meeting_id=32091 (accessed 11 April 2015).

Secretariat of the Convention on Biological Diversity (2011) *Tkarihwaié:ri Code of Ethical Respect for the Cultural and Intellectual Heritage of Indigenous and Local Communities Relevant to the Conservation and Sustainable Use of Biological Diversity*, Montreal: Secretariat CBD. Available: www.cbd.int/traditional/code/ethicalconduct-brochure-en. pdf (viewed 20 June 2015).

UNEP (2000) COP 5 Decision V/16, Art.8(j) and Related Articles, adopted May 2000.

UNEP (2002) COP 6 Decision VI/10, Art.8(j) and Related Articles, adopted April 2002.

UNEP (2003) Governing Council Decision 22/16 on the Environment and Cultural Diversity, in UNEP, Report of the 22nd Session of the Governing Council/Global Ministerial Environment Forum, 7 February 2003, p. 63. Available: www.unep.org/gc/gc22/REPORTS/K0360710English.pdf (viewed 23 June 2015).

UNEP (2004) Akwé: Kon Voluntary Guidelines for the Conduct of Cultural, Environmental and Social Impact Assessment regarding Developments proposed to take place on, or which are likely to impact on, sacred sites and on lands and waters traditionally occupied or used by Indigenous and Local Communities, COP 7 Decision adopted 13 April 2004, UNEP/CBD/COP/DEC/VII/16, Part F, p. 10.

UNEP (2010a) COP 10 Decision X/40, adopted 29 October 2010, UNEP/CBD/COP/DEC/X/40.

UNEP (2010b) Target 18, Strategic Goal E: Enhance Implementation Through Participatory Planning, Knowledge Management, and Capacity Building, Aichi Biodiversity Targets, Revised and Updated Strategic Plan for Biodiversity 2011–2010, COP 10 Decision X/2. Available: www.cbd.int/decision/cop/?id=12268 (viewed 24 June 2015).

UNEP (2011) Indicative List of Indicators for the Strategic Plan for Biodiversity 2011–2020, COP XI/3, UNEP/CBD/COP/DEC/XI/3, Annex

UNEP (2013) Message from B. Ferreira De Souza Dias, Executive Secretary CBD, 9 August 2013. Available: www.un.org/en/events/indigenousday/2013/cbd.shtml (viewed 20 June 2015).

UNESCO (1999) *A Global Assessment of the 1989 Recommendation on the Safeguarding of Traditional Culture and Folklore: Local Empowerment and International Cooperation.* Available: http://folklife.si.edu/resources/Unesco/index.htm (viewed 12 March 2015).

UNESCO (2002) First Preliminary Draft of an International Convention for the Safeguarding of the Intangible Cultural Heritage, 26 July 2002, UNESCO Doc.CLT-2002/CONF.2003/3

UNESCO (2009) Role and Participation of Civil Society, Operational Guidelines, adopted by the Conference of the Parties, 2nd session, June 2009. Available: http://en.unesco.org/creativity/sites/creativity/files/Conv2005_DO_Art_11_EN.pdf (viewed 24 June 2015).

UNESCO (2012) Operational Directives for the Implementation of the Convention for the Safeguarding of the Intangible Cultural Heritage, adopted by the General Assembly of States Parties to the Convention in 2008, and amended in 2010 and 2012, UNESCO Doc.4.GA(2012)

UNESCO (2013) Evaluation of UNESCO's Standard-setting Work of the Culture Sector, Part I – 2003 Convention for the Safeguarding of the Intangible Cultural Heritage, B Toggler, E Sediakina-Rivière and J Blake, Final Report, (October 2013), UNESCO Doc. IOS/EVS/PI/129 REV

UNESCO (2014a) Report of the Subsidiary Body on its work in 2014, 25 November 2014, UNESCO Doc.ITH/14/9.COM/10 Add.3

UNESCO (2014b) Operational Directives for the Implementation of the Convention for the Safeguarding of the Intangible Cultural Heritage, adopted by the General Assembly of States Parties, June 2014

UNESCO (2014c) Evaluation of UNESCO's Standard-Setting Work of the Culture Sector, Part IV-2005 Convention on the Protection and Promotion of the Diversity of Cultural Expressions, Final Report, April 2014, J. Baltà and IOS, UNESCO Doc.IOS/EVS/PI/134 Rev.2

UNESCO and WIPO (1985) Model Provisions for National Laws on the Protection of Expressions of Folklore on the Protection of Expressions of Folklore against Illicit Exploitation and other Prejudicial Action. Available: unesdoc.unesco.org/images/0006/000684/068457mb.pdf (viewed 10 March 2015).

United Nations Expert Mechanism on the Rights of Indigenous Peoples (2011b) Final Report of the Study on Indigenous Peoples and the Right to Participate in Decision-Making, Expert Mechanism on the Rights of Indigenous Peoples, 17 August 2011, UN Doc.A/HRC/18/42

United Nations (2002) Special Rapporteur on the Rights of Indigenous Peoples (2002) Situation on the Human Rights and Fundamental Freedoms of Indigenous Peoples. R. Stavenhagen. 4 February 2002. UN Doc.E/CN/4/2002/97

United Nations Expert Mechanism on the Rights of Indigenous Peoples (2015) Study on Cultural Heritage. Available: www.ohchr.org/EN/Issues/IPeoples/EMRIP/Pages/Study-onculturalheritage.aspx (viewed on 26 June 2015).

United Nations Independent expert in the field of cultural rights (2011a) Right of Access to and Enjoyment of Cultural Heritage, Report of the Independent Expert in the Field of Cultural Rights, 21 March 2011, UN Doc.A/HRC/17/38

United Nations Officer of High Commissioner of Human Rights. (1996b). Submission to WIPO Secretariat to IGC, Participation of Observers, 30 November 2011; and Review of the Existing Mechanisms, Procedures, and Programmes Within the United Nations concerning Indigenous Peoples, 14 October 1996, UN Doc.A/51/493

United Nations Secretary General (1996a) Review of the Existing Mechanisms, Procedures and Programmes Within the United Nations concerning Indigenous People. Report of the Secretary-General, 14 October 1996, UN Doc.A/51/493

United Nations Working Group on Indigenous Populations (WGIP) (1994) Draft UN Declaration on the Rights of Indigenous Peoples, adopted by the Working Group on Indigenous Peoples, 26 August 1994, UN Doc.E/CN.4/Sub.2/Res/1994/56

UNPFII (2003) Report on the Second Session, Permanent Forum on Indigenous Issues, May 2003, UN Doc.E/2003/43

Vrdoljak, A.F. (forthcoming) 'Defining Indigenous Peoples' Participation in Respect of International Legal Protection of Cultural Heritage', in S. Valkonen, L. Heinamaki, P. Nuorgam, and A. Xanthaki (eds), Indigenous Cultural Heritage.

Weiner, J. (1987) 'Protection of Folklore: A Political and Legal Challenge', International Review of Industrial Property and Copyright Law, 18(1), 57–92.

World Heritage Committee (1994) Revised Operational Guidelines for the Implementation of the World Heritage Convention, February 1994, UNESCO Doc.WHC/2 Revised. Available: whc.unesco.org/archive/opguide94.pdf (viewed 25 May 2015).

World Heritage Committee (1998) Decision CONF 203 VII.28 Kakadu National Park (Australia)

World Heritage Committee (2001a) Report on the Proposed World Heritage Indigenous Peoples Council of Experts, 14 June 2001, Doc.WHC-2001/CONF.205/WEB.3

World Heritage Committee (2001b) Responses to Circular Letter 9 (August 2001), concerning World Heritage and Indigenous Peoples – proposal to establish a World Heritage Indigenous Peoples Council of Experts (WHIPCOE). Available http://whc.unesco.org/en/activities/496/ (viewed 28 February 2015).

World Intellectual Property Organization (1998a) 'The Protection of Folklore: The Attempts at International Level', *Intellectual Property in Asia and the Pacific*, 56/57. Available: http://itt.nissat.tripod.com/itt9903/folklore.htm (viewed 10 March 2015).

World Intellectual Property Organization (1998b) WIPO General Rules of Procedure, revised and adopted October 1979, WIPO: Geneva. Available: www.wipo.int/freepublications/en/general/399/wipo_pub_299.html (viewed 11 April 2015).

World Intellectual Property Organization (2001) Intergovernmental Committee on Intellectual Property and Genetic Resources, Traditional Knowledge and Folklore, Rules of Procedure, 5 April 2001, WIPO/GRTKF/IC/1/2

World Intellectual Property Organization (2003) Intergovernmental Committee on Intellectual Property and Genetic Resources, Traditional Knowledge and Folklore, Report prepared by the Secretariat, 5th session, 4 August 2003, WIPO/GRTKF/IC/5/15

World Intellectual Property Organization (2006) Establishment of the WIPO Voluntary Fund. WP/GA/32/6, Annex; Participation of Indigenous Local Communities: Decision of WIPO General Assembly Establishing the Voluntary Contribution Fund, 20 March 2006, WIPO/GRTKF/IC/9/3

World Intellectual Property Organization (2011) Note on Existing Mechanisms for Participation of Observers in the Work of the WIPO Intergovernmental Committee on Intellectual Property and Genetic Resources, Traditional Knowledge and Folklore, prepared by the WIPO Secretariat, 10 October 2011. Available: www.wipo.int/export/sites/www/tk/en/igc/ . . . /note_igc_participation.pdf> (viewed on 11 April 2015).

World Intellectual Property Organization (2013) Draft Study on the Participation of Observers in the Work of the Intergovernmental Committee on Intellectual Property and Genetic Resources, Traditional Knowledge and Folklore, Prepared by the Secretariat, 13 January 2013, WIPO/GRTKF/IC/20/7

World Intellectual Property Organization (2014a) The Protection of Traditional Knowledge: Draft Articles. Document prepared by the Secretariat, 2 June 2014, WIPO/GRTKF/IC/28/5

World Intellectual Property Organization (2014b) The Protection of Traditional Cultural Expressions: Draft Articles. Document prepared by the Secretariat, 2 June 2014, WIPO/GRTKF/IC/28/6

World Intellectual Property Organization (2014c) Draft Report. Document prepared by the Secretariat, Intergovernmental Committee on Intellectual Property and Genetic Resources, Traditional Knowledge and Folklore, 28th session, 7–9 July 2014, WIPO/GRTKF/28/11 Prov.2

Yokota, Y. and Sami Council (2006) Review of draft Principles and Guidelines on the Heritage of Indigenous Peoples, 16 June 2006, UN Doc.E/CN.4/Sub.2/2006/5, Annex

Chapter 4

Cultural and intellectual property in cross-border disputes over intangible cultural heritage[1]

Christoph Antons and Lisa Rogers

Introduction: the rise of intangible heritage

Modern international mobilisation to protect tangible cultural heritage arose from twentieth-century concerns about the wartime loss of cultural treasures (Brown 2005: 41) and international disputes in specific cases such as the one between Britain and Greece about the return of the Elgin marbles.[2] International conventions introduced the concept of 'cultural property', concerned with its protection and trade.[3] This was accompanied by what has been referred to as an emerging 'discourse of monumentality' (Smith 2006: 109), reflected in the *Convention for the Protection of the World Cultural and Natural Heritage* (the 1972 Convention),[4] which defined cultural heritage as 'monuments, groups of buildings and sites' of 'outstanding universal value' to be protected as the 'world heritage of mankind as a whole' (1972 Convention, Preamble).

By comparison, the interest in immaterial cultural heritage developed more recently. It evolved from early concerns about the appropriation of expressions of folklore in developing countries (Intergovernmental Copyright Committee 1973).[5] Such 'expressions of folklore' were defined for the purposes of the UNESCO-WIPO Model provisions (1985) as 'elements of the traditional artistic heritage developed and maintained by a community of [name of the country] or by individuals reflecting the traditional artistic expectations of such a community' (UNESCO -WIPO Model Provisions 1985: Section 2). Due to negative post-colonial associations with the term 'folklore', it fell into disfavour in an international context, resulting in the more frequent use by WIPO of the term 'traditional cultural expressions' (WIPO undated: 2).

Concepts of culture subsequently became redefined at the World Conference on Cultural Policies in Mexico in 1982[6] (known as Mondiacult), which asserted a new egalitarian axis for culture, rejecting a hierarchy between world cultures and proclaiming instead that intangible heritage covered 'all the values of culture as expressed in everyday life' (UNESCO 1982; Logan et al. 2010: 6).[7] This conference referenced 'intangible heritage' (UNESCO 2011b: 6), one of the earliest official uses of the term, which came later to be defined in the *Convention for the Safeguarding of the Intangible Cultural Heritage* (the 2003 Convention)[8] as the 'practices, representations, expressions, knowledge, skills' (2003 Convention, Article 2) manifested in such domains as oral traditions, performing arts and knowledge and practices. The inclusion of intangible cultural heritage in the safeguarding programs of UNESCO was designed to mitigate the Eurocentric perspective of what constitutes heritage (Vecco 2010: 324) because developing countries were regarded as particularly rich in heritage (Forrest 2012: 365) invested in 'intangible' oral traditions and practices (Brown 2005: 41).

Heritage, including of the intangible type, has economic, political and social value for a diverse group of 'stakeholders' ranging from tourism operators, regional and national development planners to the representatives of indigenous peoples and other ethnic minorities. One of the chief reasons for the increasing interest in heritage is the embrace of culture[9] in more recent development strategies, which include the emergence of cultural and heritage tourism, as well as high hopes in various countries for the creative industries (Suharmoko 2008; Theparat 2012; *Borneo Post* 2010). Developing countries are investing in contemporary creativity using traditional expressions and materials to contribute to their economic development. This investment is seen to support job creation, skills development, tourism and revenue from cultural products (WIPO, undated).

UNESCO heritage inscriptions are markers of authenticity for natural and cultural world heritage. UNESCO heritage listings become important symbols and quality seals for tourist attractions, whether they are natural parks or entire parts of cities (see the contributions in Picard and Wood 1998). In the case of intangible cultural heritage, the skills, knowledge, crafts and performances of local people are often an attraction that is marketed in addition to the natural and cultural values of the site itself.[10] Numerous intangible cultural heritage festivals and performances are inscribed on the Representative List of the Intangible Cultural Heritage of Humanity.

The benefits to tourist industries of a World Heritage designation are well understood, and the extension to the intangible has introduced a new layer of interest and potential contestation.[11] For conceptual, historical and political reasons (Barsh 1999: 14), international law as conceptualised in the United Nations separates the tangible from the 'intangible' nature of heritage; however, they are inter-related and inter-dependent. This is also recognised in the preamble to the 2003 Convention in 'considering the deep-seated interdependence between the intangible cultural heritage and the tangible cultural and natural heritage'. In describing the artificial and misleading separation of culture and nature when examining significant cultural landscapes, Russel Barsh states that the 'Western distinction between nature and culture is reflected in the assumption that nearly all cultural and intellectual property can be completely detached from the landscapes in which they arose' (Barsh 1999: 16).

This chapter outlines the application of cultural property and intellectual property concepts to intangible cultural heritage. It will show the cross-border conflicts which have arisen from the intersection and conflation of these concepts and laws and the influence of nationalistic sentiment in pursuing claims and rights. It will further analyse the different concepts of geographical space that were used in nation-building processes in Southeast Asia on the one hand and in the legal construction of 'cultural space' for heritage conservation and intellectual property rights on the other hand.

The value of intangible cultural heritage

The use of intangible cultural heritage in tourism promotion campaigns and in other areas of commercialisation of traditional culture has led to considerable diplomatic tensions between neighbouring countries with similar or shared cultural heritage. Many of these disputes about heritage are to be found in Southeast Asia, an area that historically has always been at the crossroads of and receptive to different cultural influences (Antons 2013a). The borders in this region were drawn by European colonial powers with little knowledge of or regard for existing ethnic or cultural boundaries. In an environment with relatively fluid boundaries, cultural communities were often permanently separated into different colonies and subsequently different nation states (Antons 2012a; 2013b). Today, communities continue to adapt and reinvent cultural heritage which may be shared or which may have originated elsewhere. Competition between countries laying claim to the same or similar cultural heritage for tourism or the commercialisation of, for example, traditional medicine or music has led to a scramble to monopolise the relevant aspects of a culture, relying on a mixture of cultural property claims derived from UNESCO conventions and intellectual property rights such as copyrights and patents.

Thus, national governments often collect a variety of local cultural expressions and represent such local cultures in negotiations with neighbouring and other foreign countries. The 2003 Convention establishes lists under the Convention, but it also requires States to develop an inventory or inventories of intangible cultural heritage within their territory (Article 12, 2003 Convention). Local communities who *create, maintain and transmit* (Article 15, 2003 Convention) the intangible cultural heritage are often left on the side-lines of subsequent discussions over commercialisation. Their rights and benefits may be restricted to a form of compensation in return for the contribution their cultural expressions or their traditional knowledge have made to new products (Antons 2010).

Contestation over heritage can also occur, therefore, within States. Disputes may arise between States and their 'communities' or indigenous peoples as the creators and transmitters of intangible cultural heritage that is subsequently utilised by the State. Much has been made of the participation of 'communities', 'in particular indigenous communities, groups and, in some cases individuals' that play an important role 'in the production, safeguarding, maintenance and re-creation of the intangible cultural heritage' (Forrest 2012: 368). However, the duty to safeguard rests with the State, as only State Parties are subject to international law and the 2003 Convention (Forrest 2012: 374). In administering the 2003 Convention, UNESCO has a range of programs and training to build capacity and the participation of communities above the written consent submitted with the nomination. The ICH inter-governmental committee has decided not to inscribe elements which have not satisfactorily met the criteria with respect to, for example, the involvement and consent of the community.[12] In reality, the degree of the informed nature of the consent may often be difficult to ascertain.

In the circumstance of shared traditional knowledge, the World Intellectual Property Organization (WIPO) calls for transboundary cooperation and the involvement of indigenous and local communities.[13] The Inter-governmental Committee (IGC) for the 2003 Convention similarly encourages multi-national nominations of intangible cultural heritage, evoking the capacity to accept multinational nominations to the List of the Intangible Cultural Heritage in Need of Urgent Safeguarding and the Representative List of the Intangible Cultural Heritage of Humanity when an element is found on the territory of more than one State Party.[14] The Secretariat of the 2003 Convention has reported that there are already numerous elements inscribed on the Lists in their own right that might instead have been the subject of a multinational inscription had circumstances been different.[15] In practice, these transboundary issues are not easy. In 2016, three nominations related to multi-national nominations, including the expansion of an existing registration 'Falconry' to include five additional States Parties. Of the 391 registered elements on the Representative List, only 27 are multinational files.[16]

The relationship between intangible cultural heritage, cultural property and intellectual property

Different international discourses promoting cultural and intellectual property have been influential in the developing world. When international discourse and international models on cultural property were first promoted in post-War UNESCO Conventions, cultural property did not extend to the intangible or overlap with intellectual property. It was initially concerned in particular with the repatriation of cultural material removed in circumstances of war, occupation and colonisation. Currently, traditional knowledge and traditional cultural expressions are regarded as forms of intangible cultural heritage that are also under discussion by WIPO, and they have a wide scope.

In fact, there has been a subtle move away from the terminology of cultural property (Prott and O'Keefe 1992: 307), most notably in the 2003 UNESCO Convention for the Safeguarding of Intangible Cultural Heritage, which does not refer to 'cultural property' but to the broader concept of 'intangible cultural heritage'. At the same time, WIPO embarked upon a program of work on traditional cultural expressions, traditional knowledge and associated genetic resources in the late 1990s and has overseen negotiations for international instruments in these fields since 2001.[17] The mandate was renewed in 2017 for WIPO to continue this work on text-based negotiations for international legal instrument(s) relating to intellectual property to ensure the effective protection of traditional knowledge, traditional cultural expressions and genetic resources.[18]

As the 2003 UNESCO Convention also covers 'knowledge and skills', there is overlap with the work of WIPO. The UNESCO Convention addresses this overlap and states that nothing in the Convention shall affect intellectual property rights (Blake 2006: 43). Some international law experts (Francioni 2001, as quoted in Aikawa-Faure 2008: 29; Lixinski 2013: 8) have further argued that intangible cultural heritage can be distinguished from those aspects negotiated at WIPO, because intellectual property rights focus on the end product of a creative process, whereas intangible cultural heritage focuses on the entire process of transmission and viability. Intellectual property (IP) lawyers would not see this as the case as IP rights also recognise concepts such as patents for innovative processes, for patents are designed to promote continuous improvement and invention by encouraging innovation. The public domain consists of knowledge not covered by intellectual property rights or where protection has expired. The expansion of the intellectual property system has implications for the access and dissemination of knowledge to new creators. The public domain is 'an important reservoir for innovators and creators, and for society at large' (Melendez-Ortiz and Roffe 2009: xx). The knowledge is released back into the public domain to be used by broader society. In that sense IP lawyers would contend that IP rights can also contribute to the transmission of viability, a key requirement for 'safeguarding'.

The purpose of 'safeguarding' in the 2003 Convention is equally meant to ensure the continuance and viability of the practice or tradition in question. The inscription by UNESCO is a commitment by the State to 'take the necessary measures to ensure the safeguarding of the intangible cultural heritage' (Article 11). Unlike with the 1972 Convention, there is no equivalent of the 'List of World Heritage in Danger' designation if the heritage is not safeguarded, and the Convention does not elaborate on consequences for not safeguarding the intangible cultural heritage.

UNESCO states that the use of intellectual property rights to protect intangible heritage is 'not satisfactory' due to the characteristics of intangible cultural heritage being re-created and evolving, not being frozen in one point of time or one manifestation of it (UNESCO 2011a). For WIPO, however, 'traditional knowledge' is a 'living body of knowledge that is developed, sustained and passed on from generation to generation within a community' (WIPO 2016). As a consequence, Forrest (2012: 363–364) recognises that '[f]orms of intangible cultural heritage fall within the scope of an overlapping and multifaceted international regime' and that the overlap between IP rights and intangible cultural property in particular requires 'close collaboration between the two regimes in order to ensure consistency' and to address the overlaps 'in a way that does not undermine either one'. Blake (2015) considers that they are 'two sides of the same coin.' While the objectives of the 2003 Convention and UNESCO seem to differ, in reality, the remit of WIPO to ensure the protection of intangible cultural heritage is similar to UNESCO's safeguarding objectives.

In 1978 WIPO and UNESCO worked together to adopt a dual-track approach to protecting folklore, with UNESCO examining ICH from an interdisciplinary viewpoint, namely, addressing the definition, identification, preservation, conservation, promotion and protection of ICH and WIPO exploring the protection of expressions of folklore via intellectual property rules (Blake 2006: 10). IP law is concerned with the 'protection' of aspects of intangible cultural heritage, while cultural heritage law uses the term 'safeguarding' as defined under the 2003 Convention (Blake 2015: 11). The view in UNESCO was that safeguarding intangible cultural heritage needed a broader cultural approach since IP protection would only respond to certain situations (Blake 2015: 230). As we shall see further in what follows, some States have utilised IP protection and cultural heritage laws simultaneously to claim, use and market their intangible cultural heritage. In the absence of an international treaty concluded by WIPO, some States have adopted national intellectual property mechanisms or *sui generis* regimes and combined them with the international law principles derived from the 2003 Convention. These claims to the exclusive use or "ownership" of intangible cultural heritage have triggered disputes between countries, as will be discussed in the following section.

Contested heritage and claims to intangible cultural heritage

Disputes can arise at the intersection of intangible cultural heritage and its use or appropriation, for 'while heritage can unite, it can also divide' (Ruggles and Silverman 2007), particularly in countries where the politics of land and intangible cultural 'property' are closely related (Blomley 2003: 122). Where the continuance of the ICH is dependent on access to real property or disputed resources, claims may also arise. In the *Navigational Rights* Case (2010)[19] the International Criminal Court (ICJ) advocated for the rights of local nomadic people to cross State boundaries to undertake customary fishing. Judge Bennouna,

> the focus should perhaps be on the essence of the issue, because the frontier, as predicated on the Westphalian model, is far removed from the cultural heritage of this region of the world. In the framework of a good-neighbourliness relation, it is for the Parties to rediscover this heritage by deepening, as encouraged by the Court, their co-operation.
>
> (Polymenopoulou 2014: 455)

Obviously, there is opportunity for disputes to arise between States laying claim to similar intangible cultural heritage, derived from a shared history. Indeed, disputes have arisen between Malaysia and Indonesia, for example, over the use of a rap version of the folk song 'Rasa sayang' in several languages of ethnic communities in Malaysia. This song was used for the international tourism campaign 'Malaysia truly Asia'. Indonesian commentators regarded the song as originating in the Moluccan islands, in the eastern part of the Indonesian archipelago. Malaysia asserts that the song is *kebudayaan Nusantara*, common heritage of the entire Southeast Asia archipelago (*The Star* Online 2007: Antons 2009). Similarly, two years later, another Malaysian tourism campaign utilised *pendet*, a temple dance from the Indonesian Island of Bali, for the 'Enigmatic Malaysia' campaign on the Discovery Channel (Abdussalam 2009; *Asia Sentinel* 2009; Fitzpatrick 2009; Antons 2009; Chong 2012). Other contested elements of heritage include the shadow puppet theatre of *wayang kulit*, the ceremonial dagger *kris*, the Malaysian national anthem 'Negaraku', the music instruments *gamelan* and *angklung* (Chong 2012 with further references) and the patenting by the Massachusetts Institute of Technology together with the Malaysian government of the bioactive fraction of *pasak bumi*, a plant used in traditional medicine in both countries and known in Malaysia as *tongkat Ali* (Antons 2015; Antons and Antons-Sutanto 2009 with further references). The inscription of batik on the 2003 Convention's *Representative List of the Intangible Cultural Heritage of Humanity* was widely celebrated in Indonesia (Chong 2012; Clark and Pietsch 2014), with Tourism Minister Jero Wacik proclaiming 'we will keep fighting for our heritage one tradition at a time' (Clark and Pietsch 2014: 85).

In the field of agriculture, both countries have used geographical indications to market organic red rice varieties from the borderlands of Sarawak and North Kalimantan, triggering claims that the organic rice sold in Malaysia under a Malaysian Geographical Indication was in fact grown in Indonesia (Susilo 2012). These rice varieties are grown by related communities on both sides of the border. However, the Indonesian community is landlocked, with easy access to border towns in Malaysia but no road access to the Indonesian provincial capital. As a result, the cheapest way for growers to sell their rice is on the Malaysian side of the border (Ardhana et al. 2004).

The shared history, common origin of languages and consequently cultural expressions means that transboundary issues between culturally similar countries such as Indonesia and Malaysia have and will continue to arise and trigger negotiations of competing claims.

When commenting on such cases and using the term 'copyright' to justify Indonesian claims, Indonesian politicians were probably thinking of Article 10 of the Copyright Act of 2002. It provided in Article 10(2) that the state should hold the copyright in folklore and so-called products of popular culture which become common property and listed a whole range of examples that included also songs and dances. Article 10(3) provided further that foreigners needed permission from the relevant authorities to use such material. Further, Article 10(1) effectively attempted to create a copyright in heritage by providing that the state would also hold the copyright in pre-historical and historical works and 'other national cultural objects' (Antons 2009). Article 10 was introduced into the Copyright Act as early as 1982 (Antons 2000) but in practice never implemented, because a Government Decree to regulate the details was never issued. In 2014, the Indonesian copyright law was revised, and a new provision on 'traditional cultural expressions' replaced Article 10. The new Copyright Act (Law No. 28 of 2014 on Copyright) deleted the subsection related to pre-historical and historical works and 'other national cultural objects' but retained the copyright of the state to traditional cultural expressions.

Such provisions constitute a symbolically powerful claim of the government to administer and control traditional cultural expressions at the central level. This is in accordance with the Indonesian Constitution, which provides in Article 32(1) that 'the state shall advance the national culture of Indonesia among the civilisations of the world by assuring the freedom of society to preserve and develop cultural values'. The use of intangible cultural heritage to represent the identity of a cohesive nation raises the question of when precisely does culture become 'national', and how does this process relate to cultural expressions that are essentially 'regional' or 'local'?

The Indonesian writer Ajip Rosidi, who followed the debate around Indonesia's first national Copyright Act of 1982,[20] pointed out that the idea to place the copyright to expressions of folklore into the hands of the state encountered 'sharp protests' at the time (Rosidi 1984: 79). The government ultimately settled on a compromise, that it would only exercise the copyright 'with regard to foreign countries' (see the official government response in Simorangkir 1982: 196). Copyright experts concluded from this that Indonesian citizens remained generally free to use their respective folkloristic material (Rosidi 1984: 79–80; Simorangkir 1982: 136). In various revisions that followed, this position has slowly been eroded (Antons, in print). The new Copyright Act now no longer focuses on foreign users and instead speaks of the duty of the state to make an inventory of and to protect and conserve traditional cultural expressions and to remain conscious of the values of the communities from which the material originated (Article 38 Copyright Act).

By way of comparison, at the regional level in Africa, the *Swakopmund Protocol on the Protection of Traditional Knowledge and Expressions of Folklore* (the Swakopmund Protocol) adopted by the African Regional Intellectual Property Organisation (ARIPO) of 2010 vests exclusive rights to authorise the use of traditional knowledge in the holders of the knowledge, namely, local and traditional communities and recognised individuals within such communities who create, preserve and transmit knowledge in a traditional and intergenerational context. (Sections 6 and 7). The beneficiaries of expressions of folklore are the local and traditional communities in accordance with local customary law and practices (Section 18). Section 12, however, provides for a 'competent national authority' in the State to intervene if the traditional knowledge holder is not sufficiently exploiting the traditional knowledge or granting economic licences with reasonable conditions. The State may, in the interests of public safety or public health, grant a compulsory licence to fulfil 'national needs'. ARIPO also acts to resolve disputes between member countries in relation to shared heritage across borders (Swakopmund Protocol, article 22.4).

International models and the conflation of concepts in intellectual property and heritage laws

Earlier discussions in the WIPO and UNESCO about folklore protection and the protection of national cultural property culminated in the WIPO/UNESCO–sponsored Tunis Model Law on Copyright of 1976 (Weiner 1987) and in the 1970 UNESCO Convention on the Means of Prohibiting and Preventing the Illicit Import, Export and Transfer of Ownership of Cultural Property (Hoffman 2006). The 1970 UNESCO Convention reflected the concerns of developing countries during the early post-colonial period when they were seeking the return of cultural objects looted from their territories by colonial powers. This discussion would soon become extended to the relationship of indigenous peoples with both former colonial powers and the governments of post-colonial settler societies (Hoffman 2006; Vrdoljak 2008: 206–11). In relation to copyright, the Tunis Model Law was drafted by a Committee of Governmental Experts convened by the Tunisian government with assistance from WIPO and UNESCO (International Bureau of WIPO 1998). With its focus on 'works of national folklore', it reflected the view at the time that economic development was state led and state planned (Antons 2012b: 147–8). Such international models became influential at a time when developing countries were drafting their first national copyright laws. As explained in the previous section, early versions of the Indonesian copyright law, for example, conflate intellectual property models for folklore protection with nationalistic cultural property claims based on the principles of UNESCO conventions drafted for tangible objects. The protection of 'national cultural objects', which remained as part of the legislation until the reform in 2014, turned up in early drafts of Indonesian copyright laws for the first time in 1966 (Simorangkir 1979: 19 and 151).

Other countries mixing intellectual and cultural property concepts include Laos, where the Law on National Heritage of 2005 provides that the State asserts copyright ownership of Lao national and cultural historic heritage if it is outside Laos in the illegitimate possession of other countries or if other countries have in an illegitimate manner asserted copyright ownership. In the Philippines, the community intellectual rights of indigenous peoples are protected under the Indigenous Peoples' Rights Act of 1997. They include the right to the restitution of cultural, intellectual, religious and spiritual property taken without free and prior informed consent or in violation of customary laws and traditions (Section 32), and the right to special measures to control, develop and protect indigenous knowledge systems and practices, sciences and technologies and cultural manifestations (Section 34 Indigenous Peoples Rights Act). These rights sit alongside the National Cultural Heritage Act of 2009, which uses both 'cultural property' and 'cultural heritage' and prescribes consultation with the National Commission on Indigenous Peoples in cases of indigenous claims.

From 'tradition' to cultural and intellectual property

What is further remarkable in this field is the strong role of the state and the appropriation of heritage material by national governments. This has a long tradition going back to the early days of the discussion about folklore. Thus, when Bolivia requested UNESCO's intervention in the international protection of folklore in 1973, it viewed folklore as 'belonging to the culture of people' and claimed State ownership of anonymous folk music (Van Balen and Vandesande 2015: 16). As heritage is seen as a powerful tool in development and tourism and important in nation building, it is not surprising that states want to control it and seek to absorb the intangible cultural heritage of communities within their borders and to represent them in the international arena.

Academic commentators have described how governments use intellectual property and cultural property concepts in ways that seek to empower young nation states (Antons 2005; 2009; 2012a; 2013a, b; 2015; Aragon 2012; Aragon and Leach 2008). Although their origins are very different, with international law in the case of cultural property and commercial law in the case of intellectual property, both concepts are understood as helping to strengthen national culture and enhance development goals. In the implementation, the cultural property concept developed for tangible material is applied to 'intangible' heritage, and the intellectual property becomes national property with all of its potential benefits.

The notion of cultural property has also been important for indigenous peoples seeking restitution of their cultural material from former colonial powers as well as from nation states succeeding former colonial governments. The international legal discourse emphasises the common nature of heritage; the 'world heritage of mankind' (as expressed in the 1972 World Heritage Convention) and intangible cultural heritage as a 'common concern of humankind' (as expressed in the 2003 Convention). Both downplay any notions of contestation (Smith 2015: 138). However, discourses about particular community rights are also emerging. Over the last few decades, the rise of an international indigenous movement commencing in North and South America, Australia and New Zealand, as well as in Scandinavian countries, has been noted. In recent years, the international indigenous movement has come to include minorities from Asia and Africa (Sissons 2005: 22–23), although this extension has been controversial, and some have questioned in how far such a broader understanding of 'indigenous peoples' could weaken the specific concerns of indigenous movements in settler societies (Niezen 2003: 74; Benjamin 2017).

The use of the international concept of 'indigenous peoples has long been resisted by governments concerned about national unity, particularly in Asia" (Kingsbury 1999: 336–377). Nations may also be selective about the level of recognition of minority cultures. This is visible in Malaysia, where a distinction is being made between the 'natives of Sabah and Sarawak' and aboriginal groups on the Malayan peninsula ('orang asli'), categorised as one group by British colonial administrators and subsequently by Malaysian authorities (Khor Manickam 2015: 99–101). Demonstrating the ambiguity of the term 'indigenous' in Malaysia, the former share with the Malay 'indigenous' majority the special position and access to preferential treatment under Article 153 of the Constitution, while the *orang asli* are not mentioned and have to be content under Article 8(5)(c) with the administrative 'provision for the protection, well-being or advancement of the aboriginal peoples of the Malay peninsula (including the reservation of land) or the reservation to aborigines of a reasonable proportion of suitable positions in the public service' (Harding 2012: 73, 186). In recent years, aboriginal communities have turned to the courts to improve their situation. Landmark cases from elsewhere in the Commonwealth such as the *Mabo* decision of the Australian High Court (Russell 2005) were referred to in a string of cases in Malaysia since 1997 recognising 'customary community title' at common law to their lands (Harding 2012: 188–91). Legal practitioners working with *orang asli* communities, however, have pointed to the considerable challenges of claiming these rights in the (for aboriginal people) alien environment of the Malaysian courts, the failure of federal and state governments to recognise these rights in legislation and the attempts of governments to eliminate communal land ownership through the granting of individual titles (Subramaniam 2016).

In Indonesia, the discourse on community rights continues to be connected to the recognition of *adat* law communities, as recognised in the revised Constitution of 1945. *Adat* is a very complex concept. It is often superficially equated with custom (Utrecht and Djindang 1983: 99) but is actually, in the words of adat scholar Koesnoe (1971: 3; as quoted in von Benda-Beckmann (1979: 113), 'the whole body of teaching and their observance which governs the way of life of the Indonesian people and which has emerged from the people's conception of man and world'. Initially covering both the supernatural and secular social reality, as von Benda-Beckmann points out (1979: 114), its sacred aspects have been to varying degrees superseded by the established religions. Utrecht and Djindang (1983: 99) define *adat istiadat* as a 'collection of social principles' with the purpose of regulating the order of Indonesian society. *Adat* law, on the other hand, is widely regarded as a Dutch colonial creation (Lev 2000: 20). Jaspan (1965: 252–3, as quoted in Holleman 1981: LII) explains that before Dutch adat scholar Van Vollenhoven at the University of Leiden and his school, 'adat law was not a separate and independent entity but was in most cases intertwined with the history, mythology and institutional charters . . . of each ethnic or cultural unit'.

While playing only a marginal role in law reform for many decades after independence, *adat* and *adat* law returned to prominence after the end of the many years of authoritarian rule centred on Jakarta of Indonesia's second President Suharto. A constitutional revision strengthened the position of local government units and recognised the unity of adat law communities and their traditional rights 'as long as they are still in existence and in accordance with the development of society and the principles of the unitary Republic of Indonesia regulated by law' (Article 18B(2) of the revised Constitution of 1945). It also introduced in a new part on human rights recognition of the cultural identity and rights of traditional communities 'in accordance with the development of the times and civilization' (Article 28(3) Constitution of 1945). Some *adat* communities have begun to test the strength of such recognition in the courts. In a landmark decision in 2013, the Indonesian Constitutional Court reinterpreted a key provision of the Forestry Act so that *adat* forests were no longer categorically included in state forests under the control of the Ministry of Forestry but were henceforth forests 'subject to rights' (Rachman and Siscawati 2017: 224). Some regional governments responsible for the recognition of customary law communities have meanwhile issued regulations to provide the basis for the implementation of these rights.[21]

A regional response to the longstanding centralisation of heritage and traditional culture can further be seen in the emergence of regional intellectual property laws with specific rules for regional cultural heritage, genetic resources and traditional cultural expressions. For example, the Special Regional Regulation of the Province of Papua No. 19 of 2008 on the Protection of Intellectual Property Rights of Indigenous Papuans includes 'indigenous Papuan geographical indications' and the protection for original and local Papuan plant varieties (Antons, in print). At the same time, the revised national Copyright Act of Indonesia interprets the control of the national government over 'traditional cultural expressions' as extending to *adat* rituals and ceremonies (Explanatory memorandum to Article 38(2) of the Copyright Act of 2014), apparently reducing such rituals to copyright-protected performances (Antons 2017a: 256).

Heritage, rights and territorial boundaries

In their recent work on space and legal pluralism, von Benda Beckmann et al. (2009: 4) found that '[t]he ways in which physical spaces, boundaries or borderlands are conceived and made legally relevant varies considerably within and across legal orders' (Benda-Beckman et al. 2009: 4). The discourse about maps and cartography is, therefore, a political one (Benda-Beckmann et al. 2009: 19). There are historical as well as current examples of the politics of cartography. A historical example from Southeast Asia that is likely to exemplify the experience of many feudal kingdoms with the arrival of the European colonial powers is the way modern geography came to influence the Kingdom of Siam's negotiations with Britain and France as the new rulers in neighbouring British Burma and French Indochina (Winichakul 1994). Prior to the arrival of the Europeans with their concepts of national borders, political power in Southeast Asia was organised according to tributary relationships. Ancient Southeast Asian kingdoms organised in this manner have been described as *mandalas*, with each of them constituting a 'vaguely definable geographical area without fixed boundaries and where smaller centers tended to look in all directions for security' (Wolters 1999: 28).

In view of this history of empire building on the basis of overlapping power relationships rather than territorial control, some of the modern-day conflicts about the symbolic relationship between cultures and certain territories are easier to understand. Disputes about heritage between Thailand and Cambodia have also to be seen against a background of the Thai view of the Thai monarchy and ethnic Khmer population in the North Eastern provinces of Thailand as heirs of the ancient Angkor civilisation (Denes 2015). In the disputes between Indonesia and Malaysia described earlier, Malaysia's understanding of a 'Malay' world (*Dunia Melayu*) encompassing parts of several Southeast Asian nations and inhabited by people of 'Malay stock' encounters a narrower interpretation in multi-ethnic Indonesia, in which 'Malay' is just one of many ethnic categories (Reid 2004: 20). As in the case of Thailand and Cambodia, both interpretations evoke ancient kingdoms of the region. The 'Malay world' follows in the footsteps of *Srivijaya*, an ancient kingdom on the Indonesian island of Sumatra, and the Sultanate of Melaka, while Indonesian history reading focuses on Java and on a pre-colonial 'Greater Indonesia' established by the ancient Java-based kingdom of *Majapahit* (Liow 2008: 50).

However, the differences in legal boundaries drawn by different legal orders have implications not just at the international level. Decentralisation policies promoted by the international financial institutions (Wittayapak and Vandergeest 2010) have led to a resurgence of traditions and forms of traditional laws also within nation states. The recognition of traditional or indigenous communities and their rights, discussed in the previous section of this chapter, is usually accompanied by the mapping of the community territory, in which such rights can be exercised. Examples are the drafting of community maps for *orang asli* land in Malaysia (Subramaniam 2016: 434) and of maps of the community land of Papuan customary law communities in Indonesia (Savitri and Price 2016: 349).

Apart from such recognitions of customary laws and the spaces associated with them (von Benda-Beckmann et al. 2009), there are now also national laws that introduce different conceptions of space. The protection of geographical indications (GIs) as a form of intellectual property is a good example. GIs were introduced by the World Trade Organisation Agreement on Trade-related Intellectual Property Rights (TRIPS) to 'identify a good as originating in the territory of a Member, or a region or locality in that territory, where a given quality, reputation or other characteristic of the good is essentially attributable to its geographical origin' (Article 22 WTO TRIPS Agreement). GIs have been lauded for their potential in promoting traditional cultural expressions, the creative industries and rural and regional development (Wong and Fernandini 2010: 193–6; Dutfield 2013) and the safeguarding of cultural heritage (Gangjee 2012). They have been adopted in many developing countries (Blakeney 2009: 104) with high hopes for tourism and industries involving heritage, crafts and agricultural products (Antons 2017b: 504). However, the commercialisation of products related to certain 'cultural spaces' and traditions also raises the question as to who will be allowed to operate in the space and to benefit from the commercialisation. Adams (1997) reports for the popular tourism destination of the *Toraja* highlands in the Indonesian province of South Sulawesi tensions between ethnic *Torajans*, on the one hand, and the provincial government and neighbouring ethnic groups about who should be allowed to represent *Toraja* culture. Clearly, local authorities in this context may often have different interests than the central government, as the mentioned emergence of Regional Regulations on intellectual property in several Indonesian provinces demonstrates (Antons 2017b: 492–494; Ayu Palar in this volume).

Conclusion

For young nation states in the developing world with a sometimes still relatively fragile national unity, intangible cultural heritage provides a valuable resource to promote national unity and identity. Nations may inventorise and promote forms of heritage which are consistent with national goals for development. More recently, however, decentralisation policies in many countries are also leading to a revival of local cultural expressions and heritage. With the simultaneous revival of customary and religious laws, different legal orders can relate to different spaces for which they can claim validity. Such alternative legal orders may go beyond the boundaries of the nation state or attempt to create relatively exclusive spaces with preferential rights for some within nation states. In many cases, therefore, tradition, custom and religion are not only important symbols of identity, but they are also identity markers related to boundaries, resources and the question of who can control them.

States are selectively using elements from various UNESCO Conventions and national intellectual property laws to construct powerful claims to cultural and intellectual property vis-à-vis neighbouring countries. Although relevant laws are often not implemented in regards to the local use of cultural symbols, indigenous and local communities may become more critical towards this gradual process of centralisation and State control of their intangible cultural heritage. An international movement of indigenous peoples, which has long been seeking recognition in various countries' court systems and in international organisations, is also extending its reach to communities in the democratising environment of Asia and Africa.

With its powerful role in nation building and national myth making, heritage still relatively rarely leads to the international collaboration that UNESCO envisaged in the 2003 Convention. Heritage remains contested, however, also at the national level. The emergence of local intellectual property rights to elements of heritage shows that local governments are becoming very active in seeking their share of the income generated from its commercialisation. Under these circumstances, current bargaining processes about conservation and/or commercialisation are likely to continue for some time at the international level as well as between national and local governments and communities. With their relationship to democratisation, recognition of minority rights and distribution of political and economic power, these are very sensitive discussions that state authorities watch with some nervousness and seek to manage as far as possible.

Notes

1 Research for this chapter was supported under the Australian Research Council's *Discovery Projects* funding scheme (project number DP130100213).

2 For examples of disputes about tangible heritage, including the Elgin marbles, see Gillman (2010: Ch. 1, 9–40) and Merryman (2009: 24–80).

3 See the *Convention for the Protection of Cultural Property in the Event of Armed Conflict* (the Hague Convention, 1954), opened for signature 14 May 1954, UNTS 249 (entered into force 7 August 1956) and the *Convention on the Means of Prohibiting and Preventing the Illicit Import, Export and Transfer of Ownership of Cultural Property* (the 1970 Convention) opened for signature 14 November 1970, UNTS 823 (entered into force 24 April 1972).

4 See the *Convention for the Protection of the World Cultural and Natural Heritage*, opened for signature 16 November 1972, UNTS 1037 (entered into force 17 December 1975).

5 In 1973 the Government of Bolivia requested UNESCO consider an international instrument for the protection of folk arts and cultural heritage of nations of the world because '[f]olklore, viewed as the cultural substratum of human groups with expressions characterised by anonymous authorship, traditionality and popular origin (International Congress of Folk Arts held in Buenos Aires), constitutes part of the cultural heritage of the peoples and so far has not rated specific attention either by the international organizations or by the majority of States.' (UNESCO, Committee of Experts on the Legal Protection of Folklore, 1997).

This request arose from concerns about 'melodies being wrongfully appropriated by persons unconnected with their creation who register them as their own compositions . . . to secure . . . benefits conceded by the copyright regulations'. See the Intergovernmental Copyright Committee, *Proposal for International Instrument for the Protection of Folklore,* IGC/X11/12, 12th sess, 1A-73/CONF.005/12 (December 1973) published at http://unesdoc.unesco.org/images/0000/000058/005845eb.pdf.

6 See the World Conference on Cultural Policies, Final Report, Mexico City, 26 July–6 August 1982 at http://unesdoc.unesco.org/images/0005/000525/052505eo.pdf and the Declaration, Mexico City Declaration on Cultural Policies, World Conference on Cultural Policies, Mexico City, 26 July–6 August 1982 at http://portal.unesco.org/culture/en/files/12762/11295421661mexico_en.pdf/mexico_en.pdf which states at Principle 23 that 'The cultural heritage of a people includes the works of its artists, architects, musicians, writers and scientists and also the work of anonymous artists, expressions of the people's spirituality, and the body of values which give meaning to life'. It includes both tangible and intangible works through which the creativity of that people finds expression: languages, rites, beliefs, historic places and monuments, literature, works of art, archives and libraries.

7 See the World Conference on Cultural Policies, Final Report, Mexico City, 26 July–6 August 1982 at http://unesdoc.unesco.org/images/0005/000525/052505eo.pdf

8 See the *Convention for the Safeguarding of the Intangible Cultural Heritage*, opened for signature 17 October 2003, UNTS 2368 (entered into force 20 April 2006).

9 Rosemary Coombe has referred in so far to the 'cultural turn in development policies' (Coombe, 2009).

10 The 1972 Convention recognises the relationship of intangible heritage to tangible heritage and the intangible values associated with tangible heritage places (Blake, 2006: 26).

11 See Coombe & Aylwin (2014) discussing the 'growing possessiveness in relation to cultural forms'.
12 See for example the discussion of the 'free, prior and informed consent' of various elements which were not inscribed on the Representative List of the Intangible Cultural Heritage in the *Decisions* report of the eighth session of the Intergovernmental Committee (8.COM) for the Convention for the Safeguarding of the Intangible Cultural Heritage, held from 2 to 7 December 2013, Retrieved www.unesco.org/culture/ich/en/8com.
13 See Article 12 of the draft text of the WIPO Inter-governmental Committee, The Protection of Traditional Knowledge: Draft Articles Rev. 2 (Annex B) WIPO/GRTKF/IC/28/5 June 2 2014, www.wipo.int/edocs/mdocs/tk/en/wipo_grtkf_ic_28/wipo_grtkf_ic_28_5.pdf.
14 See paragraphs 13–15 of the 2014 Operational Directives for the Implementation of the Convention for the Safeguarding of the Intangible Cultural Heritage adopted by the General Assembly of the States Parties to the Convention at www.unesco.org/culture/ich/en/directives and the introduction of the mechanism for a State Party to publish their intention, in advance, of submitting files in order to raise awareness about the existence of a given element in the territory of more than one State Party and to facilitate multi-national nominations in consequence, as resolved at the 7 COM, UN Doc ITH/12/7.COM, Paris, *Decisions* (7 December 2012).
15 Inter-governmental Committee for the Convention on the Safeguarding of the Intangible Cultural Heritage, 7th Session, UN Doc ITH/12/7. COM, (7 December 2012).
16 See statistics on the Lists of the Intangible Cultural Heritage published by UNESCO at   www.unesco.org/culture/ich/en/lists?multinational=2&display1=inscriptionID#tabs.
17 For a discussion of the work of WIPO, see Antons (2012b).
18 See draft articles for the protection of traditional knowledge, traditional cultural expressions and genetic resources and the work of WIPO at http://www.wipo.int/meetings/en/details.jsp?meeting_id=42302.
19 *Dispute Regarding Navigational and Related Rights* (Costa Rica v. Nicaragua), Judgment of 13 July 2009. For a discussion of cultural rights arising in case law of the International Court of Justice see Polymenopoulou (2014).
20 The 1982 Copyright Act replaced an outdated Dutch colonial law that had survived the declaration of independence but not been relevant in practice (Antons 2000: 53–4).
21 See, for example, the Regional Regulation of the District of Lebak, Province Banten, No. 8 of 2015 on the Recognition, Protection and Empowerment of the *Adat* Law Community of the *Kasepuhan*.

Bibliography

Abdussalam, A. (2009) 'Malaysia to Reprimand Pendet Dance Clip Producer', August 26. Available: www.antaranews.com/en/news/1251222710/malaysia-to-reprimand-pendet-dance-clip-producer?FORM=ZZNR (accessed 29 June 2016).
Adams, K.M. (1997) 'Touting Touristic "Primadonas": Tourism, Ethnicity and National Integration in Sulawesi, Indonesia', in M. Picard and R.E. Wood (eds.), *Tourism, Ethnicity and the State in Asian and Pacific Societies*, Honolulu, HI: University of Hawai'i Press, 155–180.
African Regional Intellectual Property Organisation (ARIPO) (2010) *Swakopmund Protocol on the Protection of Traditional Knowledge and Expressions of Folklore*, ARIPO, Swakopmund, Namibia. Available: www.wipo.int/wipolex/en/other_treaties/text.jsp?file_id=201022 (accessed 20 July 2016).

Aikawa-Faure, N. (2008) 'From the Proclamation of Masterpieces to the Convention for the Safeguarding of Intangible Cultural Heritage', in L. Smith and N. Akagawa (eds), *Intangible Heritage*, Oxon: Routledge, 13–44.

Antons, C. (2000) *Intellectual Property Law in Indonesia*, London-The Hague: Kluwer Law International.

Antons, C. (2005) 'Traditional Knowledge and Intellectual Property Rights in Australia and Southeast Asia', in C. Heath and A. Kamperman Sanders (eds), ,, Oxford and Portland, OR: Hart Publishing, 37–51.

Antons, C. (2009) 'What Is "Traditional Cultural Expression"? International Definitions and Their Application in Developing Asia', *The WIPO Journal*, 1(1), 103–116.

Antons, C. (2010) 'The Role of Traditional Knowledge and Access to Genetic Resources in Biodiversity Conservation in Southeast Asia', *Biodiversity and Conservation*, 19(4), 1189–1204.

Antons, C. (2012a) 'Geographies of Knowledge: Cultural Diffusion and the Regulation of Traditional Knowledge/Cultural Expressions in Southeast Asia', *The WIPO Journal*, 4(1), 83–91.

Antons, C. (2012b) 'Intellectual Property Rights in Indigenous Cultural Heritage: Basic Concepts and Continuing Controversies', in C.B. Graber, K. Kuprecht and J.C. Lai (eds), *International Trade in Indigenous Cultural Heritage: Legal and Policy Issues*, Cheltenham, UK-Northampton, MA: Edward Elgar, 144–174.

Antons, C. (2013a) 'At the Crossroads: The Relationship Between Heritage and Intellectual Property in Traditional Knowledge Protection in Southeast Asia', *Law in Context*, 29, 74–94.

Antons, C. (2013b) 'Asian Borderlands and the Legal Protection of Traditional Knowledge and Traditional Cultural Expressions', *Modern Asian Studies*, 47, 1403–1433.

Antons, C. (2015) 'Epistemic Communities and the "People without History": The Contribution of Intellectual Property Law to the safeguarding' of Intangible Cultural istory": The Contribution of Intellectual Property Law to the "Safeguarding" of Intangible Cultural Heritage', in I. Calboli and S. Ragavan (eds), *Diversity in Intellectual Property: Identities, Interests and Intersections*, Cambridge: Cambridge University Press, 453–471.

Antons, C. (2017a) 'Legal and Cultural Landscapes: Cultural and Intellectual Property Concepts, and the 'Safeguarding' of Intangible Cultural Heritage in Southeast Asia', in C. Antons (ed.), *The Routledge Handbook of Asian Law*, London New York: Routledge, 250–268.

Antons, C. (2017b) 'Geographical Indications, Heritage and Decentralization Policies: The Case of Indonesia', in I. Calboli and W.L. Ng-Loy (eds), *Geographical Indications at the Crossroads of Trade, Development and Culture: Focus on Asia-Pacific*, Cambridge: Cambridge University Press, 485–507.

Antons, C. (in print) 'Copyright Law in Indonesia: From a Hybrid to and Endogenous System?', in B. Fitzgerald and J. Gilchrist (eds), *Copyright, Property and the Social Contract – the Reconceptualisation of Copyright*, Berlin-Heidelberg: Springer.

Antons, C. and Antons-Sutanto, R. (2009) 'Traditional Medicine and Intellectual Property Rights: A Case Study of the Indonesian *jamu* Industry', in C. Antons (ed.), *Traditional Knowledge, Traditional Cultural Expressions and Intellectual Property Law in the Asia-Pacific Region*, Alphen aan den Rijn: Kluwer Law International, 363–384.

Aragon, L.V. (2012) 'Copyright Culture for the Nation? Intangible Property Nationalism and the Regional Arts of Indonesia', *International Journal of Cultural Property*, 19, 269–312.

Aragon, L.V. and Leach, J. (2008) 'Arts and Owners: Intellectual Property Law and the Politics of Scale in Indonesian Arts', *American Ethnologist*, 35(4), 607–631.

Ardhana, I.K., Langub, J. and Chew, D. (2004) 'Borders of Kinship and Ethnicity: Cross-Border Relations Between the Kelalan Valley, Sarawak, and the Bawan Valley, East Kalimantan', *Borneo Research Bulletin*, 35, 144–79.

Asia Sentinel (2008) 'Thailand and Cambodia Agree to Cool Things Off', October 17.

Asia Sentinel (2009) 'Indonesian Outrage over a Dance', August 25.

Barsh, R. (1999) 'How Do You Patent a Landscape?' *International Journal of Cultural Property*, 8(1), 14–47.

Benda-Beckmann, F. von (1979) *Property in Social Continuity: Continuity and Change in the Maintenance of Property Relationships Through Time in Minangkabau, West Sumatra*, The Hague: Martinus Nijhoff.

Benda-Beckmann, F. von, Benda-Beckmann, K. von and Griffiths, A. (2009) 'Space and Legal Pluralism: An Introduction', in F. von Benda Beckmann, K. von Benda-Beckmann and A.M. Griffiths (eds), *Spatializing Law: An Anthropological Geography of Law in Society*, Surrey: Ashgate, 1–29.

Benjamin. G. (2017) 'Indigenous Peoples: Indigeneity, Indigeny or Indigenism?', in C. Antons (ed.), *The Routledge Handbook of Asian Law*, New York-London: Routledge, 363–377.

Blake, J. (2006) *Commentary on the 2003 UNESCO Convention on the Safeguarding of the Intangible Cultural Heritage*, Leicester, England: Institute of Art and Law.

Blake, J. (2015) *International Cultural Heritage Law*, Oxford: Oxford University Press.

Blakeney, M. (2009) 'Protection of Traditional Knowledge by Geographical Indications', in C. Antons (ed.), *Traditional Knowledge, Traditional Cultural Expressions and Intellectual Property Law in the Asia-Pacific Region*, Alphen aan den Rijn: Wolters Kluwer, 87–108.

Blomley, N. (2003) 'Law, Property, and the Geography of Violence: The Frontier, the Survey, and the Grid', *Annals of the Association of American Geographers*, 93(1), 121–141.

The Borneo Post Online (2010) 'Creative Industries a Major Driver of Economic Growth', 1 January. Available: www.theborneopost.com/2010/01/01/creative-industries-a-major-driver-of-economic-growth (last accessed 28 May 2015).

Brown, M. F. (2005) 'Heritage Trouble: Recent Work on the Protection of Intangible Cultural Property', *International Journal of Cultural Property*, 12, 40–60.

Calboli, I. and Ragavan, S. (eds.) (2015) *Diversity in Intellectual Property: Identities, Interests and Intersections*, Cambridge: Cambridge University Press.

Carpenter, K.A., Katyal, S.K. and Riley, A.R. (2009) 'In Defense of Property', *Yale Law Journal*, 118, 1022.

Chong, J.W. (2012) ' "Mine, Yours or Ours?" The Indonesia-Malaysia Disputes Over Shared Cultural Heritage', *SOJOURN: Journal of Social Issues in Southeast Asia*, 27(1), 1–53.

Clark, M. and Pietsch, J. (2014) *Indonesia-Malaysia Relations: Cultural Heritage: Politics and Labour Migration*, vol. 37, London: Routledge.

Coates, K.S. (2004) *A Global History of Indigenous Peoples*, Houndmills, Basingstoke, Hampshire and New York: Palgrave Macmillan.

Coombe, R. (2009) 'The Expanding Purview of Cultural Properties and Their Politics', *Annual Review of Law and Social Science*, 5, 393–412.

Coombe, R. and Aylwin, N. (2014) 'Marks Indicating Conditions of Origin in Rights-Based Sustainable Development', *U. C. Davis Law Review*, 47(3), 753–786.

Denes, A. (2015) 'Foklorizing Northern Khmer Identity in Thailand: Intangible Cultural Heritage and the Production of "Good Culture" ', *SOJOURN: Journal of Social Issues in Southeast Asia*, 30(1), 1–34.

Dutfield, G. (2013) 'Geographical Indications and Agricultural Community Development: Is the European Model Appropriate for Developing Countries?', in C. Lawson and J. Sanderson (eds), *The Intellectual Property and Food Project: From Rewarding Innovation to Feeding the World*, Farnham, Surrey-Burlington, VT: Ashgate, 175–200.

Fitzpatrick, S. (2009) 'Malaysia "Steals" Bali Dance', *The Australian*, 26 August 2009.

Forrest, C. (2012) *International Law and the Protection of Cultural Heritage*, Oxon: Routledge.

Francioni, F. (2001) *Intangible Cultural Heritage – Working Definitions*, unpublished meeting paper, Turin: UNESCO, cited in Aikawa-Faure, N. (2008: 43) 'From the Proclamation of Masterpieces to the Convention for the Safeguarding of Intangible Cultural Heritage', in L. Smith and N. Akagawa (eds), *Intangible Heritage*, Oxon: Routledge, 13–44.

Gangjee, D. (2012) 'Geographical Indications and Cultural Heritage', *The WIPO Journal*, 4(1), 92–102.

Gillman, D. (2010) *The Idea of Cultural Heritage*, revised edition, Cambridge: Cambridge University Press.

Harding, A. (2012) *The Constitution of Malaysia: A Contextual Analysis*, Oxford and Portland, OR: Hart Publishing.

Hoffman, B.T. (2006) 'Exploring and Establishing Links for a Balanced Art and Cultural Heritage Policy', in B.T. Hoffman (ed.), *Art and Cultural Heritage: Law, Policy and Practice*, Cambridge: Cambridge University Press, 1–18.

Holleman, J.F. (1981) *Van Vollenhoven on Indonesian Adat Law*, The Hague: Martinus Nijhoff.

Intergovernmental Copyright Committee (1973) *Proposal for International Instrument for the Protection of Folklore*, IGC/X11/12, 12th sess, 1A-73/CONF.005/12 (December 1973) published at http://unesdoc.unesco.org/images/0000/000058/005845eb.pdf

International Bureau of WIPO (1998) 'The Protection of Expressions of Folklore: The Attempts at International Level', *Intellectual Property in Asia and the Pacific*. Available: http://itt.nissat.tripod.com/itt9903/folklore.htm (last accessed 28 May 2015).

Jaspan, M.A. (1965) 'In Quest of New Law: The Perplexity of Legal Syncretism in Indonesia', *Comparative Studies in Society and History*, 7(3), 252–266.

Keyes, C.F. (2002) 'The Case of the Purloined Lintel: The Politics of a Khmer Shrine as a Thai National Treasure', in C.J. Reynolds (ed.), *National Identity and Its Defenders: Thailand Today*, Chiang Mai: Silkworm "Books, 212–237.

Khor Manickam, S. (2015) *Taming the Wild: Aborigines and Racial Knowledge in Colonial Malaya*, Singapore: NUS Press.

Kingsbury, B. (1999) 'The Applicability of the International Legal Concept of "Indigenous Peoples" in Asia', in J.R. Bauer and D.A. Bell (eds), *The East Asian Challenge for Human Rights*, New York: Cambridge University Press, 336–377.

Kosnoe, M. (1971) *Introduction into Indonesian Adat Law*, Publikaties over Adatrecht, vol. 3, Nijmegen: Instituut voor Volksrecht, Universiteit van Nijmegen.

Lev, D.S. (2000) *Legal Evolution and Political Authority in Indonesia: Selected Essays*, The Hague: Kluwer Law International.

Liow, J.C. (2008) *The Politics of Indonesia-Malaysia Relations: One Kin, Two Nations*, London and New York: Routledge.

Lixinski, L. (2013) *Intangible Cultural Heritage in International Law*, Oxford: Oxford University Press.

Logan, W., Langfield, M. and Craith, M.N. (2010) 'Intersecting Concepts and Practices', in M. Langfield, W. Logan and M. Nic Craith (eds), *Cultural Diversity, Heritage and Human Rights: Intersections in theory and practice*, London-New York: Routledge, 3–20.

Manderson, D. (2005) 'Interstices: New Work on Legal Spaces', *Law Text Culture*, 9, 1–10.

Melendez-Ortiz, R. and Roffe, P. (2009) 'The New International Intellectual Property Architecture', in Melendez-Ortiz, R. and Roffe, P. (eds), *Intellectual Property and Sustainable Development, Development Agendas in a Changing World*, The International Centre for Trade and Sustainable Development, Cheltenham and Northampton, MA: Edward Elgar Publishing Limited, xix–xxix.

Merryman, J. H. University of California Press (2009) *Thinking About the Elgin Marbles: Critical Essays on Cultural Property, Art and Law* (2nd ed.), Alphen aan den Rijn: Wolters Kluwer Law & Business.

Nafziger, J.A.R., Paterson, R.K. and Renteln, A.D. (2010) *Cultural Law: International, Comparative and Indigenous*, New York: Cambridge University Press.

Niezen, R. (2003) *The Origins of Indigenism: Human Rights and the Politics of Identity*, Berkeley, CA: University of California Press.

Picard, M. and Wood, R.E. (eds) (1998) *Tourism, Ethnicity and the State in Asian and Pacific Societies*, Honolulu, HI: University of Hawai'i Press.

Polymenopolou, E. (2014) 'Cultural Rights in the Case Law of the International Court of Justice', *Leiden Journal of International Law*, 27(2), 447–464.

Prott, L.V. and O'Keefe, P.J. (1992) ' "Cultural Heritage" or "Cultural Property"?' *International Journal of Cultural Property*, 1(2), 307–320.

Rachman, N.F. and Siscawati, M. (2017) 'Forestry Law, *masyarakat adat* and Struggles for Inclusive Citizenship in Indonesia', in C. Antons (ed.), *The Routledge Handbook of Asian Law*, Oxon-New York: Routledge, 224–44.

Reid, A. (2004) 'Understanding *Melayu* (Malay) as a Source of Diverse Modern Identities', in T.P. Bernard (ed.), *Contesting Malayness: Malay Identity Across Boundaries*, Singapore: Singapore University Press, 1–24.

Rosidi, A. (1984) *Undang-Undang Hak Cipta 1982 – Pandangan Seorang Awam*, Jakarta: Penerbit Djambatan.

Ruggles, D.F. and Silverman, H. (eds), (2007) *Cultural Heritage and Human Rights*, Cultural Heritage in a Globalized World, New York-London: Springer.

Russell, P.H. (2005) *Recognising Aboriginal Title: The Mabo Case and Indigenous Resistance to English-Settler Colonialism*, Sydney, University of New South Wales Press.

Savitri, L. A. and Price, S. (2016) 'Beyond special autonomy and customary land rights recognition: examining land negotiations and the production of vulnerabilities in Papua', in McCarthy, J.F. and Robinson, K., *Land and Development in Indonesia: Searching for the People's Sovereignty,* Singapore: ISEAS Publishing, 343–361.

Simorangkir, J.C.T. (1982) *Undang-Undang Hak Cipta 1982 (UHC 1982)*, Jakarta: Penerbit Djambatan.

Simorangkir, J.C.T. (1979) *Hak Cipta Lanjutan*, Jakarta: Penerbit Djambatan.

Sissons, J. (2005) *First Peoples: Indigenous Cultures and Their Futures*, London: Reaktion Books.

Smith, L. (2006) *The Uses of Heritage*, Oxon: Routledge.

Smith, L. (2015) 'Intangible Heritage: A Challenge to the Authorised Heritage Discourse?' *Revista d'etnologia de Catalunya*, 40, 133–142.

The Star Online (2007) 'Rasa Sayang Belongs to All', October 3.

Subramaniam, Y. (2016) 'Orang Asli, Land Rights and the Court Process: A "Native Title" Lawyer's Perspective', in K. Endicott (ed.), *Malaysia's Original People: Past, Present and Future of the Orang Asli*, Singapore: NUS Press, 423–45.

Suharmoko, A. (2008) 'Govt Plans Blueprint for Creative Industries', *Jakarta Post*, March 10.

Susilo, H. (2012) 'Beras Adan Resmi Dipatenkan', *Kompas.com*. Available: http://regional.kompas.com/read/2012/01/15/18453496/Beras.Adan.Resmi.Dipatenkan, 15 January 2012 (on file with the author; last accessed 17 March 2015).

Theparat, C. (2012) 'New Agency to Give Creative Industries an Infusion of Funds', *Bangkok Post*, August 27. Available: www.bangkokpost.com/print/309507 (last accessed 28 May 2015).

UNCTAD-ICTSD (2005) *Resource Book on TRIPS and Development*, Cambridge: Cambridge University Press.

UNESCO (1977) Committee of Experts on the Legal Protection of Folklore, *Study of the various aspects involved in the preparation of folklore'*, Tunis, 11–15 July 1977, Appendix A, Annex p. 3, FOLK/3/3 PARIS, 1 June 1977, Retrieved 26 June 2017, http://unesdoc.unesco.org/images/0002/000280/028098eb.pdf).

UNESCO (1982) *A World Conference on Cultural Policies: Final Report, Mexico City, 26 July–6 August 1982*. Available: http://unesdoc.unesco.org/images/0005/000525/052505eo.pdf

UNESCO-WIPO (1985) *Model Provisions for National Laws on the Protection of Expressions of Folklore Against Illicit Exploitation and Other Prejudicial Actions*. Available: www.wipo.int/wipolex/en/text.jsp?file_id=184668

UNESCO (2011a) *Kit of the Convention of the Safeguarding of the Intangible Cultural Heritage, Questions and Answers*. Available: www.unesco.org/culture/ich/index.php?pg=00451#5 (accessed 26 June 2017).

UNESCO (2011b) *Working Towards a Convention, Intangible Cultural Heritage*. Available: www.unesco.org/culture/ich/index.php?pg=00451#1 (accessed 26 June 2017).

Utrecht, E. and Djindang, M.S. (1983) *Pengantar Dalam Hukum Indonesia*, Jakarta: Penerbit Sinar Harapan.

Van Balen, K. and Vandesande, A. (eds) (2015) *Community Involvement in Heritage*, Antwerp: Garant.

Vecco, M. (2010) 'A Definition of Cultural Heritage: From the Tangible to the Intangible', *Journal of Cultural Heritage*, 11(3), 321–324.

Vrdoljak, A. (2008) *International Law, Museums and the Return of Cultural Objects*, Cambridge: Cambridge University Press.

Weiner, J. (1987) 'Protection of Folklore: A Political and Legal Challenge', *International Review of Industrial Property and Copyright Law*, 18(1), 56–92.

Winichakul, T. (1994) *Siam Mapped – a History of the Geo-Body of a Nation*, Honolulu, HI: University of Hawai'i Press.

WIPO (2001) *Intellectual Property Needs and Expectations of Traditional Knowledge Holders: WIPO Report on Fact-finding Missions on Intellectual Property and Traditional Knowledge*, WIPO: Geneva.

WIPO (2015) *Intellectual Property and Genetic Resources, Traditional Knowledge and Traditional Cultural Expressions: An Overview*, 14, WIPO Publication No. 933E. Available: www.wipo.int/edocs/pubdocs/en/tk/933/wipo_pub_933.pdf (accessed 28 June 2016).

WIPO (2016) *Traditional Knowledge and Intellectual Property, No 1 Background Brief.* Available: www.wipo.int/edocs/pubdocs/en/wipo_pub_tk_1.pdf

WIPO (2017) *Protect and Promote Your Culture: A Practical Guide to Intellectual Property for Indigenous Peoples and Local Communities*, WIPO: Geneva.

WIPO (undated) *Intellectual Property and Traditional Cultural Expressions/Folklore*, Booklet No. 1, WIPO Publication No. 913E, p. 6. Available: www.wipo.int/edocs/pub docs/en/tk/913/wipo_pub_913.pdf (accessed 28 June 2016).

Wittayapak, C. and Vandergeest, P. (2010) *The Politics of Decentralization: Natural Resource Management in Asia*, Chiang Mai: Mekong Press.

Wolters, O.W. (1999) *History, Culture and Region in Southeast Asian Perspective* (revised ed.). Ithaca, NY, and Singapore: Cornell Southeast Asia Program Publications/Institute of Southeast Asian Studies.

Wong, T. and Fernandini, C. (2010) 'Traditional Cultural Expressions: Preservation and Innovation', in T. Wong and G. Dutfield (eds), *Intellectual Property and Human Development: Current Trends and Future Scenarios*, New York: Cambridge University Press, 175–217.

Chapter 5

The failed case for property rights in intangible indigenous cultural property

Dennis S. Karjala and Robert K. Paterson

Introduction

In an earlier work,[1] we argued that resolving the problem of protecting intangible indigenous cultural heritage should not take the form of defining a new class of "indigenous cultural property" that would be subject to rights under or analogous to those recognized by the intellectual property regimes of patent and copyright. We concluded instead that a "one size fits all" approach was incapable of balancing the tensions between understandable demands from indigenous peoples to have control over their cultural heritage on the one hand and fundamental policy values reflected in the intellectual property regimes and in basic notions of free expression on the other. We outlined a number of specific situations in which careful judicial interpretation of existing laws or modest amendments to existing statutory regimes could meet many of the needs and demands of indigenous peoples. In many cases, there is no fundamental clash between Western legal traditions and the legitimate demands for privacy, confidentiality, or recognition that indigenous claimants might make. In some cases, however, especially those involving outsider use of publicly available but "old" indigenous works (that is, those works no longer protected by copyright), attempting to give control to the group is fundamentally antithetical to basic notions of free expression and the overall development and dissemination of culture. For such cases, a value judgment must be made. We concluded that a regime of perpetual rights in the indigenous group from which the work derived is both practically impossible and theoretically unsound: Indigenous cultural tradition must in certain respects give way to the modern creative spirit.[2]

Since our article appeared, there has been a good deal of activity at the international, regional, and national levels.[3] In addition, the commentators have been active. Most, however, continue down the path of asserting that Western legal concepts are "inappropriate" to meet the needs of indigenous peoples and therefore must be modified in one way or another. An implicit assumption in many of these commentaries is that "indigenous peoples" do, in fact, have some common needs or demands that are in conflict with "Western" traditions. They also seem to assume that all members within a particular indigenous culture have the same goals with respect to the use, by insiders or outsiders, of the group's intangible heritage. To the extent a given proposal does rely on inter- or intra-group homogeneity, we are sceptical that it can provide a meaningful general resolution. Some groups might find, for example, that the commodification of their music or certain artistic images is offensive on religious grounds. Others might find the same use offensive simply because it is, in their opinion, in bad taste. Others might not object to the commodification so much as to their exclusion from the profits derived from it.[4]

Another problem that remains extant in the literature is the general assumption that "indigenous cultural property" can be defined in a meaningful way and that the individuals or groups who are to be given a certain degree of control rights can be identified. There is also an implicit assumption that these control rights can be appropriately circumscribed to assure that those in control do, in fact, exercise their power with the goals and needs of the group in mind.[5]

One of the more important commentaries on these topics attempts to obviate some of these difficulties by reframing rights in indigenous cultural property within traditional Western property law concepts.[6] Professor Kristen Carpenter et al. offer the notion of "stewardship" as a limitation on ownership rights in cultural property, both tangible and intangible, so that an "owner" of property might not necessarily be able to use it to the full extent otherwise allowed but would negotiate with relevant cultural groups or their representatives over uses that impinge on aspects of the group's cultural heritage that the group has an obligation to maintain. Unfortunately, however, while Professor Carpenter et al. give a number of examples to show how their stewardship model would work, they actually pay scant attention to the problem of intangible cultural property (discussing in detail only the problem of sports mascots). Professor Carpenter et al. supply no definition of what property is covered, who exercises the rights of stewardship, or how such rights are to be determined or delimited (except by way of ad hoc example). We believe that it is imperative to distinguish carefully between tangible and intangible property. We do not see how the stewardship model – as a limitation on a property right – applies even to the main intangible property problem that they address, which is that of sports mascots. More important, for traditional designs, music, dance, literature, and other graphic arts, we must distinguish between a demand for regulation on offensiveness grounds and a demand for revenue sharing. Not only must we decide who does the "stewarding" and on what basis, but we must also decide on what basis, if any, a new design based on an indigenous "style" gives rise to a claim. For plants or even human DNA, what is there to "steward" except a stream of profits, to a part of which indigenous people are assumed to be entitled? The failure to distinguish tangible from intangible property in these situations is, in our mind, fatal to the enterprise insofar as intangible cultural heritage is concerned.

The basic problem of intangible cultural heritage protection

It is important to emphasize that here we are considering the problem of control over *intangibles* – most broadly speaking, information. We are not dealing with real property, such as geographical locations that are sacred or otherwise culturally meaningful to one or more indigenous groups. Nor are we dealing with tangible personal property, such physical things as carvings, baskets, rugs, pots, jewellery, clothing, paintings, and the like. Rather, we address whether and under what circumstances an indigenous group may justifiably assert control rights over such intangibles as music, designs, pictures, stories, and traditional methods of medical treatment.

There are important reasons why we single out information for special treatment in the discussion of protecting indigenous cultural heritage. Rights in information – especially *property rights* in information – are a relatively new concept in human development. Copying successful behaviour is something humans have done from time immemorial, and indeed copying successful behaviours has been shown to be a strategy that can win over a strategy of innovating.[7] Until the invention of the printing press, it was so difficult to copy an extensive work of literature that no need was seen for anything like copyright. In other words, over most of human history, the absence of exclusive rights in information was the default position.

The legal community has seen ongoing debate over the reasons that we *do*, in fact, recognize intellectual property rights (IPRs). The reasons are important, because they determine not only whether information of a particular type is protected at all but also the *scope* of any protection that is afforded, including the *term* of such protection. Thus, traditional trademark law protects against the unauthorized use of a mark to "pass off" goods or services as those of the mark owner, but only if there is a likelihood of confusion by the consuming public. This allows mark owners to invest in building their reputations with good-quality products and services and assists consumers in rapidly finding products and services in whose quality they have confidence. While the term of trademark protection is indefinite (and therefore potentially infinite), the very narrow scope of protection severely limits trademark's encroachment into the public domain. In the case of trademark law, therefore, we know what the protection goals are, and this informs the decision concerning what types of information to protect, how such protection should be limited and by what means, and against what actions by third parties protection will be available.

Intangible property – information – is given certain degrees of legal protection depending on the nature of the information and overall social goals. The default position is that information is free for anyone to use as he or she will. With trade secret law, society seeks to improve economic efficiency with respect to information that, in any event, would not be made available to the public, by reducing the effort the possessor of the information must make to keep the information of value. With trademark law, society cabins off a tiny bit of information so that it can serve a signalling function for offerors of goods and services and their customers. With patent and copyright, society seeks to supply an incentive to create new and desirable works, with the details depending crucially on whether the information relates to technological function or to the non-functional world of art, literature, and music. Thus, any call to protect information that does not fall within traditional information-protection regimes needs to supply a reason both for protection at all and for the specific scope and duration of such protection. We do not believe that a single rationale exists for a broad category of information under the rubric of "indigenous cultural heritage." We do believe, however, that reasons can be given for a degree of protection of specific types of information that many would classify as "indigenous cultural heritage." It is simply a matter of articulating the need for protection in terms beyond "I would like to have exclusive rights in X." Once the necessity or desirability case has been made, we can set about limiting both the scope and duration of protection to meet the articulated need, subject to countervailing interests in the public for allowing the information to remain in the public domain.

The basic problem for cultural heritage protection does not, therefore, lie in the absence of a known single author or group of authors. If a legitimate basis for protection can be articulated, it is relatively easy to write statutory language that accomplishes the task.[8] Similarly, the problem does not inhere in the absence of a writing or other fixation of the work, such as stories handed down by means of oral tradition. The real problem for intangible cultural heritage protection, as a general matter, is that it requires us to go beyond patent and copyright and beyond the default position that information is in the public domain to protect information for an indefinite, potentially infinite time. We know why non-protection is the default position for information, and we know why (more or less) we make limited exceptions to that position for patent and copyright. If we are to go beyond the boundaries of these two paradigms, we must know why we are doing so.[9]

Two proposals for indigenous cultural heritage protection

The stewardship model

Recently, a good deal of attention has been directed toward the so-called stewardship model for cultural property proposed by Professors Carpenter et al.[10] This ambitious proposal argues that many problems of cultural heritage protection can be analyzed and resolved using traditional concepts of property law. These authors correctly observe that title to property, tangible or intangible, has never given the property owner an absolute right to use or even to exclude others from the property. "Stewardship" is seen as a limitation on owners' rights designed to reconcile the interests of owners and nonowners. The notion is that indigenous people often have a fiduciary or custodial duty with respect to certain tangible and intangible properties and that the cultural survival of a group may depend on its ability to fulfil such duties.[11] Consequently, legal ownership rights would be modified or curtailed to some extent, presumably to the degree needed to permit the indigenous groups to fulfil their custodial duties.

We have no objection as a general matter to limitations on owners' rights in tangible or intangible property that are designed to permit the carrying out of inherited custodial duties, especially if the survival of an entire culture depends on it. The problem is in the details, few of which Professor Carpenter et al. supply, especially for intangible property. Their basic idea stems from the claim that "certain property deserves legal protection because it is integral to the collective survival and identity of indigenous groups."[12] This is followed by the claim that "Indigenous peoples, rather than holding property rights delineated by notions of title and ownership, often hold rights, interests, and obligations to preserve cultural property irrespective of title."[13] The stewardship model would transfer some of the sticks in the traditional property rights bundle to nonowners, who would exercise certain rights sometimes in conjunction with and sometimes in place of their exercise by the formal property owners.[14] Importantly, the stewardship model does not predetermine outcomes in favor of indigenous groups. Rather, the principle mandates that the interests of indigenous people be taken into consideration "as raising legal claims that are equal to, and in some unique cases superior to, those of title-holders."[15] Finally, stewardship itself is divided into "dynamic and static stewardship,"[16] whose "trajectories"[17] serve as "prisms"[18] for viewing the role of stewardship in protecting indigenous cultural property.

Static stewardship under the model of Professor Carpenter et al. involves four interests of indigenous people: conserving a sacred resource from overuse or pollution; placing an object, such as funerary remains, to rest; imposing rules against alienation to preserve the "physical and spiritual integrity" of an object; and access to and preservation of a cultural resource, such as a sacred site.[19] Static stewardship thus seems to apply largely, if not wholly, to tangible property. To that extent it lies outside our specific concern here with intangible property. Dynamic stewardship, however, involves at least one of three "rights": rights of "commodification that govern the production of downstream cultural properties"; rights governing the acquisition and use of downstream cultural goods, including the sharing of information with nonindigenous groups; and more limited rights of "representation and attribution" with respect to commercial use of indigenous religious practices and identities.[20] Professor Carpenter et al. concede that indigenous rights like attribution and commodification should not always win over the claims of a legitimate creator with respect to intellectual property.[21] They do claim, however, that stewardship is "a uniquely powerful normative framework" for considering the claims of indigenous people to intangible property.[22] They do not seek, for example, to deny outsider access to traditional medical information but rather seek to play a role in the development and distribution of products developed from such information and compensation for revealing it. They claim that this type of information is "commonly" associated with sacred or confidential indigenous information,[23] but they do not say that the stewardship model would be restricted to sacred or confidential information. Confidential information, at least, *does* stand on different ground from information that may be learned simply from observing open practices of the group or has already been disclosed, without coercion or deception, outside the group.[24] It is quite a different problem, however, if the objection is that outsiders are making an allegedly profane or otherwise objectionable use of known but "sacred" information. And while the notion of "stewardship" can be sufficiently broad to cover the protection of confidential information that has been improperly released, it is very difficult to see how "stewardship" applies to non-confidential information. Finally, while one can understand the desire to share in the market benefits from worldwide distribution of a pharmaceutical product based on some aspect of indigenous but non-confidential medical knowledge, it is difficult to see what "stewardship" adds to the claim.

To fill this gap, Professor Carpenter et al. make a second questionable move. They correctly note that indigenous people are among the developing world's poorest. Traditional medical knowledge and genetic resources may be the economically most important contribution that a given group can make to the world's economy. Therefore, "indigenous peoples increasingly request to share in the profits from the products that are created through the use of indigenous traditional knowledge, primarily as a matter of survival and basic equality."[25] This ties in with their earlier definition of cultural property as property deserving of protection because it is integral to indigenous group survival and identity.[26] But if participation in the commercialization of a downstream product based on indigenous knowledge is necessary to the group's survival, it is not stewardship of the knowledge itself that permits the group survival but simply the assumed economic claim against knowledge that, in any other context, would be in the public domain. Moreover, this reasoning would not apply to commercial products derived from indigenous knowledge where the indigenous group is independently well off economically, say, by reason of mineral resources on their land or perhaps the operation of gaming casinos. It is insufficient simply to say that the descendants of knowledge creators are poor so we should give them permanent exclusive rights to commercialize such knowledge. Grand-nephews of Jane Austen have been heard to complain about their inability to share in the commercial benefits from the recent spate of Austen adaptations into television and film.[27] And even if indigenous groups were to share in the commercialization of traditional medicinal knowledge, how can we know that the group will in fact use this survival benefit to preserve their culture, as opposed to simply joining the mainstream of society? Finally, Professors Carpenter et al. do not provide even a conceptual schematic for what kinds of commercializable knowledge would be subject to stewardship restrictions or profit sharing[28] or for how profits from commercialization are to be calculated and divided.[29] In short, if we are to take information out of the public domain by giving even "stewardship" rights of participation in its commercial development, we need a reason other than "the group is poor and this is their only potential source of subsistence." This is not to belittle the problem of poverty among indigenous people or anybody else. It is, rather, to say that the problem of poverty is much more important than and cannot be meaningfully addressed through ad hoc recognition of intellectual property rights in what is otherwise public-domain information.

The main intangible property application that Professors Carpenter et al. make of their theory is to trademarks. They thereby side-step the difficult problem of how to apply copyright or copyright-like protection to indigenous cultural works of art, music, and literature, as well as the problem of applying patent or patent-like protection to indigenous information related to technology, such as herbal medicines or human or other genetic makeup. As discussed earlier, including trademark law under the rubric of "intellectual property" and then expanding conclusions from trademark analysis to patent and copyright is an unjustifiable leap. The indefinite period of trademark exclusivity is ameliorated by the extremely narrow scope of traditional trademark protection (using the mark falsely to signal the identity of the supplier of goods or services, and only then if consumers are confused) that essentially does not impinge on the public domain.

Professor Carpenter et al. assert that, "It is its unique flexibility and capacity for giving voice to claims of both owners and nonowners that make stewardship a uniquely powerful normative framework for considering indigenous peoples' intangible property claims."[30] However, they never explain exactly what this "normative framework" actually is, and they concede that the complexity of intellectual property law will require variances in indigenous approaches to disputes relating to intangible property.[31] We commend them for avoiding the "one size fits all" trap for all intangibles related to indigenous cultural heritage, but we query whether they have moved the ball very far forward in applying their stewardship notion to intangible cultural property. In each case or set of circumstances in which indigenous people demand an exception to the default rule that anyone may freely use information lawfully obtained, we need to articulate reasons for making such an exception. Only then can we tailor the type and scope of protection to the circumstances at hand.

The New Zealand "Wai 262 report"

An important report concerning the cultural rights of New Zealand's indigenous Maori people was published in 2011. With no written constitution, New Zealand law furnishes only statutory and common law rights for its large Maori population. Nevertheless, the Waitangi Tribunal report in *Ko Aotearoa Tenei: A Report Into Claims Concerning New Zealand Law and Policy Affecting Maori Culture and Identity* (the "Wai 262 report") is likely to significantly influence future legal developments in New Zealand, as well as attract interest elsewhere.[32] The Wai 262 report was in response to a claim originally filed in 1991 by six Maori tribes (*iwi*) regarding flora, fauna, and intellectual property issues and may be seen to represent a variant of the stewardship model that Carpenter et al. have put forth.[33]

The Wai 262 report focused on the concept of Maori stewardship or guardianship (*kaitiakitanga*) – a concept of caring for natural and physical resources (human and non-human) for their overall benefit. The object of the report was to address Maori claims that the New Zealand government (the Crown) had failed to adequately protect, preserve, and respect various aspects of Maori culture and traditional knowledge. This included addressing the ongoing tension between indigenous rights and existing intellectual property laws. The Wai 262 report centered on the language of Article 2 of the Treaty of Waitangi.[34] The Maori version of Article 2 emphasizes traditional knowledge, whereas the English version affirms Western concepts of property, with its use of such terms as "pre-emption" and "alienation."

The Wai 262 report addressed the concept of the public domain by noting that while Maori possession of its traditional knowledge was, prior to European settlement, undisturbed, it is now a shared resource and, in that sense, irretrievable. While this may seem self-evident, it was an important conclusion, since it implicitly rejected the idea of creating *sui generis* intellectual property rights for Maori traditional knowledge.[35] Instead, the Tribunal's report focused on the stewardship principle, which it saw as a key component of Maori culture. In so doing the report also sided with the majority of contemporary legal scholarship, which sees indigenous traditional knowledge is an ill fit with Western intellectual property concepts.

The Tribunal thought that there needed to be restrictions to prevent the offensive or derogatory public use of Maori forms of cultural expression.[36] While New Zealand law already protects against such use to a certain extent, the Tribunal recommended enhanced protection where someone had an existing custodial or guardianship relationship (*kaitiaki)* to the objects and beliefs in question. The report proposed a new Commission that would establish guidelines for prospective users of Maori cultural expressions. This Commission could also serve as a register of the guardians of particular works, but such registration would not be compulsory. The idea of a prohibition on offensive or derogatory use of Maori works seems appropriate enough and has well-established precedents in other countries with significant indigenous populations – such as Canada and the United States. What is more problematic is what exactly it is that can be subject to a "guardianship" relationship and afforded legal protection on that basis. Since such relationships appear to be subject to definition on a case-by-case basis, it would seem that there could be a good deal of uncertainty surrounding when a certain use is protected, along with the precise level of protection itself.

The most controversial aspect of the report's recommendations surrounds its suggestion that any commercial use of Maori culture that is subject to a "guardianship" relationship requires consultation with *kaitiaki* and possibly their consent before use. It should be stressed, however, that this recommendation is based on the Tribunal's understanding of the obligations of the New Zealand Crown under the Treaty of Waitangi. As explained in the report, while Western-based intellectual property concepts define specific legal rights connected to certain forms of property, Maori focus on relationships towards their cultural objects (*taonga*) and the duties and responsibilities that surround these relationships. The recommendation that consent be required to allow the commercial use of Maori cultural objects is basically that New Zealand law make such consent mandatory – whether or not the works concerned are in the public domain. It remains unclear how such a requirement would be implemented and what sort of recognition, if any, it would receive outside New Zealand.

Even if this requirement of consent for expressions of Maori traditional knowledge were made part of New Zealand law, it is not clear what it exactly entails. The report does not explain what would happen if consent were refused – even assuming there had been prior consultation. Furthermore, the report recommends that the Commission have the power to limit commercial use of Maori cultural expressions in a form that the would-be user already has intellectual property rights over – like a photograph. Would this mean, for example, that the owner of copyright in a photograph could not display it for sale in a gallery if the *kaitiaki* of its subject matter objected?

The report grapples with this problem by suggesting that while existing intellectual property rights cannot be compromised, any future rights would be subject to decisions of the Commission. Thus, a design might be refused registration under the existing statutory scheme if the Commission decided that there had been inadequate or no consultation or an absence of consent. In effect, existing intellectual property rights might be made subject to laws giving effect to Treaty of Waitangi principles.

The report distinguished between what it described as "*taonga*-works" (Maori treasures or highly prized possessions) and "*taonga*-derived works." While the former are assumed to always have living individuals or communities that are responsible for them, the latter are works that have a Maori element, but this is combined with other non-Maori influences.[37] For these, there is no *kaitiaki* relationship. The report suggests that while derivative works be made subject to restrictions on offensive or derogatory use, they not be subject to any obligation to consult or prior consent because of the absence of guardians. In her analysis of the report, Dr Jessica Christine Lai has said,

It would seem to the author here that the distinction cannot be made objectively and that the line between the two seems conceptually porous. As has been stated elsewhere, the opinion of Maori is by no means lacking in diversity, making it difficult to objectively and consistently answer the question of how much Western or "modern" material must make up a work for it to no longer be considered a *taonga* work but a *taonga*-derived work. Considering that Maori culture should be viewed as dynamic and constantly developing, how does one differentiate between this acceptable development (which may involve incorporating in aspects not of traditional Maori culture) and hybrids that cross the line and become *taonga*-derived works? This further begs the question of whether the racial descent of the creator is important towards this end. In other words, is one more willing to consider something a *taonga* work, rather than a *taonga*-derived work, if its creator is Maori in descent? If so, is that a justifiable distinction to make? Notably, this would not go both ways, as non-Maori can only make *taonga*-derived works, due to the requirement of a *kaitiaki* relationship.[38]

Given the significance of the consultation and consent requirement, it is surprising that the report did not address these inherent problems more closely. In effect, the report is dealing here with the concept of "fair use" or its equivalent, which in most legal systems is seen as ensuring a basis for new interpretations and other creative expressions. If the concept of "*taonga*-derived works" were interpreted narrowly, it would place a significant and undesirable restriction on such creativity. This example illustrates the need to articulate the basis for limiting the right to use information freely. The justification for any right of refusal must inhere in some kind of offensive use of the underlying work. Assuming we can actually identify what is "offensive" and quantify how much "offensiveness" must be present to justify a refusal to allow commercial exploitation – each an extraordinarily difficult problem in a society that believes in rights of free expression – any refusal should be predicated not on the quantity of underlying indigenous content that finds its way into the challenged work but on the aspects of the challenged work that are seen as offensive.

Another controversial aspect of the report is its suggestion that certain Maori traditional knowledge (*matauranga Maori*) that is "closely held" be afforded additional protection beyond merely a prohibition on offensive or derogatory use. This is the nearest the report gets to canvassing what level of legal protection could be afforded intangible Maori culture. While unable to exhaustively define the content of such Maori culture, the Tribunal thought that traditional knowledge that was specific to particular Maori communities should enjoy some level of protection – possibly against offensive or derogatory use, as well as a requirement of consultation and consent. As with Maori works, there are troubling questions here surrounding how and when such use should or could be controlled. In addition, as Dr Lai has pointed out, there is a good deal of uncertainty as to what exactly "closely held" means.[39] She ponders from whose perspective such intangible cultural heritage would be considered as "closely held." In her view, the report also fails to address the possible misuse by Maori of Maori culture. The report discusses the rights of Maori versus non-Maori, but it does not explain how its recommendations apply in other contexts – such as Maori misuse of Maori culture.[40] Again, articulation of the reason justifying *any* deviation from the default rule that information should be freely useable by anyone is necessary both in determining the existence and scope of the right and in the basis, if any, for distinguishing between Maori and non-Maori use of the knowledge.

Some aspects of the Tribunal's report do speak to general issues concerning the basis for affording legal protection to indigenous cultural heritage in general. What is most striking about the report is that it completely avoids any suggestion that new forms of property rights be created in respect of Maori cultural heritage. The explanations for this are probably many, but the most likely must be the daunting task of defining the content of such rights and explaining how they would co-exist with pre-existing norms. New Zealand has struggled over the last few decades to resolve its identity through a new kind of engagement between its Maori and non-Maori (*pakeha*) populations. The Wai 262 report is just one facet of this tortuous journey. It would seem its authors chose "stewardship," together with all its attendant uncertainties, over ownership with the aim of avoiding the sort of confrontation that a rights-based approach might have engendered. In so doing they may have merely designed a roadmap with its own particular set of problems concerning implementation and dissonance.

Concluding thoughts on *sui generis* approaches

We have suggested approaches to the protection of intangible cultural heritage outside the framework of IPRs, such as through tort law, contract law, rights of privacy, and analogies to trademark and trade secret law.[41] We will not reiterate that discussion here. Rather, we wish to reaffirm the need to focus on and articulate specific legitimate interests that some indigenous people or groups may have in certain information or classes of information. Sacred information relating to religious rites that is not generally known provides one of the clearest examples. To the extent such information exists and the groups in question wish to maintain its secrecy, we can imagine a statutory solution modelled on privacy and trade secret protection that could serve the legitimate interests of the group. On the other hand, where the information is publicly known and not otherwise eligible for protection under the existing IPR regimes, it is difficult for us to see *any* case for general control rights, exclusive or nonexclusive, in the group that was the original source of the information. Between these two extremes, arguments can and should be made on a case-by-case basis, with focus always on the harm that is being suffered by outsider use of the information in question and whether that harm justifies limitations on free speech and the dissemination of knowledge.

We recognize that, at bottom, we are choosing sides in a fundamental value conflict. The default position of most Western societies is that publicly available information, being nonrival, is free for all to use, subject to the IPR regimes for new information and subject to specific uses of information that threaten identifiable harms (e.g. crying "Fire!" in a crowded theatre, even if there is an actual fire). Many defenders of exclusive rights in intangible indigenous cultural property disagree that this default position should apply to indigenous groups. The reasons these defenders have thus far given for their position, however, are not convincing. That many wrongs have been perpetrated against many indigenous groups all over the world, often over the course of centuries, is undeniable. How to compensate for these wrongs to the extent possible is a vital subject of public discourse and potential legal development. Recognizing exclusive control rights, or even more limited "stewardship" rights, in old information, however, is simply not a remedy that in any way, except by chance, relates to the wrong.

In each case, we need to ask whether a right equivalent to the one proposed for indigenous groups should be recognized for nonindigenous groups otherwise similarly situated. Can and should we afford exclusive control over the origin stories of indigenous groups while denying such control to the Greeks over Homer? There is a clear and easily articulated basis for the default position that information is and must be free, with at least articulated reasons for the exceptions relating to traditional IPRs. There is nothing in that basis that distinguishes between information deriving from particular groups, indigenous or otherwise. The burden is therefore on those seeking stronger indigenous group rights in old information to articulate clearly whatever basis they see for deviating from this solidly based default position that information is free.

Notes

1 Robert K Paterson & Dennis S. Karjala, "Looking Beyond Intellectual Property in Resolving Protection of the Intangible Cultural Heritage of Indigenous Peoples", (2003) 11 *Cardozo J. Internat'l & Comp. L.* 633.
2 *Id.* at 670.
3 For an overview of some of these developments, see "Intangible Cultural Heritage", in James A.R. Nafziger, Robert K. Paterson, and Alison Dundes Renteln, *Cultural Law: International, Comparative, and Indigenous* (Cambridge Univ. Press, 2010), 614.
4 *See* Jin Yuqin, Note, "Necessity: Enacting Laws to Protect Indigenous Intellectual Property Rights in the United States", (2011) 19 *Transnat'l L. & Contemp. Probs.* 950, 956–59 (reporting disputes between related Native American tribes over ownership of the knowledge in question and raising the question of who can legitimately represent indigenous people).
5 *See* M. Strathern, "Multiple Perspectives on Intellectual Property", in K. Whimp & M. Busse (eds.), *Protection of Intellectual, Biological and Cultural Property in Papua New Guinia*, (Oceania 2000), at 47, and 52.
6   Kristen A. Carpenter, Sonia K. Katyal & Angela R. Riley, "In Defense of Property", (2009) 118 *Yale L.J.* 1022 [hereinafter referred to as Carpenter et. al.].
7 Elizabeth Pennisi, "Conquering by Copying", 328 *Science* 165 (Apr. 9, 2010) and Dennis S. Karjala, "Copying" and "Piracy" in the Digital Age", (2013) 52 *Washburn L.J.* 245, 247 n.7.
8 For example, Article 15(4)(a) of the Berne Convention provides that members may designate an author's representative to enforce the copyright rights of an unknown author from that country. *Berne Convention for the Protection of Literary and Artistic Works* (Paris Act 24 July 1971) article 15(4)(a).
9 Professor Michael Brown has proffered an "ecological approach" to draw an appropriate balance between the two desirable goals of protecting cultural heritage and promoting free and open expression throughout society. Michael F. Brown, "Heritage Trouble: Recent Work on the Protection of Intangible Cultural Property", (2005) 12 *Int'l J. Cultural Prop.* 40, 51.
10 *Supra*, n. 6.
11 *Id.* at 1124–25.
12 *Id.* at 1046. Except in their specific examples, Professor Carpenter et al. do not supply a definition of what property is included in the "certain property" they refer to here.
13 *Id.* at 1067.
14 *Id.* at 1080.
15 *Id.* at 1083.

16 *Id.* at 1083–7
17 *E.g., id.* at 1084, 1085, 1086, 1087.
18 *E.g., id.* at 1086, 1087.
19 *Id.* at 1085.
20 *Id.* at 1084.
21 *Id.* at 1087.
22 *Id.* at 1102.
23 *Id.* at 1102.
24 See *supra* n. 1, at 665 to 666.
25 Carpenter et al., *supra* n. 6, at 1103–4.
26 *Id.* at 1046.
27 See Amy Stevens, "Poor Jane Austen Didn't Live to See "Sense and Sensibility", *Wall St. Journal*, March 25, 1996.
28 In what sense, for example, would the use of a plant to treat a given medical condition be "integral" to the identity or survival of the group that discovers the useful property?
29 Because the stewardship model supplements rather than replaces traditional property concepts, Professor Carpenter et al. concede "the need for regulatory oversight or mediation when title-holders and nonowners disagree." *Supra* n. 6 at 1080. However, what standards does the mediator or regulator apply in deciding these and the many subsidiary questions that they raise? In the case of pharmaceuticals, in particular, what part of the risk of unsuccessful commercialization should be borne by the group supplying the initial information? See Dennis S. Karjala, "Sustainability and Intellectual Property Rights in Traditional Knowledge", (2012) 53 *Jurimetrics J.* 57, 64 n.25.
30 Carpenter et al., *supra* note 6, at 1102.
31 *Id.* at 1100–1.
32 The report was published in three volumes, the first of which summarizes its findings and recommendations. See David V. Williams, "Ko Aotearoa Tenei: Law and Policy Affecting Maori Culture and Identity", (2013) 20 *Int'l. J. of Cultural Prop.* 311.
33 See Graeme W. Austin, "Re-Treating Intellectual Property? The Wai 262 Proceeding and the Heuristics of Intellectual Property Law" (2003), 11 *Cardozo J. of Int'l. and Comp. Law*, 333.
34   The 1840 Treaty of Waitangi was neglected by the New Zealand legal system but achieved constitutional status through the establishment of the Waitangi Tribunal in 1975; see Austin, id., at 341 to 351. The tribunal is a quasi-judicial body which hears claims by Maori alleging violations by the Crown of the principles contained in the Treaty. Its findings are not legally binding but are often implemented by changes to laws.
35 See Jessica Christine Lai, "Maori Traditional Cultural Expressions and the WAI 262 Report: Looking at Details", University of Lucerne, Switzerland, i-call Working Paper No. 02, at 8 (2012).
36 See Owen Morgan, "Protecting Indigenous Signs and Trade Marks – the New Zealand Experience", *Intel. Prop. Q.*, 58 (2004).
37 This assumption itself seems questionable given that there are thousands of Maori artifacts in New Zealand and foreign museums whose tribal affiliation is unknown.
38 See Lai, *supra* n. 35 at 12.
39 *Id.* at 13.
40 *Id.* at 13–14.
41 Robert K Paterson & Dennis S. Karjala, *supra* note 1, at 652–69.

Chapter 6

The Alliance of Small Island States

Intellectual property, cultural heritage, and climate change

*Matthew Rimmer**

Introduction

There has been significant debate over intellectual property, cultural heritage, and traditional knowledge in respect of small island states in recent international discussions over climate change and sustainable development.

In June 2012, Ambassador Marlene Moses, Nauru's Permanent Representative to the United Nations and the then-chair of the Alliance of Small Island States (AOSIS), gave a stirring address on the topic of sustainable development, the Green Economy, and climate change (Moses, 2012b). Her paper was a position piece in the lead up to the Rio+20 Summit on Sustainable Development. In her discussion, Moses commented upon the impact of climate change upon small island states:

> For many of the world's island and coastal communities, climate change has grown into an existential threat. Kiribati and the Maldives have already lost some of their islands to rising seas and more territory loss has been reported in the Pacific and Caribbean. Shoreline erosion and flooding has caused major damage to roads, public utilities and homes. Saltwater intrusion has degraded agricultural lands and freshwater supplies. Tackling climate change, in other words, cannot be separated from sustainable development.
>
> (Moses, 2012b)

She concluded in her address: 'Given the stakes, we cannot afford to ignore the overarching problem of the emissions gap, here or in any discussions that involve international environmental or development policy' (Moses, 2012b).

AOSIS is a 'transnational', 'polyglot' grouping of like-minded countries, to use the language of Professor Margaret Chon (2012). AOSIS is a coalition of island states and coastal countries, which share common concerns about development, the environment, and climate change. AOSIS serves as an ad hoc lobbying group for small island states within the United Nations system. AOSIS does not have a formal charter; a budget; or a secretariat. AOSIS has a membership of 43 states and observers from all parts of the world. A significant number of its members come from the Pacific region – including the Cook Islands, Fiji, the Federated States of Micronesia, Kiribati, Palau, Papua New Guinea, Samoa, the Solomon Islands, Timor-Leste, Tuvalu, and Vanuatu. The observers include American Samoa, Netherlands Antilles, Guam, and U.S. Virgin Islands. The AOSIS has been in operation for over two decades – with a rotation of the chair-person position.

In *Climate Change and Small Island States*, Jon Barnett and John Campbell (2010) commented that there are fractures between the members of AOSIS in the international debates over climate change. The pair observed,

> There are tensions between those AOSIS members who are members of G77 or have aligned themselves with the G77, which holds the view that emissions reductions should be restricted to the Annex 1 parties, and those that are not part of the G77 (such as the Cook Islands, Niue and Tuvalu) or which hold the view that the large developing countries must also begin reducing their emissions.
>
> (Barnett and Campbell 2010: 101)

Such schisms have also been evident in the debates over intellectual property, sustainable development, and the Green Economy.

Michael Gerrard and Gregory Wannier's (2013) collection *Threatened Island Nations* surveys the various impacts of climate change and sea level rise on small island states. The work considers a number of existential legal questions:

> If a country is under water, is it still a state? Does it still have a seat at the United Nations? What becomes of its exclusive economic zone, and the fishing rights on which it depends for much of its livelihood? What countries will take in its displaced people, and what rights will they have when they arrive? Do they have any legal recourse against those states whose greenhouse gas emissions caused this plight?
>
> (Gerrard and Wannier 2013: xvii)

Gerrard and Wannier maintained, 'It is our moral duty as a society to prevent anthropogenic climate change to the extent that we can and to help these threatened nations cope with the climate change that will occur despite our best efforts' (Gerrard and Wannier 2013: 14). The collection focuses upon the threats posed by climate change to sovereignty and territorial lands.

Jenny Grote Stoutenburg (2013: 57) noted that

> the failure of the post-Copenhagen era to produce new meaningful greenhouse gas emission reduction obligations for States renders it more likely that

unmitigated climate change and its potentially most destructive consequence, sea level rise, will threaten the sovereign existence of low-lying island States such as the Marshall Islands.

Maxine Burkett (2013b: 120), an expert on climate justice from the University of Hawaii, comments, 'Climate change has introduced the potential for a seismic shift in the way we have organized human systems on our planet' (Burkett 2013b: 120). She observes that 'our thorough reworking of our environment will necessarily affect the legal, political, and economic systems in which they were conceived, developed, and globalized' (Burkett 2013b: 120). She suggests that 'we are embarking on a postclimate era in law and human society' (Burkett 2013b: 120).

In her book *This Changes Everything*, Naomi Klein (2014) considers the plight of Nauru, a small island state, which has suffered from various kinds of exploitation by other countries. Extrapolating from the case of Nauru, Naomi Klein wonders whether the rest of the planet suffers from a similar malady. She suggests, 'Nauru isn't the only one digging itself to death; we all are' (Klein 2014: 168). Naomi Klein observes that Nauru teaches us not only about the dangers of fossil fuel emissions, but it also highlights the mentality of 'extractivism'. Klein is critical of the 'narrative that assures us that, however bad things get, we are going to be saved at the last minute – whether by the market, by philanthropic billionaires, or by technological wizards – or best of all, by all three at the same time' (Klein 2014: 187). She wistfully hopes for a shift in the discourse: 'Only when we dispense with these various forms of magical thinking will we be ready to leave extractivism behind and build societies we need within the boundaries we have – a world with no sacrifice zones, no new Naurus' (Klein 2014: 187).

This chapter will consider the role of AOSIS in debates over intellectual property, the environment, and climate change. It will consider questions of technology transfer, climate justice, and intergenerational equity. This chapter has three main parts. It first explores Indigenous intellectual property and small island states. It then considers intellectual property, climate change, and small island states. It finally explores intellectual property, sustainable development, and small island states.

This chapter will conclude that there is a need for AOSIS to bolster its position on intellectual property, technology transfer, access to genetic resources, and Indigenous Knowledge. Moreover, the group could seek to benefit from the development of international networks – such as the Technology Mechanism established under the *United Nations Framework Convention on Climate Change* 1992, the Global Indigenous Network announced by Australia at the Rio+20 discussions on sustainable development, and Sustainable Development Goal Partnerships. As discussed by Peter Drahos (2012), there is potential in establishing development Indigenous networks and engaging in the adaptive management of intellectual property. There will be a need for small island states to develop frameworks for intellectual property and cultural heritage in light of the *Paris Agreement* 2015 and the *United Nations Sustainable Development Goals* 2015. Small island states will need to respond to the twin challenges of climate change and sustainable development.

Indigenous intellectual property, small island states, and climate change

Although historically they have borne little responsibility for the increase in carbon emissions, small island states and Indigenous communities have suffered disproportionately from the impact of climate change. Climate change poses significant threats to territoriality and nationhood. Climate change also raises challenges in respect of food security, health care, water security, and access to genetic resources. In addition to there being significant impacts upon physical property and territory, climate change also poses threats to traditional knowledge, Indigenous knowledge, and local knowledge. A literature review reveals that Indigenous communities in small island states are on the front lines of climate change. There is a need to provide for stronger protection in respect of Indigenous Intellectual property. There should be greater protection of cultural heritage. The regime for access to genetic resources and benefit sharing should be applied to include traditional knowledge relating to the environment and climate change.

Climate change and Indigenous peoples

There are a host of legal issues in respect of climate change and small island states. There has been much concern about resettlement (Lagan 2013). The issue of intellectual property, Indigenous Knowledge, and climate change is one of many confronting issues.

In an overview of climate change, legal governance, and the Pacific Islands, Erika Techera (2013: 343) comments, 'Because indigenous peoples comprise the majority of the populations of each Pacific Island Country, and as high percentages of these people continue to live traditional lifestyles, they are likely to be vulnerable to the impacts of climate change'. She elaborates,

> Essentially, most people in the majority of Pacific Island Countries are indigenous. For example, in Samoa over 85 per cent of the population is indigenous and in Vanuatu about 94 per cent of people are indigenous (known as ni-Vanuatu). The exception is Fiji where just over half of the people are indigenous Fijians and 36 per cent are of Indian origin (having been brought from India to work as plantation labourers). Importantly, it has been noted that unlike the Indian Ocean island nations and Caribbean countries, 'Pacific indigenous cultures have remained strong' and this includes their profound cultural and spiritual connection to nature.
>
> (Techera 2013: 342–3)

Techera observes, 'The Pacific Island Countries are legally pluralist with often fragmented legal frameworks that include customary law and community-based governance, colonial-era statutes and post-independence legislation' (Techera 2013: 343). She emphasizes that such a situation 'creates considerable complexity when legal strategies are being developed to address contemporary environmental challenges such as climate change' (Techera 2013: 343). Techera worries, 'The Pacific Island Countries are some of the least responsible for global greenhouse gas (GHG) emissions yet are likely to suffer the worst effects of climate change' (Techera 2013: 345).

Techera (2013: 347) stressed that climate change will have an impact upon traditional knowledge: '[The] physical impacts will be compounded by damage to intangible heritage, as traditional knowledge and cultural practices depend on sacred sites, animals and plants'. She feared, 'Changes to species habitats, abundance and movement will also result in the loss of traditional knowledge about ecology, medicine, arts and crafts' (Techera 2013: 347).

Maxine Burkett (2013a) has noted, 'In regions across the world, including the Pacific, an appeal to Indigenous knowledge is also emerging'. She comments upon the relevance of Indigenous environmental knowledge to the question of climate change adaptation:

> Integration of Indigenous Ecological Knowledge, in the adaptation context, describes at least two different phenomena. It describes the indigenous methods used to respond to historical extremes that climate forecasts portend with greater frequency and severity – such as floods and drought – and suggests proven adaptations. It can also describe a lens, or worldview, with which decisions should be made that might facilitate long-range, multi-generational adaptive governance.
>
> (Burkett 2013a: 96)

Burkett has argued, 'It would serve us well to continue to look to Indigenous environmental knowledge as a source for specific management practices and alternative worldviews that might inspire and support practices that will support us through the greatest challenge to human adaptation' (Burkett 2013a: 118). In this context, it is important to think about the intersections and interconnections between intellectual property, environmental law, and Indigenous rights.

There has been research on the impacts of climate change on particular island states, such as Fiji (Sutton 2013), Tuvalu (Boom 2013), and other small island states (Mulalap 2013), as well as Indigenous communities in New Zealand (Johnstone 2013) and Australia (Davis 2013). The United States National Climate Assessment 2014 featured significant research on the impact of climate change on Indigenous communities, particularly in the United States (Bull Bennett et al. 2014, 297–317).

Weathering Uncertainty

The *Weathering Uncertainty* report provides a consideration of Indigenous Knowledge and climate change in a range of regions (United Nations University 2012). In chapter 8, the report focuses upon small islands. The report noted that 'small island societies have lived for generations with considerable and often sudden environmental change' (United Nations University 2012: 88). The report stressed, 'The traditional knowledge and related practice with which small island societies have adapted to such change are of global relevance' (United Nations University 2012: 88). The report commented,

> Areas in which small island societies have developed adaptation relevant traditional knowledge include natural disaster preparedness, risk reduction, food production systems and weather event forecasting. In many small island contexts, the transmission and application of traditional knowledge is under threat from changes in consumption and migration patterns, as well as from the lack of recognition of Traditional Knowledge in the formal educational system.
>
> (United Nations University 2012: 88)

The report emphasized the potential for Pacific traditional knowledge to be applied for climate adaptation: 'Traditional knowledge systems and practices were indispensable in making the original settlement of small islands possible, and subsequently in ensuring continuous human habitation, in spite of the islands' considerable past and present exposure to both anthropogenic and non-anthropogenic environmental variation and stress' (United Nations University 2012: 90). The report also discussed traditional calendars, weather and extreme event forecasting, and food production and storage. The report also noted that 'traditional knowledge in the small island context is in many cases rapidly eroding due to the interruption of intergenerational knowledge transmission' (United Nations University 2012: 95).

Oxfam has also produced a complementary study on *Strengthening Governance of Climate Adaptation Finance* (Maclellan et al. 2012). The report emphasized that the 2007 Fourth Assessment Report of the Intergovernmental Panel on Climate Change (IPCC) stated that indigenous knowledge is 'an invaluable basis for developing adaptation and natural resource management strategies in response to environmental and other forms of change' (Maclellan et al. 2012: 44). The report noted that 'one valuable way research participants identified to improve the effectiveness of climate funding was to support more applied research in the Pacific on the generation, protection and transfer of traditional knowledge in response to the effects of climate change' (Maclellan et al. 2012: 44). This involves 'integrating indigenous ecological knowledge and practice into contemporary western methodologies of climate observation, research, assessment and response' (Maclellan et al. 2012: 44). The study observed, 'Across the Pacific there are a number of examples that have shown the value of integrating Western and indigenous forms of scientific knowledge' (Maclellan et al. 2012: 44).

The Intergovernmental Panel on Climate Change (2014) further highlights issues in respect of intellectual property, Indigenous Knowledge, and climate change in its 2014 report on climate mitigation.

Indigenous intellectual property

There is a need for small island states to push for enhanced protection in respect of Indigenous intellectual property – particularly in respect of environmental knowledge and climate knowledge.

The Preamble of the *United Nations Declaration on the Rights of Indigenous Peoples* 2007 states that we need to 'Recognis[e] that respect for Indigenous Knowledge, cultures and traditional practises contributes to sustainable and equitable development and proper management of the environment'. Article 31 (1) acknowledges,

> Indigenous peoples have the right to maintain, control, protect and develop their cultural heritage, traditional knowledge and traditional cultural expressions, as well as the manifestations of their sciences, technologies and cultures, including human and genetic resources, seeds, medicines, knowledge of the properties of flora and fauna, oral traditions, literatures, designs . . . They also have the right to maintain, control, protect and develop their intellectual property over such cultural heritage, traditional knowledge, and cultural expressions.

Article 31 (2) recognises, 'In conjunction with Indigenous peoples, States shall take effective measure to recognise and protect the exercise of these rights'. There is also a strong emphasis upon the importance of prior, free, and informed consent for Indigenous peoples in the *United Nations Declaration on the Rights of Indigenous Peoples* 2007.

Naomi Klein (2014) has been concerned about the impact of climate change upon Indigenous communities. She comments that 'the exercise of Indigenous rights has played a central role in the rise of the current wave of fossil fuel resistance' (Klein 2014: 370). Naomi Klein also charts the development of international law to help recognise and protect Indigenous rights:

> As the Indigenous rights movement gains strength globally, huge advances are being made in recognizing the legitimacy of these claims. Most significant was the *United Nations Declaration on the Rights of Indigenous Peoples*, adopted by the General Assembly in September 2007 after 143 member states voted in its favor (the four opposing votes – United States, Canada,

Australia, and New Zealand – would each, under domestic pressure, eventually endorse it as well). The declaration states that, 'Indigenous peoples have the right to the conservation and protection of the environment and the productive capacity of their lands or territories and resources'. Some countries have even taken the step of recognizing these rights in revised constitutions.

(Klein 2014: 377)

Activist Martin Lukacs had hoped that 'implementing Indigenous rights on the ground, starting with the *United Nations Declaration on the Rights of Indigenous Peoples*, could tilt the balance of stewardship over a vast geography: giving Indigenous peoples much more control, and corporations much less' (Klein 2014: 383).

In the Pacific, a Regional Framework for the Protection of Traditional Knowledge and Expressions of Culture was developed in 2002. Miranda Forsyth has written extensively about intellectual property, Indigenous Knowledge, and the Pacific (Forsyth 2012a; Forsyth 2012b; Forsyth 2013a; Forsyth 2013b; Forsyth and Farran 2013). She has been concerned about whether Western-style TRIPS regimes are appropriate or well-adapted for small island developing states, given their capacities and needs. Bronwyn Parry (2002) has expressed concerns that 'empirical evidence from the Pacific illustrates how the TRIPs regime facilitates the commodification and appropriation of intellectual, cultural and biological resources in the region'. She also highlights 'the development of sui generis systems of IPR protection that challenge the normativity and hegemony of this regime'.

A 2014 report on *Pacific Trade and Human Rights* (WHO, OHCHR, and UNDP 2014: 31) concluded that 'in general Pacific Island Countries are net importers of intellectual property and introducing new IPR regimes will therefore result in increased costs to individuals and governments'. The report observed,

TK cannot be adequately protected by current IPR systems. Although there have been treaty negotiations to develop a treaty that would do this for over a decade, there is no current international system for the protection of TK, or one likely in the immediate future. Any reference to the protection of TK in a trade agreement is highly likely to be merely aspirational and non-binding, and should not be seen as a worthwhile trade-off for agreeing to high IPR standards . . . To avoid such problems arising, it is essential that any national IPR laws that are agreed to as a result of trade agreements are drafted having regard to the local conditions, including the cultural context, rather than relying only on model laws.

(WHO, OHCHR, and UNDP 2014: 32)

Peter Drahos (2014) argues in *Intellectual Property, Indigenous People and their Knowledge* that there is a need for development networks for the better protection of Indigenous intellectual property.

Cultural heritage

There will also be a dramatic impact of climate change upon the cultural heritage of small island states and Indigenous communities. The World Heritage Committee of UNESCO has been concerned 'that the impacts of Climate Change are affecting many and are likely to affect many more World Heritage properties, both natural and cultural in the years to come'.

Kim Hee-Eun (2011) – a scholar from Stanford Law School under the supervision of John Merryman – has contended that we need to add a climate change dimension to the protection of intangible cultural heritage. The scholar observes that the topic has been sadly neglected thus far:

> The impact of climate change on cultural heritage hardly figures in current climate change policymaking, with its dominant focus on greenhouse gas emissions and their direct consequences. Likewise, the conventional perspective of cultural heritage risk management concerns especially the loss of tangible heritage sites and structures, and to a lesser extent how such loss will affect communities and the intangible aspects of culture. However, as climate change displacement materializes, these human dimensions will demand increasing attention.
>
> (Hee-Eun 2011: 290)

Kim Hee-Eun suggests that 'the emergence of international climate change issues in cultural heritage, intangible as well as tangible, could complicate such distinction of interests' (Hee-Eun 2011: 290). The writer argues,

> Accommodation may need to be made for climate change–related regulation, international human rights law concerning climate change refugees, and intellectual property rights or sui generis rights relevant to the protection and promotion of traditional knowledge and traditional cultural expressions, especially in terms of cross-border protection.
>
> (Hee-Eun 2011: 290)

The impact of climate change will further complicate the regulation of tangible and intangible cultural heritage – particularly Indigenous cultural heritage (Graber et al. 2012).

Access to genetic resources

There have also been significant issues with small island developing states dealing with the demands of policing biodiversity regimes (Rimmer 2009).

Climate change poses significant additional threats to the biodiversity and genetic resources of small island developing states.

The United Nations Under-Secretary General and UNEP Executive Director, Achim Steiner (2014), highlighted the threats posed to small island developing states. He commented, 'Small island developing states contribute little to the problem of climate change – the combined annual carbon dioxide output of these nations accounts for less than one per cent of global emissions'. Steiner noted that 'Overall, climate change adaptation is a top priority in Small Island Developing States, but lack of financial resources is an obstacle'. He contended, 'The right enabling conditions are vital to generate and stimulate both public and private sector investments that incorporate broader environmental and social criteria, and thus address this growing challenge'.

Braulio Ferreira de Souza Dias (2014), the Executive Secretary of the Convention on Biological Diversity, said, 'Small Island Developing States have learned, often the hard way, that their long-term quality of life will depend on keeping healthy nature as the most cost effective provider of critical ecosystem services and protection against climate change and disaster vulnerability'.

The *Convention on Biological Diversity* 1992 provides a framework for access to genetic resources, informed consent, and benefit sharing. The regime also provides recognition for the protection of traditional knowledge. Small island states face a number of heightened concerns in respect of biodiversity and climate change.

The *Nagoya Protocol* 2012 elaborates upon the protection of traditional knowledge. Article 7 notes, 'In accordance with domestic law, each Party shall take measures, as appropriate, with the aim of ensuring that traditional knowledge associated with genetic resources that is held by indigenous and local communities is accessed with the prior and informed consent or approval and involvement of these indigenous and local communities, and that mutually agreed terms have been established'.

Article 12 (1) comments, 'In implementing their obligations under this Protocol, Parties shall in accordance with domestic law take into consideration indigenous and local communities' customary laws, community protocols and procedures, as applicable, with respect to traditional knowledge associated with genetic resources'. Article 12 (2) insists that

> Parties, with the effective participation of the indigenous and local communities concerned, shall establish mechanisms to inform potential users of traditional knowledge associated with genetic resources about their obligations, including measures as made available through the Access and Benefit-sharing Clearing-House for access to and fair and equitable sharing of benefits arising from the utilization of such knowledge.

Article 12 (3) provides that

> Parties shall endeavour to support, as appropriate, the development by indigenous and local communities, including women within these communities,

of: (a) Community protocols in relation to access to traditional knowledge associated with genetic resources and the fair and equitable sharing of benefits arising out of the utilization of such knowledge; (b) Minimum requirements for mutually agreed terms to secure the fair and equitable sharing of benefits arising from the utilization of traditional knowledge associated with genetic resources; and (c) Model contractual clauses for benefit-sharing arising from the utilization of traditional knowledge associated with genetic resources.

Article 12 (4) emphasizes,

> Parties, in their implementation of this Protocol, shall, as far as possible, not restrict the customary use and exchange of genetic resources and associated traditional knowledge within and amongst indigenous and local communities in accordance with the objectives of the Convention.

There remain tensions within the regime between the interests of states and the concerns of Indigenous communities.

There has been a special focus by the Secretariat of the *Convention on Biological Diversity* 1992 on 'island diversity' and 'protecting paradise on earth': 'Islands and their surrounding near-shore marine areas constitute unique ecosystems often comprising many plant and animal species that are endemic – found nowhere else on Earth'. The Secretariat stressed that island diversity was 'key to the livelihood, economy, well-being and cultural identity of 600 million islanders – one-tenth of world population'. The Secretariat was concerned about extinction in island biodiversity, 'Over the past century, island biodiversity has been subject to intense pressure from invasive alien species, habitat change and over-exploitation, and, increasingly, from climate change and pollution'. The Secretariat was worried. 'Among the most vulnerable of the developing countries, small island developing States (SIDS) depend on the conservation and sustainable use of island biodiversity for their sustainable development'.

A networked approach has been promoted for small island states. The Global Island Partnership is intended to promote 'action for island conservation and sustainable livelihoods by inspiring leadership, catalysing commitments and facilitating collaboration among all islands'.

There has been much concern about 'carbon cowboys' who engage in the misappropriation of the property and intellectual property of Indigenous communities and small island states. This debate raises the question – is 'carbon piracy' the new biopiracy? There has been a longstanding debate over traditional knowledge and access to genetic resources. An elaborate regime for access to genetic resources, prior informed consent, and benefit-sharing has been established under the *Convention on Biological Diversity* 1992. There could be scope for expanding the protection afforded to traditional knowledge within this regime to Indigenous climate knowledge.

Intellectual property, climate change, and small island states

Reviewing the history of AOSIS, Marlene Moses (2013) has emphasized the constructive role of the transnational group in the international climate negotiations, 'Early on, AOSIS earned reputation for advocating for policies that are rigorously based in science and calculated to reduce emissions to a level that is consistent with the survival of all our members'. She commented that AOSIS played an important role at the climate negotiations, 'as both intellectual leader and voice of the most vulnerable'. Moses (2009) has maintained that 'developed countries have created a global crisis based on a flawed system of values'. She suggested that 'there is no reason we should be forced to accept a solution informed by that same system'.

Erika Techera (2013: 361) comments that 'the technology transfer and financial assistance offered through the UNFCCC framework and Global Environmental Facility are beneficial for Pacific Island States, many of whom are also Least Developed Countries'.

It is worthwhile tracing the influence of AOSIS in a number of recent international climate conferences – including the *Copenhagen Accord* 2009, the *Cancun Agreements* 2010, the *Durban Decisions* 2011, the *Doha Climate Gateway* 2012, the *Warsaw Opportunity* 2013, the *United Nations Climate Summit* 2014, the *Lima Call to Climate Action* 2014 and the *Paris Agreement* 2015.

The Copenhagen Accord *2009*

At the Copenhagen Summit, the AOSIS (2009) put forward a comprehensive proposal in respect of the survival of the *Kyoto Protocol* 1997 and a Copenhagen protocol to enhance the implementation of the *United Nations Framework Convention on Climate Change* 1992. The text emphasized that

> Climate change has significant negative implications for human society and ecosystems that are already occurring and pose an existential threat to particularly vulnerable developing countries, especially the least developed countries and small island developing countries and countries in Africa affected by drought, desertification and floods who have contributed least to the problem.

Article 8 looked at reducing emissions from deforestation and forest degradation in developing countries. Article 8 (4)(e) stressed the need to ensure that 'all actions are consistent with the *United Nations Declaration on the Rights of Indigenous Peoples* and respect the knowledge and rights of indigenous peoples including ensuring their free, prior and informed consent'. Such a statement alludes to the regime for access to genetic resources, prior informed consent, and benefit sharing under the *Rio Convention on Biological Diversity* 1992.

Article 11 of the proposal by the AOSIS (2009) addressed technology development and transfer. Article 11 (1) emphasized that

> All Parties shall enhance cooperation and joint development to promote the development, deployment, diffusion and transfer of climate friendly technologies, in particular to take effective measures to encourage and provide incentives for technology transfer to developing countries, remove relevant barriers, and appropriately address issues of intellectual property rights.

Article 11 (2) proposed, 'A mechanism for technology development and transfer, the Technology Mechanism, is hereby established to fully implement the commitments on technology development and transfer under the Convention, in particular Article 4, paragraphs 3, 5, and 7 of the Convention'.

Tuvalu (2009) argued, 'Parties shall cooperate to develop and deploy patent sharing and/or intellectual property free renewable energy and energy efficiency technologies'.

The debate over intellectual property and climate did not progress far at the Copenhagen meeting (see Rimmer, 2011a). Developed countries such as the United States, Japan, and members of the European Union pushed for strong protection of intellectual property rights. China and the G77 argued for intellectual property flexibilities – such as technology transfer, public-sector licensing, patent pools, compulsory licensing, and patentable subject matter exclusions. There was also a discussion about the use of genetic resources. Small island states and least developed countries highlighted the need for a commons for clean technologies. Although the countries could not agree on text on intellectual property, a proposal for a Technology Mechanism was supported.

The Cancun Agreements 2010

The *Cancún Agreements* 2010 helped clarify the establishment of a new Climate Technology Centre and Network. Dr Al Binger of AOSIS argued that the function of the Technology Mechanism should be to create an environment for more technology development and transfer (Raman 2011). He hoped that the Climate Technology Centre and Network would increase the availability of green technologies for development including social development. Binger also stressed that the Climate Technology Centre and Network should be Party driven and that there should be sufficient financial resources to support projects.

The Durban Decisions 2011

The AOSIS entered into a strategic alliance with Least Developed Countries and the European Union at the Durban meeting (Common Statement by the European

Union, Least Developed Countries, and the Alliance of Small Island States 2011). This combination of countries released a common statement emphasizing

> We believe that the world has had a lot of time to think. What we need is not more thinking. What we need is more action. The gap between our ambitions and the current pledges is simply too wide. And we need not to remind anyone of the scale of climatic threats facing the most vulnerable countries in the world as a result of climate change. The facts are clear and we are still too far from where we need to be to secure the most vulnerable countries' right to sustainable development.

The AOSIS, the Least Developed Countries, and the European Union pushed for ambitious outcomes in the *Durban Decisions* 2011 (see Rimmer 2011b).

The Doha Climate Gateway 2012

There was further deadlocked debate over intellectual property and climate change at the Doha talks (Rimmer 2012). The UNFCCC Climate Technology Centre and Network was formally established, with the United Nations Environment Programme winning the competition to host the Centre.

At the Doha discussions in 2012, AOSIS sought to raise a new international mechanism for Loss and Damage. Spokesman Ronald Jumeau was critical of developed nations for their dilatory approach to climate change:

> The Doha caravan seems to be lost in the sand. As far as ambition is concerned, we are lost. We're past the mitigation (emissions cuts) and adaptation eras. We're now right into the era of loss and damage. What's next after that? Destruction? Disappearance of some of our islands? We're already into the era of re-location. But after loss and damage there will be mass re-locations if we continue with this loss of ambition.
>
> (Harrabin 2012)

The issue of compensation in respect of climate losses became a critical issue in the discussions over the text of the *Doha Climate Gateway* 2012.

The United States Chief Negotiator, Todd Stern, resisted the proposal in respect of Loss and Damage, emphasizing, 'I will block this. I will shut this down' (Parnell 2013).

Marlene Moses (2013), ambassador for Nauru and chair of AOSIS, discussed the significance of the concept of Loss and Damage. She emphasized that ' "Loss and Damage" refers to impacts of climate change that can no longer be addressed by mitigating emissions or helping countries adapt to environmental changes – when our coral reefs fade away, gardens turn to dust, and sea walls succumb to ferocious waves' (Moses 2013). Moses suggested that 'our proposal on Loss and Damage' 'addresses the "new normal" of climate change' (Moses 2013). She observed that the proposal 'draws on numerous principles of international law, including the responsibility of a state, polluter pays, common but differentiated responsibilities and respective capabilities, intergenerational equity, trans-boundary harm and others' (Moses 2013).

Moses reflected that

> the very fact we have to talk about Loss and Damage – not hypothetically but out of necessity – after over two decades of negotiations in some way concedes that we have failed to achieve the ultimate objective of the Convention; that, for some, mitigation and adaptation are no longer enough.
>
> (Moses 2013)

Yeb Sano and Julie-Anne Richards (2014) have argued that levy should be imposed on fossil fuel companies to pay for the loss and damage caused to people the world over from the burning of their products.

The Warsaw Opportunity 2013

There were further talks in Warsaw in 2013. Tony de Brum – Minister-in-assistance to the president of the Republic of the Marshall Islands – wrote a piece on climate justice, with Mary Robinson and Kelly Rigg (de Brum et al. 2013). The three called for the adoption of clean energy to promote a safe climate: 'This is why island states at the negotiations in Poland are proposing a "Warsaw Workplan" to quickly reduce emissions by accelerating the uptake of renewable energy and improve the efficiency of energy use and supply'. AOSIS (2013) called for urgent climate action.

The United Nations Climate Summit 2014 and the Lima Call to Climate Action 2014

At the United Nations Climate Summit in 2014 in New York, Kathy Jetnil Kijiner spoke on behalf of civil society (Rimmer 2014). The Marshall Islands resident warned of the impact of climate change upon small island states: 'We deserve to do more than just survive. We deserve to thrive' (reported by Visentin 2014). Jetnil-Kijiner (2014) delivered a moving poem to her daughter – lyrically expressing the profound impact that climate change would have on future generations (Jetnil-Kijiner 2014). This was a striking use of cultural expression to address the impact of climate change upon small island states.

Intellectual property was a contentious topic in the lead-up to the Paris climate talks. At talks at Bonn in October 2014, Australia, the United States, and Japan opposed the inclusion of provisions on intellectual property rights in the 2015 agreement (International Institute for Sustainable Development 2014).

Tuvalu – representing Least Developing Countries – suggested exploring schemes to make some technologies free of intellectual property rights. China and the G77 maintained that the agreement should support technology transfer modalities. Bangladesh stressed the role of the Green Climate Fund in supporting technology transfer.

The *Lima Call to Climate Action* 2014 agreed that 'the least developed countries and small island developing States may communicate information on strategies, plans and actions for low greenhouse gas emission development reflecting their special circumstances in the context of intended nationally determined contributions'.

In her book *Hard Choices*, Hillary Clinton (2014: 569) emphasized that 'the most important voices to be heard on this issue are those of the many people whose lives and livelihoods are most at risk from climate change'. She was particularly affected by the messages of 'leaders of island nations trying to raise the alarm before their homes are submerged together' (Clinton 2014: 569).

The President of Kiribati, Anote Tong, feared that climate action will be too slow to save small island developing states: 'The world is finally listening, but sometimes it all feels futile, you know' (Van Tiggelen 2014/2015).

The **Paris Agreement** *2015*

AOSIS played a significant role in calling for a strong *Paris Agreement* 2015. At the international talks, AOSIS lectured the other nation states:

> We must now seize every opportunity to make renewable energy accessible for every person and every community. We must use it more efficiently. And we must implement smart climate policies faster and more broadly . . . The international community has a responsibility to ensure that those who suffer from climate change impacts that are now unavoidable will have the resources they need to adapt when possible and rebuild their lives when all else fails.
>
> (AOSIS, 12 December 2015)

AOSIS emphasized that 'history will judge us not by what we did today, but by what we do from this day forward'. AOSIS stressed, 'That is how the Paris agreement will be measured: by future generations'.

Small island states played a critical role in the debate over loss and damage at the Paris international climate talks (Simonelli 2015).

There was substantial but inconclusive debate over the treatment of intellectual property and climate change during the Paris climate talks.

The United Nations Secretary-General Ban Ki-Moon commented, 'Intellectual property, technology transfer, and financing are among a wide range of topics that must be addressed in the context of climate change and sustainable development' (*The Tribune India* 2014). The Paris Climate Talks considered a number of issues related to intellectual property, technology transfer, finance, and climate change

Draft Article 56.3 laid down a number of options (Ad Hoc Working Group on the Durban Platform for Enhanced Action 2015). The first option called for a number of possibilities to facilitate technology transfer. Item A suggests that developed countries

> provide financial resources to address barriers caused by intellectual property rights (IPRs) and facilitate access to and the deployment of technology, including inter alia, by utilizing the Financial Mechanism and/or the establishment of a funding window under the Green Climate Fund/the operating entities of the Financial Mechanism.

Item B asked for 'an international mechanism on IPRs to be established to facilitate access to and the deployment of technology to [developing country Parties]'. Item C promoted other arrangements to be established to address intellectual property rights – such as 'collaborative research and development, shareware, commitments related to humanitarian or preferential licensing, fully paid-up or joint licensing schemes, preferential rates and patent pools'. Item D suggested that

> funds from the Green Climate Fund will be utilized to meet the full costs of intellectual property rights (IPRs) of environmentally sound technologies and know-how and such technologies will be provided to developing country Parties free of cost in order to enhance their actions to address climate change and its adverse impacts.

The second option was that 'Parties recognize that IPRs create an enabling environment for the promotion of technology innovation in environmentally sound technologies'.

The third option favoured by developed countries was that 'IPRs are not to be addressed in this agreement'.

The fourth option was for 'Developed country Parties to make available Intellectual Property (IP) through multilateral institutions as public good, through purchase of intellectual property'. For its part, AOSIS – along with other countries vulnerable to climate change – promoted public-interest approaches to intellectual property.

The final text of the *Paris Agreement* 2015 avoided dealing with intellectual property and climate change directly. Nonetheless, there are glancing references to traditional knowledge in the context of a larger debate about Indigenous Knowledge. There is some extensive text, more generally, about technology research, development, and dissemination in the *Paris Agreement* 2015. The Paris Climate Talks also saw a number of announcements on innovation – including

Mission Innovation, the Breakthrough Energy Coalition, and the International Solar Alliance.

AOSIS played a key role in calling for countries to ratify the *Paris Agreement* (AOSIS, 21 September 2016). Dr Mohamed Asim – the Minister of Foreign Affairs for the Maldives and the chair of AOSIS – said, 'Climate change is a truly international problem and solving it requires all of us to do our part'.

There has been consternation from small island states about the new United States administration of President Donald Trump withdrawing from the *Paris Agreement* 2015. AOSIS has stressed that the *Paris Agreement* 2015 is not 'renegotiable' (AOSIS, 1 June 2017). Thoriq Ibrahim, Environment and Energy Minister for the Maldives and chair of AOSIS, commented,

> The *Paris Agreement* was almost three decades in the making. It was designed for maximum flexibility and universal participation. It even allows countries to adjust their climate plans based on national circumstances. If the US wishes to change its contribution, that would be unfortunate but is its prerogative. Renegotiating the entire agreement, however, is not practical and could be a setback from which we never recover.

The implementation of the *Paris Agreement* 2015 will proceed, even without the involvement of the United States.

Intellectual property, sustainable development, and small Island states

There has been much discussion about appropriate legal remedies for small island states and Indigenous communities, given the impacts of climate change (Abate and Kronk 2013, and Techera 2013). What should be the negotiating position of AOSIS in respect of intellectual property, Indigenous Knowledge, and climate change? Small island developing states – and Indigenous communities – have a number of distinctive intellectual property interests. First, it is critical that small island developing states receive access to clean technologies and renewable energy, as well as climate mitigation and adaptation technologies. Second, there is a need to promote sustainable development policies and practices in small island developing states. Third, the *2030 Agenda for Sustainable Development* and the *United Nations Sustainable Development Goals* 2015 provides an important framework for future discussions over intellectual property, sustainable development, and climate change.

Technology transfer

It is also imperative that innovation policies promote the research, development, and diffusion of clean technologies to small island states and Indigenous communities.

There has been a significant debate over policy settings in respect of intellectual property and clean technologies (Lane 2011; Rimmer 2011a; Brown 2013; and Menell and Tran 2014). Small island developing states have come under a great deal of political pressure to provide for heightened protection of intellectual property rights, particularly under international trade agreements (Forsyth and Farran 2015).

There has been a push for countries vulnerable to climate change to be able to make use of flexibilities within intellectual property to obtain access to clean technologies. In the context of intellectual property and clean technologies, Jerome Reichman et al. (2014) have recently reviewed strategies and alternatives for intellectual property and green innovation. The writers commented, 'If climate change is going to be addressed successfully, clean technology must be adopted globally' (Reichman et al. 2014: 383).

Keith Maskus and Ruth Okediji (2014: 392–414) have provided legal and economic perspectives on international technology transfer in environmentally sound technologies. The pair comment,

> To date international climate-change negotiations under the aegis of the UNFCCC have achieved some successes with respect to technology transfer, most notably the establishment of a funding mechanism that remains largely unfulfilled. These talks have made little progress, however, in determining means by which such funding may be effectively deployed or patent regimes may be used or modified to enhance global access.
>
> (Maskus and Okediji 2014: 410)

Maskus and Okediji (2014: 410) observed that there is a need to make use of flexibilities within existing trade agreements: 'Within the patent arena we reaffirm the importance of taking advantage of flexibilities offered by the *TRIPS Agreement* in terms of IP standards, limitations, and exceptions'.

Maskus and Okediji (2014: 410) also recommend the implementation of complementary measures: 'Outside the realm of intellectual property rights, our suggestions range from allocating funding to prize mechanisms and targeted interventions of demonstrated effectiveness, to greater use of voluntary patent pools and research networks, often based on concessional licensing terms for use in poor countries'. In this context, innovation networks and finance mechanisms are particularly important. The UNFCCC Climate Technology Centre and Network will play a key role in encouraging research, development, and deployment of clean technologies. The Green Climate Fund needs to be properly supported to facilitate access to renewable energy and clean technologies.

The *Barbados Declaration on Achieving Sustainable Energy for All in Small Island Developing States (SIDS)* 2012 emphasized the need to achieve 'sustainable energy for all in Small Island Developing States', including 'providing all households with access to modern and affordable renewable energy services, while eradicating poverty, safeguarding the environment and providing new opportunities for sustainable development and economic growth'.

In September 2012, the AOSIS (2012) issued a leaders' declaration. The Declaration emphasized that 'Small Island Developing States remain a special case for sustainable development in view of our unique and particular vulnerabilities, including our small size, remoteness, narrow resource and export base, and exposure to global environmental challenges and external economic shocks, including to a large range of impacts from climate change and more frequent and intense natural disasters'. The Declaration stressed, 'We are gravely concerned that climate change poses the most serious threat to our territorial integrity, viability and survival, and that it undermines our efforts to achieve sustainable development goals and threatens our very existence'. The Declaration emphasized, 'We reaffirm the sovereign rights of all Small Island Developing States in light of the adverse impacts of climate change'. The Declaration called upon

> the international community, with developed countries taking the lead, to undertake urgent, ambitious and decisive action to significantly reduce emissions of all greenhouse gases, including fast action strategies, and to support Small Island Developing States, and other particularly vulnerable countries, in their efforts to adapt to the adverse impacts of climate change, including through the provision of increased levels of financial and technological resources.

The *Majuro Declaration for Climate Leadership* 2013 recognises the commitment of Pacific countries to take climate action. The Declaration highlights that Climate change is 'the greatest threat to the livelihoods, security and well-being of the peoples of the Pacific and one of the greatest challenges for the entire world'. The Declaration affirms,

> We, the Leaders of the Pacific Islands Forum, underline the need for urgent action at all levels to reduce greenhouse gas emissions commensurate with the science and to respond urgently and sufficiently to the social, economic and security impacts of climate change to ensure the survival and viability of all Pacific small island developing States, in particular low-lying atoll States, and other vulnerable countries and regions worldwide.

The Declaration also acknowledged, 'At the same time, we recognize that the necessary energy revolution and economic transformation to low-carbon development is an unprecedented opportunity to enhance our security, protect and ensure the sustainability of our natural resources and environment, and to improve our people's health'. The statement observes, 'We confirm the responsibility of all to act to urgently reduce and phase down greenhouse gas pollution in order to avert a climate crisis for present and future generations'.

The *Pacific Agreement on Closer Economic Relations (PACER Plus)* 2017 will also have a bearing on trade and investment rules for small island states in the Pacific. This agreement was the subject of longstanding negotiations, which commenced in 2009 and were concluded in 2017. The Agreement was signed in Nuku'alofa in Tonga on 14 June 2017 by Australia, New Zealand, and eight Pacific island countries – Cook Islands, Kiribati, Nauru, Niue, Samoa, Solomon Islands, Tonga and, Tuvalu. A number of other countries – such as Fiji and Papua New Guinea – refused to join the agreement. After consultation, Vanuatu joined the agreement in September 2017.

The Future We Want

Another approach would emphasize the need to support sustainable development for small island states, particularly in respect of development issues, such as food security, biodiversity conservation, environmental protection, and access to health care.

Discussing *The Future We Want* negotiations, Ambassador Marlene Moses (2012b) observed, 'Challenges to be considered have been identified: over a billion people live in poverty, food and water are becoming increasingly scarce, and two-thirds of the earth's ecosystems are in decline, to name a few'. She lamented, though, that the humanitarian and environmental crisis of climate change was not explicitly addressed: 'The fact is we cannot achieve fair and sustainable development unless we dramatically reduce the greenhouse gas emissions responsible for climate change'.

The AOSIS expanded upon its submission at Rio+20. Moses (2012a) maintained, 'It is important to Small Island Developing States that the Rio+20 outcome document addresses the special challenges of island nations'. She stressed, 'We would welcome more concrete language on how countries can work towards a Green Economy, including stronger language on the commitment of the international community to provide new and additional financial resources, technology transfer and capacity building'.

The final *Future We Want* text contains a number of paragraphs on small island states. Paragraph 178 emphasizes,

> We reaffirm that small island developing States remain a special case for sustainable development in view of their unique and particular vulnerabilities, including their small size, remoteness, narrow resource and export base, and exposure to global environmental challenges and external economic shocks, including to a large range of impacts from climate change and potentially more frequent and intense natural disasters.

The document warned,

> Sea-level rise and other adverse impacts of climate change continue to pose a significant risk to small island developing States and their efforts to achieve

sustainable development, and for many represent the gravest of threats to their survival and viability, including for some through the loss of territory.

Paragraph 179 called for 'continued and enhanced efforts to assist small island developing States in implementing the Barbados Programme of Action and the Mauritius Strategy' and 'a strengthening of United Nations System support to small island developing States in keeping with the multiple ongoing and emerging challenges faced by these States in achieving sustainable development'. Paragraph 180 suggested that there should be an international conference on small island developing States.

Paragraph 175 concerned oceans and sea. It stressed,

> We commit to observe the need to ensure access to fisheries and the importance of access to markets, by subsistence, small-scale and artisanal fisherfolk and women fish workers, as well as indigenous peoples and their communities, particularly in developing countries, especially small island developing States.

Such text, though, falls well short of there being binding commitments supporting the development of a 'Blue Economy'.

Tuilaepa Lupesoliai Sailele Malielegaoi (2012), the prime minister of the Independent State of Samoa, addressed the Rio+20 summit. He emphasized that 'Rio holds special significance for small island developing states like mine'. The prime minister noted, 'It is where our unique and specific vulnerabilities deserving of special case treatment, were given due recognition by the international community'. The prime minister contended, 'It is why we need a stronger global commitment to its sustainable management and development through a "Green Economy in a Blue World" '.

The former president of the Republic of Maldives, Mohamed Nasheed, and the former president of East Timor, José Ramos-Horta, (2014) have written about the need for Asian leadership in respect of climate policy. The two leaders observed that 'climate change has become malignant' and 'threatens to blunt Asia's growth and upend our development'. Nasheed and Ramos-Horta emphasized that 'Asian countries should focus on building clean economies to boost growth, increase wealth and reduce pollution'. The pair stressed, 'By strengthening our natural defences, embracing clean growth, and leading the push for a global climate deal, Asian leaders can secure a more stable climate – and safeguard our development'.

United Nations Sustainable Development Goals

On 5 June 2014, United Nations Secretary-General Ban Ki-Moon (2014) highlighted the precarious position of small island states on World Environment Day. He observed of the position of small island states, 'The world's small island nations . . . play an important role in protecting the oceans and many are biodiversity hotspots, containing some of the richest reservoirs of plants and animals on the planet'.

Ban Ki-Moon observed that small island states face significant challenges: 'Many are increasingly vulnerable to the impacts of climate change – from devastating storms to the threat of sea level rise'. He noted that

> Small Island Developing States have contributed little to climate change: Their combined annual output of greenhouse gases is less than one per cent of total global emissions, but their position on the front lines has projected many to the fore in negotiations for a universal new legal climate agreement in 2015.

He hoped that small island states could become 'leaders in disaster preparedness and prevention' and would 'achieve climate neutrality through the use of renewable energy and other approaches'. In his view, 'Small island nations share a common understanding that we need to set our planet on a sustainable path'.

Secretary-General Ban Ki-Moon provided leadership in establishing the *2030 Agenda for Sustainable Development* and the *United Nations Sustainable Development Goals* 2015. His successor, Antonio Guterres, who took office in 2017, is committed to supporting the implementation of the goals.

Francis Gurry (2017), the Director-General of WIPO, has spoken about the intersection between intellectual property and the Sustainable Development Goals (SDGs).

Francis Gurry suggested that there is a strong connection between intellectual property and SDG 9 dealing with industry, innovation, and infrastructure. Gurry also observed that innovation has an impact on a number of other SDGs – including SDG 2 Zero Hunger, SDG 3 Good Health and Well-Being, SDG 6 Clean Water and Sanitation, SDG 7 Affordable and Clean Energy, SDG 8 Decent Work and Economic Growth, SDG 11 Sustainable Cities and Communities, and SDG 11 Climate Action. He also suggests that innovation as a policy can assist in realizing other SDGs – notably SDG 1 No Poverty, SDG 8 Decent Work and Economic Growth, SDG 14 Life Below Water, and SDG 15 Life on Land. Gurry also observed that certain SDGs are relevant to the settings of an innovation policy framework – SDG 5 – Gender Equality; SDG 8 – Decent Work and Economic Growth, SDG – 10 Reduced Inequalities, and SDG 12 – Responsible Consumption and Production. Moreover, SDG 17 is a modality in terms of partnerships for the goals.

Francis Gurry also commented that there is an important linkage between intellectual property and SDG 4 dealing with quality education. This has a number of dimensions. Gurry commented that copyright law played a role as the principal mechanism for financing cultural production – in terms of the legal framework in treaties and normative discussions. There was also an important role in terms of partnerships – such as the Accessible Books Consortium and enhancing publishing capacity. Gurry also stressed the importance of capacity building – legal and technical advice, collective and individual rights management, and human resource capacity building.

Francis Gurry also notes that intellectual property is connected to SDG 3 – Good Health and Well-Being. There are relationships with health and innovation, upstream R&D activities, and the operational use of activities. Notably, access to medicines and tobacco control are significant issues, which raise larger matters about intellectual property, good health, and well-being.

The United Nations (2016) is seeking new partnerships for small island developing states to advance the SDGs.

Conclusion

The international summits on the environment, biodiversity, and climate change have sought to reconcile such tensions over intellectual property and the global commons. In *Climate Change and Small Island States*, Jon Barnett and John Campbell (2010) discuss the position of small island states in the popular imagination in debates over climate change. The pair observed,

> Pacific Island countries, particularly small and low-lying ones, are central figures in popular understandings and the politics of global warming. Because of climate change, countries like Tuvalu, which previously had low international profiles, have appeared in numerous press articles, television documentaries, and news accounts around the world. In many ways, representations of the islands as being vulnerable to climate change have been helpful in leveraging international support.
>
> (Barnett and Campbell 2010: 155)

In this context, it is worthwhile considering how small island states could address matters of intellectual property and climate change. AOSIS should develop a comprehensive platform on intellectual property and climate change. There is a need to address questions of the protection of Indigenous intellectual property – particularly relating to knowledge about the environment and climate. There should be protection for tangible and intangible cultural heritage. Access to genetic resources is an important means of protecting biodiversity in an age of climate change. There should be provision for access to clean technologies. Moreover, AOSIS and Indigenous communities should seek to take advantage of the potential of global development networks – such as the Climate Technology Centre and Network, the Global Indigenous Network, and Sustainable Development Goal Partnerships. There is also a need to ensure sustainable development policies and practices are put into action in small island developing states.

AOSIS has engaged with major, landmark international agreements in respect of the *Paris Agreement* 2015 and the *United Nations Sustainable Development Goals* 2015. AOSIS has sought to face the twin challenges of climate change and sustainable development. In a presentation to the United Nations headquarters in New York, Ambassador Ahmed Sareer (2017) considered the inter-relationship between climate change and sustainable development. He commented, 'Unless we decouple economic growth from the burning of fossil fuels, worsening climate change impacts will undermine our development gains and make it difficult, if not impossible, to create a healthy and prosperous future for all'. Sareer reflected that small island developing states were on the 'frontline of climate change':

> We know all too well the toll that climate impacts will have drastic effects on our economies. Warming seas have already shifted the fish stocks that we rely on; back-to-back coral bleaching episodes have [been] undermining essential marine habitats as well as our critical ecotourism industries. At the same time, rising seas, worsening coastal erosion, and increasingly powerful storms have forced us to climate-proof our infrastructure projects both in the Caribbean and the Pacific and even threaten the territorial integrity of some of our low-lying members.

The Ambassador stressed that 'the world has to do more to rapidly scale up the deployment of renewable energy and to ensure effective adaptation'. He promised that 'AOSIS will continue to work to accelerate adaptation and mitigation efforts to set our development pathways to a low greenhouse gas and climate-resilient development'. The ambassador observed, 'The reality is, addressing the dual climate change and sustainable development challenge rests on the provision of means of implementation'. He noted the huge burdens faced by small island states: 'This is urgent for small islands [and] developing states where the cost of adapting to climate change is so high relative to population size; and yet, the impact of extreme events on gross domestic product in SIDS is disproportionately large'. The ambassador emphasized the need for public finance to accelerate climate action: 'Meeting the climate agreement's $100 billion annually by 2020 commitment is absolutely essential and new partnerships with the private sector, non-government organisations, and other institutions can help to mobilise the resources immediately'.

Increasingly, small island states and Indigenous communities will play a significant role in the fossil fuel resistance. In October 2014, the Pacific Climate Warriors travelled to Australia to protest against the expansion of the coal industry (Garrett 2014). The group consisted of a number of young Pacific Islanders, representing 13 countries and including the daughter of the Marshall Islands president, Christopher Loeak. The group used five traditional canoes to lead a flotilla of boats to blockade the coal port of Newcastle. Milan Loeak explained the protest: 'We just want to share our stories and make sure that people are aware that the decisions that are being made over here are directly affecting our islands back home'. Fiji Climate Warrior George Nacewa commented, 'These expansions will affect us and I live in a generation that has inherited a perfect environment but I am not too sure if I can pass this on to my kids and future generations to come'.

From Vanuatu, Iasoa Chief Kawea Sausiara emphasized that there was a close connection between climate change and cultural heritage: 'If climate change is not stopped we will lose our cultural activities'. The climate group 350.org (2014) supported the action of the Pacific Climate Warriors: 'Together we are calling for an end to the industries that are threatening their homes and their culture'. Fenton Lutunatabua (2014) – one of the Pacific Climate Warriors stressed, 'We all have a piece of the solution to climate change. It's time to start putting them together'.

In the future, there could well be the prospect of climate litigation by small island states and Indigenous communities to protect intellectual property and cultural heritage as well as lands and territories if there is further climate inaction by developed countries.

Note

* This chapter has been developed at a number of conferences. The author would like to thank Dr Miranda Forsyth for the invitation to participate in the conference Innovation, Creativity, Access to Knowledge and Pacific Island Countries held by Regnet at the ANU College for Asia and the Pacific in September 2012; and Professor Christoph Antons for the invitation to participate at the conference at Deakin Law School in November 2012.

Bibliography

350.org (2014) *Stand with the Pacific Climate Warriors*. Available http://act.350.org/sign/pacific_solidarity_petition/

Abate, R. and Kronk, E.A. (ed.), (2013) *Climate Change and Indigenous Peoples: The Search for Legal Remedies*, Cheltenham, UK-Northampton, MA: Edward Elgar.

Ad Hoc Working Group on the Durban Platform for Enhanced Action (2015) 'Work of the Contact Group on item 3, Negotiating Text', February 12. Available: http://unfccc.int/files/bodies/awg/application/pdf/negotiating_text_12022015@2200.pdf

The Alliance of Small Island States (2009) 'Proposal for the Survival of the Kyoto Protocol and Copenhagen Protocol to Enhance the Implementation of the *United Nations Framework Convention on Climate Change* 1992', Ad-Hoc Working Group on Long-Term Cooperative Action Under the Convention, Agenda Item 3, 11 December. Available: http://unfccc.int/files/kyoto_protocol/application/pdf/aosis121209.pdf

The Alliance of Small Island States (2013) 'Small Islands Call for Urgency in Warsaw in Wake of Deadly Typhoon', November 11. Available: http://aosis.org/for-immediate-release-small-islands-call-for-urgency-in-warsaw-in-wake-of-deadly-typhoon/

The Alliance of Small Island States (2015) 'Closing Statement – Paris Agreement', December 12. Available: http://aosis.org/closing-statement-paris-agreement/

The Alliance of Small Island States (2016) 'Press Release: Small Islands Call on All Countries to Ratify Paris Agreement as Entry into Force Threshold Nears', September 21, http://aosis.org/press-release-small-islands-call-on-all-countries-to-ratify-paris-agreement-as-entry-into-force-threshold-nears/

The Alliance of Small Island States, http://aosis.org/about-aosis/

Barnett, J. and Campbell, J. (2010) *Climate Change and Small Island States: Power, Knowledge and the South Pacific*, London-Washington, DC: Earthscan.

Boom, K. (2013) 'The Rising Tide of International Climate Litigation: An Illustrative Hypothetical of Tuvalu v Australia', in R. Abate and E.A. Kronk (eds), *Climate Change and Indigenous Peoples: The Search for Legal Remedies*, Cheltenham, UK and Northampton, MA: Edward Elgar, 409–438.

Breakey H., Popovski, V. and Maguire, R. (ed.) (2015, November) *Ethical Values and the Integrity of the Climate Change Regime*, Farnham, Surrey: Ashgate.

Brown, A. (ed.) (2013) *Environmental Technologies, Intellectual Property, and Climate Change: Accessing, Obtaining, and Protecting*, Cheltenham, UK and Northampton, MA: Edward Elgar.

Bull Bennett, T.M., et al. (2014) 'Chapter 12: Indigenous Peoples, Lands, and Resources', in J.M. Melillo, T.C. Richmond and G.W. Yohe (eds), *Climate Change Impacts in the United States: The Third National Climate Assessment*, U.S. Global Change Research Program, 297–317. Available: http://nca2014.globalchange.gov/report/sectors/indigenous- peoples

Burkett, M. (2013a) 'Indigenous Environmental Knowledge and Climate Change Adaptation', in R. Abate and E.A. Kronk (ed.), *Climate Change and Indigenous Peoples: The Search for Legal Remedies*, Cheltenham, UK and Northampton, MA, 96–118.

Burkett, M. (2013b) 'The Nation Ex-Situ', in M. Gerrard and G. Wannier (ed.), *Threatened Island Nations: Legal Implications of Rising Seas and a Changing Climate*, Cambridge: Cambridge University Press, 89–122.

Chon, M. (2012) 'Public-Private Partnerships in Global Intellectual Property', Innovation, Creativity, Access to Knowledge and Pacific Island Countries, Regnet, ANU College of Asia and the Pacific, September 24. Available: http://asiapacific.anu.edu.au/blogs/pacificinstitute/files/2012/09/IP_Pacific_program_final_small.pdf

Cimoli, M., Dosi, G., Maskus, K., Okediji, R., Reichman, J. and Stiglitz, J. (ed.) (2014) *Intellectual Property Rights: Legal and Economic Challenges for Development*, Oxford: Oxford University Press.

Clinton, H.R. (2014) *Hard Choices: A Memoir*, London: Simon & Schuster.

Davis, M. (2013) 'Climate Change Impacts to Aboriginal and Torres Strait Islander Communities in Australia', in R. Abate and E.A. Kronk (ed.), *Climate Change and Indigenous Peoples: The Search for Legal Remedies*, Cheltenham, UK-Northampton, MA: Edward Elgar, 493–507.

de Brum, T., Robinson, M. and Rigg, K. (2013) 'Warsaw Climate Talks: The World's Poorest Cannot Wait for a 2015 Deal', *The Guardian*, November 22. Available: www.theguardian.com/environment/2013/nov/21/warsaw-climate-talks-the-worlds-poorest- cannot-wait-for-a-2015-deal

de Souza Dias, B.F. (2014) 'Seventh Plenary Session of the Third United Nations Small Island Developing States Conference', Apia, Samoa, September 4. Available: www.cbd.int/doc/speech/2014/sp-2014-09-04-unsids-en.pdf

Drahos, P. (2012) 'Indigenous Developmental Networks and the Adaptive Management of Intellectual Property', *Innovation, Creativity, Access to Knowledge and Development in Pacific Island Countries*, September 25. Available: http://asiapacific.anu.edu.au/blogs/pacificinstitute/files/2012/09/IP_Pacific_program_final_small.pdf

Drahos, P. (2014) *Intellectual Property, Indigenous People and Their Knowledge*, Cambridge: Cambridge University Press.

Drahos, P. and Frankel, S. (ed.) (2012) *Indigenous Peoples' Innovation: Intellectual Property Pathways to Development*, Canberra: ANU ePress.

European Union, Least Developed Countries and the Association of Small Island States (2011) 'Common Statement', December 9. Available: http://ec.europa.eu/commission_2010-2014/hedegaard/headlines/news/2011-12-09_01_en.htm

Forsyth, M. (2012a) 'Lifting the Lid on "the Community": Who Has the Right to Control Access to Traditional Knowledge and Expressions of Culture?', *International Journal of Cultural Property*, 19, 1–31.

Forsyth, M. (2012b) 'Do You Want It Giftwrapped? Protecting Traditional Knowledge in the Pacific Island Countries', in P. Drahos and S. Frankel (ed.), *Indigenous Peoples' Innovation: Intellectual Property Pathways to Development*, Canberra: ANU ePress, 189–214.

Forsyth, M. (2013a) 'The Developmental Ramifications of Vanuatu's Intellectual Property Commitments on Joining the World Trade Organisation', *Journal of Pacific Studies*, 36(1/2), 157–172.

Forsyth, M. (2013b) 'How Can Traditional Knowledge Best Be Regulated? Comparing a Proprietary Rights Approach with a Regulatory Toolbox Approach', *The Contemporary Pacific*, 25(1), 1–31.

Forsyth, M. and Farran, S. (2013) 'Intellectual Property and Food Security in Least Developed Countries', *Third World Quarterly*, 34(3), 516–533.

Forsyth, M. and Farran, S. (2015) 'Weaving Intellectual Property Policy in Developing States', *Intersentia*. Available: www.intersentia.com/SearchDetail.aspx?bookid=102921

Garrett, J. (2014) 'Pacific Climate Warriors in Australia to Protest Coal Industry', *ABC News*, October 13. Available: www.abc.net.au/news/2014-10-13/pacific-climate-warriors-to-protest-newcastle-coal-port/5809392

Gerrard, M. and Wannier, G. (ed.) (2013) *Threatened Island Nations: Legal Implications of Rising Seas and a Changing Climate*, Cambridge: Cambridge University Press.

Gerrard, M. and Wannier, G. (ed.) (2013) 'Overview', in Gerrard, M. and Wannier, G. (ed.), *Threatened Island Nations: Legal Implications of Rising Seas and a Changing Climate*, Cambridge: Cambridge University Press.

Global Island Partnership, http://glispa.org/

Graber, C., Kuprecht, K. and Lai, J. (ed.) (2012) *Indigenous Trade in Indigenous Cultural Heritage: Legal and Policy Issues*, Cheltenham, UK and Northampton, MA: Edward Elgar.

Green Climate Fund, http://unfccc.int/cooperation_and_support/financial_mechanism/green_climate_fund/items/5869.php

Gurry, F. (2017) 'WIPO and the Sustainable Development Goals', *World Intellectual Property Organization*, February 9. Available: www.wipo.int/export/sites/www/about-wipo/en/dgo/speeches/pdf/wipo_sdgs_022017.pdf

Harrabin, R. (2012) 'Climate Compensation Row at Doha', *BBC News*, December 5. Available: www.bbc.co.uk/news/science-environment-20613915

Hee-Eun, K. (2011) 'Changing Climate, Changing Culture: Adding the Climate Change Dimension to the Protection of Intangible Cultural Heritage', *International Journal of Cultural Property*, 18, 259–290.

Intergovernmental Panel on Climate Change. (2014) 'Chapter 15 – National and Sub-National Policies and Institutions', *Mitigation of Climate Change*, IPCC WGIII AR5. Available: http://report.mitigation2014.org/drafts/final-draft-postplenary/ipcc_wg3_ar5_final-draft_postplenary_chapter15.pdf

International Institute for Sustainable Development (2014) 'Bonn Climate Change Conference', *Earth Negotiations Bulletin*, 12(604). Available: www.iisd.ca/vol12/enb12604e.html

Jetnil-Kijiner, K. (2014) 'Dear Matefele Peinam', *Responding to Climate Change*, RTCC, September 23. Available: www.rtcc.org/2014/09/23/marshall-islands-poet-we-deserve-to-do-more-than-just-survive/#sthash.81K1tNIG.dpuf

Johnstone, N. (2013) 'Negotiating Climate Change: Maori, the Crown and New Zealand's Emission Trading Scheme', in R. Abate and E.A. Kronk (ed.), *Climate Change and*

Indigenous Peoples: The Search for Legal Remedies, Cheltenham, UK-Northampton, MA: Edward Elgar, 508–31.

Ki-Moon, B. (2014) 'Raise Your Voice, Not the Sea Level', The United Nations Secretary-General Message on World Environment Day, June 5. Available: www.unep.org/wed/messages/SG-WED-Message.asp#.U5AAchDLMQo

Klein, N. (2014) *This Changes Everything: Capitalism vs The Climate*, New York: Simon & Schuster.

Lagan, B. (2013) 'Australia Urged to Formally Recognise Climate Change Refugee Status', *The Guardian*, April 16. Available: www.guardian.co.uk/environment/2013/apr/16/australia-climate-change-refugee-status

Lane, E. (2011) *Clean Tech Intellectual Property: Eco-Marks, Green Patents and Green Innovation*, Oxford: Oxford University Press.

Lutunatabua, F. (2014) 'Take It From the Pacific: To Win on Climate, You've Got to Fight', *The Huffington Post*, August 8. Available: www.huffingtonpost.com/fenton-lutunatabua/take-it-from-the-pacific-_b_5660583.html

Maclellan, N., Meads, S. and Coates, B. (2012) *Owning Adaptation in the Pacific: Strengthening Governance of Climate Adaptation Finance*, Auckland, New Zealand: Oxfam Australia and Oxfam New Zealand, August. Available: www.oxfam.org.nz/news/owning-adaptation-pacific

Malielegaoi, T.L.S. (2012) 'Statement by the Prime Minister of the Independent State of Samoa', United Nations Conference on Sustainable Development, Rio de Janeiro, Brazil, 22 June. Available: www.uncsd2012.org/content/documents/1036samoa1.pdf

Maskus, K. and Okediji, R. 2014. 'Legal and Economic Perspectives on International Technology Transfer in Environmentally Sound Technologies', in M. Cimoli, G. Dosi, K. Maskus, R. Okediji, J. Reichman, and J. Stiglitz (eds), *Intellectual Property Rights: Legal and Economic Challenges for Development*, Oxford: Oxford University Press, 392–414.

Menell, P. and Tran, S. (ed.) (2014) *Intellectual Property, Innovation, and the Environment*, Cheltenham, UK and Northampton, MA: Edward Elgar.

Moses, M. (2009) 'Statement on Behalf of Pacific Small Island Developing States', Presented at Youth Delegates Demand Climate Justice, New York, 13 October.

Moses, M. (2012a) 'Permanent Representative of the Republic of Nauru to the United Nations on behalf of the Alliance of Small Island States at the Preparatory Committee for the United Nations Conference on Sustainable Development, Consultations on zero draft of the outcome document of the Conference', New York, January 25. Available: www.forumsec.org/resources/uploads/attachments/documents/AOSIS%20-%20Final%20statement%20on%20Rio20%20Zero%20Draft%20%28Jan%202012%29.pdf

Moses, M. (2012b) 'The Choice is Ours', *The Huffington Post*, 11 June 2012. Available: www.huffingtonpost.com/ambassador-marlene-moses/the-choice-is-ours_b_1586540.html

Moses, M. (2013), 'The Role and Influence of the Alliance of Small Island States (AOSIS) in UN Climate Change Negotiations', *ANU Climate Change Institute and ANU Pacific Institute*, 19 February, http://aosis.org/amb-moses-gives-climate-talk-at-australia-national-university/

Mulalap, C.Y. (2013) 'Islands in the Stream: Addressing Climate Change from a Small Island Developing State Perspective', in R. Abate and E.A. Kronk (ed.), *Climate Change and Indigenous Peoples: The Search for Legal Remedies*, Cheltenham, UK and Northampton, MA, 377–408.

Nasheed, M. and Ramos-Horta, J. (2014) 'The Need for Asian Climate Leadership', *The Jakarta Post*, May 10. Available: www.thejakartapost.com/news/2014/05/10/asia-must-show-way-climate-change.html

Parnell, J. (2013) ' "Loss and Damage" to Make or Break Doha Climate Talks', *Responding to Climate Change (RFCC)*, February 5. Available: www.rtcc.org/doha-climate-change-talks-close-in-on-low-ambition-deal/

Parry, B. (2002) 'Cultures of Knowledge: Investigating Intellectual Property Rights and Relations in the Pacific', *Antipode: A Radical Journal of Geography*, 34(4), 679–706.

Raman, M. (2011) 'New Technology Transfer Mechanism Raises Many Issues', *Third World Network*, May 9. Available: www.twnside.org.sg/title2/climate/info.service/2011/climate20110503.htm

Reichman, J., Rai, A., Newell, R. and Wiener, J. (2014) 'Intellectual Property and Alternatives: Strategies for Green Innovation', in M. Cimoli, G. Dosi, K. Maskus, R. Okediji, J. Reichman and J. Stiglitz (eds), *Intellectual Property Rights: Legal and Economic Challenges for Development*, Oxford: Oxford University Press, 356–91.

Rimmer, M. (2009) 'The Sorcerer II Expedition: Intellectual Property and Biodiscovery', *Macquarie Journal of International and Comparative Environmental Law*, 6, 147–189.

Rimmer, M. (2011a) *Intellectual Property and Climate Change: Inventing Clean Technologies*, Cheltenham, UK-Northampton, MA: Edward Elgar, September.

Rimmer, M. (2011b) 'Climate Justice for Intellectual Property at Durban', *The Conversation*, December 8. Available: http://theconversation.edu.au/climate-justice-for-intellectual-property-at-durban-4572

Rimmer, M. (2012) 'The Doha Deadlock: Intellectual Property and Climate Change', *The Conversation*, December 11. Available: http://theconversation.com/the-doha-deadlock-intellectual-property-and-climate-change-11244

Rimmer, M. (2014) ' "We are Here to make History": The United Nations Climate Summit 2014', *Medium*, September 23. Available: https://medium.com/intellectual-property-and-climate-change/we-are-here-to-make-history-the-united-nations-climate-summit-2014-bf9292d5b6c5

Sano, Y. and Richards, J-A. (2014) 'A Small Price to Pay for Climate Justice,' *ABC Environment*, June 11. Available: www.abc.net.au/environment/articles/2014/06/11/4022486.htm

Sareer, A. (2017) 'Climate Change and Sustainable Development Statement', *AOSIS*, March 23. Available: http://aosis.org/transcript-of-climate-change-and-the-sustainable-development-statement/

Secretariat for the Convention on Biological Diversity. *Island Biodiversity*. Available: www.cbd.int/island/

Simonelli, A. (2015) 'The Ethical Responsibility of the Loss and Damage Mechanism: A Consideration of Non-Economic Loss and Human Rights', in H. Breakey, V. Popovski and R. Maguire (ed.), *Ethical Values and the Integrity of the Climate Change Regime*, Farnham, Surrey: Ashgate, November, 2013–224.

Steiner, A. (2014) *Messages for World Environment Day*. Available: www.unep.org/wed/messages/#.U5AAPBDLMQp

Stoutenburg, J.G. (2013) 'When Do States Disappear? Thresholds of Effective Statehood and the Continued Recognition of "Deterritorialized" Island States', in M. Gerrard and G. Wannier (ed.), *Threatened Island Nations: Legal Implications of Rising Seas and a Changing Climate*, Cambridge: Cambridge University Press, 57–88.

Sutton, V. (2013) 'Fiji: Climate Change, Tradition and *Vanua*', in R. Abate and E.A. Kronk (ed.), *Climate Change and Indigenous Peoples: The Search for Legal Remedies*, Cheltenham, UK and Northampton, MA: Edward Elgar 363–76.

Techera, E. (2013) 'Climate Change, Legal Governance and the Pacific Islands: An Overview', in R. Abate and E.A. Kronk (ed.), *Climate Change and Indigenous Peoples: The*

Search for Legal Remedies, Cheltenham, UK and Northampton, MA: Edward Elgar 339–62.

The Tribune India (2014) 'Unfair to Expect Same Commitment from All Nations on Climate', *The Tribune India*, December 8. Available: www.tribuneindia.com/news/world/-unfair-to-expect-same-commitment-from-all-nations-on-climate/15638.html

Tuvalu (2009) *"Copenhagen" Protocol to the United Nations Framework Convention on Climate Change.* Available: http://unfccc.int/files/kyoto_protocol/application/pdf/tuvalu200509.pdf

UNESCO. *Climate Change.* Available: http://whc.unesco.org/en/climatechange/

UNFCCC Climate Technology Centre and Network. Available: http://unfccc.int/ttclear/jsp/CTCN.jsp

United Nations (2016) *New Partnerships for Small Island Developing States to Advance SDGs.* Available: www.un.org/sustainabledevelopment/blog/2016/09/new-partnerships-for-small-island-developing-states-to-advance-sdgs/

United Nations University (2012) *Weathering Uncertainty: Traditional Knowledge for Climate Change Assessment and Adaptation*, Paris: UNESCO and Darwin: United Nations University Report, http://unu.edu/publications/policy-briefs/weathering-uncertainty-traditional-knowledge-for-climate-change-assessment-and-adaptation.html

Van Tiggelen, J. (2014/2015) 'Cold Comfort: The President of Kiribati Goes on a Fact-Finding Mission in the Arctic', *The Monthly.* Available: www.themonthly.com.au/issue/2014/december/1417352400/john-van-tiggelen/cold-comfort

Visentin, L. (2014) 'Poet Brings World Leaders to Tears at UN Climate Summit', *The Sydney Morning Herald*, September 25. Available: www.smh.com.au/environment/climate-change/poet-brings-world-leaders-to-tears-at-un-climate-summit-20140925-10lq5x.html

World Health Organization, United Nations Office of the High Commissioner for Human Rights, and the United Nations Development Programme (2014) *Pacific Trade and Human Rights*, Geneva: United Nations, http://infojustice.org/wp-content/uploads/2014/11/rbap-hhd-2014-pacific-trade-and-human-rights.pdf

International Law

The Alliance of Small Island States Leaders' Declaration 2012 http://aosis.org/wp-content/uploads/2012/10/2012-AOSIS-Leaders-Declaration.pdf

Barbados Declaration on Achieving Sustainable Energy for All in Small Island Developing States (SIDS) 2012 http://aosis.org/wp-content/uploads/2012/10/2012-Barbados-Declaration.pdf

Cancún Agreements 2010 *Outcome of the Work of the Ad Hoc Working Group on Long-Term Cooperative Action Under the Convention*, CP.16, http://unfccc.int/files/meetings/cop_16/application/pdf/cop16_lca.pdf and *Outcome of the Work of the Ad Hoc Working Group on Further Commitments for Annex I Parties under the Kyoto Protocol at its Fifteenth Session*, http://unfccc.int/files/meetings/cop_16/application/pdf/cop16_kp.pdf

Convention on Biological Diversity 1992, opened for signature 5 June 1992, 1760 UNTS 143 (entered into force 29 December 1993).

Copenhagen Accord 2009, UN Doc. FCCC/KP/CMP/2009/L.9 (December 18, 2009).

Durban Decisions 2011, CP.17, http://unfccc.int/meetings/durban_nov_2011/meeting/6245/ php/view/decisions.php

Doha Climate Gateway 2012, COP. 18/CM 18, https://unfccc.int/key_steps/doha_climate_
gateway/items/7389.php; and

Durban Decisions 2011, CP.17, http://unfccc.int/meetings/durban_nov_2011/meet-
ing/6245/ php/view/decisions.php

The Future We Want, UN Doc A/RES/66/288 (11 September 2012).

Kyoto Protocol to the United Nations Framework Convention on Climate Change 1997,
Opened for signature 16 March 1998, 2303 UNTS 148 (entered into force 16 February 2005) ('Kyoto Protocol').

Lima Call for Climate Action 2014, CP. 20, http://unfccc.int/meetings/lima_dec_2014/
meeting/8141/php/view/decisions.php

The *Majuro Declaration for Climate Leadership*, 5 September 2013, www.majurodeclara-
tion.org/

*Nagoya Protocol on Access to Genetic Resources and the Fair and Equitable Sharing
of Benefits Arising from their Utilization to the Convention on Biological Diversity
('Nagoya Protocol')* Adopted 29 October 2010, opened for signature 2 February 2011
to 1 February 2012.

Pacific Agreement on Closer Economic Relations (PACER Plus) 2017 http://dfat.gov.au/
trade/agreements/pacer/pages/pacific-agreement-on-closer-economic-relations-pacer-
plus.aspx

Paris Agreement of the United Nations Framework Convention on Climate Change 2015
[2016] ATNIF 31.

*Regional Framework for the Protection of Traditional Knowledge and Expressions of Cul-
ture* (2002), www.forumsec.org/resources/uploads/attachments/documents/PacificMode
lLaw,ProtectionofTKandExprssnsofCulture20021.pdf

United Nations Climate Summit 2014, New York, 23 September 2014, www.un.org/
climatechange/
summit/2014/09/2014-climate-change-summary-chairs-summary/ and www.un.org/cli-
matechange/ summit/action-areas/

United Nations Declaration on the Rights of Indigenous Peoples 2007, 61st sess, UN Doc
A/61/L.67, Adopted by General Assembly Resolution 61/295 on 13 September 2007.

United Nations Framework Convention on Climate Change 1992, Opened for signature 9
May 1992, 1771 UNTS 107 (entered into force 21 March 1994).

United Nations Sustainable Development Goals 2015 www.un.org/sustainabledevelopment/
sustainable-development-goals/

Warsaw Opportunity 2013, CP. 19, http://unfccc.int/meetings/warsaw_nov_2013/meeting/
7649.php

Part II

The regulation of heritage and indigenous rights

The placelessness of property, intellectual property and cultural heritage law in the Australian legal landscape[*]

Engaging cultural landscapes

Kathy Bowrey and Nicole Graham

Part One explores the reasons why the Australian legal space is necessarily place-less due to our colonial history and the dominant legal conception of property rights. Rights are conceived in abstract terms as 'dephysicalised', with interests realised in terms of market value that fosters the economic growth priorities of federal and state governments. When the legal space is pre-occupied with this particular economic logic, there is little room for 'place' and in particular for Aboriginal knowledges and laws, which are intimately connected to place, to be recognised.

Part Two shows this problem in action, reviewing the legal machinations surrounding property development at Kumarangk, which involved an unsuccessful attempt to prevent the construction of the Hindmarsh Island Bridge under state and federal heritage laws.[1] We argue that Aboriginal interests and heritage are made especially vulnerable as a consequence of legal investment and reinvestment in a placeless property paradigm. If there is little within Australian jurisprudence that can recognise place, there cannot ever be any political settlement that is different to where we are now – no decolonisation – whatever the attempted discussion or reimagining of the political or legal space.

Having framed this problem, Part Three takes a strategic turn by exploring concepts that are currently present within our existing laws and jurisprudence that house some, albeit undeveloped, capacity to confront and disrupt the reproduction of placelessness. We explore the potential productivity of the notion of "cultural landscape" under the UNESCO World Heritage Convention (WHC), ratified by Australia on 22 August 1974. The term 'cultural landscape' has developed with the implementation of the WHC. In 1992 the World Heritage Committee adopted a very broad definition. It includes cultural properties that "represent the 'combined works of nature and of man" designated in Article 1 of the Convention. They are illustrative of the evolution of human society and settlement over time, under the influence of the physical constraints and/or opportunities presented by their natural environment and of successive social, economic and cultural forces, both external and internal.[2] Though 'cultural landscape' is not a judicially considered concept in Australia, it is well established in numerous scholarly disciplines, including geography, ethnography, anthropology and environmental studies.[3] The notion already comes to life in Australian legal processes through the input of disciplinary expertise that informs protection obligations conferred by federal and state environmental and heritage laws, whether or not there is a connection to the WHC.

Part Four looks at the significance of the Uluru-Kata Tjuta (Ayers Rock-Mount Olga) National Park listing as an 'associative cultural landscape' under the WHC in 1994. While there are problems with the capacity for Indigenous governance at Uluru, the cultural landscape idea has provided a mechanism whereby Aboriginal laws have achieved some recognition and practical impact upon decision making that can undermine the dominant property paradigm.

In conclusion, we argue that in order to better fulfil its capacity to bridge discordant legal traditions, the concept of cultural landscape needs to be hierarchically repositioned. At present cultural landscape is primarily defined by non-lawyers – the non-legal experts who by "asking the Aborigines"[4] then inform Australian legal institutions and governing bodies about Aboriginal culture: the relevant spiritualism, belief, practices, customs and protocols. This 'cultural' knowledge has a ghostly presence in the way it interacts with the Australian legal space. Stripped of the priority and authority of Aboriginal laws and traditional modes of recognition and repositioned as cultural knowledge, meanings are distorted and Aboriginal laws are misrepresented.

However, reconsidering the cultural landscape construct as *a priori* a juridical construct both facilitates the possibility of living in accordance with Aboriginal laws by Aboriginal Peoples within the Australian legal system and better develops the potential to reconnect people, culture, place and law more generally. Regarded in terms of recognising law, not just people and their culture, it houses some capacity as a postcolonial form of governance that can dislodge the historical 'placelessness' of the Australian legal system. Further, in starting to redress the problem with our legal space, there is a far greater potential to seed mainstream Australian laws that are more respectful of the environment and sustainability through forging the connections between all people and places as part of the ordinary processes of land management and resource development.

The placelessness of Australian law

Place is a concept that combines the particular physical characteristics of a specific part of the Earth's surface with a human relationship to it.[5] That relationship can take many forms: economic, familial, political, aesthetic, psychological and so forth. Place can be also a sentient experience of living in, as part of, attached to and dependent on the material world. However, in contemporary Australian life, place is often regarded in somewhat reductive terms as a set of coordinates on a map or a description of a piece of real estate. Even so, the idea of place refers to human engagement with a specific physical location including any anthropogenic structures such as buildings, dams and bridges and any cultural narratives such as significant and sacred 'natural' features. For this reason, the concept of place is a radical concept in Anglo-American cultural discourse because it reveals the possibility of the synthesis of apparently separate realms: 'natural' and 'cultural' within a single site.

The reason it is important to understand the radical potential of the idea of place is because we are concerned here with problems arising from the removal of place from law and particularly from property law. Placelessness is not unique to modern law – it is part of the deeper paradigm of anthropocentrism on which the project of colonisation was premised.[6] Anthropocentric thought facilitated the gradual transformation of inalienable relationships between peoples and places into the intra-human transactions of rights over commodities both corporeal and incorporeal with regard to land. These transactions reflected a radically changed legal order in which people became alienable from lands and people could alienate lands.[7] The history of English diaspora through the enclosure of the commons and the transportation of convicts to foreign lands is one side of that transformation – the colonisation of the lands and peoples of those foreign lands is the other side – both were premised on the anthropocentrism of the dominant culture and the attendant placelessness of law.

The removal of place from colonial Australian property law was part of the strategy of political invasion and the imposition of foreign sovereignty. It fed deeply rooted cultural anxieties surrounding justification for invasion and colonisation of Australia. These were reflected in Letters Patent acknowledging pre-existing Aboriginal rights in South Australia,[8] reception of Aboriginal protest in Europe,[9] landscape themes explored in late-nineteenth-century Australian art,[10] and in portrayals of dispossession in major twentieth-century Australian literature and films.[11] It was this cultural history that contributed to the *Mabo* decision's partial reappraisal of the doctrine of *terra nullius* and its applicability to the Australian situation: "The fiction by which the rights and interests of indigenous inhabitants in land were treated as non-existent was . . . an unjust and discriminatory doctrine of that kind can no longer be accepted".[12] However despite ongoing political and legal overtures toward recognition of Aboriginal Peoples, none of this has led to any fundamental reappraisal of the sovereignty of the Anglo-Australian notions of property. Letters Patent suggestive of pre-existing Aboriginal rights have been read down to mean that a "principle of benevolence" should be exercised in the governance of Aboriginal people;[13] absolute Crown ownership and prerogative to dispose of title to land remains intact;[14] native title claims are determined by common law and Parliamentary rules of recognition.[15]

Although this chapter refers to the placelessness of Australian law, it is important to recognise that the absence of place is not accidental or insignificant but critical to the operation and logic of Australian property law as a rights-based discourse and as a technology of colonisation.[16] What this means is that restoring place to Australian law is not as simple as adding it in at potentially suitable points. Restoring place to Australian law means challenging and overcoming the ongoing convention of a colonising, if no longer colonial, legal discourse and outdated legal categories that entrench the priority of property rights over increasing environmental regulation designed to address the consequences of the placeless-ness of property law.[17] The work of such restoration therefore begins with a recollection and critique of the status quo.

Contemporary property law is essentially a set of equations designed to determine and allocate the access, benefits and other entitlements to land and natural resources. It is articulated as a series of 'rights' which are regarded as existing between people, as separate individual legal 'persons'. Property rights are not absolute, but relative to each other subject to a logic that facilitates the twin overarching goals of individual liberty and economic growth. Jeremy Bentham understood that the equations and language of property law, as rights, produces a necessarily 'dephysicalised' relation between humans and the environment. From his perspective it was important to a capitalist economy that property rights were disconnected from 'any exterior reality'.[18] For Bentham, this was necessary to provide for the security of wealth derived not (only) from land and its resources (which had been locked into feudal power relations) but from any number of more liquid 'things' including especially abstract notions such as shares, options and futures. This is why Bentham claimed that 'property is entirely a creature of law'[19] and that its origins were entirely 'metaphysical'.[20] Although long gone, Bentham's crystalline articulation of the dephysicalisation of English property law (back when it was known as land law) is as true a statement of property law as it ever was. Indeed, the High Court of Australia referred to this definition amongst others in a 1999 case[21] which above all others presented the Court with an opportunity to depart from this logic of dephysicalisation – a native title determination. However, the Court repeated the notion that property law is a series of rights, and the rights of native title were merely an addition to them rather than a fundamental challenge or a conundrum. A similar logic is evident in the intellectual property recognition of Aboriginal 'customary law'.[22]

The dephysicalisation of property law is important to understand because in addition to explaining the economic and political rationale of property as a rights-based institution, it also serves to remind legal scholars that property law is self-referential and self-authorising. Dephysicalised property conceals the real, material consequences of its operation. Whether the 'thing' of property is a natural resource, a public utility or a sign of an abstract commodity, it is intrinsically immaterial to an account of property law as dephysicalised. Australian property law has no regard for place; rather, it makes a space for commodification in which 'things' are dematerialised and denatured to facilitate the process of exchange. Australian property law refers to itself rather than to the (experiences of the) physical places it protects, shapes and destroys. The adverse environmental effects of the absence of place from law are in part addressed by a separate subordinate body of law, environmental law. But for the most part, the effects of a placeless or atopic property law are "eclipsed by a fetishism of its technicalities".[23] As Valerie Kerruish has stated, however:

'Things' may be intangible; they are no less created as things by conceptualisation and exchangeability. It is certainly a consequence of the dynamic of wealth that forms of property less-connected to wealth creation than to use in everyday life tend to be seen as consumer goods, to be protected by consumer rather than property law, or in the case of Aboriginal ideas of property to be virtually unprotected and increasingly seen as non-proprietary.[24]

Modern Australian property law excludes non–rights-based relationships between people and place, which renders invisible to it the 'things' that make life possible. This poses a considerable challenge for Australian cultural heritage laws that seek to make sense of place and for Aboriginal laws which are often structured around the "laws of reciprocity and obligation".[25] Proprietary relationships here are not defined by the subordination and irrelevance of place to people, but by human responsibilities for and from place. In her critique of the growth-oriented economy facilitated by modern Australian property law, Irene Watson states that the separation between the physical and metaphysical, between people and place, is antithetical to Indigenous jurisprudence:

> The non-indigenous relationship to land is to take more than is needed, depleting *ruwi* [land] and depleting self. Their way with the land is separate and alien, unable to understand how it is that we communicate with the natural world. We are talking to relations and our family, for we are one.[26]

The viability of knowledge-based land laws is evident in the long-established and successful Aboriginal legal regimes. These regimes are neither inherently superior (on a romantic conflation of race and environmentally sustainable law) nor were they rapid in development. Aboriginal legal regimes connected knowledge of places to laws on the basis of experience of specific geographic conditions, over very long periods of time and across a vast continent of diverse and dynamic climatic conditions. The point is not to essentialise and racialise law but to identify and respect the intellectual integrity and practical success of laws that have been and remain locally viable and authoritative. By contrast, as modern Australian property law increasingly exceeds the physical conditions of its own existence, what local authority can it be said to have? Its anthropocentrism and placelessness render potent obstacles to the development of enduring laws founded on knowledge of and responsibility for places.

The failure of culture heritage laws at Kumarangk

The dominance of the placeless property paradigm in Australian law is well illustrated in the failed cultural heritage protection actions surrounding development at Kumerangk in South Australia (SA).[27] These legal events are infamous due to a complexity that was, at least in part, derived from the overt politicisation of the associated approval process at both state and federal levels.[28]

Property developers Tom and Wendy Chapman had obtained planning permission for a marina to be built on Hindmarsh Island dating from the 1980s, and it had been partially built. The Chapmans later sought a bridge to facilitate access to the island. However, the financier, the Westpac bank, declined to fund the bridge. The SA State Bank had recently collapsed. The SA state Labor government, approaching an election, was keen to be seen to be sponsoring major developments. This led to a peculiar financing arrangement whereby the Westpac bank and the Labor government entered into a financing arrangement whereby the State government provided a guarantee and agreed to build the bridge.[29]

SA planning law required consideration of the environmental and cultural heritage significance of the site that would be affected by the bridge and marina. However, the processes of heritage law mirror the monarchical power of the Crown that determines original land grants in Australia. Under both state and federal heritage laws, heritage protection is determined ultimately by the relevant minister who reviews applications, orders investigations, determines facts and makes relevant protection orders. Ministerial advice is dependent upon expert input to the collection and presentation of relevant evidence. There is considerable discretion with respect to who is consulted and what processes should be implemented. As such, while Aboriginal people may give evidence to anthropologists, in court, Aboriginal knowledge, law and identity based in place are miscategorised. 'Evidence' of 'culture' is taken, removed and abstracted from its lived context and authority. It is rendered an ethereal knowledge, repositioned as mythic, spiritual, backward-facing immemorial custom and oral traditions. So constructed, this knowledge can appear to require materialisation through expert transcription. Positioned as *a priori* 'other worldly', it now needs to be translated, officially reported, verified, allowing it to be linked back to specific map co-ordinates to be potentially made relevant to ministerial determinations about particular geographical 'sites'. As Sneddon argues:

> It is clear from numerous judgements across several jurisdictions that the courts and tribunals of Australia have little time for evidence that lacks detail and precision when determining matters relating to Aboriginal heritage values of a spiritual kind. Broad assertions of sacredness or spirituality are not well-received by courts/tribunals, who have stated on many occasions that they cannot make a determination on the basis of generalities.[30]

It is a colonising logic that presumes Aboriginal knowledge comes into the world as abstract and dematerialised. This fiction allows it to be presented as Other to *homo economicus*, who, in place of an original mysticism, practises modern reason in order to accumulate private property rights and deliver us 'material' progress.[31] Aboriginal knowledges and laws are thus boxed in by their cultural and legal positioning, an exception to the economic rationality that might 'normally' prevail in planning law.

The Chapmans appointed an expert, Nadia McLaren, to compile an archaeological report for the Aboriginal Heritage Branch of the South Australia Department of Environment and Planning. The developers were consequently asked to consult with traditional owners, referred to as the Ngarrindjeri people. However, the adoption of the term 'Ngarrindjeri' as a descriptor for those whose interests were affected disguises a contested history that flows from the violent dispossession that characterises this land.[32]

There were some discussions with some Ngarrindjeri people, the content of which remains unclear. These did not conclude anything. Following public concerns, another survey was also sought by the state's chief archaeologist, Mr Neil Draper. He identified different significant Aboriginal sites to those noted previously and recommended these be protected. The Draper report was received by an incoming conservative government that sought to avoid the financial obligation to build the bridge.[33] Unsuccessful, the State Minister for Aboriginal Affairs then authorised damage to any heritage sites as was necessary to enable construction.

In response, the Aboriginal Legal Rights Movement, based in South Australia, applied to the Federal Labor Minister for Aboriginal Affairs, Hon Robert Tickner, on behalf of some affected women, seeking an urgent order prohibiting construction of the bridge under the *Aboriginal and Torres Strait Islander Heritage Protection Act* 1984 (Cth). The Minister appointed Professor Cheryl Saunders, a University of Melbourne constitutional law expert, as reporter. Professor Saunders cited the cosmological significance of the area. Her report had appended to it two envelopes containing 'secret women's business'. The envelopes were only read by the minister's female advisor. She informed the minister there was nothing in the evidence in the envelopes that conflicted with the report. The minister then issued an emergency declaration to stop work on the bridge. The Chapmans appealed this decision under the *Administrative Decisions (Judicial Review) Act 1977* (Cth), claiming lack of procedural fairness, including bias, a failure to take relevant considerations into account in the making of decisions (including the evidence of men) and unreasonability, and they were successful.[34]

Another group of 'dissident women' then came forward, claiming that the secret women's business was fabricated. The South Australian government set up a Royal Commission to inquire into the authenticity of secret women's business. Legal issues thus became enshrined in questions about the genuineness of evidence about 'sites' and the veracity of belief and the reliability of Aboriginal witnesses, who must recount into evidence 'relevant details' and particulars of how they came to know it. The women who had initiated the original inquiries and were at the centre of the allegations refused to appear and be subjected to the state inquiry. The inquiry subsequently determined that the evidence of 'secret women's business' was fabricated.[35]

A further application was made to the Federal Minister for Aboriginal Affairs to ban the bridge. Another report was initiated, this time to be investigated by Justice Jane Matthews of the Federal Court. Her report was not released due to a challenge to her appointment. Apparently it determined the undisclosed information was significant but not sufficient for a declaration under the Act.[36]

With a new conservative federal government coming into office, development was then facilitated by the passing of a special law, the *Hindmarsh Island Bridge Act 1997* (Cth) (the Bridge Act), which allowed for the by-passing of the

Commonwealth heritage act altogether. Infamously, the Bridge Act overcame a constitutional challenge, with the Court failing to agree whether the race power of the *Constitution* restricted the Commonwealth Parliament to making laws for the *benefit* of the 'Aboriginal race'. Accordingly, it was found that the government could in fact enact laws to the detriment of any particular race.[37]

While the legal events surrounding development at Kumarangk suggest an epic failure of cultural heritage laws, the case is productive in suggesting future paths for development of a different kind. Firstly, in scholarly accounts of anthropology and law, there was considerable unease at the political machinations. Though political interference expedited the process that led to the bridge development, this was widely disparaged as a legal perversion and corruption. There remained confidence that 'fairly considered' cultural heritage laws could have succeeded in protecting important 'sites'. More importantly, the events also highlight where the deeper problems lie in Australian laws. One of the biggest limitations rests in the containment of cultural heritage laws and the way they are nestled within a dephysicalised property paradigm. It is thus toward addressing the problem of dephysicalised property through cultural heritage laws that this chapter now turns.

The productivity of the cultural landscape concept

Critiques of property are not new to law. As a matter of legal classification, property law is seen as a system that regulates the private rights of persons in things. Legal theorists problematise the legal relationship between persons and things.[38] There is also property law scholarship informed by anthropology, in particular the work of Marilyn Strathern.[39] These critical analyses of property law provide important insights into socio-economic problems associated with modern, alienable property such as the philosophical separation between persons and things. However, they also reproduce the abstractness of modern property law by naturalising dichotomies between public/private, private property/communal property and reason/ nature. Here in contrast to the dephysicalised paradigm of modern property Indigenous property is also reproduced in conventionally abstract terms of 'tradition', 'identity' and race-based 'customs' rather than with physical and 'place-based' laws. This assignment is very pernicious and self-serving. It allows lawyers to suspend consideration of what happened to Aboriginal law under conditions of invasion and to distance us from consideration of how 'progressive' scholarship reproduces the status quo through acts of categorisation and subjection.

The turn to cultural heritage is motivated out of a concern to investigate whether it is still possible to imagine a space for 'raw law'- the Aboriginal way of knowing law through living, emanating from the ruwe, currently buried beneath layers of colonialism.[40] Yet this strategy may strike some as somewhat perverse. Law that straddles public and private domains occupies a marginal legal space in Australia, and its jurisprudence remains relatively underdeveloped. Heritage law is no exception, having a problematic relationship to property law, where it regulates a class of interests subordinate to property. Heritage laws create procedural rights that can lead to restrictions on the freedom of movement and exchange of objects and protection orders preventing the destruction of parts of the built and/or natural landscape. In Australia heritage law is not a distinct legal specialisation. Rather it is a sub-set spread across four other legal specialisations related to the natural environment (environmental law), built environment (planning law), culture (intellectual property laws) and human rights (international law). However, since the 1980s there has been a shift away from scholarship that essentialises a nature/culture distinction.[41] This has undermined the conceptual foundation of these traditional taxonomic separations and, in turn, led, at least in part, to a merging of natural heritage/cultural heritage concepts and to heritage laws that embody aspects of a 'cultural landscape' approach. The historic marginalisation of heritage law and its late development arguably provides it with advantages over other doctrinally established categories that were once thought to be more productive, such as native title and copyright law. Through links with Australian environmental studies, critical geography and anthropology, heritage scholars are comparatively well informed by Aboriginal knowledges and can demonstrate an awareness of the problem with the mainstream confinement and distortion of Aboriginal laws within the Australian legal space.

'Cultural landscape' is now a preferred legal construct developed under the WHC that is valued for its potential to bridge the nature/culture divide. It has wider resonance through its circulation within the disciplinary knowledges of archaeology, geography, land use planning and ecology.[42]Further, the international endorsement of this term helps legitimate local experience and authorise a particular way for relevant contemporary Australian experts to acknowledge the importance of an Aboriginal sense of place. It is thus a term that houses some capacity to reconnect people, things, memories, geographies and identities, and it is a concept that can grow meaning and authority through its local circulation and reinscription.

The concept of cultural landscape links mental geographies (including ways of knowing), social landscapes and the natural environment. For example, John Barrett defines cultural landscape as:

> The entire surface over which people moved and within which they congregated. That surface was given meaning as people acted upon the world within the context of the various demands and obligations which acted upon them. Such actions took place within a certain tempo and at certain locales. Thus landscape, its form constructed from natural and artificial features, became a culturally meaningful resource through its routine occupancy.[43]

Barrett's reference to the cultural landscape as a 'resource' is problematic if it is taken to prioritise growth-based exploitation over other relations. However, the term needs to be understood in the context of broader national policy discussion of land use:

> From the end of the nineteenth century to the mid-twentieth century, and during a period of federation, war and slowing immigration Frawley (1999) and Heathcote (1972) trace the emergence of a national vision which, although

it remained developmentalist, sought to make 'wise use' of the nation's resources. By the late Twentieth century, however they claim to discern the beginnings of an ecological vision which draws on elements of the earlier scientific, Romantic and national visions and on Aboriginal concepts of place an environment, and seeks a more sustainable future for Australia.[44]

Jessica Weir also notes the relevance of the idea of cultural landscape to traditional owners:

> One of the most common characteristics of Indigenous peoples' knowledge in comparison to modern thinking, is an emphasis on knowledge coming from a specific place. This place is known as 'country'. Country is profoundly important to traditional owners, who are generally the people who have inherited the rights and responsibilities to country from their ancestors and ancestral beings. For them, these are innate ties between particular people, land, law and language.[45]

The term has connections with Australian federal and state environmental protection and heritage laws which pay regard to 'place', defined expansively.[46] For example, the *Environment Protection and Biodiversity Conservation Act* 1999 (Cth) (EPBC Act) protects places of World Heritage, National Heritage and Commonwealth Heritage. Section 3 defines the objects as including:

- a co-operative approach to the protection and management of the environment involving governments, the community, land-holders and indigenous peoples;
- assisting in the co-operative implementation of Australia's international environmental responsibilities; and
- recognising the role of indigenous people in the conservation and ecologically sustainable use of Australia's biodiversity; and
- promoting the use of indigenous peoples' knowledge of biodiversity with the involvement of, and in co-operation with, the owners of the knowledge.

The act encourages use of governance structures that incorporate Indigenous management to help identify places requiring protection at first instance[47] and in ongoing day-to-day decision making affecting relevant places. In the latter role there is some explicit recognition of the significance of Aboriginal law to decision making about access to and culturally appropriate use of particular places.

The cultural landscape concept is open to further jurisprudential development. There is a broadly based academic interest in exploring its potential, and, if thoughtfully engaged, it could help support the survival of 'raw law' when there are very few other obvious options. In the spirit that it is a path 'worth trying', in the last substantive section we critically discuss how the cultural landscape approach has been working in practice.

The Uluru-Kata Tjuta National Park as a cultural landscape

> First we got that World Heritage listing for that flora and fauna and now we got
> that cultural landscaping . . . first in Australia and second in the world!
> Yami Lester, Chair, Uluru-Kata Tjuta Board of Management.[48]

The Uluru (Ayers Rock-Mount Olga) National Park was first listed as a (natural) world heritage site in 1987. The Uluru-Kata Tjuta National Park renomination as an associative cultural landscape in 1994 was on the basis of it meeting four criteria.[49] These took into account the landscape being: (v) an outstanding example of a traditional human settlement that is representative of a culture or human interaction with the environment; (vi) directly or tangibly associated with events or living traditions, ideas and beliefs, with artistic and literary works of outstanding universal significance; (vii) containing superlative natural phenomena or areas of exceptional natural beauty and; (viii) outstanding examples representing major stages of earth's history and significant geomorphic or physiographic features.[50] The supporting text refers to the landscape somewhat differently:

> the landscape . . . is the outcome of millennia of management under tradi-
> tional Anangu procedures governed by the *tjukurpa* (law) . . . To write that
> the landscape is *associated with* the narratives, songs, and art of the *tjukurpa*,
> while accurate from a western perspective, does not do full justice to Anangu
> ontology and is a poor translation of Anangu concepts. For the Anangu this
> landscape is the product of the heroic ancestors' actions and can be read as a
> text specifying the relationship between the land and its indigenous inhabit-
> ants laid down by the *tjukurpa*. The very rock of Uluru and Kata Tjuta is
> proof of the heroes' actions and being.[51]

The objection to the focus being on proof of 'association' with a cultural landscape points to a problem with the wording of the WHC. The criteria suggest an initial boundary between persons/things, legal subjects/objects that, in exceptional heritage cases, can be infilled by 'culture' when there is sufficient tangible evidence of living traditions, ideas and beliefs associated with the surrounding geography. The criteria reproduces a concept of place (as landscape) in which 'nature' and 'culture' remain separate and can at best interact or co-exist rather than exist synthetically or holistically. This peculiar framing is entirely contrary to Anangu ontology and diminishes the significance of Tjukurpa as a knowledge system. Tjukurpa is far more than a 'belief system'. Elder Tony Tjamiwa refers to it this way:

> Government law is on paper. Ananguku Law is held in our heads and kurunpa
> [spirit]. You can't put Aboriginal law on paper; it's the rules that grandfathers
> and grandmothers and that fathers and mothers gave us to use, that we hold in

our hearts and in our heads. National park are government rule, paper laws, but in Uluru we've got both laws working together, running side by side. Government might try and give you a flat tyre, just a national park without the title. Don't take it. Only talk one way, the straight way. Don't compromise your law for a Flat tyre.[52]

From an Anangu perspective law, property law and Anangu identity are one and the same thing. The flat tyre analogy points to the uselessness of forms of 'recognition' and, in particular forms of land title, that are emptied of Aboriginal jurisprudence. While, as Yami Lester puts it, "we know we had Uluru and Kata Tjuta all the time but it helps having it in writing",[53] under Australian law land title remains linked to a colonial legacy.

The area in which the park is now situated was excised from an Aboriginal reserve in 1958 and reserved by the Crown for use as a national park. In 1977 the Uluru (Ayers Rock- Mount Olga) National Park was declared under the *National Parks and Wildlife Conservation Act* 1975 (Cth) with title vesting in the Director of National Parks and Wildlife. A land claim was lodged by the Central Land Council under the *Aboriginal Land Rights (Northern Territory) Act* 1976 (Cth). This claim was partly successful in relation to land adjoining the National Park. However, the prior vesting of title in the Director of National Parks meant that this land was not available under the Land Rights Act.[54] In 1985 title was granted by the Governor General to the Uluru-Kata Tjuta Aboriginal Land Trust, and in 1993 the park was renamed. Since 1986 the park has been managed by the Australian National Parks and Wildlife Service (Parks Australia) within the Commonwealth Department of the Environment, Water, Heritage and the Arts and the Uluru-Kata Tjuta Board of Management.

Declaration of the park continued under the introduction of the EPBC Act in 1999. In addition to the WHC listing, the National Park is also included on the Commonwealth Heritage and National Heritage Lists established under the EPBC Act. Joint management is based on Aboriginal title to the land, which is supported by a legal framework laid out in the EPBC Act discussed in Part Three. The Nguraritja and relevant Aboriginal people and the Director of National Parks are formally lessees of the park. Management plans are published by the Director of National Parks.

Strelein argues that:

> Joint management allows indigenous people to be involved in habitat preservation within the confines of the Australian political system. Donna Craig notes that the evolution of joint management models under our system of land law rather than by recognition of traditional land tenure and title is a fundamental flaw.[55]

The Uluru-Kata Tjuta Board of Management are involved in key planning and everyday decision making about the park, and "respect for Tjukurpa" is a principle that guides management practice.[56] This operates within an imposed alien structure of land title. However, we argue that it is not simply the form of title but rather more importantly the particular economic relation to place that informs it, in which the landscape is valued primarily as a tourist resource, that poses a major confinement of Tjukurpa.

The extent and limitations of current practice can be seen from how sensitive issues are handled by park management. The Uluru-Kata Tjuta National Park Management Plan 2010–2020 notes that:

> Tjukurpa requires that Nguraritja take responsibility for looking after visitors to their country and each time a visitor is seriously or fatally injured at Uluru, Nguraritja share in the grieving process. It is this 'duty of care' under Tjukurpa that is the basis of Nguraritja's stress and grieving for those injured. Although climbing Uluru is an attraction for some visitors, it is the view of Nguraritja that visitors should not climb as it does not respect the spiritual and safety aspects of Tjukurpa . . . In the past, many people have been injured and more than 30 people have died attempting to climb the very steep Uluru path.[57]

The Uluru-Kata Tjuta National Park visitor site advises:

> That's a really important sacred thing that you are climbing . . . You shouldn't climb. It's not the real thing about this place. And maybe that makes you a bit sad. But anyway that's what we have to say. We are obliged by Tjukurpa to say. And all the tourists will brighten up and say, 'Oh I see. This is the right way. This is the thing that's right. This is the proper way: no climbing.'
>   Kunmanara, traditional owner

However, climbing is still not prohibited under the EPBC regulations. For visitor safety and cultural and environmental reasons the official policy is to work toward closure, but only:

> when the Board, in consultation with the tourism industry, is satisfied that adequate new visitor experiences have been successfully established, or the proportion of visitors climbing falls below 20 per cent, or the cultural and natural experiences on offer are the critical factors when visitors make their decision to visit the park.[58]

Whilst figures fluctuate from year to year, the numbers climbing Uluru appear to be slowly trending downwards. Yet a 2006 study showed 38% of visitors still climbed Uluru despite the clear signage and knowledge that this was not considered by traditional owners as appropriate.[59]

The prioritising of tourist interests over Tjukurpa is seen through the management of ceremonial business. Uluru is not closed to outsiders for rituals including, importantly, Sorry Business. Rather there are short, partial closures "effected in a way that minimises disruption to visitors".[60] The visitor as consumer takes priority over the needs and interests of Uluru citizens. The Management Plan treats ceremonial obligations as more a complication affecting the work practices of its Indigenous employees than as a matter of obligation that should be adhered to because of the protocols or laws of the landscape.[61]

This is not to suggest that there is no genuine interest in or commitment to respect for Tjukurpa. However, currently when it clashes with the commercial imperatives, Tjukurpa is reduced to esoteric knowledge associated with traditional owners' spiritual beliefs, primarily of relevance to traditional owners and perhaps of interest as exotica for tourists. The problem here rests with seeing Tjukurpa through a veil of alienated property, as a 'cultural' demand on Indigenous subjects rather than as a legal imperative that establishes and requires a lawful way of living with the landscape. This flows from the lack of development of the cultural landscape idea as jurisprudence, informing the practice of law at Uluru.

Nonetheless, there are developments elsewhere worth noting in other related domains where residential developments were involved. For example, the Blue Mountains City Council (a body that governs an area of which about 70% is incorporated into the World Heritage Blue Mountains National Park, listed for its natural features), denied planning permission for a large sculpture that had already been erected out the front of a privately owned art gallery situated in a Village Tourist zone. The gallery owner had commissioned a non-Aboriginal person to make a new and 'original' Aboriginal-themed work, which led to doubts that intellectual property laws could prevent the appropriation.[62] This led to a large sandstone structure being erected on site which, without permission, depicted Wandjina imagery, spirit figures from the Kimberley region of Western Australia, causing great offence. As part of the ordinary planning process, Council received objections from many people including non-Indigenous and Indigenous residents, custodial owners from the Kimberley represented by the Ngarinyin Aboriginal Corporation, the Arts Legal Centre of Australia and New South Wales National Parks Service.

Section 4 of the *Environmental and Planning Assessment Act* 1977 (NSW) defines environment as including consideration of "all aspects of the surroundings of man, whether affecting him as an individual or in his social groupings", and s79C(b) refers the consenting authority to evaluate environmental impacts on both the natural and built environments, and social and economic impacts in the locality. While the legislation does not adopt the 'cultural landscape' terminology, the concepts are clearly present in the evaluative criteria applied to developments, in particular in the concept of social impact. In the Land and Environment Court it was noted that a s79C evaluation could include consideration of the religious or cultural values of an immediately affected and identifiable group who may be affected by a development. Here evidence taken, including from council planners and an anthropologist, was sufficient to "objectively" prove the sculpture was highly offensive to Aboriginal religious and cultural beliefs and that their objection was based in more than a mere "fear or concern without rational or justified foundation". Due to the prominent street location the sculpture was thus found to produce a negative social impact which justified the denial of planning permission and an order for its removal.[63]

This is not a unique approach to decision making under s79C in the NSW Land and Environment Court. For example, members of the Numbahjing clan within the Bundjalung nation successfully challenged council approval for a path associated with a new housing development where the proposed route travelled across the site of an 1853/4 massacre. Consent had been based on a heritage report that focused too closely on archaeological evidence without duly sufficiently considering the weight of anthropological evidence of the cultural significance of the massacre site.[64] Related claims were not successful in relation to protection of Aboriginal "objects" under the *National Parks and Wildlife Act 1974* (NSW), with destruction authorised in light of "the reality that Aboriginal objects are found across the NSW landscape".[65] The difference in outcome only reinforces the importance of heritage protection law recognising the particularity of place.

Though still limited, there is clearly some relevant jurisprudence that establishes the need to consider mental geographies in conjunction with the physical geography of heritage sites. The failure to fairly consider the two in conjunction can, in some cases, lead to planning approvals being overruled under administrative law. The combination of the existing presence of the cultural landscape idea dispersed across federal and state environmental, planning and heritage legislation, affecting many different kinds of land holdings and uses that provide a platform for further jurisprudential development. The capacity to develop it further is supported by the deployment of relevant disciplinary expertise operating in a context in which there has been a significant shift in the cultural sensibility of the law, at least in some quarters – from anxiety about placelessness to a degree of acceptance of a history of colonisation. There may now be room for a stronger and formal recognition of the necessary relationship between peoples, mental geographies and places within the daily operation of Australian laws, including especially Aboriginal knowledges as law.

The development of the cultural landscape idea within mainstream Australian environmental law casts doubt on the relevance or necessity of separate protection under the UNESCO Convention for the Safeguarding of the Intangible Cultural Heritage, a convention to which Australia is not a signatory. To the extent that the cultural landscape concept provides a critique of dephysicalised property, it also provides a mechanism for refreshing reform agendas with respect to intellectual property laws affecting Aboriginal Peoples. This is sorely needed given current impasses which lead to ongoing appeals for *sui generis* laws for protection of traditional knowledge, traditional cultural expressions and initiatives against biopiracy.[66] These calls only further reify the unhelpful and unsustainable dichotomy between tangible/intangible property rights, ignoring the placelessness that is fundamental to both legal concepts.

There will, of course, be further pushback and opposition to change from those who benefit most from investment in the dephysicalised property paradigm, in particular from representatives of the mining, coal seam gas, land clearing, property developers and animal hunting lobby groups. However, there are also strategic linkages to be forged with a broader environmentalist constituency who are sympathetically engaged in related pathways of resistance. Due to ongoing environmental crises – increasingly severe and recurrent bushfires, droughts, floods, losses of biodiversity, losses of arable land and high-profile doomed predictions about many of our other signature World Heritage properties including the Great Barrier Reef [67] – there are productive anxieties to be nurtured and engaged, raising concerns about the irresponsibility inherent in the very idea of dephysicalised property when we live in a material world of contaminated and depleting resources.

Conclusion

Of late, in seeking to explain the difficult social challenges we face, critical legal studies has turned toward addressing the spatiality of law. In this literature law is constructed as a mechanism that secures the infrastructure necessary for extended capital accumulation, and in line with a neoliberal sensibility, it operates to eliminate spatial constraints to accumulation.[68] This analysis offers a totalising view of law even whilst plotting marginal pockets of resistance, because, in adopting the pursuit of capital as the inner logic of all law, the possibility of other ideas of law is *a priority* excluded. In essence in ignoring the survival of Aboriginal laws, critical legal theorists suspend taking responsibility for colonialism.

Colonialism houses political and economic imperatives within a legal framework in which there are jurisprudential choices to be made. It is clear that, as with the example of Kumerangk, law makers can choose to reinvest in dephysicalised property. By so doing the law continues to disembody the emancipatory potential within cultural heritage law. Australian law remains a technology of governance,[69] in which the state legitimates planning decisions that accord with the colonial project. This priority is also present to some extent in the governance structures and practices at Uluru-Kata Tjuta National Park. It is only when the cultural landscape concept is taken to provide an access point to an alternate way of thinking about the materiality of law, identity and place that the capacity to challenge the legal status quo arises. This requires us to stop thinking about cultural landscape in terms of exceptional cases and in terms of embodying only procedural rights that permit a consideration of cultural claims. We need to develop a jurisprudence in which the particular economic logic of dephysicalised property does not predetermine the legal space. This requires us to stop thinking and talking about cultural landscape in terms of culture and repositioning it as being about law.

Colonialism is perpetuated through the embeddedness of dephysicalised property concepts because it currently confines other political and legal agendas. This creates an intractable political situation whereby Aboriginal demands for survival are misconstrued as disembodied cultural claims. Because of the hold of this way of thinking, calls to open up the Australian legal space to accommodate cultural difference, for constitutional recognition, for reconciliation are all compromised from the outset. Human rights law has a fractious relationship with the domestic legal space. There is no treaty discussion. Native title jurisprudence has failed to fulfil its own limited potential. Intellectual property laws replace sovereign claims with rights to protect 'traditional knowledge', 'traditional cultural expressions' and 'benefit-sharing' from innovation instead of engaging with Aboriginal law as law. These are sideshows that divert attention from the poverty of the property model in securing a way of living with the landscape. The nourishing of cultural landscape law offers greater possibility in a lawscape currently occupied by very few other viable pathways.

Notes

* Thanks to Irene Watson, Valerie Kerruish, Lucas Lixinski and Christoph Antons; and to Kendy Ding for research assistance.
1 The event is often referred to as the Hindmarsh Island Bridge controversy, the Ngarrindjeri 'secret women's business' or with reference to associated High Court litigation, *Kartinyeri v. Commonwealth* [1998] HCA 22.
2 See Expert Group on Cultural Landscapes (La Petite Pierre, France, 24–26 October 1992) WHC-92/CONF.202/10/Add. The text was subsequently approved for inclusion in the Operational Guidelines by the World Heritage Committee at its 16th session (Santa Fe 1992), WHC-92/CONF.002/12; WHC. 13/01, July 2013.
3 See Graeme Aplin (2007) 13(6) 'World Heritage Cultural Landscapes' *International Journal of Heritage Studies* 427–446.
4 Ask the Aborigines: the process is complexly embedded in politics, history, ethics and stereotypes. The temptation is to conceptualise Aboriginal people as guides – a familiar cultural icon which we all know how to grasp. Stereotypically, the black person indicates the terrain, the white person makes notes on maps, describes, sketches, consults documents, and finally defines the meanings which transforms a piece of geographical space into a cultural and historical place. The white person imposes meaning, and the worlds of meaning are lost." Deborah Bird Rose and Darrell Lewis, 'A bridge and a pinch' (1992) (1) *Public History Review* 26–36, 29.
5 Tim Creswell, 'Place' in (ed) Barney Warf *Encyclopedia of Human Geography* Sage Publications 2006, 357.
6 Nicole Graham, *Lawscape: Property, Environment, Law* Routledge 2011, 5–6.
7 Ibid., 41–47.
8 The establishment of the colony of South Australia provided, "nothing in those our Letters Patent contained shall affect or be construed to affect the rights of any Aboriginal Natives of the said Province to the actual occupation or enjoyment in their own Persons or in the Persons of their Descendants of any Lands therein now actually occupied or enjoyed by such Natives". *Letters Patent for the setting up of the new colony of South Australia*, 19 February 1836.
9 Fiona Paisley, *The Lone Protestor. AM Fernando in Australia and Europe* Aboriginal Studies Press 2012.
10 Tim Bonyhady, *Images in opposition: Australian landscape painting 1801–1890* Oxford University Press 1991.
11 For example, James Vance Marshall, *Walkabout* Penguin Books 1963; *Walkabout* Film Director: Nicolas Roeg, Producer: Si Litvinoff 1971, See <http://aso.gov.au/titles/features/walkabout/notes/>; Thomas Keneally, *The Chant of Jimmy Blacksmith* Angus and Robertson 1972; *The Chant of Jimmy Blacksmith,* Film Director: Fred Schepsi, Producer: Fred Schepsi 1978, <http://aso.gov.au/titles/features/chant-jimmie-blacksmith/notes/>

12 Brennan J. in *Mabo v. Queensland (No 2)* ("Mabo case") [1992] HCA 23 at [42].
13 *Milirrpum and Others v. Nabalco Pty. Ltd. and The Commonwealth of Australia* (1971) 17 FLR 141, 255–258.
14 *Attorney-General v. Brown* (17) (1847) 1 Legge, 317–320); *Seas and Submerged Lands Case* (1975) 135 CLR 337; *Mabo v. Queensland* [1988] HCA 69; (1988) 166 CLR 186; *Mabo v. Queensland* (No 2) [1992] HCA 23; (1992) 175 CLR 1.
15 *Native Title Act* 1993 (Cth).
16 Graham above n.6, 91.
17 Nicole Graham, 'This is not a thing: land, sustainability and legal education' (2014) 26(3) *Journal of Environmental Law* 395–422.
18 Peter Fitzpatrick, *The Mythology of Modern Law* Routledge 1992, 56.
19 Jeremy Bentham (1838) *The Works of Jeremy Bentham,* Vol. I (ed. J. Bowring), William Tate, 308.
20 Jeremy Bentham, [1864] 'A Theory of Legislation' in (ed) C.B. Macpherson, *Property: mainstream and critical positions,* University of Toronto Press, 1978, 51.
21 *Yanner v. Eaton* (1999) 201 CLR 351. For a detailed discussion of the role of dephysicalised definitions of property in the case see: Graham, above n.8, 166–170.
22 *Bulun Bulun v. R & T Textiles Pty Ltd* [1998] 41 IPR 513; Kathy Bowrey, 'The Outer Limits Of Copyright Law – Where Law Meets Philosophy And Culture' (2001) 12(1) *Law and Critique* 1–24.
23 Alain Pottage, 'Foreword' in Graham above n.8, x.
24 Valerie Kerruish, 'Property and equity', unpublished lectures, Macquarie University 1999.
25 Irene Watson, 'Buried Alive' (2002) 13 *Law and Critique* 256.
26 Watson, ibid, 256.
27 For an Aboriginal history of Kumerangk, see Irene Watson, *Aboriginal Peoples, Colonialism and International Law. Raw Law* Routledge 2014.
28 International lawyer Prof Hilary Charlesworth noted that it "will surely enter Australian folklore as one of the most complex, and litigated, of disputes". Hilary Charlesworth, 'Little Boxes: A Review of the Commonwealth Hindmarsh Island Report by Jane Mathews' (1997) 3(90) *Aboriginal Law Bulletin* 19.
29 This view was based on advice received by Samuel Jacobs QC, who was appointed by Premier Brown to determine the legal responsibilities arising out of the contracts into which the parties entered.
30 Andrew Sneddon, 'Aboriginal objections to development and mining activities on the grounds of adverse impacts to sites of spiritual significance: Australian judicial and quasi-judicial responses', (2012) 29(3) *Environmental and Planning Law Journal* 217, 218.
31 See generally Meyers, Diana, 'Feminist Perspectives on the Self', *The Stanford Encyclopedia of Philosophy* (Spring 2010 Edition), Edward N. Zalta (ed.), <http://plato. stanford.edu/archives/spr2010/entries/feminism-self/>.
32 For the history of the term 'Ngarrindjeri', see Irene Watson, 'First Nation Stories, Grandmother's Law: Too Many Stories to Tell' in (eds) Heather Douglas, Francesca Bartlett, Trish Luker, Rosemary Hunter, *The Australian Feminist Judgments Project. Righting and Re-writing Law* Hart Publishing 2014, 46–53.
33 Statement by the Hon. Diana Laidlaw, Legislative Council, South Australia, Debates, 15 February 1994, 25–28.
34 *Chapman v. Tickner* (1995) 55 FCR 316.
35 South Australia, Hindmarsh Island Bridge Royal Commission, *Report* (1995). Based on the Royal Commission report, there was further action for damages in the Federal Court against Robert Tickner, Cheryl Saunders and others associated with the Tickner report. These claims were dismissed. See *Chapman v. Luminis Pty Ltd (No 4)* (2001) 123 FCR 62; *Chapman v. Luminis Pty Ltd (No 5)* [2001] FCA 1106 (21 August 2001).

36 *Wilson v. Minister for Aboriginal and Torres Strait Islander Affairs* (1996) 189 CLR 1;
Alexander Reilly, 'Finding an Indigenous Perspective in Administrative Law' (2009)
19 *Legal Education Review* 271, 284.
37 *Kartinyeri v. Commonwealth* [1998] HCA 22.
38 Margaret Davies and Ngaire Naffine, *Are Persons Property? Legal Debates about
Property and Personality*, Ashgate, 2001; Margaret Radin, *Reinterpreting Property*,
University of Chicago Press, 1993.
39 Marilyn Strathern, *Property, substance and effect: anthropological essays on persons
and things*, Althone Press 1999; (eds) Alain Pottage and Martha Mundy, *Law, Anthropology, and the Constitution of the Social: Making Persons and Things* Cambridge
University Press 2004.
40 Irene Watson, above n.27, 12–13.
41 See Sarah M. Titchen, 'Changing perceptions and recognition of the environment-
from cultural and natural heritage to cultural landscape' in J. Finlayson and A. Jack-
son-Nanko, *Heritage and Native Title: Anthropological and Legal Perspectives* Native
Title Research Unit AIATSIS 1996, 40.
42 See, for example, C.O. Sauer, 'The Morphology of Landscape' (1929) 2(2) *University
of California Publications in Geography* 19–53. And, A.J. Rose, 'Australia as a Cultural Landscape' in Rapoport, Amos (ed) *Australia as Human Setting: Approaches to
the designed environment* Angus & Robertson 1972.
43 Quoted in Rodney Harrison, *Shared Landscapes. Archeologies of Attachment and the
Pastoral Industry in New South Wales* University of New South Wales Press 2004, 10–11.
44 Roy Jones & Christina Birdsall-Jones, 'The Contestation of Heritage: The Coloniser
and the Colonised in Australia', in (ed) Brian Graham and Ian Howard, *The Ashgate
Research Companion to Heritage and Identity* Ashgate 2008, 374.
45 Jessica Weir, *Murray River Country. An ecological dialogue with traditional owners*
Aboriginal Studies Press 2009, 11.
46 E.g. s4 *Heritage Act* 1977 (NSW) defines environmental heritage as including buildings, works, relics or places of historic, scientific, cultural, social, archaeological,
architectural, natural or aesthetic significance for the state.
47 For example, *Aboriginal Heritage Act* 1988 (SA) provides for the protection and conservation of Aboriginal sites, Aboriginal objects and Aboriginal remains, defined in
relation to significance according to Aboriginal tradition; or of significance to Aboriginal archaeology, anthropology or history, with the minister advised by an Aboriginal
representative body, the Aboriginal Heritage Committee.
48 Quoted in Sarah M. Titchen, above n.41, 46.
49 World Heritage listing No. 447 (1987); Renomination WH No. 447rev (1994). For
the deficiencies of the original nomination see Rodney Harrison, *Heritage. Critical
Approaches* Routledge, 2003, 122–5.
50 Operational Guidelines for the Implementation of the World Heritage Convention,
WHC-92/CONF.002/12; WHC. 13/01, July 2013
51 Ibid.
52 Tony Tjamiwa 'Tjunguringkula Waakaripai: Joint Management of Uluru National
Park', translated by Jon Willis, in (ed) John Birckhead, Terry De Lacy, Laura-Jane
Smith, *Aboriginal Involvement in Parks and Protected Areas* AIAITSIS 1992, 7, 10.
53 Quoted in Sarah M. Titchen, above n.41, 46.
54 Office of the Aboriginal Land Commissioner, *Uluru (Ayers Rock) National Park and
Lake Amadeus/Luritja Land Claim: Report by the Aboriginal Land Commissioner, Mr.
Justice Toohey to the Minister for Aboriginal Affairs and to the Minister for Home
Affairs*, Australian Government Printing Service 1980.
55 Lisa M. Strelein, 'Indigenous people and protected landscapes in Western Australia',
(1993) 10 *Environmental Planning & Law Journal* 380, 390. (note omitted).

56 Uluṟu Kata-Tjuṯa National Park Management Plan 2010–2014, Director of National Parks (2010).
57 Ibid., 90.
58 Ibid., 92.
59 Hannah Hueneke, *To climb or not to climb? The sacred deed done at Australia's mighty heart*. Thesis. Bachelor of Arts/Science with Honours, School of Resources, Environment and Society, ANU, 2006, 36.
60 Uluṟu Kata-Tjuṯa National Park Management Plan 2010–2014, Director of National Parks (2010), 7.
61 "Where Anaŋgu have been required to go away for several weeks at a time for religious ceremonies or to honour other social or family responsibilities, Parks Australia has been able to adapt work requirements so as not to disadvantage Anaŋgu and not to affect overall park management responsibilities. The park was closed for three hours in 1987 to allow the unobserved transit through the park of Anaŋgu who were engaged in ceremonial activity. Since this time parts of the park have sometimes been closed for ceremonial reasons." Ibid. See also Department of the Environment, 'A Mark of Respect for the Passing of Senior Uluṟu Elder' Media Release, 21 September 2001 <www.environment.gov.au/archive/media/dept-mr/dp21sep01.html>
62 For a discussion of the intellectual property aspects of the case, see Kathy Bowrey, 'An Australian Perspective' in Christoph Beat Graber, Karolina Kuprecht & Jessica Lai (eds), *International Trade in Indigenous Cultural Heritage: Legal and Policy Issues* Edward Elgar 2012, 396, 412–414.
63 *Tenodi v. Blue Mountains City Council* [2011] NSWLEC 1183.
64 *Anderson v. Ballina Shire Council* [2006] NSWLEC 76; *Anderson (behalf of Numbahjing Clan within the Bundjalung Nation) v. Minister for Infrastructure Planning & Natural resources* [2006] NSWLEC 725.
65 *Anderson & Anor v. Director-General of the Department of Environment and Climate Change & Anor* [2008] NSWLEC 182, [27], [28].
66 See Kathy Bowrey, 'Economic rights, culture claims and a culture of piracy in the Indigenous art market: what should we expect from the western legal system?' (2009) 13(2) *Australian Indigenous Law Review* 35, 43; Daniel Robinson, 'Traditional Knowledge and Biological Product Derivative Patents: Benefit-Sharing and Patent Issues Relating to Camu Camu, Kakadu Plum and Açaí Plant Extracts – a discussion paper', United Nations University Traditional Knowledge Initiative (UNU-TKI) 2010, www.unutki.org/news.php?doc_id=174.
67 UNESCO, 'Decision on Australia's Great Barrier Reef Deferred until 2015' <http://whc.unesco.org/en/news/1149>
68 See generally Chris Butler, "Critical Legal Studies and the Politics of Space" (2009) 18 *Social and Legal Studies* 313, 321.
69 Laurajane Smith, 'Archeology of the Governance of Material Culture: A Case Study from South Eastern Australia' (2001) 34 (2) *Norwegian Archaeological Review* 97–105; Libby Porter, *Unlearning the Colonial Cultures of Planning* Ashgate 2010, 108–109.

Chapter 8

Protection of Sámi intangible cultural heritage and intellectual property rights and its relation to identity politics in a postcolonial Norway

Gro B. Ween

As I will show, in Norway, over the past several decades, the state has taken initiatives to decolonize Sámi areas. Compared to other parts of Sápmi, the area inhabited by the Sámi in the Northern parts of Scandinavia and the Kola Peninsula, the indigenous rights situation in Norway is progressive; rights to self-determination, culture, language and land are acknowledged. Still, as my story from the Tana Valley on the border between Norway and Finland will illustrate, protection of Sámi intangible heritage is not straightforward. I will explain the complexity of how nature and its resources figure in Sámi intangible heritage by means of the story of Anja and her family. An outline of the annual activities that her family engages in illustrates the nature–culture entanglements in Sápmi. The story displays not only cultural continuities but also the developments necessary to maintain a Sámi lifestyle.

The Sámi institutions, established within the last few decades of Sámi rights development, have been able to establish procedures to safeguard heritage and provide a level of self-management of that heritage. Nevertheless, this chapter describes three critical challenges to the protection of Sámi intangible heritage. Most significant for Sámi lives is the challenge associated with the lack of legislative and bureaucratic efforts to acknowledge Sámi nature practices as cultural heritage. The second challenge regards the effects of legislative and bureaucratic work on Sámi heritage. The third challenge relates to the postcolonial ambitions in later generations of cultural heritage conventions.

Nature practices in Sápmi

Anja is on her way out. It is late July, an early summer morning in East Finnmark, in the far north of Norway, close to the borders of both Russia and Finland. She will have to go to work at the nursing home shortly. I see her walking purposefully at great speed towards the mountaintop some kilometres behind our houses. As I do every time I see her move through the landscape, I marvel at the differences in the way she and I move. She walks straight through the small bushy birches and juniper that increasingly crowd the tundra. Anja needs no tracks but rather knows that tracks should be treated with suspicion: most likely they are made by sheep, not the most trustworthy of animals to follow. As she starts walking up hill she turns and responds to my silent question. 'I am just going to quickly check the ripening of the cloudberries. You know it's all about getting there first!'

Outside her house, there is the snowmobile, the sledge, the caravan and the ATV (all-terrain vehicle). An outdoor benchtop is made ready to clean the salmon that her husband brings back from the river at the bottom of the valley. Anja's family spends summers on the banks of the Tana River. For centuries, the start of the salmon season has signalled spring and a moratorium on all other subsistence activities. Towards the end of summer, people will start to joke about being sick of the taste of salmon. Sometimes men, but also women, will go trout fishing in the mountain lakes and come back with fat mountain trout for dinner, or they will go to the fjord and spend a week or so fishing pollock, stocking up whitefish for the coming winter. In autumn, Anja's husband and kids move reindeer from the summer grazing areas, first to the autumn- and later to the winter land. On arrival at the winter land, the reindeer are counted and selected for slaughter. For local men, the autumn season is not just about reindeer but also about moose. After the moose, the newly white grouse resting on patches of new snow become the focus of the hunt. Some weekends after Christmas, the caravan outside Anja's house is loaded onto the snowmobile sledge and driven up to a nearby mountain lake, close to the tents and caravans of friends and relatives. Entire days are spent outside in scooter clothes, ice fishing, tobogganing, skiing, grouse trapping, driving snowmobiles and hanging out. For many Sámi, this is the best time of the year. After Easter, reindeer are moved back to the coast. In the spring, people collect firewood for the winter. Then people will start waiting for the ice on the river to break up so that the salmon fishing season can begin. This cycle of events is a common, regular pattern that marks the seasons and seasonal changes for many inhabitants of Finnmark. Not everyone takes part in all these activities, but most people take part in some (Ween and Lien 2012).

Anja's family is like most families in the Sámi core areas, the areas of Sápmi where the majority of the population in some way identify as Sámi. In these areas, most people spend a considerable amount of their time engaging with nature. Here, subsistence production is not only a guarantee of cultural survival but also a necessary contribution to household budgets in a region where regular incomes are scarce, particularly for men. Hunting, fishing and gathering concerns more than food production. Anja and her mother, like most of her female relatives, knit and make leather goods, such as *nuvttohat* (reindeer fur shoes), *gákti* (the traditional Sámi costumes) and everything else that goes with it—the woven leg bands for the shoes, the silk shawls, the embroidered leather bags. Anja's father and her husband, like her grandfather before them, like the women, are *duojárs* or craft workers; they make objects such as knives from bone shafts, bowls, tools and decorative objects. Her husband, her uncles and her grandfather, among other family members, all do traditional Sámi singing—the *joik*—and some of her relatives have made considerable careers from it.

Figure 8.1 Anja's family.
Photograph by Ande Somby

New skills, needed to maintain Sámi culture and lifestyles, have also been introduced (see also Kischenblatt-Gimblett 2004: 55). Anja is a midwife with a vast knowledge of traditional medicine. She promotes home birth in a county where hospitals are few and far between. She is also dedicated to bringing to public attention the difficulties caused by mainstream Norwegian health services' lack of awareness of the need to develop cultural interfaces for Sámi patients, particularly the elderly and those in psychiatric care. Other members of her family are journalists, filmmakers and lawyers. Arguably, all do work that is necessary to maintain a Sámi way of life in Finnmark, Norway's northernmost county.

I describe Anja's family to give the reader an impression of Sámi lives, to point out that in a Sámi world, as in most indigenous worlds, cultural practices are inseparable from what we call nature: in subsistence activities such as hunting, gathering and fishing; in economic activities; in religious activities; and in crafts, such as storytelling, singing or other ongoing engagements. The skills needed to maintain cultural engagements with nature must develop and adapt and, these days, arguably include politics, journalism, law and midwifery. I will return to how Anja's year illustrates core issues of intangible heritage, but first we must consider how heritage is legally construed.

Heritage operationalized

As I have previously described, heritage work offers new opportunities for emancipation, co-management, economic development, the writing of postcolonial histories and identity politics (Ween 2002; 2006; 2010; Ween and Lien 2012; Ween and Risan 2014). One such emancipatory potential relates to the inherent reflexivity within the UNESCO system and the subsequent ongoing evolution of heritage legislation. As an example, just following one singular line of development, intangible heritage is inscribed as the third generation of heritage, brought about by the postcolonial efforts of UNESCO to self-reflectively evolve and improve and to include what was previously missing from UNESCO collection of the outstanding heritage of mankind.

This potential for reflexivity is maybe not what is normally associated with law. Anja's story hints at the difficulties of fitting indigenous practices within the structures of international law. Legal regimes have spheres of influence, outside of which what is protected becomes less significant or even invisible. Legal fixity intervenes in cultural transmission, diffusion, development and appropriation, creating ongoing debates over legitimacy and questions of ownership and authenticity (Coombe 1998), with consequences for Sámi understandings of nature, cultural knowledge, property and identity. On a larger scale, legal work twists or re-narrates context and purpose, even the ontological and epistemological framework of cultural practice in itself. Let me illustrate this with examples from Sámi heritage protection, Sámi knowledge and cultural practices.

Sámi heritage protection

Prior to 1978, cultural heritage in Norway was synonymous with historical relics of the Norwegian majority's society. The automatic protection of remains from periods prior to the year 1537 CE offered little protection to Sámi remains, as Sámi remains usually were made of organic perishable materials. In 1978, however, the Cultural Heritage Act was revised to include the automatic protection of Sámi Cultural Heritage objects and sites more than 100 years old, in acknowledgement of the perishable nature of Sámi material culture (Ween 2006; 2010; Section 4, *Lov om kulturminner*, [Cultural Heritage Act] 1978). According to Myrvoll, the revised Cultural Heritage Act manifested significant changes that had taken place in Norwegian politics concerning the Sámi people (Myrvoll et al. 2012). After the establishment of the Sámi Parliament in 1989, Sámi cultural heritage became self-managed. From a Sámi perspective, this was an important political milestone. In the coming years, extensive documentation of Sámi history and cultural heritage was initiated, contributing to the protection of Sámi lands against development and nurturing the Sámi sense of identity and belonging (Ween 2006; Myrvoll et al. 2012: 7).

As already mentioned, Sámi cultural rights have also been protected by other means. In the 1980s, national Sámi Rights processes were initialized. Next to the establishment of the Sámi Parliament, the first significant state concessions included a new paragraph in the Norwegian constitution acknowledging the state's responsibility to ensure that the Sámi are able to secure and develop their language, culture and society (§108, previously §110a). At the time, the Sámi Rights Commission emphasized that state obligations according to this constitutional paragraph could not be fulfilled without securing fundamental access to land and its resources (NOU 1984: 18).

In this time period, Norway was also, internationally speaking, at the forefront of indigenous rights development. It was the first nation to sign the Indigenous and Tribal Convention (1989), also called the ILO 169, and the first leader of the UN Permanent Forum on indigenous issues, Ole Henrik Magga, was Norwegian Sámi. Despite international recognition, Sámi legal protection within the Norwegian state has only partly been implemented. A pronounced gap remains between the grand formulations in the constitution and the larger bureaucratic machinery that constitutes its practice (Ween 2010). As has already been hinted, one significant gap concerns the significance of nature for culture.

In international legal work, this has been pronounced; for example, Article One of the UNESCO Universal Declaration on Cultural Diversity acknowledges the importance of preserving *all* kinds of heritage, the tangible, cultural and natural, and the intangible, on equal terms, recognising that cultural diversity is as necessary as for humanity as biodiversity is for nature (Kirshenblatt-Gimblett 2004: 143). It is not just that cultural and natural heritage are equally important; the two are also connected. Awareness of the significance of necessary ties between cultural and natural diversity had been confirmed on numerous occasions in international legislation, such as in the Biodiversity Convention (1992) and the UN Declaration of the Rights of Indigenous Peoples (2007; Maffi 2005: 612).

Also in Norwegian legislation, the significance of culture to nature is noted. Most significantly, the Nature Diversity Act of 2009 notes that 'although scientific knowledge shall remain the foundation for Norwegian nature management, local knowledge, and particularly Sámi knowledge should be consulted' (§8). The noted right to be consulted only pertains to the Sámi Parliament, however. Although the Sámi Parliament does make efforts to include locals, Sámi experiences of being consulted are usually restricted to partaking in short surveys, participating in meetings or having local opinions included as an attachment to scientific reports (Ween and Risan 2014). Sámi knowledge, in other words, is not consulted as expert knowledge on par with scientific contributions. This provides local knowledge with little opportunity to engage or intervene in the scientific foundation for natural resource management. The significance of nature to culture is also noted by the state in the work of the Sami Rights Commission (NOU 1997: 4). The consequences of this natureculture are, however, *not* carried through into cultural heritage work. I will illustrate this legal disconnect with two examples from core Sámi subsistence practices: salmon fishing and reindeer herding.

Salmon and reindeer

As evidenced by Anja's story, reindeer herding and salmon fishing structure the year for many in Sápmi. Besides being essential to the Sámi diet and to cultural gifting practices, these are also activities essential to Sámi identity production. Both reindeer herding and salmon fishing are sources of large fields of knowledge and specialized vocabulary about interrelations between species, that are only articulated and transferred in the course of these practices. Many of these details will disappear if reindeer herding or fishing can no longer be practiced (Magga et al. 2001). It is, as I will return to, not just parts of a vocabulary that are threatened by extinction but also a cultural way of thinking (see Oskal 1995; Sara 2004; 2009; Kuokkanen 2006; Guttorm 2011).

While the Reindeer Herding Act (2007) and its predecessor, the Reindeer Herding Act of 1978, protect reindeer herding as a Sámi industry, there is no legal protection of Sámi rights to salmon fishing nor other access to significant natural resources. The Reindeer Herding Acts must be considered with an eye to Norway's colonial history. Although the current act has decolonizing intentions, acknowledging the need to protect Sámi reindeer herding with its foundation in 'Sámi culture, tradition and customary law,' this has not always been the case. When the first reindeer herding act was introduced towards the end of the nineteenth century, it existed to protect Norwegian settler farmers from the reindeer that habitually returned to the land that was once theirs. A much later revision, that of 1978, forced industrialization upon the reindeer herding industry, hence intervening in its organization, ownership structures, herd structure, understanding of ecology and connections between reindeer and other natural and social relations, including ethical and spiritual connections between human beings and animals or other beings in nature (Oskal 1995; Sara 2004; 2009; Ween 2006). In terms of the protection of reindeer herding as intangible heritage, the various

Figure 8.2 Reindeer at summer pastures, Ifjordfjellet.

Photograph by Gro Ween

approaches of the Norwegian state through its reindeer herding legislation have obviously caused great damage, but the protection has also contributed to a living and thriving industry.

Classified as heritage, this, intervened-in, contemporary reindeer herding practice becomes problematic in terms of UNESCO expectations. In the inscription of Laponia, a World Heritage cultural site in Swedish Sápmi (UNESCO 1996) reindeer herding was articulated as one of the grounds for inscription, but with an obvious traditionalist bias. In the long description of Laponia, it was written that

> the area has been occupied continuously by the Sámi people since prehistoric times, and is one of the last and unquestionably the largest and best preserved area of transhumance, involving summer grazing by large reindeer herds, a practice that was widespread at one time and which dates back to an early stage in human economic and social development (UNESCO 1996).

Through the early years of the process of becoming a World Heritage area, reindeer owners in the Laponia area fought hard to be allowed to continue their contemporary herding practices, making use of snowmobiles and helicopters. Without these adaptations, reindeer herding could not remain a livelihood (Dahlström 2003; Green 2009; Ween 2012; Ween and Risan 2014).

Figure 8.3 Local salmon fisherman trawling on the Tana River in a locally made boat.

Photograph by Gro Ween

Much has been written about the naturecultures of Sámi relations with their reindeer. Little however has been written about the tangible and intangible heritage of Sámi salmon fishing. Salmon fishing has been practiced amongst both the coastal Sámi and the River Sámi since time immemorial. As is the case with Sámi relations with reindeer, linguistics provide evidence of immemorial intimate relations between Sámi and salmon. Sámi vocabulary contains words concerning the details of salmon physiognomy, its movements and travels that are significant to particulars of fishing in the Tana, as well as for the upkeep and development of the Sámi language. This finely tuned knowledge tradition involves intricate knowledge of the capabilities of and engagements between fish, nets, iron bars, riverbank and riverbed and the relation of all these to water and weather. In the Tana River area, this is a tradition passed on from father to child (Ween 2010; 2012). Since the 1970, Sámi salmon fisheries in the Tana have been continuously restricted by the natural resource management authorities. For many Sámi, even filling the freezer for the winter is no longer possible. While salmon fishing would occupy all local men in the summer season less than thirty years ago, many today no longer consider traditional salmon fishing a viable activity. Traditional fishing practises have changed not only as a result of Norwegian prohibitions but also as a result of new technology. The most recent tradition to disappear has been the old weirs constructed from twigs. Now, only three old men insist on maintaining this tradition. New materials have been introduced, such as nylon nets and iron bars. New materials are costly, and at the same time new restrictions make it increasingly difficult to fish with more traditional technology. Fishing restrictions only allow open nets three days a week. While nylon nets can be easily closed, this is much harder to accomplish with the wooden structures in the midst of a raging river.

While the Tana River salmon fisheries, as a result of fishing restrictions, have been outside of economic markets for more than a decade, reindeer herding is a key source of income in a region that offers few employment opportunities. Comparing these two examples, it becomes clear that while it is vital, in the present, to argue for the upkeep of traditional practices and technologies when it comes to salmon fishing, the activity must be seen in the context of its economic potential. The fact that reindeer herding has been protected as an industry has allowed it to remain a vibrant lifestyle that could be culturally revitalized with the new Reindeer Herding Act of 2007. Lack of financial opportunity has the consequence that salmon fishing is rapidly losing its emblematic position within River Sámi life worlds. And this is not because people have to make money to engage in a cultural activity, but the difficult financial situation of many people does not allow spending so much time on an activity that represents a significant expense. If the present development continues, a significant proportion of existing traditional knowledge associated with fishing will be lost. The ripple effects will not only include the loss of particular vocabulary and nature knowledge, significant food and gifting objects, all central to Sámi identity practices.

Despite the lack of awareness in natural resource management structures of the need to protect Sámi intangible heritage, this need has been acknowledged by the Norwegian Sámi Rights Commissions. As part of these very thorough and long-term decolonizing processes, Sámi local knowledge and forms of subsistence were heavily documented by expert groups for the Ministries involved in Sámi affairs (published as Norwegian Official Reports, or NOUs): NOU 1984: 14; 1997: 4; 2001: 34; 2007: 13; 2008: 5). In the most recent Sámi Rights Commission, concerning coastal fisheries in Finnmark (NOU 2008: 5), it was even stressed that if fishing rights were not secured, coastal Sámi culture would face extinction (see also Smith 2004). Still, existing environmental management of Sámi key species continues to threaten Sámi intangible heritage. Reindeer herders everywhere are losing needed grazing areas. They also suffer a considerable toll on their herds as a result of the increasing numbers of predatory species that have themselves become protected as endangered. Likewise, the Tanafjord and the river is regulated to almost nothing. Additionally, the new emphasis on nature tourism poses a threat not only to reindeer herding and salmon fishing but also to other key Sámi subsistence activities; tourists are encouraged to go into areas of the tundra used for berry picking, grouse hunting and lake fishing, activities that the Sámi and other inhabitants of Finnmark previously had to themselves (Ween 2009; 2011; Ween and Lien 2012).

These two examples illustrate that despite their key positions within Sámi life worlds, reindeer and salmon practices have remained outside the focus of state efforts to protect Sámi intangible heritage. These examples demonstrate how what could be labelled intangible heritage often ends up in situations in which different kinds of legal frameworks overlap and where other aspects of the situation at hand take priority. In the case of reindeer herding, economic viability was deemed more important than culture; in the case of salmon, natural resource management considers tourist angling more sustainable than local fishing. Caught by anglers, salmon can be released and fished again, while a fish caught by an indigenous fisherman not only dies but also does so without gaining a monetary value (Ween 2012). As I will show, efforts to protect Sámi intangible heritage, on the other hand, are focused on secondary issues to these core practices, practices that cannot survive without the continued presence of reindeer herding, salmon fishing and other hunting and gathering activities.

The work of the Intangible Heritage Convention in Norway

Let us move to what cultural heritage legislation is currently able to do for Sámi intangible heritage. According to the Intangible Heritage Convention (2003), state parties are obliged to define and identify cultural assets on their territory by creating inventories (art. 12.1), formulating heritage policy and creating bodies to carry out policy (art. 11b) and establishing institutions to support documentation of cultural assets and conduct research into how to safeguard them (art. 13b; see also Kirshenblatt-Gimblett 2004: 55). While the Norwegian state has been very active in its efforts to have tangible heritage sites inscribed on the UNESCO World Heritage list, the state has put little effort towards having intangible heritage listed.

At the same time, simply by existing, the Intangible Heritage Convention has provided Sámi with new political leverage (Ween 2006). The emphasis on the immaterial has enabled the Sámi Parliament to argue successfully against new land developments, with reference to such matters as past reindeer herding migratory routes or the cultural landscapes created by grazing reindeer in the past. State efforts towards fulfilling obligations to the Convention have also channelled funds to a number of cultural organizations engaging in particular heritage activities. Although most of these cultural activities represent the iconic Norwegian inland farming culture, the Norwegian parliamentary proposition (St.prp.) 73 (2005–2006) *'Immateriell Kulturarv i Norge'* (Intangible Cultural Heritage in Norway) acknowledges that the need for the protection of the intangible heritage of Sámi and other national minorities is greater than that for majority cultural practices. Interestingly, the proposition emphasizes that 'the aim is not to freeze the intangible heritage at a certain historical point, in such a way that it remains as unchanged as possible, but rather to see intangible heritage in a dynamic and meaningful interaction with contemporary people' (KUD 2010: 65).

To fulfill the stated obligations to protect Sámi intangible heritage, the Directorate of Cultural Heritage has channelled funding to Sámi Allaskuvla, the Sámi University College in Kautokeino, to establish a project seeking to articulate the foundations of Sámi knowledge on the basis of key cultural practices called *Arbediehtu*, meaning 'traditional knowledge' in Northern Sámi (Guttorm 2011). Means were also provided to support educational programs on reindeer herding, uses of natural resources and *duodji* (crafts), as well as to Sámi Arkiiva, to create a 'holistic documentation of Sámi civil society' including interviews, stories and joiks in Sámi, the documentation of particular historical events and all Sámi dialects and languages (KUD 2010: 66).

Aside from providing the means to nurture and vitalise existing cultural knowledge, the Norwegian state contributes funds to ensure the protection of elements of Sámi cultural heritage as Intellectual Property Rights (IPR). IPR, however only offers protection in later parts of cultural processes, when particular knowledge or cultural expressions are both set apart from the originating nature practices and considered economically valuable in themselves. For example, IPR protect Sámi intangible heritage through the organization Sami Kopiija. This non-governmental organization protects Sámi artists, composers and writers all over Sápmi by making use of the label Sámi Duodji©, certifying Sami Kopiija members and authenticating Sámi crafts for buyers. Similarly, IPR have been put into use to secure the protection of particular joiks (Gaski 2007; Lassen 1999) or Sámi ornamentation, such as the sun wheel (Guttorm 2007), from illegal commercial use. IPR have also been discussed as a measure to protect against future fears of biomedical prospecting in Sámi areas (Solbakk 2007).

The question is, however, whether funding for or protection of particular expressions of iconic activities can maintain the many heterogeneous, entangled nature–culture activities that make up Sámi intangible heritage. As Anja's story shows, cultural practices are ultimately all related. The use of intellectual property rights to protect indigenous intangible heritage has been the subject of a long-term debate, first initiated at a time when an intangible heritage convention did not seem to be a future prospect (Coombe 1998; Daes 2001). In these debates as in the case of both reindeer herding and salmon practices, discourses of authenticity represent a recurring problem. Indigenous cultural artefacts are, as Sámi professor of duodji Gunvor Guttorm (2007) points out, products in a process of cultural development that involves diffusion and appropriation and both fluidity and fixity. A related fact often noted is that in most cases the originator is unknown, and tales or stories are understood as belonging to no one individual. Stories and myths are collective property. Guttorm points out that, when connected with IPR, the knowledge or object in question is already taken out of its original context. The meaning of cultural heritage, with its complex webs of rights and obligations, does not prevail outside these circumstances. The collective opinion of renowned Sámi scholars (Guttorm 2007; Gaski 2007, Vars 2007) with regard to intellectual property rights, is in line with Coombe's and Daes's opinion that IPR manifests a European possessive individualism based upon personal property relations and that it is unable to embrace the unique relationship between indigenous people and their knowledge system. As Laila Susanne Vars (1997) argues, Sámi customary law does not easily merge with the Nordic legal system (see also Somby 1999). The differences in the legal understanding of heritage practices means that indigenous use of IPR must involve a considerable translation effort to be of use to the Sámi (Coombe 1998; Shand 2002: 68). The issue of translation will become my topic in the later parts of this text.

Culture from above and below

As the case of Sámi heritage exemplifies, Norwegian heritage bureaucracy singles out particular fields of knowledge without attending to overarching cultural practices and logics. There are several difficulties with this approach, all relating to Rosemary Coombe's point that human rights legislation seeks to protect something holistic through piecemeal legislation (1998). The narrow focus of what is to be protected is problematic in the sense that apprenticeships or other educational programs in reindeer herding training and duodji are not in themselves enough to save reindeer herding as an industry. The knowledge of such subsistence activities is so specialized that it can only be maintained by engaging in the activities themselves. It is also not just that the knowledge of species and landscapes in themselves are threatened, but as Anja's story along with the examples of salmon fishing and reindeer herding illustrated, these subsistence activities are also the foundation of a number of other kinds of knowledge and activities, including knowledge of other species, knowledge of subsistence technologies and knowledge of how to make use of what is procured, as well as understanding of the necessary engagements with animals and non-human beings (Gaski 2007; Solbakk 2007) understandings of ethics and morality (Ween 2012).

I will argue that the Sámi University College *Árbediehtu* project attempts to counter the effects of such piecemeal protection. At first paid for by the Directorate of Cultural Heritage, this pilot project could at first be seen as a tokenistic handout to Sámi intangible heritage. With Árbediehtu, meaning 'traditional knowledge,' the Sámi University College was able to frame an approach to Sámi cultural practice that encompassed a greater whole. Árbediehtu has since its early beginning expanded and aims to articulate a Sámi science as the foundation of Sámi knowledge by drawing together a wide variety of Sámi intangible culture, such as duodji, joik, storytelling, nature management and relations among humans, animals and landscapes, including this science's consequences for religion, ethics and morals (Guttorm 2011; Riseth et al., 2010, Ween and Risan 2014). The articulation of such foundational knowledge in turn is put into use to re-articulate the interaction between Sámi and Norwegian knowledge in the interfaces between Sámi and Norwegian law in areas such as cultural heritage and nature management.

Efforts to protect Sámi intangible heritage stress the importance of Norwegian legislative efforts' being adapted to fit Sámi customary law. Legal authority Laila Susanne Vars points to the potential for ontological and epistemological conflicts in the interfaces between international law and indigenous cultural knowledge practices. In response, Árbediehtu seeks to map culture *from below* by way of heritage practices, connecting practices with their knowledge foundations and carving out a new space for the articulation of ontological and epistemological difference. For example, the project illustrates the point to which this chapter has returned several times: that culture and nature are not kept apart in Sámi life worlds, and therefore they should not be kept apart in Norwegian heritage management (see also Byrne and Ween 2015). Sámi nature practices similarly stress different understandings of ownership (Magga et al. 2001). Nature used for subsistence activities is *meahcci* (Schanche 2001) – that is, land that for most practical purposes is held in common and used according to unwritten rules agreed upon by local communities (Schanche 2001; Riseth et al. 2010; Rybråten 2014).

The landscape consists not only of relationships between people which one must try to cooperate with but also with other living things (Magga et al. 2001). All relations in nature are, as Ingold (2000) has described, based upon trust, but not in a fatalist trust. As Liv Østmo has described in her work and films, people complement each to make sure that the necessary nature's work gets done. This trust has as its foundation an ongoing sharing between humans, animals and other non-humans (Ingold 2000: 69). Kuokkanen (2006) elaborates on this by use of the Sámi term *láhi* (Guttorm 2012). Láhi describes ongoing relations to nature that must be upheld. Láhi is about giving nature and what is in it its share; it is about what we receive from nature and our ability to share what we receive (Magga et al. 2001). An important sentiment is that one must be humble if lucky in hunting and fishing activities. At the same time, one must also be satisfied with bad luck (Kuokkanen 2006 in Guttorm 2012: 69).

Relationships with nature involve other kinds of causal relations. A much-repeated Sámi saying is that 'one year is not the brother of the next.' Humans cannot control nature; one must simply try to be on the good side of nature (Oskal 1995). The same inherent openness and fluidity can be found in descriptions of Sámi kinship and other kinds of human relationships (Pehrson 1957; Paine 1960). Reciprocities play a similar part in relations between people as they do between humans, animals and other-than-human beings. Gift exchange has the capacity to integrate people across differences; it is an open, transgressing practice (Lien 2001; Kramvig 2006: 177).

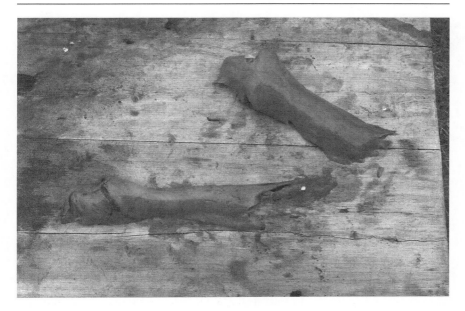

Figure 8.4 The salmon livers are used to read seasonal water flows, then the livers are re-gifted to local animal life.

Photograph by Gro Ween

Particular kinds of gifting, involving craft objects or joiks, are also enacted within similar transgressive ownership structures: it is not the creator that owns the joik or the craft made but rather the one to whom it is gifted (Guttorm 2007; Gaski 2007). This does not mean that the person who has made the joik becomes insignificant, but the gift does not imply expectations of a return gif, or a kind of confirmation of the relationship. In Sápmi there is an openness to all such relations; people may choose, or not, to confirm or further particular relations. As is the case with reciprocal relations with nature, there is no obligatory return. Multiple beginnings and ends can be brought to the heterogeneous mass of potential stories or relations to be told and retold.

Conclusion

Sámi rights in Norway have been developed through a long and thorough process. There are a number of mechanisms in place to correct for the difference between Sámi and the non-Sámi Norwegian majority, such as the Cultural Heritage Act (1978) or the Reindeer Herding Act (1978). The implementation of the Intangible Heritage Convention into Norwegian legislation (2003) provided new possibilities for the protection of Sámi heritage, initially by enabling the Sámi Parliament to argue for the protection of Sámi cultural landscapes, land and resources.

Compared to the efforts made on behalf of tangible heritage, the Norwegian state has not been active in working to have Norwegian intangible heritage, Sámi or non-Sámi, inscribed on the UNESCO Representative List. Initiatives towards supporting Sámi intangible heritage practices have been made, but these are limited and piecemeal. This also includes Norwegian initiatives with regard to IPR, which primarily protects the aspects of Sámi knowledge that interface with commercial circulations.

This chapter describes how Sámi institutions arguably work towards resisting the logic of Norwegian heritage legislation and make use of limited resources to build a more overarching and viable knowledge framework. Árbediehtu at the Sámi University College, for example, makes use of what was piecemeal funding to map and articulate heritage from below, insisting on its larger entangled relations. This initiative speaks to the fact that Sámi are not satisfied with simply having their cultural practices placed in a 'global museum.' It aspires not only to nurture and protect key Sámi cultural practices but also to articulate a larger Sámi knowledge as Sámi science, emphasizing local communities, knowledge holders and their control over their own knowledge production. Through this mapping exercise, the project is able to articulate cultural foundations, including their ontological and epistemological differences, enabling this to become a resource for Sámi knowledge production, politics or decision-making processes.

This does not mean that Sámi intangible heritage is well protected. To return to Anja's story and my examples of reindeer and salmon, this chapter emphasizes that all Sámi cultural practices, the tangible as well as the intangible, rely on a foundation of key nature practices. As Rosemary Coombe (1998: 93) points out, cultural knowledge can only be conserved by keeping it alive and in use. This cannot be achieved by the provision of limited funding for piecemeal practices. The main challenge for Norwegian intangible cultural management is to bridge the divide between cultural and natural heritage. As most Sámi cultural heritage has its foundations in relations to landscape and core animals, it is difficult to envision a way that intangible heritage can be nurtured and protected if Sámi relations with core animals cannot be maintained.

References

Aikawa, N. (2004) An Historical Overview of the Preparation of the UNESCO International Convention for the Safeguarding of the Intangible Cultural Heritage, *Museum*, 221–222: 56(1–2): 137–149.

Byrne, D. and Ween, G.B. (2015) 'Bridging Natural and Cultural Heritage', in L. Meskell (ed.), *Global Heritage: A Reader*, New York: John Wiley & Sons, Inc., 94–111.

Convention on Biological Diversity (1992) (online). Available: www.cbd.int/convention/text/default.shtml (accessed 1 April 2015).

Coombe, R. (1998) 'Intellectual Property, Human Rights and Sovereignty: New Dilemmas in International Law Posed by Recognition of Indigenous Knowledge and the Conservation of Biodiversity', *Indiana Journal of Global Legal Studies*, 6(1), 59–119.

Daes, E.I. (2001) 'Intellectual Property and Indigenous Peoples', *Proceedings of the Annual Meeting (American Society of International Law)*, 95, 143–150.

Dahlström, Å.N. (2003) *Negotiating Wilderness in a Cultural Landscape. Predators and Sámi Reindeer Herding in the Laponian World Heritage Area.* Uppsala Studies in Cultural Anthropology no. 32. Uppsala.

Gaski, H. (2007) 'Samisk musikk i verden eller verdensmusikk', in J.T. Solbakk (ed.), *Tradisjonell kunnskap og opphavsrett*, Karasjok: Callidlagadus and Samikopiia (online). Available: www.samikopiija.org/web/index.php?sladja=7&giella1=nor (accessed 1 April 2015).

Gjessing, G. (1940) *Lappedrakten. En skisse av dens opphav*, Oslo: Instituttet for sammenlignende kulturforskning.

Green, C. (2009) *Managing Laponia. A World Heritage as Arena for Sámi Ethno-Politics in Sweden.* Ph.D. Thesis, University of Uppsala.

Guttorm, G. (2007) 'Duodji – hvem eier kunnskapen og verkene?' [Duodji- Who Owns the Knowledge and the Crafts?] in J.T. Solbakk (ed.), *Tradisjonell kunnskap og opphavsrett*, Karasjok: Callidlagadus and Samikopiia (online). Available: www.samikopiija.org/web/index.php?sladja=7&giella1=nor (accessed 1 April 2015).

Guttorm, G. (2011) 'Árbediehtu – as a Concept and in Practice', in J. Porsanger and G. Guttorm (eds), *Working with Traditional Knowledge: Communities, Institutions, Information Systems, Law and Ethics*, Diedut, vol. 1, 59–73.

Ingold, T. (2000) *The Perception of the Environment*, London: Routledge.

Kalland, A. and Sejersen, F. (2005) *Marine Mammals and Northern Cultures*, Edmonton: CCI Press.

Kirke og Undervisningsdepartementet (2010) *Utredninger. Immateriell kulturarv i Norge.* Available: www.regjeringen.no/upload/KUD/Kulturvernavdelingen/Rapporter_Utredninger/Immateriell_kulturarv_i_Norge_AMBU_2010.pdf (last accessed 1 April 2015).

Kirshenblatt-Gimblett, B. (2004) 'Intangible Heritage as Metacultural Production', *Museum*, 1–2, 221–222, 52–65.

Kramvig, B. (2006) *Finnmarksbilder*, PhD. Thesis, University of Tromsø.

Kuokkanen, R. (2006) 'The Logic of the Gift – Reclaiming Indigenous Peoples' Philosophies. Re-Ethnicizing the Mind?' in T. Botz-Bornstein (ed.), *Cultural Revival in Contemporary Thought*, Amsterdam–New York: Rodopi, 251–71.

Lassen, B.S. (1999) 'On Copyright in Sami Joiks', *Scandinavian Law* (online). Available: www.scandinavianlaw.se/pdf/38-5.pdf (accessed 1 April 2015).

Lien, M. (2001) 'Likhet og verdighet. Gavebytter og integrasjon i Båtsfjord', in M.E. Lien, H. Vike and H. Lidén (eds.), *Likhetens paradokser, Antropologiske undersøkelser i det moderne Norge* [Pardoxes of Similarity. Anthropological Investigations in Modern Norway]. Oslo: Universitetsforlaget.

Lov om kulturminner, [Cultural Heritage Act] 1978.

Lov om naturmangfold [Nature Diversity Act] 2009 (§ 8).

Lov om reindrift [Reindeer Herding Act] 1978, 2007 (§4).

Maffi, L. (2005) 'Linguistic, Cultural, and Biological Diversity', *Annual Review of Anthropology*, 29, 599–617.

Magga, O.H., Oskal, N. and Sara, M.N. (2001) *Dyrevelferd i samisk kultur* [Animal Welfare in Sami Culture], Guovdageaidnu: Sámi Allaskuvla.

Myrvoll, M., Thuestad, A., Myrvoll, E.R. and Holm-Olsen, I.M. (2012) 'Unpredictable Consequences of Sámi Self-Determination: Rethinking the Legal Protection of Sámi Cultural Heritage in Norway', *Arctic Review on Law and Politics*, 3(1), 30–50.

Norwegian Constitution §108, *Sameparagrafen* [The Sámi Paragraph] §108 (previously §110a).

NOU 1984:18 *Om sameness rettstilling* [About the Rights of the Sámi]. Ministry of Local Government and Modernisation.

NOU 1993:34 *Rettigheter til land og vann i Finnmark* [The Rights to Land and Waters in Finnmark]. Ministry of Justice and Public Security.

NOU 1997:4 *Naturgrunnlaget for samisk kultur* [Nature as the Foundation for Sámi Culture]. Ministry of Justice and Public Security.

NOU 2001:34 *Samiske sedvaner og rettsoppfatninger – bakgrunnsmateriale for Samerettsutvalget* [Sámi Customary Law and Legal Perceptions – background material for the Sámi Rights Commission]. Ministry of Justice and Public Security.

NOU 2007:13 *Den nye sameretten. Utredning fra Samerettsutvalget* [the New Sámi Rights Legislation. An inquiry from the Sámi Rights Commission]. Ministry of Justice and Public Security.

NOU 2008:5 *Retten til å fiske på kysten utenfor Finnmark* [The Rights to the Fisheries on the Coast of Finnmark], Ministry of Fisheries and Coastal Affairs.

Oskal, N. (1995) *Det rette, det gode og reinlykken* [The Right and the Good and Reindeer Luck], Ph.D. thesis, University of Tromsø.

Paine, R. (1960) Emergence of a Village as a Social Unit in a Coastal Lappish Fjord. *American Anthropology*, 62(6), 1004–1017.

Parliamentary proposition (St.prp.) 73 (2005–2006) *Immateriell Kulturarv i Norge* [Intangible Cultural Heritage in Norway] (online). Available: www.regjeringen.no/ globalassets/upload/kud/kulturvernavdelingen/rapporter_utredninger/immateriell_ kulturarv_i_norge_ambu_2010.pdf [accessed 1 April 2015]

Pehrson, R. (1957) *The Bilateral Network of Social Relations in Könkämä Lapp District*, Indiana: Bloomington.

Pottage, A. and Mundy, M. (2004) *Law, Anthropology, and the Constitution of the Social: Making Persons and Things*, Cambridge: University of Cambridge Press.

Riseth, J.Å., Solbakken, J.I. and Kitti, H. (2010) *Naturbruk i Kautokeino. Fastboendes bruk av meachhi i Kautokeino kommune og konsekvenser av etablering av naturvernområder* [Uses of Nature in Kautokeino. Local Residents' Use of Meachhi in the Municipality of Kautokeino and the Consequences of the Establishment of Nature Protection Areas], Sámi Allaskuvla: Utredning 1/2010.

Rybråten, S. (2014) *'This Is Not a Wilderness. This is Where We Live.' Enacting Nature in Unjárga-Nesseby, Northern Norway*, PhD Thesis, University of Oslo.

Sara, M.N. (2004) 'Land Usage and Siida Autonomy', *Arctic Review on Law and Politics*, 3, 2138–2158.

Sara, M.N. (2009) 'Siida and Traditional Reindeer Herding Knowledge', *The Northern Review*, 30, 153–178.

Schanche, A. (ed.) (2001) *Naturressurser og miljøverdier i samiske områder: forvaltnings- og forskningsutfordringer* [Natural Resources and Environmental Values in Saami Areas: Challenges for Management and Science], Diedut: Kautokeino, Nordisk samisk institutt.

Shand, P. (2002) 'Scenes from the Colonial Catwalk: Cultural Appropriation, Intellectual Property Rights, and Fashion', *Cultural Analysis*, 3, 47–88.

Smith, C. (2004) *Samerettsutvalget- tyve år etter* [Sami Rights Commission, Twenty Years After], Innledning på Torkel Opsahls minneseminar, Norsk Senter for Menneskerettigheter.

Solbakk, A. (2007) 'Samisk mytologi og folkemedisin' [Sami Mythology and Folk Medicine], in J.T. Solbakk (ed.), *Tradisjonell kunnskap og opphavsrett*, Karasjok: Callidlagadus and Samikopiia online. Available: www.samikopiija.org/web/index. php?sladja=7&giella1=nor (accessed 1 April 2015).

Somby, A. (1999) *Juss som retorikk*, Oslo: Tano Aschoug.

UNESCO (1996) *Laponia World Heritage site* (online). Available: http://whc.unesco.org/en/list/774 (accessed 1 April 2015).

UNESCO Convention for the Safeguarding of Intangible Cultural Heritage (2003) (online). Available: http://portal.unesco.org/en/ev.php-URL_ID=17716&URL_DO=DO_TOPIC&URL_SECTION=201.html (accessed 1 April 2015).

Vadi, V. (2007) 'Intangible Heritage: Traditional Medicine and Knowledge Governance', *Journal of Intellectual Property Law*, 2(10), 682–691.

Vars, L.S. (2007) 'Hvorfor bør man og hvordan kan man bevare samenes tradisjonelle kunnskap?' [How and Why Should One Keep Sámi Traditional Knowledge?]. In J.T. Solbakk (ed.), *Tradisjonell kunnskap og opphavsrett*, Karasjohka: Callidlagadus and Samikopiia (online). Available: www.samikopiija.org/web/index.php?sladja=7&giella1=nor (accessed 1 April 2015).

Vars, L.S. (1997) Hvordan bør man og hvordan kan man bevare sameness tradisjonelle kunnskap? [Why is it important to preserve Sami traditional knowledge and how can it be done?] in J.T. Solbakk (ed), Tradisjonell kunnskap og opphavsrett, Karasjok: Callidlagadus and Samikopiia online. Available: http://www.samikopiija.org/web/index.php?sladja=&giella1=nor" www.samikopiija.org/web/index.php?sladja=&giella1=nor (accessed 1 April 2015)

Ween, G.B. (2002) *Bran Nue Dae: Indigenous Rights and Political Activism, in Kimberley, Western Australia: A Study of Indigenous Activism*. D.Phil. in Social Anthropology, Oxford University.

Ween, G.B. (2010) Making Places and Politics: Indigenous Uses of cultural Heritage Legislation in Norway and Australia. In Minnerup, G. & Solberg, P (eds.). *First World First Nations. Internal Colonisation and Indigenous Self-determination in Northern Europe and Australia*. Sussex Academic Press: Sussex.

Ween, G.B. (2006) *Sørsamiske Sedv aner: Tilnærminger til Rettighets for Ståelser* [Southern Sámi Customary Law, Approaches to Rights Perceptions], Diedut: Nordisk samisk institute.

Ween, G.B. (2011) 'Performing Indigeneity in Human-Animal Relations', in R. Ellefsen, G. Larsen and R. Sollund (eds), *Eco-Global Crimes: Contemporary and Future Challenges*, London: Ashgate, 295–312.

Ween, G.B. and Lien, M.E. (2012) 'Decolonialization in the Arctic? Nature Practices and Land Rights in the Norwegian High North', *Journal of Rural and Community Development*, 7(1), 93–109.

Ween, G.B. and Risan, L. (2014) 'Exploring Heritage Lives, Indigenous Peoples in World Heritage Sites', *Primitive tider*, 2, 55–67.

Weiss, L. (2007) 'Heritage-Making and Political Identity', *Journal of Social Archaeology*, 7(3), 413–431.

Wendland, W. (2004) 'Intangible Heritage and Intellectual Property: Challenges and Future Prospects', *Museum*, 56(1–2), 97–107, 221–222.

Acknowledgements

This article could not have been written without the kindness and generosity of the Somby family in Sirma, but also the inspiring comments from staff at Sámi Allaskuvla in Kautokeino. Also, much is owed to the editors, William Logan and Christoph Antons, for their patience and sound advice.

Chapter 9

Comparative case analysis of FPIC processes for community intellectual property rights in the Philippines

Leilene Marie C. Gallardo

There are 12 million indigenous peoples in the Philippines, or 17% of the total population, who live in and lay claim to ancestral domains totalling 5 million hectares that are overlapped by the country's remaining forest and bio-diverse areas, as well as mineral- and water-rich resources. As a result of the country's Spanish and American colonial past, the indigenous peoples suffered state exploitation of their resources, rationalized by the western concept of state ownership of resources under the "Regalian Doctrine". As a result of a long struggle, the Indigenous Peoples' Rights Act (IPRA) was passed in 1997 to correct the historical injustices suffered by the indigenous peoples.

The IPRA is the first, if not the only, progressive legislation in Asia that promotes and protects the rights of indigenous peoples' ownership over their ancestral domains and lands, their right to cultural integrity, to self-governance and to social justice. The protection of cultural integrity includes recognition of community intellectual property of indigenous knowledge systems and practices; in fact it is posited as an exception to the Intellectual Property Code of the Philippines (Peria, March 21–22 2012). As such it is a *sui generis* law for indigenous peoples because it provides for their right to practice and revitalize their own cultural traditions and customs. The nature of the right is to own, control, develop and protect the following: (a) the past, present and future manifestations of their cultures, such as but not limited to, archaeological and historical sites, artifacts, designs, ceremonies, technologies and visual and performing arts and literature, as well as religious and spiritual properties; (b) science and technology, including but not limited to human and other genetic resources, seeds, medicines, health practices, vital medicinal plants, animals, minerals, indigenous knowledge systems and practices, resource management systems, agricultural technologies, knowledge of the properties of flora and fauna and scientific discoveries; and (c) language, music, dances, scripts, histories, oral traditions, conflict-resolution mechanisms, peace-building processes, life philosophy and perspectives and teaching and learning systems, as well as the right to the restitution of cultural, intellectual and spiritual property taken without their free and prior informed consent or in violation of their laws, traditions and customs.

The safeguard for protecting community intellectual property rights is that researchers, research institutions, institutions of learning, laboratories or their agents and representatives must secure Free Prior Informed Consent (FPIC).[1]

The National Commission on Indigenous Peoples (NCIP) is the mandated agency to implement the law to protect and promote the interests and well-being of the indigenous cultural communities/indigenous peoples (ICCs/IPs) with due regard to their beliefs, customs, traditions and institutions. The NCIP, in protecting the intellectual property rights of the communities, are to act in accordance with the principle of first impression first claim, the Convention on Biodiversity, the Universal Declaration of Indigenous Peoples' Rights and the Universal Declaration of Human Rights.

An analysis of four indigenous peoples' communities in the exercise of their right to their ancestral domains and to Free Prior Informed Consent (FPIC) over their community intellectual property is the subject of this chapter.

1   The first case is an ethnobotanical documentation of the ancestral domain of Bakun, peopled by the Kanakaney-Bago indigenous peoples located in the northern part of the Philippines, specifically within the province of Benguet. A Certificate of Ancestral Domain (CADT) was issued to the community in 2002 by the NCIP. The case looks into the process of how their peoples' organization, the Bakun Indigenous Tribal Organization (BITO), negotiated for local government and national agency support and recognition of their community intellectual property rights over their plant resources as a result of ethno-botanical documentation, as contained in a Memorandum of Agreement (MOA). This is hereinafter to be referred to as the Bakun Case.

2   The second case is similarly situated, relating to an FPIC process on bio-prospecting and drug discovery in the ancestral domain of the Aetas, a Negrito people in Kanawan, Bataan Province, where the proponent and the community agreed on a co-ownership of the intellectual property rights as embodied in an MOA, hereinafter to be referred to as the Kanawan case (NCIP 2004, September 21).

3   The third case is a negotiated agreement as contained in a Memorandum of Agreement pursuant to the 2012 Protection and Promotion of Indigenous Knowledge Systems and Practices (IKSP) and Customary Laws Research and Documentation Guidelines, between the publisher university, the author and the Bukidnon indigenous peoples from three areas called Garangan, Masaroy and Agcalaga Calinog, located in Iloilo, which is the largest Province of the Western Visayas. Incidentally 4% of the total population of Iloilo are indigenous peoples. The three areas were issued a Certificate of Ancestral Domain Title (CADT). This case shall hereinafter be referred to as the Calinog case.

4   The last case relates to the indigenous peoples of Kabayan, the Ibaloi-Kankanaey-Kalangoya indigenous peoples, located within the province of Benguet. The case concerned state declaration of the Kabayan Mummies as a heritage site, which vests ownership with the national government museum

as well as the subsequent proclamation of Mt Pulag, their sacred mountain, as a protected area. The declarations occurred fifty-one and twenty-eight years respectively prior to the passage of the IPRA, hence the absence of any consultation with the community. Apart from those declarations are other overlapping pieces of state legislation depriving the indigenous peoples of access to their resources. In 2005, the Kabayan were issued a Certificate of Ancestral Domain Area Title (CADT). Overlapping and conflicting laws, notwithstanding the issuance of their CADT, have caused land and legal conflict between the indigenous peoples and the local government units on the one hand and the national agencies on the other over management and access to the resources.

Case discussion

The Bakun and the Kanawan cases were undertaken under the February 19, 2002, NCIP Administrative Order No. 3, Series of 2002, which pertains to FPIC in connection with applications for programs/projects/plans/businesses or investments that do not involve issuance of licenses, permits, agreements or concessions but require the Free Prior Informed Consent of indigenous peoples in Ancestral Domain Areas. The latter applies when there is no endorsing agency, meaning the application becomes a direct application for FPIC.

The guidelines covered, among others, research on indigenous systems, knowledge and practices related to forestry, watersheds and resource management systems and technologies, medical and scientific concerns, bio-diversity and bio-processing, including the gathering of biological and genetic resources.

The Calinog Case is the first FPIC undertaken under the 2012 Indigenous Knowledge Systems and Practice (IKSP) Guidelines and Customary Laws and Research and Documentation. The Guidelines cover all research such as academic, social research and research in aid of policy pertaining to the provisions on community intellectual property rights under the IPRA. Biological and genetic prospecting and commercial research are covered by the 2012 FPIC guidelines and related processes.[2] The IKSP guidelines provide that indigenous knowledge systems are *sui generis*, that there be an MOA to embody the result of a negotiation for monetary and non-monetary benefits such as royalties or user fees, as well as a community process of validation of the research output, negotiated between the researcher and the community; ownership rights by the community to the documentation and research, whether published or communicated in any medium, is also provided.

The Kabayan case illustrates how the State through various proclamations dispossessed the community of their right to their lands, including their sacred and burial sites. Even with the issuance of their ancestral domain title, their full claim and management over their resources has been a constant struggle with national agencies.

The Bakun case

A CADT was issued to the indigenous community of Bakun, covering 29,449.3449 hectares, and registered on October 10, 2007.

The land and natural resources, including the spiritual dimension as a whole, defines the ancestral domain of the indigenous peoples and is considered as common property, or collectively owned by the Kankanaey-Bago. The land resource is "saguday" or inheritance from ancestors, passed on from generation to generation, and is to be nurtured as their ancestors did. Part of the conservation and protection of the environment is the belief that deities and spirits (*anitos*) guard the environment, and if they are disturbed, this results in sickness; this is where the living mediums for deities and spirits, called the *Mansip-oc* or *Mankutom*, perform rituals to cure ailments. The uses of the medicinal plants are known to the elders of the community, but the *mani-ilot*, or traditional healer, is the expert on their application.[3]

On 30 June 2004, a Memorandum of Agreement was signed for the Documentation of Biodiversity and Ethnobotanical[4] Knowledge in Bakun, Benguet, between the Department of Environment and Natural Resources (DENR), the Department of Agriculture-Cordillera Highland Agricultural Resources Management (DA-CHARMP), the Benguet State University, Benguet State University-Highland Agricultural Resources Research and Development Consortium, World Agroforestry Center, the University of the Philippines-Baguio City and the National Commission on Indigenous Peoples (NCIP).

The ethnobotany documentation was a replication of a process facilitated in Lakewood, Zamboanga del Sur, among the indigenous community of the Subanen. The stages involved in ethnobotanical documentation as carried out in Lakewood were as follows: (1) consensus building of stakeholders; (2) technical preparation of the documentation team; (3) data gathering; (4) alphanumeric and digital data processing; (5) production of informational materials; and (6) registering finished products with the appropriate Intellectual Property Rights Office (Sumingit, p. 2).

The NCIP-Cordillera Administrative Region recommended the protection of the community intellectual property rights over the indigenous knowledge systems and practices of the indigenous community as provided in the Indigenous Peoples' Rights Act or Republic (IPRA) Act 8371. Prior to the ethnobotany documentation, there were several community and inter-agency discussions on the IPRA provision on community intellectual property rights and the FPIC in relation to the prevailing laws on intellectual property rights, such as the copyright and patent law. The participation of other government agencies with mandates for conserving, protecting and developing environmental resources, including the local government unit of Bakun, was undertaken.[5] The Kanankaney-Bago indigenous community in Bakun, represented by the Bakun Indigenous Tribes Organization (BITO), expressed their interest and at the same time apprehension as to how the information collected could be owned by the community. The BITO is composed of the "Papangoan" or Council of Elders/leaders of the Bakun community.

It was realized that the concept of community intellectual property rights (CIPR) as provided in the IPRA was "sui generis" and the indigenous knowledge systems and practices of the indigenous peoples could not be the subject of ownership under the prevailing national laws on Patenting and Copyright. The FPIC under the IPRA served as the means of recognizing CIPR, resulting in an MOA providing for its recognition and protection by government agencies.

Finally, after discussion among the elders, and as embodied in the MOA, among others, the BITO, in ensuring preservation of their cultural traditions and customs for the benefit of the community under Section 32 of the IPRA, communicated their need for support in the documentation of their plant biodiversity and ethnobotanical knowledge. The BITO waived the FPIC only for the ethno-botanical documentation, since the same would be made part of the BAKUN Ancestral Domain Sustainable Development Protection Plan (ADSDPP).[6] However, the FPIC would have to be obtained among others on the release of any information derived from the study or for commercial purposes.

The MOA then contained the following relevant provisions in sum:

> BITO as representative of the Bagu-Kankanaey tribe was responsible for ensuring that all aspects of the documentation was made known to the community, to organize a documentation team, to be the owner and sole repository of the documented ethno-botanical study, and as custodian to be the body authorized to release information on the data of the study upon written request by interested parties to the MOA.

All assisting government agencies, including the NCIP, in recognition of the CIPR of the community, made themselves responsible and accountable for any breach of the following provisions of the MOA, such as:

1   to ensure that the Indigenous Peoples Rights were observed and respected and to provide translations of relevant documents into a format understandable to the majority of the community;
2   to help establish a mechanism for securing the full ownership and control of the community in the use of the findings of the documentation process;
3   to endorse all persons acting on its behalf for the community and to detail the extent of representation and activities in order to prevent unscrupulous persons from using the terms therein to steal indigenous knowledge for their own purposes;
4   to ensure that no biological specimens or genetic resources leave the area without the FPIC of the community;
5   to recommend options to the community for securing benefits from any future commercial or beneficial use of data obtained from the study;
6   to keep in full confidence the results of the documentation and secure the FPIC of the community if the results are to be shared with any individual or entity, whether or not such sharing is in accordance with contracts with third persons.

7   The assisting organizations agree in recognition of the communities' intel-
     lectual property rights to give full and complete information in case of any
     development of any portion of the documentation or a derivative therefrom.
8   The rights of the Bago-Kankanaey indigenous community are not deemed
     waived or compromised by the MOA.

In order to make the MOA binding, it was decided by BITO and NCIP to push
for local legislation for the MOA. The local province and municipality represented by the governor and mayor respectively were requested to be made part
of the MOA. The local municipal government of Bakun, represented by the local
mayor, supported the MOA by ratifying the same in a legislative Resolution num-
bered 232–2004 but stated that they be made co-owner and co-repository of the
information. As a result of the documentation the provincial government, with
a mandate to review resolutions of the municipal government, also ratified the
Memorandum of Agreement through legislative Resolution No. 05–46, under
its mandate in Section 447(vi) to protect the environment and impose appropriate penalties for acts which endanger the environment, such as dynamite fishing
and other forms of destructive fishing, illegal logging and smuggling of logs and
smuggling of natural resources, products and endangered species and fauna.

The documentation was finished but the digital processing of the documentation was not continued for lack of funding. It was also agreed with the assisting
facilitator that the indigenous names and uses of the plant species would be submitted for digital processing, but not the scientific names, to protect the traditional
knowledge.

To date the establishment of a community registry has yet to be completed.

The Aetas case

The focus of this case is on the FPIC process by the Aeta people regarding research
on biodiversity and drug discovery. Although the Aetas were dispossessed from
their ancestral domain because of the State declaring their area as the Bataan
National Park, their right to FPIC was recognized and respected by the local government unit and the proponents because of their rich traditional knowledge of
their medicinal plants.

The Aetas were forcibly relocated to an area called Sitio Kanawan as a result
of the declaration of their ancestral domain as the Bataan National Park. Subsequently, in 1987, by virtue of Presidential Proclamation 192, Kanawan was
declared as a Negrito Reservation area, covering 165 hectares, and issued a Certificate of Land Ownership Application (CLOA) by the Department of Agrarian
Reform in the same year. As a result, Kanawan was segregated from the 23,688
hectare Bataan National Park, declared under Presidential Proclamation 192, also
in 1987. The Aetas' application, which remains pending with the NCIP, is for
the return of their ancestral domain, covering an area of 10,970 hectares, 50% of
which is within the Bataan National Park (Regpala 2010).

The proponents in this case are the University of the Philippines and Michigan State University. The project is intended to serve as the pilot study for succeeding projects by the University in other areas in the Philippines, such as in Marinduque, Samar, Bohol and the Palawan underground River.

Initially, the proponents were complying with the provisions of EO 247 Prescribing Guidelines and Establishing a Regulatory Framework for the Prospecting of Biological and Genetic Resources, their By-Products and Derivatives, for Scientific and Commercial Purposes and other Purposes managed by the Department of Environment and Natural Resources. After several consultations, they were informed by the NCIP in the area that they had to comply with the FPIC process under the IPRA, a process which they realized was different from EO 247. The endorsing agency was the local Protected Area Management Board (PAMB)[7] of the Bataan National Park.

The project was funded by the US National Institute of Health, the National Science Foundation (NSF) and the US Department of Agriculture (USDA) under the International Cooperative Biodiversity Groups and was a 2-year exploratory/planning phase as a prelude to assessing feasibility for requesting a 5-year research grant from the ICBG.

The 2-year exploratory project was aimed at surveying Philippine biodiversity, with emphasis on medicinal plants, as well as on microorganisms found in various terrestrial and aquatic environments, with the following objectives: to establish intellectual property and commercial research agreements between the MSU and UP in accordance with Executive Order 247 and the Wildlife Act; to document, collect, screen and analyze poorly-studied medicinal plants listed in the Philippine Registry of Medicinal Plants and Herbs or identified as traditionally used by indigenous herbalists; and to determine the complexity of terrestrial and marine microbial communities and other organisms using various molecular techniques.

In view of the various consultations previously conducted by the proponents, the NCIP decided to validate the process instead of going through a new process under the FPIC Guidelines. The validation report confirmed the conduct of consultation and community consensus towards achieving a signed MOA.

It was affirmed by the NCIP that a total of 13 consultations were undertaken with the Aetas of Kanawan, and in a validation process conducted by the NCIP in a community assembly the Aetas affirmed that they understood the content of the Memorandum of Agreement. The assembled Aetas were asked by NCIP to sign and thumbmark an authority for their leaders to sign the MOA on their behalf and that of their indigenous peoples organization, called the *Samahan ng Katutubong Negritos ng Kanawan* (SAKANEKAN). Further, a community Resolution[8] affirming their approval of and consent to the project was submitted to the NCIP.

The Certificate Precondition was issued by the NCIP on June 18, 2005, in Quezon City, affirming the MOA.

Among the more important provisions was co-ownership of the intellectual property rights and that patents on drugs derived from traditional medicine plants of the Kanawan Aetas by the University of the Philippines (UP) and the Michigan State University (MSU) should provide benefits to the Aetas.

The royalty shares from patents on such drugs derived from the traditional medicinal plants of the Kanawan Aetas are based on the International Cooperative Biodiversity Groups (ICBG) accepted rates involving similar projects, with royalties to be split between the Kanawan Aetas, MSU and UP as follows, after costs for patent expenses are recovered: Aetas 40%, MSU 30%, UP 30%.

The provisions on Intellectual Property Protection state that the MSU shall control pursuit of intellectual property rights in the United States for any intellectual property arising out of this project. Prosecution costs for such protection in the United States shall be paid by MSU but shall be recovered out of any licensing fees prior to royalty distribution as outlined in the MOA. The UP shall control pursuit of intellectual property rights in the Philippines for any intellectual property arising out of this project. Prosecution costs for such protection in the Philippines shall be paid by UP but shall be recovered out of any licensing fees prior to royalty distribution as outlined in Section I. (2) and I. (3) of the MOA, and finally the intellectual property protection and cost sharing for such protection in countries other than the United States and the Philippines shall be deducted by mutual agreement among the parties.

On the one hand, the Aetas agreed to be responsible for assisting and cooperating with UP and MSU researchers regarding sample collection and sharing of traditional knowledge on medicinal plants. In addition, the proponents agreed to be responsible for implementing measures for the protection of the IP rights and values of the Kanawan Aetas, such as the respect of customary laws, practices and tradition and community ownership of ancestral domains/land. However, based on available funds UP, to be assisted by MSU, is to be responsible for among other things a census of the residents of Kanawan Negritos Reservation, for conducting and recording a genealogy survey, for determination of the socio-cultural development index before and after the project, and the empowerment of the community through education and capability building. Further, again based on available funds, UP and MSU shall again provide specific measures among other things for the conservation/protection of the ancestral domain of Kanawan Aetas such as assistance in the formulation of a sustainable development plan for the Kanawan Negritos Reservation and the ancestral domain.

Noteworthy is that MSU, in concert with UP, shall be responsible for a survey of the abundance of relevant species prior to collection, the collection of minimal amounts of species, particularly those that are of low abundance in the area, and ensuring that the collection of plant parts will not endanger the life of any threatened species.

Kabayan case

Etched in the minds of the indigenous peoples of Kabayan is a history of dispossession as a result of state legislation, starting with the granting of permits to big logging concessionaries who conducted logging from 1950–1972 in six local areas (ONKASKA-IPO 2006: 12). In fact, it was during the logging activities that the caves containing the Kabayan mummies were discovered. As a result of the logged-off areas, there was massive erosion, water shortage and flooding in Kabayan. In 1987, without community consultation, 35% of Kabayan was declared a National Integrated Protected Area (NIPAS), and President Corazon Aquino then declared Mt. Pulag, the communities' sacred site, as a National Park.

It was only in 2005 that the long-fought struggle of the Ibaloi, Kankanaey and Kalangoya indigenous communities for recognition of possession by the communities since time immemorial resulted in the NCIP issuing a CADT, covering an area of 27,252 hectares. The CADT was supported by the local government council by its passing legislative Resolution No. 172 for the recognition of Kabayan as an Ancestral Domain. The body further passed Resolution No. 34–06 requesting then-President Gloria Macapagal Arroyo to return and recognize the Mt. Pulag National Park to the municipal government of Kabayan and its people.

In an interview with the municipal Mayor Faustino M. Aquisan[9] and the elder/leader and indigenous mandatory representative of the indigenous peoples' organization, Mr. James Arroco, (Arroco 2014), the IP elder stated that the national government, apart from exploiting their domain, also stole the rights of the ICC/IPs of Kabayan as the rightful owners of their mummies by declaring them as national treasures without the consent of the people. This is because the community is spiritually connected to their dead, in a sense that a man has two souls, the *adia* and the *kaanjongan*. The adia spirit travels, and should any misfortune befall it while it is out of the body, the person either gets sick or dies. The *kaanjongan* is the lifeline or guardian spirit which goes to Mt. Pulag at death. (ONKASKA-IPO citing 2006 LeBar, Frank, Ethnic Group of Insular South east Asia 1978: 90). Mt. Pulag is a sacred site and is believed to be the resting place of their ancestors.

Calinog case

A CADT was issued on January 22, 2005, to the indigenous peoples covering 1,748.8972 hectares. An MOA was based on the NCIP 2012 IKSP and Customary Law Research Guidelines.

The Memorandum of Agreement between the University of the Philippines (UP), Dr. Alicia P Magos, Professor Emeritus, University of the Philippines in the Visayas, and the indigenous cultural communities/indigenous peoples (ICCs/IPs) of *barangays* Garangan, Masaroy and Agcalaga of the municipality of Calinog, lloilo, among others, states that:

1   The Certificate of Ancestral Domain Title (CADT) issued by the National Commission on Indigenous Peoples (NCIP) is based on evidence of their ethnicity by the oral tradition known as the Sugidanon Epic. The Sugidanon is one of the indigenous knowledge systems and practices and is owned by

the ICCs/IPs as their collective property and an inherent part of their cultural patrimony. They voluntarily and freely gave their consent to the publication of the work to the first party for the nurturing of indigenous education and preservation of their cultural heritage.[10]

2   The author and the ICC/IP community agreed that they shall have moral rights over the work, which shall include the right to claim authorship of the work, the right to the integrity of the work and the right to object to distortion, mutilation or unauthorized alteration of the work. The publisher shall ensure that these moral rights are upheld;

3   The sharing of the royalties shall be as follows: 85% of the net receipt of sales shall be given to UP as publisher, 7.5% of the gross sales to Dr. Magus and 7.5% of the gross sales to the IP communities;

4   The publisher shall render consultancy or technical services to the IP community and render technical assistance in the formulation of their community royalty development plan (CRDP), and lectures or workshop on the development of programs such as preparation of reports and project proposals, among others;

5   The IP community shall exclusively utilize its share of the royalties for programs and projects that will redound to the well-being and benefits of the ICCs/IPs in accordance with their CRDP.

6   The author and IP community grant the publisher the exclusive right to publish the works established in this agreement through the UP Press, not only in the Philippines but also even in other territorial jurisdictions, including the right to reproduce, reprint, republish, distribute, display, transmit, store or sell the said works in all forms, formats, and media, whether now known or hereafter developed and to administer requests for licensing by other parties, subject only to the sharing of royalties thereof. The right to publish of the FIRST PARTY entails the restriction/prohibition of any author to have the works established in this Agreement published elsewhere in any format or media without its express consent;

7   The author and the IP community authorize the publisher to use the works for its teaching, research and extension tasks, including the use thereof in course packs, e-learning/online courses.

This is the first negotiated agreement undertaken under the 2012 IKSP Guidelines. The term "moral rights" is not specified as such under the IKSP guidelines but essentially adapted from the Intellectual Property Rights Law. Notwithstanding the sale of the publication, to date the provision on royalty shares has not yet been implemented, perhaps because the community royalty development plan (CRDP) is not yet in place. Further, there has not yet been any monitoring by the NCIP on the implementation of the agreement.

There has yet to be an established Registry of IKSP and Customary Law by NCIP as a depository of all ethnographic information, research and documentation under the guidelines.

Challenges and lessons

In the Philippines, there are layers of legal frameworks defining property regimes and, hence, distinct types of "management" by the state, by its agencies and by private citizens that are contrary to the indigenous peoples' worldview of customary and collective ownership over their land and now even over their community intellectual property rights. The situation has become problematic because the different regimes operate over the same piece of land/domain or community intellectual property right as defined under the IPRA. The conflict is that state laws, including the newly enacted National Cultural Heritage Act of 2009, are grounded in the western concept of treating domains/lands and community intellectual property rights as objects and subject to appropriation, hence to be regulated, conserved and protected, whereas the IPRA defines the concept of ownership as spiritual in nature because domains and resources are the material bases of their cultural integrity, considered as private but community property belonging to all generations, and thus cannot be sold, destroyed or disposed of. This is related to sustainable resource use.

The National Cultural Heritage Act of 2009 specifically provides that as far as indigenous properties are concerned, the appropriate cultural agency, in consultation with the National Commission on Indigenous Peoples, shall establish a program and promulgate regulations to assist indigenous people in preserving their particular cultural and historical properties. The IRR under Section 35(f) states that the National Commission on Indigenous peoples on behalf of the country's indigenous peoples shall coordinate with the national agencies on matters pertaining to cultural property under its jurisdiction. As defined, cultural property shall refer to all products of human creativity by which a people and a nation reveal their identity, including churches, mosques and other places of religious worship, schools and natural history specimens and sites, whether public or privately owned, movable or immovable and tangible or intangible. The definition of cultural property approximates the definition under the IPRA of what are considered as CIPR. However, while the intent of the Heritage Act is to conserve and protect for the nation, but treats the cultural property as objects, the intent of the IPRA is to emphasize the significance of the collective, spiritual and life-giving importance of the CIPR to the indigenous peoples.

The 2012 FPIC Guidelines provides for no-go zones for any activity except for the exclusive purposes for which they are identified, *viz* sacred grounds and burial sites of indigenous communities, identified international and local cultural and heritage sites, critical areas identified or reserved by the ICCs/IPs for special purposes and other areas specifically identified by ICCs/IPs in their ADSDPP.

The provisions on cultural property and the no-go zones have yet to be properly mapped out and recognized by other concerned agencies. The most crucial aspect is the dearth of culturally appropriate programs and projects for indigenous communities to provide incentives for them to preserve and conserve the no-go zones while improving their economic status and benefiting the entire nation in the process, since the no-go zones are the only remaining areas rich in biodiversity.

The FPIC is a special measure to protect the right to CIPR. Specifically, the FPIC process results in a legally binding document, in which the proponent, in recognizing collective/community ownership over the physical resources of the domain, must include intellectual ownership by the community over its IKSP. Further, the MOA also legally binds the community in relation to legal representation, responsibilities/accountabilities of the proponent and the community and all other stakeholders on the manner of access of the proponent to traditional medical knowledge (TMK), the manner of the benefit-sharing agreement, the percentage of the profits that goes to the community and the commitment of the proponent to non-monetary benefits.

However, it goes against customary law to declare the proponent as well as the local government unit as co-owners, since the proponent is not a member of the community and the local government unit has a totally different personality from the community. The proponent can only be a partner for a prospective commercial agreement.

Despite the attempt of one community not to reveal the indigenous names and uses of a plant species to prevent exploitation, it is very apparent that the community lacks the technical know-how as far as assessing the value of their traditional knowledge, such as raw materials and, for instance, understanding and monitoring the technical development of their traditional knowledge into a drug. It is also left to the proponent(s) to develop and enforce the intellectual property within and outside the country. At the same time, there exists no mechanism for technically enabling the community or NCIP with oversight powers to monitor this aspect of the project.

There must be a more practical complaints mechanism for the beneficiaries and proponent(s) that can address issues and concerns to be taken cognizance of by local and international bodies. The IPRA has penal provisions on violations of rights, but again the mechanism to prosecute is under the jurisdiction of another branch of government, namely the judiciary not the NCIP. Perhaps a special court for handling CIPR could be established.

There is a need to interface with international bodies regarding mechanisms such as the FPIC and standards for safeguarding databases on TMK so that they cannot be mis-appropriated and rendered as non-patentable or regarded as prior art.

In both cases, the documentation is linked to the development of the community/domain as contained in an Ancestral Domain Sustainable Development Protection Plan (ADSDPP) or community plan to maintain the biodiversity of the community. The importance of the ADSDPP as a tool in protecting CIPR should be highlighted in all documentation and utilization endeavours.

Notes

1 Section 15. Protection and Promotion of Indigenous Knowledge Systems and Practices (IKSPs). "The following guidelines, inter alia, are hereby adopted to safeguard the rights of IPs to their indigenous knowledge systems and practices:

  a) The ICCs/IPs have the right to regulate the entry of researchers into their ancestral domains/lands or territories. Researchers, research institutions, institutions of

learning, laboratories, their agents or representatives and other like entities shall secure the free and prior informed consent of the ICCs/IPs, before access to indigenous peoples and resources could be allowed;
b) A written agreement shall be entered into with the ICCs/IPs concerned regarding the research, including its purpose, design and expected outputs;
c) All data provided by the indigenous peoples shall be acknowledged in whatever writings, publications, or journals authored or produced as a result of such research. The indigenous peoples will be definitively named as sources in all such papers;
d) Copies of the outputs of all such research shall be freely provided to the ICC/IP community; and
e) The ICC/IP community concerned shall be entitled to royalty from the income derived from any of the research conducted and resulting publications.

To ensure effective control of research and documentation of their IKSPs, the IPOs' initiatives in this regard shall receive technical and financial assistance from sources of their own choice".
2 NCIP Administrative Order No. 3, Series of 2012.
3 Betaa, A. (2012, April 18). Interview. (L. M. Gallardo, Interviewer) Baguio City.
4 Ethnobotany refers to the field of study that examines the interaction between human societies and the plant kingdom, especially how indigenous peoples perceive, manage, and utilize the plants around them (Cotton 1996). Like most fields of studies, ethnobotany is multidisciplinary in nature, involving not only scientists from the fields of anthropology, botany, forestry, and other related sciences but also community members, especially their herbalists, and support organizations. (Sumingit, 2006, p. 7)
5 Participating and assisting agencies and signatories to the MOA included the Department of Environment and Natural Resources (DENR), Department of Agriculture-Cordillera Highland Agricultural Resources Management (DA-CHARMP), Benguet State University, Benguet State University-Highland Agricultural Resources Research and Development Consortium, World Agroforestry Center and the University of the Philippines-Baguio City.
6 "RULE VIII Part II, Section 2 of the IRR of the IPRA. Preparation and Adoption of Ancestral Domains Sustainable Development and Protection Plans (ADSDPP). With the assistance of the NCIP, the ICCs/IPs concerned shall prepare their own ADSDPP in accordance with their customary practices, laws and traditions. The ADSDPP shall contain the following basic information:

a) Manner by which the ICCs/IPs will protect the domains;
b) Kind or type of development programs adopted and decided by the ICCs/IPs, in relation to livelihood, education, infrastructure, self governance, environment, natural resources, culture and other practical development aspects;
c) Basic community policies covering the implementation of all forms of development activities in the area; and
d) Basic management system, including the sharing of benefits and responsibilities among members of the concerned ICC/IP community.

All ADSDPPs shall be disseminated among community members in any mode of expression appropriate to the customs and traditions of the ICCs/IPs including, but not limited to, writings in their own language, oral interactions, visual arts, and analogous modes.
The ICCs/IPs shall submit to the municipal and provincial government unit having territorial and political jurisdiction over them their ADSDPP in order for the said LGU to adopt and incorporate the same in the Municipal Development Plan, Municipal Annual Investment Plan, Provincial Development Plan, and Provincial Annual Investment Plan.

Section 3. Basic Steps in the Formulation of an ADSDPP. For purposes of ensuring the authenticity and effectiveness of the Plan, the community members, through their PO and/or Council of Elders, and with the assistance of the NCIP, shall follow the following basic steps in the formulation process:

a) Information Dissemination. The Council of Elders/Leaders, with the assistance of the NCIP, shall conduct intensive information-dissemination on the Indigenous Peoples Rights Act (IPRA) among the community members. For the purpose of information-dissemination, the NCIP may engage the services of an authorized NGO or IPO;

b) Baseline Survey. The Council of Elders/Leaders, with the assistance of the NCIP, shall conduct a participatory baseline survey of the ancestral domain focusing on the existing population, natural resources, development projects, land use, sources of livelihood, income and employment, education and other concerns. For the purpose of the baseline survey, the NCIP may engage the services of an authorized NGO or IPO;

c) Development Needs Assessment. The Council of Elders/Leaders, with the assistance of the NCIP, shall conduct workshops in every village within the ancestral domain to determine the will of the community members regarding the kind of development the community should pursue in terms of livelihood, education, infrastructure, self-governance, environment, natural resources, culture and other aspects. For the purpose of the Development Needs Assessment, the NCIP may engage the services of an authorized NGO or IPO;

d) Formulation of Ancestral Domain Sustainable Development and Protection Plan (ADSDPP). The concerned ICC/IP, through its IPO and/or Council of Elders, and with the assistance of the NCIP, shall formulate its Ancestral Domain Sustainable Development and Protection Plan;

e) Validation of ADSDPP. With the assistance of the NCIP, the IPO and/or Council of Elders shall conduct assemblies among the ICC/IP members for the validation and approval of the ADSDPP;

f) Submission of ADSDPP to NCIP. Upon validation and approval, the IPO and/or the Council of Elders shall submit the ADSDPP to the NCIP for their information and concurrence. The ADSDPP shall form part of the data base on ICC/IP communities in the country, in relation to development projects, programs and activities within the ancestral domain, which the NCIP is mandated to establish.

7 Created by virtue of Republic Act 7586 otherwise known as the National Integrated Protected Areas System (NIPAS) Act of 1992 provides the legal framework for the establishment and management of protected areas in the Philippines. The law defines protected areas as the identified portions of land and/or water set aside by reason of their unique physical and biological significance, managed to enhance biological diversity and protected against destructive human exploitation. The NIPAS Act requires the creation of a respective Protected Area Management Board (PAMB), which is a multi-sectoral and decision making body for each of the protected area established under the NIPAS. Also, in PAMB Resolution No. 5, Series of 2003, the proponents were asked to adhere to Section 4–8 of DENR Administrative Order No. 96–20, *viz* SECTION 5 C BIOPROSPECTING WITHIN ANCESTRAL LAND,

DOMAIN AND LOCAL COMMUNITIES

5.1. Prospecting of biological and genetic resources within areas of local communities, including ancestral lands and domains of Indigenous Cultural Communities/Indigenous Peoples (IPs) shall be allowed only with the prior informed consent of such communities obtained through the procedures prescribed under Section 7 hereof.

5.2. The government agency concerned in the areas, including the PAMBs in Protected Areas (PAs), shall see to it that the consent required is obtained in accordance with the customary traditions, practices and mores of the concerned communities and, where appropriate, concurrence of the Council of the Elders in a public consultation/meeting in the site concerned.

6.1.3. Prennlior Informed Consent (PIC) Certificate obtained in accordance with Section 7 hereof from the following:

a) Indigenous Cultural Communities/Indigenous Peoples (IPs) in cases where the prospecting of biological and genetic resources will be undertaken within their ancestral domains/lands.

8 Resolusyon Bilang Serye CY 2005 (Resolution Number Series).

9 Arroco, F. M. (2014, May 31). Issues and Concerns about Mt Pulag and the Kabayan Mummies as Heritage. (L. M. Carantes-Gallardo, Interviewer)

10 There are only a few remaining culture -bearers of the indigenous peoples of Bukidnon with the role of recounting their epic. The written epic is a way of preserving the history of the community before it disappears.

Bibliography

(ONKASKA-IPO), O.N. (2006) *Ancestral Domain Sustainable Development and Protection Plan (ADSDPP)*, Benguet: Provincial Government of Benguet, Local Government of Kabayan, NCIP.

BITO Organization funded by the ILO-INDISCO (1998) *A Baseline Survey Report on the Kankanaey-Bago Ancestral Domain in Bakun, Benguet*, Bakun, Benguet, 38–141.

Cotton, C.M. (1996) Ethnobotany: Principles and Application, John Wiley and Sons: New York.

NCIP (2004) *Application for FPIC in Connection with the University of Michigan State University and the University of the Philippines on Biodiversity and Drug Development*, September 21, Quezon City: NCIP.

Peria, A.E. (2012). Paper Presented: An Overview of Philippine Initiatives and Policy on the Sui Generis Protection of Traditional Knowledge and Biological Resources. *National Forum on Intellectual Property and Traditional Knowledge*, 3, March 21–22. Manila. (unpublished)

Regpala, Elena, B.M. (2010) *Philippine Indigenous Peoples and Protected Areas*, Tebtebba Foundation, Baguio City.

Sumingit, (2006)V. Ethno-Botanical Documentation: Users Guide: COMMUNITY INTELLECTUAL PROPERTY RIGHTS SENSITIVE. *Asia-Pacific Database on Intangible Cultural Heritage (ICH)*. International Fund for Agricultural Development, Quezon City.

Part III

Intangible cultural heritage, law and nation building

Chapter 10

Culture by decree

Thailand's Intangible Cultural Heritage bill and the regulation of Thai-ness

Alexandra Denes

The promulgation of the 2003 UNESCO Convention for the Safeguarding of the Intangible Cultural Heritage (ICH Convention) was heralded as marking a historical turning point in terms of how cultural heritage is defined and managed. In contrast to the World Heritage Convention, which emphasizes monumentality and espouses notions of 'outstanding universal value' and authenticity as determined by experts, the ICH Convention purports to shift the focus of heritage conservation to communities and their living cultural practices. The commitment to a participatory, community-based heritage management approach is expressed in Article 15, which states that 'each State Party shall endeavour to ensure the widest possible participation of communities, groups, and where appropriate, individuals that create, maintain and transmit such heritage, and to involve them actively in its management.' Also embedded in the ICH Convention is an affirmation of the cultural rights of local communities to maintain their identity as well as to determine what constitutes heritage and how it should be documented and represented (Blake 2009).

Reading the Thai 2016 Law for the Safeguarding of Intangible Cultural Heritage, which established the national legal framework prior to Thailand becoming signatory to the UNESCO ICH Convention in June 2016, one is struck by the divergence from the community-based, participatory language of the ICH Convention. While the definition of intangible cultural heritage found in Article 3 of the Thai law is broadly consistent with the UNESCO Convention's definition in Article 2,[1] the Thai definition excludes the important statement that intangible heritage provides communities "with a sense of identity and continuity, thus promoting respect for cultural diversity and human creativity (UNESCO 2003)." Moreover, whereas the UNESCO Convention contains Article 15, which calls upon States Parties to involve communities in all aspects of ICH management, the Thai law lacks any specific article on communities. Rather, the Thai law focuses on defining the scope of responsibilities of a bureaucratic apparatus comprised of national, provincial and expert committees tasked with establishing selection criteria, listing elements for the national inventory and developing safeguarding plans, but only mentions briefly that these committees should "consider the participation of civil society and communities (Art. 15.3)."

The disjuncture between the participatory principles expressed in the UNE-SCO ICH Convention and the Thai ICH bill are neither surprising nor unique to Thailand. Heritage scholars such as Askew (2010) and Bendix et al. (2012) have observed the tendency for international heritage instruments to be misconstrued as their universal, humanistic abstractions about the value of cultural diversity are localized by state authorities and brought into conformity with existing 'heritage regimes' (Bendix et al. 2012) and discourses. In the case of Thailand, the heritage regime is one which values performances of cultural difference that reinforce rather than challenge established national narratives, geo-political boundaries and symbolic and social hierarchies. In other words, the 'good' heritage that is awarded with national recognition and funding is heritage that conforms to hegemonic constructions of Thai culture.

The widespread adoption and implementation of UNESCO's heritage instruments has spawned a multitude of academic critiques of these conventions as Eurocentric tools of standardization and rationalization (Kirshenblatt-Gimblett 2004; Smith 2006; Turtinen 2000). In the *Uses of Heritage*, Smith (2006) argues that UNESCO's heritage conventions constitute part of an 'authorized heritage discourse' (AHD)[2] that enables state heritage authorities and experts to determine which cultural artifacts, sites and practices should be selected and authorizes them to decide how they should be interpreted and conserved, thereby eclipsing local meanings and values. Herein lies the paradox of UNESCO's international heritage project; that is, while UNESCO's aims are cosmopolitan and progressive in their effort to foster respect for cultural diversity and conserve the heritage of humanity, in practice, the UNESCO conventions have been widely deployed to advance the nationalist, political agendas of member states. As Askew (2010), Logan (2012) and Bendix et al. (2012) have argued, since UNESCO actually has only limited legal leverage with States Parties, national elites and state heritage authorities are ultimately at liberty to carry out the branding, management and interpretation of intangible culture according to their own political and ideological agendas.

In *Heritage Regimes and the State*, Bendix et al. (2012) offer a collection of fine-grained analyses of what actually happens when states adopt international heritage conventions. Culminating from two conferences, the volume centers on two important observations:

1   a great deal of UNESCO's agenda is 'lost in translation' or invariably transformed as heritage conventions enter the level of state governance, and
2   the implementation of the international heritage regime on the state level brings forth a profusion of additional heritage regimes, endowing actors at state, regional and local levels with varied levels of power over selective aspects of culture that prior to the UNESCO initiatives had rarely seen attention or control on the part of the state (Bendix et al. 2012, p. 14)

In keeping with Bendix's call for critical investigations of the interface between international law and state bureaucracies, this chapter aims to demonstrate how the UNESCO ICH Convention has been transformed through its translation into Thai law and its incorporation into an existing national heritage regime which values the orderly expression and hierarchical management of culture.

In the first section, I begin by retracing the etymological roots and construction of the Thai concept of 'culture' (*watthanatham*) in the early twentieth century, which equated Thai-ness with modernity, public order and national sovereignty. I will then look at how the Thai notion of culture has been contested and expanded over time but ultimately reclaimed and maintained by the state heritage authorities – particularly the Ministry of Culture – who are beholden to a narrow, nationalist conception of culture as an index of civility. Turning to an analysis of the Thai 2016 Law for Safeguarding Intangible Cultural Heritage, I will demonstrate that while Thailand's quest to ratify the UNESCO ICH Convention seemingly endorses the cosmopolitan commitment to cultural rights and diversity, the language and bureaucratic mechanisms stipulated in the law are not about strengthening communities but rather about producing 'good culture' and asserting nationalistic claims of heritage ownership in contestation with neighbouring states, particularly Cambodia.

The roots of *watthanatham*: a brief history of Thailand's heritage regime

In order to understand the significance of the Thai ICH law, it is first necessary to provide some context and historical background about Thailand's heritage regime and the official definition of culture (*watthanatham*). As Askew (1994), Barmé (1993), Connors (2005), Jackson (2004) and Peleggi (2002) have all shown, the nationalist ideology of 'Thai-ness' and the modern Thai concept of culture first emerged as a response to the threat of colonial domination in the late nineteenth century. In order to legitimate their rule and maintain sovereignty in the face of European colonial discourses of civility, history and progress, Siam's monarchs carefully fashioned a refined image of Thai culture as being modern while at the same time maintaining historical continuity with a culturally sophisticated ancient past. Recognizing the need for new language to encapsulate this notion, in the 1930s, Prince Wanwaithayakorn coined the neologism for culture – *watthanatham* – which is a combination of the Pali-derived terms *watthana*, meaning progress, growth or to flourish, and the term *tham* or dharma, meaning morality or righteousness. Taken together, the term referred to the good character exhibited by Thailand's ancestors (industriousness, neatness, constructiveness and endeavour), classical works of art, performance, archaeology and architecture, as well as the capacity to appreciate such refinements (Limapichart 2003, p. 156).

It was not until after the 1932 overthrow of the absolute monarchy, however, that the ideology of Thai-ness began to penetrate public consciousness through the expanding system of modern education and the proclamation of cultural policies. A leading statesman who has had an enduring influence in defining and disseminating Thai national identity in the 1930s and 1940s was Luang Wichit Wattakan (1898–1962). A historian, politician and novelist, Luang Wichit drew on examples of Japan, Italy and Germany to fashion a brand of official nationalism cantered on proper Thai conduct (*khwam riaproy*), artistic refinement, progress and civility and loyalty in the defence of the nation from foreign threats (Barmé 1993). In his position as the Director General of Fine Arts (1932–1942) under the military rule of Field Marshall Phibul Songkram (1938–1944, 1948–1957), Luang Wichit spearheaded his campaigns to mobilize the Thai populace in the service of the nation. Two landmarks of this period were the pronouncement of the Cultural Act of 1940 and the establishment of the National Cultural Council in 1942. As summarized by Connors (2005),

> The Act defined culture as those characteristics that expressed development and order, national unity, and the morality of the people, and it covered such things as wearing appropriate dress, abiding by ethics and manners in public places, orderliness around the home, and honoring the nation and Buddhism. People who failed to abide by the new culture were to be fined.
>
> (p. 528)

While most of the Cultural Acts and Decrees disappeared in 1944 following the collapse of the Phibul regime towards the end of World War II, Phibul returned to power four years later through a coup and established the Ministry of Culture in 1952. Seeking to balance political factions during his second term (1948–1957), he toned down the ultra-nationalist rhetoric and shifted to the promotion of Buddhism (Connors 2005, p. 529).

Thailand's heritage regime was modified significantly under another military leader, Field Marshall Sarit Thanarat (1958–1963), who abolished the Ministry of Culture and National Culture Council and instead launched a cultural campaign to center Thai-ness around the monarchy and Buddhism through the revival of royal ceremonies, royal visits to the provinces, Buddhist holidays and the centralization of the Buddhist ecclesiastical order of monks, or Sangha. Concomitantly, Sarit promoted the rhetoric of community development coupled with infrastructural and economic expansion into rural areas aimed at combatting communism through modernization (Chaloemtiarana 2007).

The 1970s were a period of socio-political ferment, and in 1973, popular student protests against military rule ushered in a period of democratic openness. With the growing fear of communism, however, there was a reconsolidation of the right, and in October 1976, student protests over the return of a military strongman from exile led to a brutal crackdown and massacre of students on the Thammasat University campus by border police and paramilitaries. This crisis of hegemony indexed the need for a recalibration of the ideology of Thai-ness to include more democratic and pluralistic aspirations, and in 1979, the National Culture Commission (NCC) was established under the Ministry of Education, followed one year later by the National Identity Board (NIB) under the Office of the Prime

Minister. In the midst of the boom years of economic transformation that defined the 1980s, the NCC researched and celebrated local cultures and rural lifeways, while the NIB employed media campaigns to ensure that a more plural conception of Thai-ness emerging during this period was still subordinate to the three pillars of nation, religion and monarchy (Connors 2005, p. 531).

The rise of new business networks and interests within Thai politics in the 1990s challenged the longstanding military and bureaucratic power base, creating space for a reconceptualization of Thai-ness that aspired to diversity and democracy. Buoyed by new social movements, NGOs, international organizations and academics, the call for liberalizing reforms culminated in the 1997 People's Constitution, which included an unprecedented legal enshrinement of community and cultural rights.

> Persons so assembling as to be a local traditional community shall have the right to conserve or restore their customs, local knowledge, arts or good culture of their community and of the nation and participate in the management, maintenance, preservation and exploitation of natural resources and the environment in a balanced fashion and sustainably as provided by law (Section 46).

In spite of these developments, the state's official cultural policy from the 2000s to the present has continued to advocate a more conservative definition of Thainess, which maintains the triad of nation, religion and monarchy at the zenith while accommodating and celebrating cultural difference and regional diversity so long as it can be subsumed under the symbolic hierarchy. Thailand's official heritage regime was re-consolidated with the formation of the Ministry of Culture in 2002, which included the Fine Arts Department, the National Culture Commission and several smaller cultural organizations and agencies. In 2010, the National Culture Commission, responsible for the drafting and implementation of the Thai Intangible Cultural Heritage bill, changed its name to the Department of Cultural Promotion but retained its mandate as the key office for ICH.

In his discussion of the new Ministry of Culture, Connors identifies two ideological strands, namely Royalist-Nationalist, which espouses an elitist view of culture whose high standards must be maintained by a select minority, and Nationalist-Localist, a brand of 'cultural populism' which celebrates local cultures in a manner described (2005, p. 541). Connors asserts that the first strand of Royalist-Nationalist is by far the strongest, as evidenced by the Ministry's many projects focused on the surveillance and protection of Thai culture from corrupting foreign influences and sponsorship of royalist historiographies. Nevertheless, a more diversified image of Thai-ness is now promoted via the Department of Cultural Promotion, whose mandate is to research, document and protect local cultures threatened by the forces of globalization. It is this particular mandate of localism which corresponds in principle with the objectives of the UNESCO ICH Convention.

It's our intangible culture: the Department of Cultural Promotion as arbiters of contested heritage

To get a sense of how the Department of Cultural Promotion interprets its role as the key arbiter of the ICH Convention, it is helpful to analyze an official Thai-language document that was compiled by the agency and distributed at a 2011 meeting to garner opinions about Thailand's proposal to become signatory to the ICH Convention. The first part of the document features a lengthy background paper entitled 'Questions and Answers about the UNESCO ICH Convention and the Listing of the Royal Ballet of Cambodia and the *Sbek Thom* Shadow Play.' Written by the former Permanent Vice-Secretary of Education and a senior advisor to the Ministry of Culture, Ms. Sawitri Suwansathit, the paper traces the history and rationale leading up to the drafting of the Thai ICH bill. The author begins by reviewing the differences between the World Heritage and Intangible Cultural Heritage Conventions, pointing out that Thai state authorities, including the National Commission to UNESCO and the Ministry of Culture, have been closely following the development of UNESCO's policies around intangible heritage since well before the 2003 ICH Convention was adopted. Testifying to the Ministry of Culture's mastery of international heritage discourses and legislation, the background paper details the precursors to the ICH Convention, including the 1989 Recommendation on the Safeguarding of Traditional Culture and Folklore, the 1997 Proclamation of Masterpieces of the Oral and Intangible Heritage of Humanity and the 2001 Declaration on Cultural Diversity and also explains that the core objectives of the UNESCO ICH Convention are to safeguard the world's living cultures through recognition and awareness raising at the national and international levels.

While this historical background attests to the Ministry of Culture's grasp of the aims of the ICH Convention, a telling indicator of the agency's particular motivation for ratification of the Convention is the paper title, which refers to two elements of Cambodian intangible culture – the Royal Ballet of Cambodia and the *Sbek Thom* Shadow Play – which were added to the UNESCO Representative List of the Intangible Cultural Heritage of Humanity in 2008. In the paper, the author poses a rhetorical question: 'Why did the Cambodians list the Royal Ballet of Cambodia and the Sbek Thom Shadow Play before the Thais? Is this a case of "stealing" the heritage of Thailand?' Sawitri answers obliquely by describing the listing process for these two elements, detailing the content of nomination files which included academic research by foreign scholars, sketches of Khmer dancers by the French artist Auguste Rodin and photographic images from French colonial archives. The author then states that the Cambodian nomination file for the Royal Ballet did not include any reference whatsoever to Thai dance forms.

Though the author does not elaborate this point further, inclusion of this issue in the background report is highly significant, because it signals the longstanding and often bitter disputes between Thailand and Cambodia over claims to cultural heritage shared by both countries as a result of centuries of mutual influence and emulation (Denes 2006; 2012; Kasetsiri 2003; Keyes 1991; Sasagawa 2005). In the case of Khmer and Thai classical dance, Miettinen (2008) has shown how a vocabulary of Indian-derived dance forms was first localized by early kingdoms in mainland Southeast Asia, including the Dvaravati kingdom (sixth through eleventh centuries) and the Khmer kingdom of Angkor (ninth through fifteenth centuries C.E.). Many of the dance poses and performance traditions represented in the bas-reliefs and sculptures of Angkor Wat later appeared in temple mural imagery and *Khon* classical dance performances of the Siamese courts of Ayuthaya and Bangkok, thus substantiating Siam's emulation of earlier Khmer dance forms. The cultural borrowing was not one way, however, and as Sasagawa (2005) has argued, since the nineteenth century, Cambodian classical court dance had been strongly influenced by Siamese dance forms as a result of the Cambodian court's political status as vassal to the Siamese court during the reign of the Khmer King Ang Duong (1847–1859 CE). Furthermore, Sasagawa (ibid.) maintains that the Siamese influence on Khmer classical dance in the nineteenth century was intentionally erased by early French scholars such as George Groslier (2011), who traced Khmer dance forms to Angkorian bas-reliefs. While a detailed discussion of this complex issue is beyond the scope of this chapter, suffice it to say that the very mention of the fact that Cambodia had already listed these elements without acknowledging Thailand is clear indication of the nationalist concerns motivating the Department of Cultural Promotion to become a signatory to the Convention in order to 'set the record straight' in the international heritage arena.

Sawitri's background report then went on to catalog the various obstacles that delayed Thailand on the path to becoming signatory. These included the constitutional requirement of holding public forums at regional and national levels in order to garner public opinion and meetings with related government agencies to reach consensus about the ICH Convention. Participants at these meetings raised doubts about the benefits of becoming signatory and also struggled with the new vocabulary of 'intangible heritage,' which is awkward and difficult to translate into Thai.

In spite of these setbacks and delays, the report maintained that the Ministry of Culture had made significant progress in preparation for ratification, inasmuch as it had taken steps to clarify the state's cultural policy, established a responsible government agency (the Department of Cultural Promotion), prepared a legal framework and launched a national ICH registry. The national registry was launched in 2009 with the establishment of a special expert committee for each of the five domains of ICH, whose task was to select elements of intangible culture for nomination. Furthermore, following debates about the appropriate Thai translation of ICH, in 2009, the National Culture Commission selected the term *moradok phumpanya thang watthanatham*, which translates roughly as 'cultural wisdom and heritage.' The first twenty-five elements listed in 2009 included the two Thai equivalents of the Khmer performance forms mentioned earlier, namely, *Khon* classical dance-drama and *Nang Yai* shadow puppetry. Elements have been added to the ICH registry every year via the expert committee selection process.

In addition to the background paper, the 2011 Department of Cultural Promotion report also included summaries of the numerous official and public meetings that were held to discuss and debate the perceived merits or drawbacks of ratification. In its listing of the anticipated benefits, the Department of Cultural Promotion stated that becoming a signatory to the Convention would help Thailand to improve the effectiveness of its heritage safeguarding efforts, raise the international visibility of Thailand's ICH and affirm Thailand's commitment to the preservation of ICH, particularly heritage shared by neighbouring countries. It also stated that the Department of Cultural Promotion would have to be vigilant in protecting the nation's cultural heritage from commercial exploitation or other forms of misappropriation and that it would work with communities to raise their awareness on this issue. In terms of Thailand's readiness, the Department of Cultural Promotion had already initiated the national inventory process and the draft ICH bill, making it one of only twenty-nine other member states that had national ICH legislation.

A statement summarizing the views of the expert sub-committee offered a slightly different perspective on the prospect of ratification. While most committee members agreed with ratification, they offered a number of recommendations and caveats, noting, for instance, that the Department of Cultural Promotion needed to consider the UNESCO ICH Convention in relation to other international human rights and intellectual property instruments ratified by Thailand. In contrast to the Department of Cultural Promotion's statement, which said nothing explicitly about the role of communities, the sub-committee statement highlighted the importance of community participation and the need for nuanced understanding of the wider historical and social context of intangible heritage in all safeguarding efforts. Last, Thailand needed clear policies and legal frameworks enshrining the rights and roles of culture bearers, communities, NGOs and civil society in the ICH safeguarding initiative.

The last statement summarized opinions from five public forums (totalling 300 participants) held across the country, attended by culture bearers, heritage officers, academics, journalists and youth leaders. This statement indicated that by and large, forum participants supported Thailand's ratification of the ICH Convention as a means of protecting Thailand's heritage from misappropriation and recommended the establishment of a government agency responsible for the management, documentation, promotion and public outreach about the value of ICH. The summary statement also proposed that responsible state agencies should organize a public campaign to clarify the benefits of ratification and establish regional and local committees to encourage community participation in the ICH nomination process.

Thailand's ICH bill: domesticating difference and rewarding 'good culture'

This brings us to the Thai law for safeguarding ICH. Initially prepared in 2013 by a team of legal advisors to the Department of Cultural Promotion, the first draft of the law was amended in 2015 in response to widespread critiques from Thai academics and artists, who saw the law as setting unnecessarily severe constraints on cultural innovation and creativity. The most recent amended version was endorsed by the cabinet of Prime Minister Prayuth Chan-Ocha in February 2016. While the current law no longer contains the most controversial articles of the first draft, I argue that there is still much to learn about Thailand's particular interpretations of intangible cultural heritage by examining the initial and final versions of the Thai ICH law.[3]

For instance, whereas the UNESCO Convention defines ICH in Article 2 as "the practices, representations, expressions, knowledge, skills – as well as the instruments, objects, artefacts and cultural spaces associated therewith – that communities, groups and, in some cases, individuals recognize as part of their cultural heritage," Article 5 of the 2013 Thai draft law inserted a number of abstract criteria, namely, that the intangible heritage "must reflect academic, historical, artistic and spiritual values worthy of preservation." Moreover, whereas the UNESCO ICH Convention asserts that the primary objective of the international agreement is to provide support, recognition and respect for cultural diversity, the Thai draft law emphasized the selection and conservation of 'good' cultural heritage that would contribute to national unity, prosperity, morality and progress. This conservative and nationalistic conception of cultural heritage was expressed in Article 23, which stated that selected elements of intangible heritage must not threaten public order, morality or national security, and in Article 43, which proposed a mechanism for delisting registered elements of intangible heritage which contravened Article 23.

Aside from the requirements that the ICH recognized by UNESCO must constitute the identity of communities, groups and individuals and be compatible with human rights, mutual respect among communities and sustainable development, the UNESCO ICH Convention does not put forth any abstract, value-based criteria for the selection of intangible heritage. This is because using such criteria to judge the value of living culture would construct a hierarchy of value which privileges aesthetics over the embedded meanings and significance of living cultural heritage to its practitioners and would thus work against the Convention's aim of promoting diversity and ensuring respect for intangible cultural heritage and culture bearers (Hafstein 2009). However, this is exactly what was expressed in the 2013 Thai draft bill, which inserted several abstract criteria in Article 5 and again in Article 22, which stated that the element must have "outstanding character associated with creative values of intangible cultural heritage at the local and national levels."

Two of the most controversial articles in the 2013 ICH draft law were Article 39 and Article 40. Article 39 prohibited the 'distortion or modification' of registered ICH, requiring that those who intended to adapt or modify ICH would first have to acknowledge the original source communities or practitioners. While this article clearly derived from concerns with misappropriation and commercialization of intangible heritage, its inclusion in the draft Thai ICH bill represented a misunderstanding of the spirit and purpose of the UNESCO ICH Convention, which does not seek to tackle issues of intellectual property or contested claims of ownership or authenticity – issues which fall within the purview of other international organizations, particularly the World Intellectual Property Organization (WIPO). However, what the inclusion of this article in the Thai draft ICH bill revealed was that while listing ICH within the UNESCO framework was supposed to be about the promotion and recognition of ICH, Thai heritage authorities interpreted it as a legal mechanism for asserting notions of purity, origins and claims to cultural property. As critics noted, not only would this legal clause be likely to lead to conflicts between communities claiming 'ownership' and contesting the 'authenticity' of a shared cultural practice or tradition, but it would also penalize contemporary cultural forms that take their inspiration from themes and motifs in traditional culture. This clause would also potentially impact relations between Thailand and its neighbours in the region, as it could foment contestation over claims to entitlement of status as the 'authentic origin' of shared cultural traditions which cross national borders, as in the case of Thai and Cambodian dance described earlier.

Another controversial article in the 2013 draft was Article 40, which would have harshly penalized the use of registered ICH in a manner that would defame the institution of the monarchy, impact religion, threaten national security or result in the degradation of the intangible heritage. As stated in Article 45, violators of Article 40 would have been subject to up to two years in prison and a fine of 50,000 Thai baht, making the ICH draft bill reminiscent of the punitive Cultural Acts of the first Phibul government (1938–1944) described previously, which also prescribed punishments for transgressions of cultural codes of proper dress and behaviour, albeit comparatively milder than those in the current draft ICH law.

The 2013 draft law was lambasted by Thai artists and scholars and also received negative coverage in the media. To their credit, following these critiques, the Department of Cultural Promotion revised the 2013 draft law significantly, cutting out all of the mentioned articles. Nevertheless, what they retained in the 2016 law was a hierarchical bureaucratic structure for identifying and selecting intangible cultural heritage, which downplays the importance of community participation. The 2016 law calls for the establishment of a number of committees at the national and provincial levels. The first of these is the Advisory Committee. Chaired by the Minister of Culture, this national-level committee is comprised of eleven heads of government offices (Ministry of Culture, Ministry of the Interior, Ministry of Agriculture and Cooperatives, Ministry of Education, Buddhist Council, Fine Arts Department, Ministry of Tourism and Sports, Traditional and Alternative Medicine, Intellectual Property, Permanent Secretary of Bangkok Municipality and the Cultural Council of Thailand), as well as six appointed special experts in the following areas: oral literature and language; performing arts; social practices, rituals and festive events; knowledge of nature and the universe; handicrafts; and the arts of self-defence. Tasked with overseeing protection and promotion of intangible heritage, the Advisory Committee is expected to provide policy guidance in the form of regulations, criteria and guidelines for the registration of intangible cultural heritage. It is also expected to develop specific measures and standards for the conservation and transmission of intangible cultural heritage, monitor and evaluate protection initiatives, create awards and honours and issue rules for the disbursement of funding support.

Another tier in the hierarchy is the Provincial Committee. Chaired by the provincial governor, this committee is to be comprised of high-level provincial officers (president of the Provincial Administration, president of the Provincial Cultural Council or president of the District Cultural Council) as well as six special experts appointed by the Governor in the same areas described earlier. The Provincial Committee's proposed role is to provide guidance to the Department of Cultural Promotion in the following areas: to develop policies and measures for the protection and promotion of ICH; coordinate networks and collaborate with relevant agencies; select nominated ICH items for the national registry; evaluate reports on the protection and promotion of ICH; and disseminate, promote and transmit knowledge concerning ICH in the province.

At the bottom of this administrative hierarchy are the communities of culture bearers. The 2016 law mentions that the National and Provincial Committees should be aware of involving communities; however, it never explicitly addresses community rights or their roles in the safeguarding of their heritage. This absence represents a stark divergence from the participatory principles of the UNESCO ICH Convention. For instance, Article 2 of the UNESCO ICH Convention explicitly defines ICH as "the practices, representations, expressions, knowledge,

skills – as well as the instruments, objects, artefacts and cultural spaces associated therewith – that communities, groups and, in some cases, individuals recognize as part of their cultural heritage," while Article 11 (b) advocates that signatories "identify and define the various elements of the intangible cultural heritage present in its territory, with the participation of communities." Article 15 refers to ensuring "the widest possible participation of communities, groups and, where appropriate, individuals that create, maintain and transmit such heritage, and to involve them actively in its management."

In spite of the positive changes noted here, the Thai ICH bill nonetheless represents a highly centralized instrument of 'authorized heritage discourse' (Smith 2006), which sets exclusive parameters for selecting what counts as Thai national intangible cultural heritage. Rather than empowering communities to define the meaning of their heritage in their own terms and providing resources to implement safeguarding activities which support those local meanings and values, the Thai bill establishes a hierarchical system of selecting intangible culture which places decision making squarely in the hands of state authorities. Indeed, the Thai ICH bill embodies many of the potential pitfalls that were anticipated by academics in their consideration of the role of the state in implementing the ICH Convention. For instance, former Smithsonian Director Richard Kurin issued the following warning about over-reliance on the state for ICH listing and safeguarding:

> Government inventories of cultural practice may seem too much like cultural registries – officialising and de-officialising cultural practice, and allowing for all sorts of misuses of information. Having the government in charge of ICH activities could create uneven relationships of power between cultural

regulators and cultural practitioners, where the latter might feel there was undue intrusion into the life of their community.

(2007, p. 13)

Indeed, Kurin's warning points to another absence in the Thai ICH bill – recognition of cultural rights and the requirement of community consent. Whereas the Operational Directives of the UNESCO ICH Convention are explicit regarding the pre-requisite of informed consent from communities prior to the nomination of an element of intangible heritage, there is no such requirement stipulated by the Thai ICH bill. This absence authorizes state heritage agencies and their expert advisors to select and nominate according to their own judgement and runs the risk of state authorities appropriating local cultural practices for the registry of national heritage without first engaging culture bearers in an informed dialog about the consequences of listing. Indeed, this kind of top-down selection process has already been the case with the national ICH registry that was launched in 2009, as the Department of Cultural Promotion has listed many elements of heritage without dialogue with or consent of local practitioners.

Conclusion

International heritage conventions are never adopted by member states purely out of principle. Rather, as Askew (2010) and Bendix et al. (2012) have argued, international heritage instruments are always translated and deployed by state agencies within the frame of an existing heritage regime. This inevitable slippage between the original intent of a heritage instrument and its interpretation is vividly illustrated by Thailand's Intangible Cultural Heritage bill. Rather than decentralizing authority to communities and culture bearers, the ICH bill empowers state actors to selectively promote and represent local difference and ethnic diversity within a hierarchy of value. As argued in this chapter, the state agency responsible for the translation and implementation of the international UNESCO ICH Convention is beholden to an official heritage regime which espouses a particular definition of 'good culture' linked to national prosperity, progress, public morality and refinement.

As the analysis of official meeting documents in this chapter revealed, moreover, the Ministry of Culture's primary motivation for seeking UNESCO ICH Convention signatory status has far more to do with asserting Thailand's place within the global ICH discourse and contesting Cambodia's claims to a shared classical repertoire of art and performance forms than it does with supporting and collaborating with communities to safeguard their living heritage at the local level.

For local practitioners who are eager to document, revitalize and transmit their cultural heritage, this means that state recognition and financial support comes at a substantial price. Living cultural practices must be packaged and performed according to a particular script of loyalty, nationalism and refinement, with the 'difficult' or counter-hegemonic aspects downplayed or excised. In sum, the Thai state's engagement with the UNESCO ICH Convention has done little to challenge the official heritage regime which defines culture in narrowly nationalistic terms.

Notes

1 The "intangible cultural heritage" means the practices, representations, expressions, knowledge, skills – as well as the instruments, objects, artefacts and cultural spaces associated therewith – that communities, groups and, in some cases, individuals recognize as part of their cultural heritage. This intangible cultural heritage, transmitted from generation to generation, is constantly recreated by communities and groups in response to their environment, their interaction with nature and their history, and provides them with a sense of identity and continuity, thus promoting respect for cultural diversity and human creativity (UNESCO 2003).

2 'The "authorized heritage discourse" privileges monumentality and grand scale, innate artefact/site significance tied to time depth, scientific/aesthetic expert judgement, social consensus and nation building. It is a self-referential discourse, which has a particular set of consequences.'

3 The first draft of the ICH bill is available in Thai at the following link: www.culture. go.th/subculture4/index.php?option=com_content&view=article&id=71&Itemid=14.

References

Askew, M. (1994) *Interpreting Bangkok: The Urban Question in Thai Studies*. Bangkok: Chulalongkorn University Press.

Askew, M. (2010) 'The Magic List of Global Status: UNESCO, World Heritage and the Agendas of States', in S. Labadi and C. Long (eds), *Heritage and Globalisation*, London: Routledge.

Barmé, S. (1993) *Luang Wichit Wathakan and the Creation of a Thai Identity*, Singapore: Institute of Southeast Asian Studies.

Bendix, R., Eggert, A. and Peselmann, A. (eds) (2012) *Heritage Regimes and the State. Vol. 6*. Göttingen Studies on Cultural Property, Göttingen: Göttingen University. Press. Online. Available: www.networkedheritage.org/2012/12/10/heritage-regimes-and-the-state/ (accessed 29 May 2015).

Blake, J. (2009) 'UNESCO's 2003 Convention on Intangible Cultural Heritage: The Implications of Community Involvement in Safeguarding,' in L. Smith and N. Akagawa (eds), *Intangible Heritage*, London: Routledge.

Chaloemtiarana, T. (2007) *Thailand: The Politics of Despotic Paternalism*, Ithaca, NY: Southeast Asia Program Publications.

Connors, M.K. (2005) 'Hegemony and the Politics of Culture and Identity in Thailand', *Critical Asian Studies*, 37(4), 523–551.

Denes, A. (2006) *Recovering Khmer Ethnic Identity from the Thai National Past: An Ethnography of the Localism Movement in Surin Province*, PhD Anthropology dissertation, Cornell University.

Denes, A. (2012) 'The Revitalization of Khmer Ethnic Identity in Thailand: Empowerment or Confinement?' in P. Daly and T. Winter (eds), *The Routledge Handbook of Heritage in Asia*, London: Routledge.

Department of Cultural Promotion (2011) *Ekasan prakob kaan prachum rap fang khwam khid hen: kaan khaw ruam pen phakhi anusanya wa duay kaan sanguan raksa moradok watthanatham thi cap tong mai dai khong UNESCO* [Background report for a public hearing to garner opinion on Thailand's potential ratification of the UNESCO Intangible Cultural Heritage Convention], Bangkok: Department of Cultural Promotion, Thailand Ministry of Culture.

Department of Cultural Promotion (2012) *Moradok phumpanya thang watthanatham khong chat: phithi prakad khun thabian moradok phumpanya watthanatham khong chat pii 2555* [The National Intangible Cultural Heritage of Thailand: Registration Ceremony for Intangible Cultural Heritage 2012], Bangkok: Department of Cultural Promotion, Thailand Ministry of Culture.

Groslier, G. (2011) *Cambodian Dancers – Ancient and Modern*, Holmes Beach, FL: DatASIA.

Hafstein, V. (2009) 'Intangible Heritage as a List: From Masterpieces to Representation,' in L. Smith and N. Akagawa (eds), *Intangible Heritage*, London: Routledge.

Jackson, P. (2004) 'The Performative State: Semi-Coloniality and the Tyranny of Images in Modern Thailand', *Sojourn*, 19(2), 219–253.

Kasetsiri, C. (2003) 'Thailand-Cambodia: A Love-Hate Relationship', *Kyoto Review*, 3 (online). Available: http://kyotoreview.cseas.kyoto-u.ac.jp/issue/issue2/article_242.html (accessed 22 November 2013).

Keyes, C. (1991) 'The Case of the Purloined Lintel: The Politics of a Khmer Shrine as a Thai National Treasure', in C. Reynolds (ed), *National Identity and Its Defenders*, Melbourne: Centre for Southeast Asian Studies, Monash University.

Kirshenblatt-Gimblett, B. (2004) 'Intangible Heritage as Metacultural Production', *Museum International*, 56(1/2), 52–65, doi:10.1111/j.1350–0775.2004.00458.x

Kurin, R. (2007) 'Safeguarding Intangible Cultural Heritage: Key Factors in Implementing the 2003 Convention', *International Journal of Intangible Heritage*, 2(9), 10–20.

Limapichart, T. (2003) *The Public Sphere and the Birth of 'Literature' in Siam*, Madison, WI: University of Wisconsin-Madison.

Logan, W. (2012) 'States, Governance and the Politics of Culture: World Heritage in Asia', in P. Daly and T. Winter (eds), *The Routledge Handbook of Heritage in Asia*, London: Routledge.

Miettinen, J.O. (2008) *Dance Images in Temples of Mainland Southeast Asia*, Helsinki: Theatre Academy Helsinki (online). Available: https://helda.helsinki.fi/bitstream/handle/10138/33792/Acta_Scenica_20_a.pdf?sequence=1 (accessed 29 May 2015).

Peleggi, M. (2002) *The Politics of Ruins and the Business of Nostalgia*, Bangkok: White Lotus.

Sasagawa, H. (2005) 'Post/Colonial Discourses on the Cambodian Court Dance', *Southeast Asian Studies*, 42(4), 418–41.

Smith, L. (2006) *Uses of Heritage*, London: Routledge.

Turtinen, J. (2000) 'Globalising Heritage – on UNESCO and the Transnational Construction of a World Heritage', *SCORE (Stockholm Center for Organizational Research)*, 12 (online). Available: www.score.su.se/polopoly_fs/1.26651.1320939806!/200012.pdf (accessed 22 November 2013).

UNESCO. (2003) 'Cnvention for Safeguarding Intangible Cultural Heritage United Nations Educational, Scientific and Cultural Organization.' Available: http://www.unesco.org/new/en/santiago/culture/intangible-heritage/convention-intangible-cultural-heritage/.

Chapter 11

Protection of traditional knowledge in agriculture

A review of the laws in Malaysia

Rajeswari Kanniah

Introduction

Traditional knowledge (TK) occupies a highly contested space – between the nation that seeks to control it and its indigenous/local communities who possess it; between utilising it for public purposes and commercialising it for private profit; between communal and collective rights over it and claims of individual rights to it; and even competing claims between neighbouring countries as to its source/origin and ownership. TK in Malaysia is no exception.

Though Malaysia is one of the 12 mega-biodiverse countries in the world, many of its biological resources are yet to be discovered, and their distribution and potential use is still unknown. This is further exacerbated by large-scale development projects involving forest clearing, resulting in the destruction of yet-undiscovered species of flora and fauna and the loss of ancestral homelands of the native indigenous communities. Indigenous peoples and local farming communities are the preservers and conservers of wild plants and seeds of local plant varieties used for food and traditional medicines. Studies are still ongoing to discover and document the TK of these communities.

Malaysia aspires to expand, modernise and commercialise its agriculture sector. The 11th Malaysia Plan (2016–2020) targeted agriculture as a growth engine to support large-scale farming, biotechnological development, food self-sufficiency and commercialisation of bio-resources for the export market. Agriculture is an important sector in terms of foreign exchange earnings, domestic consumption and employment. In 2014, the agriculture sector contributed 8.87% to GDP and provided employment for 12.2% of the population.[1] Almost 30% of the country's total land area is dedicated to agriculture with the cultivation of 11 major crops, of which the largest acreages are taken up by oil palm (second-largest producer in the world), rubber (third-largest producer in the world), rice, coconut and cocoa and the rest made up of fruits, vegetables, flowers and pasture for animal husbandry.[2]

The drive to generate wealth from bio-resources is demonstrated by several government ministries exercising authority over different aspects of its development – the Department of Agriculture exercises authority over intellectual property rights on new plant varieties; the Ministry of Natural Resources and Environment is responsible for biodiversity, access and benefit sharing; the

Ministry of Information, Communications and Culture manages heritage matters; and the Ministry of Cooperatives, Domestic Trade and Consumer Affairs oversees intellectual property laws including geographical indications.

Though Malaysia is party to the Convention on Biological Diversity (CBD) and the International Treaty on Plant Genetic Resources for Food and Agriculture (ITPGRFA), which recognise the contribution of farmers' TK to biodiversity conservation, there is no national law protecting TK *per se* in Malaysia. This chapter will focus on the protection of TK in agriculture in Malaysia by undertaking a review of the laws in three areas – IP, heritage and biological resources.

TK in international laws

There are several international instruments dealing with rights over TK. Each of these is hosted by different international agencies of the United Nations. Each instrument has defined TK in the context of its mandate over the subject matter of protection.

The earliest call for the recognition and protection of TK was in relation to protection and conservation of plant genetic resources. The forum was the Food and Agriculture Organization during the negotiations on the International Undertaking on Plant Genetic Resources in 1989, which was later reconstituted as the ITPGRFA in 2001. The other forum was the United Nations Environment Programme, culminating in the CBD in 1992. In these instruments, the concept of farmers' rights was conceived and importance placed on the recognition and protection of the contribution of farmers' TK to the conservation and preservation of plant genetic resources and sharing the benefits from the utilisation of their knowledge. Malaysia ratified the CBD on 24 June 1994 and the ITPGRFA on 5 May 2003.

At UNESCO, Article 2 of the Convention for the Safeguarding of Intangible Cultural Heritage 2003 includes TK within its definition of "intangible cultural heritage". Malaysia has not ratified the UNESCO Convention.

At the UN Human Rights Council, the United Nations Declaration on the Rights of Indigenous Peoples (UNDRIP; adopted by UN General Assembly on 13 September 2007) explicitly recognises the rights of indigenous communities to protection of their TK. Malaysia endorsed the UNDRIP twice – first when she was a member of the Human Rights Council that approved the original draft in June 2006 and again on 13 September 2007, when it was successfully tabled at the UN General Assembly.

The WIPO Inter-Governmental Committee on Intellectual Property and Genetic Resources, Traditional Knowledge and Folklore (WIPO IGC) was formed in 2000 and began meeting in 2001. After much deliberation, the WIPO IGC proposed a demarcation between traditional cultural expressions (TCE) and TK so as to make the subject matter of protection clearer. TK *stricto sensu* is referred to as traditional intellectual knowledge manifested in the form of know-how, skills, teachings, practices, rituals, and TCE is tangible or intangible expressions of TK in the form of verbal (e.g. stories, legends), musical (e.g. songs, rhythms), action (e.g. dances, ceremonies, rituals) or material expressions of art (e.g. handicrafts, architecture).³ Negotiations are ongoing for an international treaty for the protection of TK and TCE. In this chapter, the focus of the review of the laws will be TK, while TCE will be included where the law provides for it.

Holders of TK in agriculture

The total population of Malaysia at the latest population census of 2010 is 28.3 million people, made up of the *Bumiputra* (comprising Malays [63%] and Indigenous Peoples: total [67.4%]), Chinese (24.6%), Indian (7.3%) and others (0.7%).⁴ The majority *Bumiputra* are the local inhabitants, while the Chinese and Indians are descended from immigrants brought from China and India during the colonial period.

The issue of who qualify as indigenous people in Malaysia⁵ is settled by definitions of "aborigine"⁶ and "natives"⁷ in the Federal Constitution, the Aboriginal Peoples Act 1954⁸ and the State laws of Sabah⁹ and Sarawak.¹⁰

In Peninsular Malaysia, the aborigines are the *Orang Asli* (original people or first people), numbering around 147,412, representing 0.6% of the population, living in 869 villages.¹¹ They comprise the three main groups of *Negrito*, *Senoi* and the *Proto-Malay* and are further divided into 18 distinct sub-groups. They lead diverse lifestyles and have equally diverse cultures and languages. For coastal communities, fishing is the chief occupation. Approximately 40% of the *Orang Asli* still live close to or within forested areas, engaged in swiddening, hunting and gathering. They also trade in fruits and plants collected from the forest to earn cash income. A very small number are still semi-nomadic, depending on the seasonal bounties of the forest for their subsistence, while some live in urban areas, surviving on salaried jobs (Nicholas 1996).

The indigenous people in the East Malaysian states of Sabah and Sarawak are the dominant population of these states. The indigenous people of Sabah account for about 55.54% of the total population of the state, of which the largest native ethnic groups are the Kadazan/Dusun, Bajau and Murut.¹² The indigenous people of Sarawak make up 48.2% of the total population of the state, of which the largest native ethnic groups are the Iban, Bidayuh and Melanau.¹³

The native communities of Sabah who live in the coastal and riverine areas engage in fishing and cultivation of food for their own consumption. For cash income, they sell jungle produce, surplus food and cash crops. The majority of the native communities of Sabah live in the interior as subsistence farmers, practising shifting agriculture, and plant wet padi, tapioca, fruits and vegetables and, increasingly now, cash crops (Nicholas 1996).

The native communities in Sarawak also practice shifting agriculture, mainly planting hill padi, and supplement their diet with hunting and forest produce. A small percentage of natives, the *Penan*, lead a nomadic life, hunting and gathering, while some of them lead a settled or semi-settled existence. The natives of Sarawak have been drawn into plantation projects, cultivating cash crops such as pepper, oil palm, cocoa and rubber, while others work in the timber industry or have moved into urban areas (Nicholas 1996).

Many studies have documented the TK of indigenous peoples in relation to sustainable natural resources management and agricultural practices as well as knowledge of plants for food and medicines (Baer 2009; Kardooni et al. 2013: 283–291; Gerten et al. 2015; Halim et al. 2012b: 159–163). Since the early 1960s, at least 500 local plants used by the indigenous communities have been documented to have economic or medicinal properties (Lasimbang and Nicholas 2004: 10–11). Studies show a high correlation between traditional uses of plants and their modern therapeutic uses – there is a 75% positive correlation for 120 active compounds used in modern medicines (Lasimbang and Nicholas 2004: 10–11).

Several early studies have documented that the *Orang Asli* have knowledge of the medicinal properties of wild plants and have been using these plants to cure various ailments.[14] An ethnomedical study of an *Orang Asli* tribe in Kampong Bawang, Perak, found a total of 62 species of plants belonging to 36 families, used for treating a range of ailments and even diseases such as malaria (Samuel et al. 2010: 5). Most of these species grow naturally in the wild, and their medicinal properties are well known to the *Orang Asli*, who have been using them to prepare traditional medicines.

An ethnomedical survey of the *Kadazandusun* native community (the largest ethnic group, representing half of the native communities in Sabah) in the Crocker Range of Sabah documented their TK of 50 plants used for medicinal purposes such as for treating minor wounds, skin diseases, diarrhoea, fever, coughs and malaria (Fasihuddin Ahmad and Ghazaly Ismail 2003). This native community has its own system of categorising their traditional medicines based on the complexity of their preparation for use. According to the survey, the holders of the TK are the community elders and traditional healers who are 50 years or older. Their TK is in danger of extinction, as the younger generation have access to modern medicines and are not interested in inheriting the TK of their forefathers.

Another study recorded the TK in agricultural practices and traditional medicines of the native community in the Ranau region of Sabah. The study similarly found that the holders of the TK are the elderly, and their TK is likely to disappear if efforts are not taken to document it (Halim et al. 2012a).

The Sabah Biodiversity Center (SBC) has carried out a field survey to document the distribution and use of medicinal ferns and poisonous plants in the state. The two-year study (2006–2007), which was conducted through interviews with 82 respondents from the local villages, discovered 32 medicinal ferns and 48 species of poisonous plants used by the local communities.[15] The SBC relies heavily on the TK of indigenous communities, as almost 90% of research conducted in SBC's laboratories is guided by the TK of indigenous communities. According to a press report cited in a study, the SBC has

> collected over 1500 plants from a dozen ethnic communities in 27 villages and they have performed bioassays on nearly 200-plus plants and more than 35 percent have shown good activity against cancer cell lines when tested.
>
> (Nordin et al. 2012: 19)

Apart from native indigenous communities, local communities are also holders of TK in Malaysia. Studies of the TK of medicinal plants of local Malay communities reveal a rich heritage of knowledge. For example, in a recent study conducted at a Malay village in Trengganu, the authors recorded the TK of the Malay community in relation to 53 species of medicinal plants used for various ailments (On get al. 2011: 175–185). The Ministry of Health Malaysia has also officially recognised the traditional and complementary healthcare traditions of the Malay, Chinese and Indian communities, much of which comprises TK which has been passed down from ancient traditional practices (Ministry of Health Malaysia 2011).

Malaysia ranks fourth in Asia (after China, India and Indonesia) as a mega-bio-diverse country with 15,000 flowering plants and 3,000 medicinal plants. Of the 3,000 medicinal plants, only 50 are being used commercially, and even fewer have been scientifically researched for their medicinal properties (Malaysian Biotechnology Corporation 2009: 18).

There is vast potential for Malaysia's bio-resources to be used to produce herbal medicines and healthcare products. No doubt, the TK of Malaysia's indigenous communities may have proven vital in establishing a starting point for research into their medicinal properties. There are studies being done to isolate the active ingredients of tongkat ali (*Euricoma Longifolia*),[16] which has multiple medicinal uses. A search on the Malaysian Intellectual Property Office database revealed 59 trademarks registered for tongkat ali. There were two applications for patents on tongkat ali made on 28.05.1999 and 5.1.2015. The former was found to be invalid, while the latter is currently being examined. Numerous patents on Tongkat Ali have been filed in the US by Malaysian individuals, companies and the government either in collaboration with US institutions or on their own.[17]

Another example of a local plant being investigated for possible medicinal properties is the Bintangor (*Calophyllum spp. [Guttiferae]*)[18] plant found in the tropical rainforests of Sarawak. Successful collaboration between the Sarawak Forestry Department, the US National Cancer Institute, the University of Illinois–Chicago and Medichem Research Inc. of Illinois resulted in the discovery of significant anti-HIV active ingredients in the plant. Eventually this led to the incorporation of Sarawak Medichem Pharmaceuticals Inc., a joint-venture company between the Sarawak Government and Medichem Research Inc. to develop anti-HIV drugs and to conduct clinical trials. Apparently no TK was utilised in the discovery of the anti-HIV properties of this plant.

More systematic efforts are now being undertaken to document the TK of indigenous and local communities. The Forest Research Institute of Malaysia (FRIM) is being funded by the Ministry of Natural Resources and Environment to develop a database on the TK of the *Orang Asli* in Peninsular Malaysia on the utilisation of medicinal and aromatic plants. Both the Sabah and Sarawak Biodiversity Centers are also documenting the TK of their respective native indigenous communities in respect of plants within their states. The Malaysian Intellectual Property Office (MyIPO) announced plans to develop a digital TK database called the Malaysia Traditional Knowledge Digital Library (MyTKDL).[19] It was launched in 2009 with the collaboration of the state of Sabah, the Department of Orang Asli Affairs, the National University of Malaysia and the Institute of Environment and Development. The purpose of the MyTKDL is to conserve knowledge for future generations, enable benefit sharing for rights owners, monitor and prevent biopiracy of genetic resources, and enable searches for prior art. The MyTKDL will be expanded at a later stage to include TCE and genetic resources. As at December 2013, the database had collected more than 1,600 records relating primarily to species of medicinal plants (OECD 2015: 106).

Laws relating to protection of TK

According to a survey by WIPO, there are five broad categories of policy objectives for the protection of TK. They are (WIPO 2006):

1   Objectives related directly to TK and TK holders;
2   Objectives related to biodiversity and genetic resources policy;
3   Objectives related to indigenous peoples' rights;
4   Objectives related to sustainable development and capacity building; and
5   Objectives related to innovation promotion.

In Malaysia, these policy objectives are covered in different legislation. There is no law on protection of TK in Malaysia in respect of objective (1). In respect of objective (2) and (4), though the Access and Benefit Sharing Bill has still not been passed, the biodiversity laws of Sabah and Sarawak provide somewhat for these objectives. The Aboriginal Peoples Act 1960 covers objective (3) in a limited way. The current IPR laws in Malaysia provide for objective (5).

Protection of TK in IP laws

Malaysia, like other developing countries, enacted and/or revised a range of IP laws post–TRIPS. However, TCE and TK would not meet the criteria for protection under most of the IP laws.

Patent Act 1983 (Patents [Amendment] Act 2006; Patents [Amendment] Regulations 2011)

TK *per se* and TCE in fixed form do not qualify for patent protection as the elements of novelty (i.e. no prior art), inventiveness and industrial application would not be satisfied.

Copyright Act 1987

Provided the TCE is in a fixed form, for example on canvas, paper, cloth, wood and so forth, copyright protection is available. However, the difficulty would be how to prove originality as TCE are freely available in the public domain.

Copyright can also be used to protect related rights for performers such as live performance of dances, music and so on (Section 3 – includes "performance in relation to expression of folklore"). However, the difficulty is who owns it, as TCE belong to the whole community or even several communities. Rights under copyright vest in the person responsible for fixing or documenting the TCE and not the community.

Trade Marks Act 1976 (Trade Marks [Amendment] Act 2011; Trade Marks Regulations 1997)

The TK/TCE can be protected with trademarks or trade names provided the community that developed it can be named as the owners of the trademark or trade name. However, any indigenous community that wishes to use trademarks or trade names to protect their TK/TCE would have to incorporate a business entity to take advantage of this option. Indigenous communities may avail defensive protection to challenge trademarks or trade names that exploit their TK or cause confusion about the indigenous origins of the products.

Industrial Designs Act 1996 (Industrial Designs [Amendment] Act 2002; Industrial Designs Regulations 1999; Industrial Designs [Amendment] Regulations 2012)

TCE such as craft objects or utilitarian implements may be protected. However, as with other IP rights, there are problems with novelty, identifying the creator, who should own it and the duration of protection.

Common law

The common law remedies such as the tort of passing off/unfair competition, including the Trade Descriptions Act, are available against those who make false claims as to authenticity or association or endorsement of indigenous communities or where distinctive styles, symbols or marks of indigenous communities are used in products not made by the community.

Breach of confidence can be used where the information is capable of legal protection, was obtained under circumstances of confidentiality and has been used without authorisation to the detriment of the party communicating it. The types of information capable of protection include trade secrets, personal secrets, literary and artistic works and public and government secrets. However, it is unlikely that indigenous communities would be in a position to exercise such rights.

Geographical Indications Act 2000

The objective of this act is to protect an indication that identifies goods (defined as any natural or agricultural product or any product of handicraft or industry) as originating in a country or territory or a region or locality in that country or territory, where the quality, reputation or characteristics of the goods are attributable to their geographical origin. Therefore, protection is given not to the TK directly but to TCE such as plant-based products or handicrafts provided they qualify for protection as a geographical indication. Such products must be unique and distinctive to a particular place and different when compared to the same product in the same class from another geographical area.

According to the act, the geographical indication need not be registered, hence according it automatic protection. However, non-registration will make prevention of its unlawful use more difficult.

Included in the definition of "producer" under the act is any producer of agricultural products and any person exploiting natural products. This act allows for local communities or indigenous people to apply directly as "producers" of the goods to register the geographical indication without the intervention of any authority. Since ownership under GI does not provide for individual ownership rights but rather ownership by affiliation, producers carrying out their activities in that geographical area producing goods in accordance to the quality, character or reputation specified in the GI Register have the right of use of the GI. Unlike trademarks, the same GI can be used by multiple producers as long as they conform to the standards specified for that GI.

Numerous agricultural and natural products produced by local and indigenous communities in Malaysia would be capable of protection as GI. From 2003 to 2016, 110 applications were submitted for GI registration, of which 102 were Malaysian and 8 were foreign. A total of 69 (62 Malaysian and 7 foreign) have qualified for registration.[20]

The period of protection of the GI is 10 years and renewable every 10 years as long as it is in use. The majority of the products protected with GI originate from the East Malaysian states of Sabah and Sarawak. In addition, the agricultural products protected such as barrio rice (GI registered to Department of Agriculture Sarawak) and Sarawak pepper (GI registered to Sarawak Pepper Marketing Board) are plants traditionally cultivated by indigenous communities who have special knowledge of the cultivation techniques and are the keepers and conservers of the seeds of species of barrio rice and Sarawak pepper. It is not known to what extent indigenous communities have benefitted from the GIs registered to date.

Protection of New Plant Varieties Act 2004

One of the objectives of this act as stated in the preamble is "the recognition and protection of the contribution made by farmers, local communities and indigenous people towards the creation of new plant varieties".

The act defines local community as "a group of individuals who have settled together and continuously inherit production processes and culture or a group of individuals settled together in a village or area under an eco-cultural system", while indigenous people is defined as "persons who fall within the definition of 'aborigines' or 'native' as defined respectively in Clause (2) of Article 160 and Clause (6) of Article 161A of the Federal Constitution".

The act requires a breeder of a new plant variety to disclose in the application for the new plant variety:

• Information relating to the source of the genetic material or immediate parental lines of the plant variety;
• The prior written consent of the authority representing the local community or the indigenous people where the plant variety is developed from traditional varieties; and
• Compliance with any law regulating access to genetic or biological resources.

In this manner, if the new plant variety has been developed from utilising the traditional varieties conserved by local communities or indigenous people, the disclosure made in the plant variety protection application form provides defensive protection for the TK of the local community or indigenous people. This act does not provide for disclosure of TK in the application for plant variety protection.

Indigenous and local communities may apply for the protection of their traditional varieties of plants provided they satisfy the requirement that it is new, distinct and identifiable.[21] The requirement that it is new may not be met, as most traditional varieties would have been in existence and been used, exchanged or traded.

The act does not provide for the consent of the local communities or indigenous peoples directly. This is obtained indirectly through the authority representing them.

The Plant Variety Protection Office began accepting applications for registration of new plant varieties in 2008. As of 2017, 109 new plant varieties have been approved for registration.[22] The majority of the applications are from Malaysian public research institutions, universities and private companies (both local and foreign), while a handful are from individuals. It is not known if the development of the newly registered plant varieties relied on the TK of local communities or indigenous peoples. There are no applications/registrations of new plant varieties by/of local farmers or native communities.

Protection of TK in heritage law

Traditional cultural heritage in the form of both TK and TCE is protected under the National Heritage Act 2005.

National Heritage Act 2005

The National Heritage Act 2005 replaced the Antiquities Act 1976 and certain sections of the Treasure Trove Act 1957. It came into force on 1 March 2006.

The objective of the act as set out in the preamble is to provide for the preservation and conservation of a national heritage, natural heritage, tangible and intangible cultural heritage, underwater heritage and treasure trove. In this respect, its ambit is wide, as it includes not just antiquities but also contemporary manifestations of cultural heritage.

The Act defines cultural heritage as inclusive of intangible forms of cultural property and intangible cultural heritage is defined as:[23]

> *any form of expressions, languages, lingual utterances, sayings, musically produced tunes, notes, audible lyrics, songs, folksongs, oral traditions, poetry, music, dances as produced by the performing arts, theatrical plays, audible compositions of sounds and music, martial arts, that may have existed or exist in relation to the heritage of Malaysia or any part of Malaysia or in relation to the* heritage of a Malaysian community. (emphasis added)

Thus, the Heritage Act provides for the protection of the intangible cultural heritage of a wide community of Malaysians.

In order to attract protection under the act, the intangible cultural heritage must have cultural heritage significance, which is defined as "having aesthetic, archaeological, architectural, cultural, historical, scientific, social, spiritual, linguistic or technological value".[24]

There are two avenues for recognition as a heritage "object" under the act:

1   A declaration under Section 49 as a heritage object by the Commissioner;
2   On the application of any person and registration under Section 51 where the Commissioner is satisfied that it qualifies to be registered as a heritage object.

In the case of heritage objects to be declared as National Heritage, there are two possible avenues:

1   A declaration by the Minister under Section 67(1) in respect of any heritage site, heritage object, underwater cultural heritage listed in the Register or any living person; or
2   A nomination by any person to the Minister under Section 68 in respect of any natural heritage, tangible or intangible cultural heritage, living person or underwater cultural heritage.

In deciding whether a heritage object qualifies for National Heritage status, the Minister may consider the criteria set out in Section 67(2):

(a)   the historical importance, association with or relationship to Malaysian history;
(b)   the good design or aesthetic characteristics;
(c)   the scientific or technical innovations or achievements;
(d)   the social or cultural associations;
(e)   the potential to educate, illustrate or provide further scientific investigation in relation to Malaysian cultural heritage;
(f)   the importance in exhibiting a richness, diversity or unusual integration of features;
(g)   the rarity or uniqueness of the natural heritage, tangible or intangible cultural heritage or underwater cultural heritage;

(h) the representative nature of a site or object as part of a class or type of a site or object; and

(i) any other matter which is relevant to the determination of cultural heritage significance.

Within the definition of "object" is included tangible and intangible cultural heritage.[25] Heritage objects will be registered in the National Heritage Register.[26] There are already many heritage objects listed in the National Heritage Register, which is divided into two categories: the list of National Heritage objects and the list of Heritage objects. These lists are further sub-divided into Sites (categorised as natural site, building and archaeological) and Objects (categorised as tangible and intangible) The list of National Heritage currently contains a total of 98 heritage objects, including 15 living persons declared as National Heritage. The list of Heritage objects contains 216 items, of which 180 are listed under Sites and 34 are listed under Objects.[27]

The TK of native communities qualifies as intangible cultural heritage and can be protected and conserved under this act. Indeed, currently a number of native community leaders are listed as National Heritage, as are cultural traditions, rituals and practices of the native indigenous communities such as the wedding ceremony of the *Murut Tangul* tribe in Sarawak, and the bathing ceremony of new-born babies of the *Ibans*. Others listed as intangible cultural heritage are dances, music, traditional clothes, traditional children's games and local foods.

Many of the intangible cultural heritage items listed also originate from the traditions and culture of the Chinese and Indian immigrant communities and could be easily contested by China and India and even Indonesia in respect of the similar Malay traditional and cultural practices. Some examples from the National Heritage Register are the Khatak and Kuccipudi dances from the Indian community, the Fan dance from the Chinese community and Chinese and Indian living persons who are experts in Indian and Chinese music and dance. However, since Malaysian society and culture is a conglomeration of Malay, Chinese and Indian communities, the listing of these intangible cultural heritage items serves to preserve and conserve their traditional and cultural practices, especially so of the Chinese and Indian immigrant communities in their adopted homeland. Any claims as to ownership beyond the country's borders would rightly be open to contest by China, India and Indonesia!

Though food items are listed as intangible cultural heritage, it is surprising that the TK in agriculture of native indigenous communities and local farming communities specifically relating to plant species as food and medicines has not been registered to date.

The National Heritage Department under the Ministry of Information, Communications and Culture has the responsibility to preserve and conserve cultural heritage by conducting research, documentation, education, promotional activities and registration in order to protect it from extinction. Given the wide interpretation of intangible cultural heritage, more efforts could be undertaken to protect and conserve the TK in agriculture of Malaysia's native indigenous communities and local farming communities as National Heritage before the TK is lost with the passing of time.

Protection of TK in biodiversity laws

Biodiversity laws confer access to TK and benefit sharing to the holders of TK and, to a limited extent, ownership rights over products resulting from the use of TK. This part will examine to what extent the biodiversity laws protect TK in agriculture.

Access to biological resources and benefit-sharing bill

As a signatory to the CBD, Malaysia is obliged to enact access and benefit-sharing legislation. The process for drafting of the federal Access to Biological Resources and Benefit Sharing Bill began in 1994, and the final text of the bill was completed in 2013. To date, the bill has not been enacted due to federal–state jurisdictional issues that have yet to be resolved.[28]

The bill includes within its scope biological resources found on communal or customary land occupied by indigenous communities, such as native customary lands and aboriginal reserves.

Access to biological resources and associated TK can only be obtained by application for an access permit granted by a competent authority. An access permit is necessary when there is commercial or possible commercial exploitation of the biological resources and associated TK[29] and also for access for a non-commercial purpose.[30] In the case of an access permit for non-commercial purpose, the activity undertaken must be in collaboration with a public higher education institution, public research institution or government agency.[31] In this manner, the state exercises control over access to the TK of indigenous and local communities.

In evaluating the application for an access licence, the competent authority shall take into account whether the activity contributes to conservation and sustainable use of bio-resources; impact assessment on the biological resources, environment, and ecology; impact assessment on the indigenous communities and their knowledge, innovations and practices; whether prior informed consent has been obtained from the resource owner in accordance with prescribed procedure and whether the benefit-sharing arrangement (payments, royalties, beneficiaries, etc.) is fair and equitable.[32]

Approval may be contingent upon an access agreement with stipulated conditions. Among the exemptions to access are indigenous communities and local communities, who may continue their traditional and customary practices of keeping, using, sharing, marketing and sale of biological resources by and among such communities,[33] and farmers, who may replant on their own land, exchange or sell for further propagation, seeds and other propagating materials that are grown on their own land.[34]

The bill establishes a Fund for the purpose of holding and redistributing funds obtained from commercialisation of TK where the knowledge or innovation cannot be attributed to a particular local or indigenous community. A percentage of the gross sales from the product or process shall be paid into the fund. In such an event, the competent authority shall utilise the funds for the interest generally of local and indigenous communities.[35]

The East Malaysian states of Sabah[36] and Sarawak[37] have enacted biodiversity laws to regulate access to and benefit sharing of bio-resources in their respective states. In both states, the respective laws establish a Biodiversity Council to provide advice and make policies governing conservation and exploitation of bio-resources. They have also each established a Biodiversity Centre to carry out administration and implementation of the objectives of the act.

Access to conduct research or collect genetic resources for commercial purposes in both States is controlled through access permits and research agreements. Individuals and academic and research institutions undertaking pure academic or non-profit research can apply for exemption. An important term of the agreement is the right of the government to share in the intellectual property rights over any discovery. In addition, regardless of whether such discovery is commercialised, the permit holder is required to provide payment to the indigenous communities for their TK, and where the research leads to commercialisation of any pharmaceutical or medicinal product, the IP rights in such products must be shared with the indigenous communities.

Conclusion

In this chapter, three avenues for protection of TK in agriculture have been discussed – protection of TK under IP laws, protection of TK under heritage law and protection of TK under biodiversity laws. Each has its own limitations – heritage law is more broad based and focussed on documentation for conservation and preservation rather than ownership and control; IP law seeks to confer ownership rights provided the criteria for protection are met but in most instances fails to offer protection and, even so, only defensive protection; biodiversity laws regulate access and confer benefit sharing where TK has been commercialised, but in reality indigenous communities rarely are the direct beneficiaries, and benefits are usurped by the state on their behalf. The state plays a protective and paternalistic role over the TK of these communities.

There is no law recognising and according indigenous and local communities positive rights to their TK. A *sui generis* a law on protection of TK is needed in a country like Malaysia where the population comprises local and indigenous communities practising TK and their TK is being documented for conservation, preservation and utilisation for commercial benefit. The law should provide for the participation of indigenous communities in policy- and decision-making bodies. There is a lack of participatory mechanisms for indigenous peoples to be represented and for self-determination in policies that affect or involve them – more so now that plans are underway for the development of a TK digital library.

There is also a need to have a regional mechanism for resolving disputes relating to shared cross-border endemic species, shared TK, and TCE within the ASEAN region, as there have already been acrimonious disputes between Malaysia and Indonesia over TK in tongkat ali, batik, Rasa Sayang and Balinese dance.[38] The draft ASEAN Framework Agreement on Biological and Genetic Resources, which provides for standard setting on access and benefit-sharing mechanisms, has not yet been adopted. It provides for a mechanism for resolving disputes among ASEAN member states, but details of the dispute-settlement body have not been worked out. It is imperative that the draft agreement be finalised and adopted soon to resolve future competing claims among ASEAN's neighbours.

Notes

1 www.statista.com/statistics/318732/share-of-economic-sectors-in-the-gdp-in-malaysia/; www.statista.com/statistics/319036/employment-by-economic-sector-in-malaysia/, accessed on 31.1.2017.
2 www.chm.frim.gov.my/About-CHM/CBD-Thematic-Issue/Agricultural-biodiversity. aspx (accessed on 31.1.2017).
3 See www.wipo.int/tk/en/igc/ for the current discussions on TK and TCE (accessed on 7 September 2014). For a critical analysis of the definitions of TK and TCE, see Antons, C. (2009), What is "Traditional Cultural Expression"? International Definitions and Their Application in Developing Asia, [2009] *W.I.P.O.J.* No. 1. 103. Also see Antons, C. (2010), "The role of traditional knowledge and access to genetic resources in biodiversity conservation in Southeast Asia", Biodivers Conserv (2010) 19: 1189–1204.
4 Department of Statistics Malaysia (2011), *Population and Housing Census of Malaysia – Population Distribution and Basic Demographics 2010*, Department of Statistics Malaysia: Kuala Lumpur. Pdf copy downloaded on 20.12.2014 from www.statistics. gov.my.
5 See definition of indigenous people in Malaysia by the Human Rights Commission of Malaysia in SUHAKAM (2011), *Background Paper – SUHAKAM's National Enquiry into the Land Rights of Indigenous Peoples of Malaysia*, SUHAKAM: Kuala Lumpur, 2–4.
6 Article 160 (2) Federal Constitution of Malaysia.
7 Article 160A (6) and (7) Federal Constitution of Malaysia.
8 Section 3 Aboriginal Peoples Act 1954.
9 Section2 Interpretation (Definition of Native) Ordinance Sabah (Cap 64).
10 Section 3 Sarawak Interpretation Ordinance 1958.
11 Statistics from Annual Report 2006, Department of Orang Asli Affairs, cited in Kamarulzaman Kamaruddin and Osman Jusoh. (2008), "Educational Policy and Opportunities of Orang Asli – A Study of the Indigenous People in Malaysia", The Journal of Human Resource and Adult Learning, Vol. 4. Num. 1. June 2008, 86.
12 As at the 2010 census, the total population of Sabah was 3,206,742million, of which 1,781,112 million are indigenous people. Department of Statistics Malaysia (2011), *Population and Housing Census of Malaysia – Population Distribution and Basic Demographics 2010*, Department of Statistics Malaysia: Kuala Lumpur, 45. Pdf copy downloaded on 20.12.2014 from www.statistics.gov.my.
13 As at the 2010 census, the total population of Sarawak was 2,471,140 million, of which 1,191,740 million are indigenous people. Department of Statistics Malaysia (2011), *Population and Housing Census of Malaysia – Population Distribution and Basic Demographics 2010*, Department of Statistics Malaysia: Kuala Lumpur, 48. Pdf copy downloaded on 20.12.2014 from www.statistics.gov.my.
14 See "The utilization of medicinal plants by the Aborigines in Malaysia" at www. globinmed.com/index.php?option=com_content&view=article&id=54:the-utilization-of-medicinal-plants-by-the-aborigines-in-peninsula (accessed on 7 September 2014).
15 Sabah Biodiversity Centre, Annual Report 2007, 262–263.
16 See https://iponline.myipo.gov.my/ipo/main/search_tm.cfm?CFID=2d31a70a-4b06-4a87-8f3c-892975e525f7&CFTOKEN=0 (accessed on 3.1.2017).
17 The US patents on *Eurycoma Logifolia* can be found on www.google.com/patents/.
18 See 'The Calophyllum Story' available from the official website of the Forest Department of Sarawak at www.forestry.sarawak.gov.my/modules/web/pages.php?mod=web

page&sub=page&id=603&menu_id=0&sub_id=170 (accessed on 5.2.2017); Annex-Case Studies available at www.cbd.int/financial/bensharing/several-absagree.doc (accessed on 1 Feb 2017); Gupta et al (2005), Nature's Medicines: Traditional Knowledge and Intellectual Property Management. *Case Studies from the National Institutes of Health (NIH), USA, Curr Drug Discov Technol.* December; 2(4): 203–219, at. p. 13–14.

19 "Database to Protect Traditional Knowledge", The Daily Express, October 12, 2012. Available at www.dailyexpress.com.my/news.cfm?NewsID=82849 (accessed on 5.2.2017).

20 Available at www.myipo.gov.my/en/statistic-application-registration/#toggle-id-4. (accessed on 3.2.2017).

21 Section 14(2) Protection of New Plant Varieties Act 2004.

22 See http://pvpbkkt.doa.gov.my/ (accessed on 4.2.2017).

23 Section 2, National Heritage Act 2005.

24 Section 2, National Heritage Act 2005.

25 *Ibid.*

26 Section 23, National Heritage Act 2005.

27 See www.heritage.gov.my (accessed on 5.2.2017).

28 For a discussion on the drafting process and contents of the Access and Benefit Sharing Bill, see Mohamed Osman (2004), "Malaysia: Recent Initiatives to Develop Access and Benefit-Sharing Regulations", in Carrizosa S. *et al. (eds) (2004) Accessing Biodiversity and Sharing the Benefits: Lessons from Implementing the Convention on Biological Diversity, IUCN: Gland, Switzerland and Cambridge, UK.*

29 Section 12(1) Access and Benefit Sharing Bill.

30 Section 14(1) Access and Benefit Sharing Bill.

31 Section 14(3) Access and Benefit Sharing Bill.

32 Section 13(1) Access and Benefit Sharing Bill.

33 Section 4(3) Access and Benefit Sharing Bill.

34 Section 5 Access and Benefit Sharing Bill.

35 Section 18(5) Access and Benefit Sharing Bill.

36 Sabah Biodiversity Enactment 2000; Sabah Biodiversity (Access and Benefit Sharing) Regulations 2011.

37 Sarawak Biodiversity Centre Ordinance 1997; Sarawak Biodiversity Centre (Amendment) Ordinance 2003; Sarawak Biodiversity Regulations 2004.

38 For an account of some of the regional disputes on TCE between Indonesia and Malaysia, see Antons, C. (2009), *op. cit.* p. 113–115.

References

Antons, C. (2009) What Is "Traditional Cultural Expression"? International Definitions and Their Application in Developing Asia, [2009] *W.I.P.O.J.* No. 1. 103

Antons, C. (2010) 'The Role of Traditional Knowledge and Access to Genetic Resources in Biodiversity Conservation in Southeast Asia', *Biodiversity and Conservation*, 19, 1189–1204.

Baer, A. (2009) *Borneo Biomedical Bibliography* (3rd ed.). Oregon State University, USA.

Fasihuddin Ahmad and Ghazaly Ismail (2003) "Medicinal Plants Used by Kadazandusun Communities Around the Crocker Range", ASEAN Review of Biodiversity and Environmental Conservation, Jan-March 2003, available at http://kdca.org.my/wp-content/files/medicinal_crange.pdf (accessed 7 September 2014).

Gerten, D., et al. (2015) 'Traditional Knowledge and Practices Related to Citurs, Garcinia, Mangifera and Nephelium in Malaysia', *Open Access Library Journal*, 2, e1453. http://dx.doi.org/10.4236/oalib.1101453

Gupta et al. (2005), Nature's Medicines: Traditional Knowledge and Intellectual Property Management. *Case Studies from the National Institutes of Health (NIH), USA, Curr Drug Discov Technol.* December, 2(4), 203–219, at. 13–14.

Halim, A.A., et al. (2012a) 'Indigenous Knowledge and Biodiversity Conservation in Sabah', *International Journal of Social Science and Humanity*, 2(2), March, 159–163.

Halim, A.A. et al. (2012b) *Traditional Knowledge and Environmental Conservation Among Indigenous People in Ranau, Sabah*, paper presented at UMT 11th International Annual Symposium on Sustainability Science and Management, 9–11 July 2012, Trengganu, Malaysia.

Kamaruddin, K. and Jusoh, O. (2008) 'Educational Policy and Opportunities of Orang Asli – a Study of the Indigenous People in Malaysia', *The Journal of Human Resource and Adult Learning*, 4(1), June, 86.

Kardooni, R., et al. (2013) 'Traditional Knowledge of Orang Asli on Forests in Peninsular Malaysia', *Indian Journal of Traditional Knowledge*, 13(2), April, 283–291.

Lasimbang, J. and Nicholas, C. (2004) *Deliberations on the National Roundtable on Biodiversity and Indigenous Knowledge Systems in Malaysia*, Subang Jaya: Centre for Orang Asli Concerns 10–11.

Malaysian Biotechnology Corporation (2009) *Overview – Malaysian Agricultural Biotechnology*, Kuala Lumpur: A Frost & Sullivan Whitepaper.

Ministry of Health Malaysia (2011) *Traditional and Complementary Medicine Programme in Malaysia*, Kuala Lumpur Ministry of Health.

Nicholas, C. (1996) 'The Orang Asli of Peninsular Malaysia', in C. Nicholas and R. Singh (eds) *Indigenous Peoples of Asia: Many Peoples, One Struggle*, Bangkok: Asia Indigenous Pact.

Nordin, Rohaida, et al. (2012) "Traditional Knowledge Documentation-Preventing or Promoting Biopiracy", Pertanika J. Soc. Sci. & Hum. 20 (S): 11–22, 19.

OECD (2015) *Boosting Malaysia's National Intellectual Property System for Innovation*, OECD Publishing, Paris, 106. Available: www.oecdbookshop.org/browse.asp?pid=title-detail&lang=en&ds=&ISB=9789264239227 (accessed 5 February 2017).

Ong H.C. et al. (2011) "Traditional Knowledge of Medicinal Plants Among Malay Villages in Kampong Mak Kemas, Trengganu, Malaysia", Ethno Med, 5(3): 175–185.

Osman, M. (2004) 'Malaysia: Recent Initiatives to Develop Access and Benefit-Sharing Regulations', in Carrizosa, S. et al. (eds.), *Accessing Biodiversity and Sharing the Benefits: Lessons from Implementing the Convention on Biological Diversity*, Gland, Switzerland and Cambridge, UK: IUCN.

Samuel, A.J.S.J., et al. (2010) 'Ethnomedical Survey of Plants Used by the Orang Asli in Kampung Bawong, Perak, West Malaysia', *Journal of Ethnobiology and Ethnomedicine*,6, 5. Electronic version available: www.ethnobiomed.com/content/6/1/5 (accessed 7 September 2014).

SUHAKAM (2011) *Background Paper – SUHAKAM's National Enquiry into the Land Rights of Indigenous Peoples of Malaysia*, Kuala Lumpur, SUHAKAM 2–4.

WIPO Intergovernmental Committee on Intellectual Property and Genetic Resources, Traditional Knowledge and Folklore, Ninth Session, Geneva, April 24–26, 2006, *The Protection of Traditional Knowledge: Revised Outline of Policy Options and Legal Mechanisms – Document Prepared by the Secretariat*, WIPO/GRTKF/IC/9/INF/5, March 27, 2006, 3–4.

Chapter 12

The protection of intangible cultural resources in the Indonesian legal system

Miranda Risang Ayu Palar

Intangible cultural resources

'Intangible cultural resources' is a working term used in this chapter to cover all possible objects within the scope of 'traditional knowledge', 'traditional knowledge associated with genetic resources', 'traditional medicines', 'traditional cultural expressions', 'folklore', and 'intangible cultural heritage of mankind'. 'Intangible cultural resources' are easily recognised as an economic asset in conjunction with 'natural resources' and 'human resources'.

'Traditional knowledge', 'associated traditional knowledge', 'traditional knowledge associated with genetic resources', 'traditional medicines', 'traditional cultural expressions', 'folklore', and 'intangible cultural heritage of mankind' are the technical terms used in various international legal instruments and text-based multilateral negotiations. Some of the objects are very different, while others are quite similar and complementary to each other. In the Indonesian legal system all of them are classified as communal or community-based intellectual property.

Discussions in different fora about 'traditional cultural expressions' and the 'intangible cultural heritage of mankind' sometimes refer to the same objects, but the different nature of the rights depends on the legal bases. In this regard, variations in an object could be protected as a form of traditional cultural expressions as well as the intangible cultural heritage of mankind.

Traditional batik textiles from Indonesia, for example, which are produced by a traditional wax block immersion technique, have been inscribed as an intangible cultural heritage of humanity based on the UNESCO Convention 2003 concerning the Safeguarding of the Intangible Cultural Heritage of Mankind. However, many varieties of batik can also be protected under Indonesian Law Number 28 Year 2014 concerning Copyright. If the variety is held by an indigenous or local community, it can be protected as a traditional cultural expression under Clause Article 38 of the Copyright Law. If the variety has been developed in an original way by an artist, it can be protected as an individual right under the same law. In addition, if the variety is predominantly characterised by the traditional culture in a certain locality, and so the link between the product and the social context is strong, it could also be protected under Geographical Indications, based on Chapter I, II, VIII, IX, X, and XI of Law Number 20 Year 2016 concerning Trade Marks and Geographical Indications and its implementing regulations specialising in Geographical Indications, as well as under a number of regulations at provincial level.

The importance of cultural development in Indonesia has also been highlighted by the enactment of Law Number 5 Year 2017 concerning the Development of Culture. Based on Article 5 of this law, most intangible cultural resources are protected by it, notably: oral traditions, manuscripts, traditional customary laws and protocols (*adat-istiadat*), rites, traditional knowledge, arts, languages, folk games, and traditional sports. In this regard, the protection and development of batik can be strengthened by this general law based on its articles about cultural mainstreaming, defensive protection mechanisms using an integrated database system of culture, stock taking, safeguarding, maintenance, conservation and publication programs, and the inclusion of batik in the national strategy of culture.

Last but not least, there is a specific Ministerial Regulation from the Ministry of Environment and Forestry concerning local wisdom, popularly known as the Environment and Forestry's Ministerial Regulation Number P34 Year 2017. This regulation provides the legal base for benefit-sharing arrangements for traditional knowledge and traditional cultural expressions associated with genetic resources. Batik clothes which are made by using natural colours and threads could also enjoy greater economic benefit from this regulation.

The objects of intangible cultural resources share similar characteristics, which can be clearly differentiated from the objects of conventional intellectual property rights (Blakeney 1999; Gervais 2003: 7). These objects:

1   are characterized by traditional values, traditional ways of thinking, traditional forms and fixed styles, and traditional contexts;
2   are actively used by indigenous and local communities, groups, and, in some cases, individuals as a living culture;
3   are maintained, used, developed, and transmitted from generation to generation inside and outside the community;
4   are strongly influenced by the environment on which the indigenous or local community depends for their livelihood;
5   serve the sense of social and cultural identity of the community.

Traditional knowledge, associated traditional knowledge, traditional knowledge associated with genetic resources, and traditional medicine

'Traditional knowledge' can be defined as the know-how, skills, innovations, practices, teachings, and learnings of indigenous and local communities (WIPO 2014a: 5). In particular, traditional knowledge can be associated with fields such as traditional agriculture, traditional healthcare, traditional medicine, traditional architecture and construction technology, and last but not least, with natural resources and genetic resources (WIPO 2014b: 5).

'Traditional knowledge' in a broad sense includes 'associated traditional knowledge', 'traditional knowledge associated with genetic resources', and 'traditional medicines'. 'Associated traditional knowledge' means "knowledge which is dynamic and evolving, generated in a traditional context, collectively preserved and transmitted from generation to generation, including but is not limited to know-how, skills, innovations, practices and learning, that subsist in a genetic resource" (WIPO 2014b: 1). 'Traditional knowledge associated with genetic resources' refers to intellectual interventions on certain genetic resources (Article 6 and 7, Nagoya Protocol)[1] by indigenous or local communities, for example, the interpretation of special benefits of a raw plant or fruit for cosmetics. In regard to 'traditional medicines', Padmashree Gehl Sampath argues that "Traditional knowledge is also often used to denote indigenous medicinal knowledge that is a coherent system linking social behavior, human physiology, and botanical observations" (Sampath 2005: 118).

Examples of 'traditional knowledge' in Indonesia are:

1   *Subak*, a traditional method of irrigating the rice fields in the landscape of Bali Island as a part of 'traditional agriculture';
2   *Lulur*, a traditional delicate powder used to maintain the health of the body and skin of the royal families in the traditions of Yogyakarta and Surakarta, Central Java, as a part of 'traditional health care';
3   *Jamu*, herbal medicines used for various illnesses, which can be found in almost all indigenous and local communities in Indonesia, but especially in Central and East Java, as a part of 'traditional medicine';
4   *Umma Mawinne*, a traditional architecture and construction technology for houses on Sumba Island, East Nusa Tenggara, which honours women by symbolising the house as the whole body of a woman;[2]
5   *Pasak Bumi* (earth stalks) from Kalimantan or Borneo Island to increase stamina; *Buah Merah* (red fruit) from West Papua to cure cysts, lumps, and cancer; *Bawang Berlian* (diamond onions) from volcanic areas in western Indonesia to cure blood-related diseases.

There are in fact many other examples of traditional knowledge associated with natural as well as genetic resources from almost all islands in the Indonesian archipelago.

Traditional cultural expressions and folklore

In the World Intellectual Property Organization's ongoing negotiations concerning the draft articles for the protection of traditional cultural expression, the working definition of 'traditional cultural expression' is:

> any form of expression, tangible or intangible, or a combination thereof, such as actions, materials, music and sound, verbal and written, regardless of the

form in which it is embodied, expressed or illustrated. Traditional cultural expressions may exist in written or codified, oral or other forms.

(WIPO 2014c)

Folklore is the term used as a subsidiary of traditional cultural expressions. The WIPO Glossary of Terms of the Law of Copyright and Neighboring Rights 1980 defines folklore as:

. . . works belonging the cultural heritage of a nation, created, preserved and developed in indigenous communities by unidentified persons from generation to generation. Examples for such works are folk tales, folk songs, instrumental music or dances, and the different rites of people. According to some opinions, works of folk art expressed in tangible form are not covered by the notion of folklore. In its broadest possible legal sense, however, folklore comprises all 'literary and artistic works' mostly created by authors of unknown identity but presumed to be nationals of a given country, evolving from characteristic forms traditional in the ethnic groups of the country.

(WIPO 1980: 121)

In multilateral negotiations, 'traditional cultural expressions' has become more common as a legal term because it refers to folklore as well as tangible forms of it.

In line with the general concept of 'traditional cultural expressions' substantiated in the second version of WIPO Document Number WO/GA/40/7 Annex A, the scope of traditional cultural expressions regulated in the Indonesian Copyright Law includes:

1   phonetic and verbal expressions, such as: stories, poems, words, names, symbols, legends and messages, either in textual or oral form;
2   musical expressions, including: songs, instrumental music, rhythms, sounds and rites;
3   gestures or movement expressions, including: mimes, dances and traditional sports;
4   theatrical expressions, including: wooden or leather puppet shows and folk theatre;
5   visual expressions in two and three dimensions, which exist in leather, wood, bamboo, metal, stone, ceramics, textiles or other materials;
6   material expressions, including: traditional handicrafts, masks, statues, architecture, spiritual goods and sacred sites;
7   customary law or *adat* ceremonies, including: sacred rituals and pilgrimage journeys.

Intangible cultural heritage

The intangible cultural heritage of mankind, or intangible cultural heritage, are technical terms used in the United Nations Educational, Scientific and Cultural Organization's Convention for the Safeguarding of the Intangible Cultural Heritage of Mankind 2003 (UNESCO Convention 2003). Article 2 (2) of the UNESCO Convention 2003 lists the manifestations or objects of intangible cultural heritage as:

1   oral traditions and expressions, including language as a vehicle of the intangible cultural heritage;
2   performing arts;
3   social practices, rituals and festive events;
4   knowledge and practices concerning nature and the universe;
5   traditional craftsmanship.

The discussion shows that the manifestation of intangible cultural heritage and the scope of traditional cultural expressions are substantially similar. Traditional knowledge can also be included in the manifestation of intangible cultural heritage as a part of 'knowledge and practices concerning nature and the universe'. In short, the differences in the terms are not intended to differentiate the objects in their safeguarding or protection. Rather, they indicate the differences in the nature of the legal protections.

The objectives of the UNESCO Convention 2003 are to safeguard intangible cultural heritage, to ensure respect for the intangible cultural heritage of the communities concerned, to raise awareness at the local, national, and international levels, and to provide for international cooperation and assistance. The safeguarding is intended to optimise the status of the objects as tools of awareness raising and to instil mutual respect and cooperation amongst different cultures in the different nations in the world. There is no economic right or exclusive right denoted in the safeguarding system. Neither is direct financial benefit obligated for the beneficiaries. The safeguarding system is designed to strengthen and perpetuate the social and cultural rights of the communities concerned.

From the perspective of other international legal instruments which regulate or negotiate protection for traditional knowledge and traditional cultural expressions in the World Trade Organization (WTO), World Intellectual Property Organization (WIPO), and United Nations Convention on Biological Diversity (UN-CBD), the safeguarding system of the UNESCO Convention 2003 provides the right holders with a kind of "communal moral right" or a "moral right" that is not held by an individual but by a community.[3]

In the UNESCO Convention 2003 system, the inscription of an object as an intangible cultural heritage would serve the object as well as its beneficiaries with the comprehensive history, advancements, and variations as well as the identification of communities, groups, or, in several cases, individuals, who are traditionally authorised or regarded as the guardians of the object in its geographical origin. Exclusive and economic rights are not the concern of this safeguarding system. In other words, talking about an object as intangible cultural heritage means talking about communal moral rights, not about individual, exclusive, or economic rights.

Indonesia has ratified UNESCO Convention 2003 by the endorsement of Presidential Regulation Number 78 Year 2007. The safeguarding system is now being used to protect selected objects, in conjunction with economic rights provided by other ratified international legal instruments and national laws. So far, there are eight elements from Indonesia which have successfully met the UNESCO criteria of inscription as Intangible Cultural Heritage of Mankind as follows:

1   *Wayang* Puppet Theatre, listed as the Intangible Cultural Heritage of Humanity as well as a UNESCO Masterpiece in 2008 (UNESCO 2008);
2   Indonesian *Keris*, listed as the Intangible Cultural Heritage of Humanity as well as a UNESCO Masterpiece in 2008 (UNESCO 2008);
3   Education and training in Indonesian *batik* as intangible cultural heritage for elementary, junior, senior, vocational school, and polytechnic students, in collaboration with the Batik Museum in Pekalongan, was also listed among the Best Safeguarding Practices in 2009 (UNESCO 2009);
4   Indonesian *batik*, listed as the Intangible Cultural Heritage of Humanity in 2009 (UNESCO 2009);
5   Indonesian *Angklung*, listed as the Intangible Cultural Heritage of Humanity in 2010 (UNESCO 2010);
6   *Saman* Dance from Nangroe Aceh Darussalam, Indonesia, listed as Intangible Cultural Heritage in Need of Urgent Safeguarding in 2011 (UNESCO 2011);
7   *Noken* multifunctional knotted or woven bags, handcraft of the people of Papua, listed as Intangible Cultural Heritage in Need of Urgent Safeguarding in 2012 (UNESCO 2012);
8   Three genres of traditional dance in Bali, namely sacred, semi-sacred, and that meant for enjoyment by communities at large, listed as the Intangible Cultural Heritage of Humanity in 2015 (UNESCO 2015).

Indonesian legal system to protect communal intellectual property

The Indonesian legal system is constructed in line with the civil law system. This system is mainly based on the layers of written laws and implementing regulations rather than on a set of judge-made laws and national conventions, as follows:

a   Cultural and Intellectual Property Rights in the 1945 Constitution of the Republic of Indonesia

There are several articles which can be used as the basis of the establishment of intellectual property protection.

The first article is Article 28c. Article 28c(1) of the 1945 Constitution states that everyone has the right to self-development through the fulfillment of their basic rights, has the right to education and to enjoying the benefits of the advancement of science and technology, arts and cultures, to enhance their quality of life and for the welfare of all human beings. Article 28c(2) of the Constitution also declares that the right to self-development applies not only individually, but also collectively, to develop the society, nation and state.

The second relevant article is Article 28i(3). This article ensures that cultural identities and the rights of indigenous communities are respected in line with the changes of the age and of civilization.

The third article is Article 32(1). This article, known as 'the constitutional article of culture', substantiates that the State enhances Indonesian national culture in the global world by assuring the rights of the society to maintain and to develop its own cultural values.

The fourth article is Article 33(2). This article determines that all production sectors which are important for the state and strategically predominant in fulfilling the interests of the society shall be controlled under the management of the state.

b   Indonesian Affirmation of Cultural Rights based on UDHR Article 27, ICCPR Article 27, ICESCR Article 15 and UNDRIP Article 29

Indonesia acknowledges the International Bill of Rights, which consists of the Universal Declaration of Human Rights (UDHR), the International Covenant on Civil and Political Rights (ICCPR), and the International Covenant on Social, Economic and Cultural Rights (ICESCR). In addition, with reservations on the use of a term that may lead indigenous communities in Indonesia to conduct separatist movements against the unity of the Republic of Indonesia, Indonesia also supports the human rights listed in the Universal Declaration of the Rights of Indigenous People (UNDRIP).

The Universal Declaration of Human Rights 1948 (UDHR) Article 27 (1) and (2) states that:

1) Everyone has the right freely to participate in the cultural life of the community, to enjoy the arts and to share in scientific advancement and its benefits;
2) everyone has the right to the protection of the moral and material interests resulting from any scientific, literary and artistic production of which he is the author.

The International Covenant on Civil and Political Rights (ICCPR) Article 27 states that:

In those states in which ethnic, religious or linguistic minorities exist, persons belonging to such minorities shall not be denied the right, in community with other members of their groups to enjoy their own culture, to profess and practice their own religion, or to use their own language.

The International Covenant on Economic, Social and Cultural Rights (ICE-SCR) Article 15 points (a), (b), and (c) note that the State Parties recognize the right of everyone:

a   to take part in cultural life;
b   to enjoy the benefits of scientific progress and its applications;
c   to benefit from the protection of the moral and material interests resulting from any scientific, literary, or artistic production of which he is the author.

The Universal Declaration of the Rights of Indigenous People (UNDRIP) Article 29 states that

Indigenous people are entitled to the recognition of the full ownership, control and protection of their cultural and intellectual property. They have the right to special measures to control, develop and protect their science, technologies and cultural manifestations, including human and other genetic resources, seeds, medicines, knowledge of the properties of fauna and flora, oral traditions, literatures, designs and visual and performing arts.

Articles of the International Bill of Rights and of the United Nations Declaration of the Rights of Indigenous People, therefore, imply that the scope of cultural rights includes communal intellectual property rights, especially those whose objects are still held by indigenous and local communities as the authorised guardians or custodians, based on customary law. Expressions of communal intellectual property are protected not merely for a short period to be economically beneficial for an individual. Rather, they are to be safeguarded in perpetuity, for all possible benefits, including indirect monetary benefit such as for educational purposes, research, or cultural encounters or for enhancing eco-cultural tourism. Most importantly, the safeguarding efforts should be conducted to strengthen the socio-cultural identity of the community concerned.

c   Ratifications of international intellectual property legal instruments

Indonesia has also ratified a number of international legal instruments specialised in intellectual property rights. The conventional intellectual property rights systems which can serve for the protection of certain aspects of intangible cultural resources are: Copyright, Geographical Indications and Undisclosed Information, as intellectual property subject matters in the TRIPS Agreement; Trade Names, Appellation of Origins, Indication of Source and Trade Secrets as subject matters in the Paris Convention; all copyright aspects, most importantly the individual Moral Right in the Berne Convention; and indirect protection provided by the WIPO Performances and Phonograms Treaty.

In Indonesia the use of international intellectual property legal instruments complements the safeguarding system of the UNESCO Convention 2003. This is because the intangible cultural heritage safeguarding system in the UNESCO Convention does not deal with exclusive, economic, or individual rights issues as the international intellectual property legal instruments do.

d   **Benefit-sharing arrangements in UN CBD Article 8j and the Nagoya Protocol**

New emerging issues in the intellectual property system dealing with the need for the best protection for genetic resources, traditional knowledge, and traditional cultural expressions have influenced the way the Indonesian intellectual property legal system works. This influence began when Law Number 32 Year 2009 concerning the Protection and Management of the Environment was promulgated, by gradually involving several related international legal instruments in environmental law. These legal instruments are the United Nations Convention on Biological Diversity (UN-CBD) ratified by Law Number 5 Year 1994 and the Nagoya Protocol ratified by Law Number 11 Year 2014.

These inclusions were made because the existing protection and safeguarding systems were still too partial and scattered to provide comprehensive and maximum protection for genetic resources and the potential of traditional knowledge in a country of mega biodiversity and cultural diversity like Indonesia. Sacred values, oral expressions, communal ownership, layers of management of rights, state responsibility, perpetual custodianship, and shared custodianship between several nations cannot be accommodated properly in the conventional intellectual property rights system, which mostly relies on profane originality, on inventiveness or newness values, on written expression, individual ownership, person-to-person or private legal relations, limited periods of protection, and exclusive rights of possession.

Article 8(j) of the United Nations Convention on Biological Diversity requires member states to

Subject to its national legislation, respect, preserve and maintain knowledge, innovations and practices of indigenous and local communities embodying traditional lifestyles relevant for the conservation and sustainable use of biological diversity and promote their wider application with the approval and involvement of the holders of such knowledge, innovations and practices and encourage the equitable sharing of the benefits arising from the utilization of such knowledge, innovations and practices.

The Nagoya Protocol focuses its content on regulating access to genetic resources and on the fair and equitable sharing of benefits arising from their utilisation. This Protocol also regulates access to and utilisation of traditional knowledge associated with genetic resources.

Article 6 (1) of the Nagoya Protocol concerning Access to Genetic Resources states that

In the exercise of sovereign rights over natural resources, and subject to domestic access and benefit-sharing legislation or regulatory requirements, access to genetic resources for their utilization shall be subject to the prior informed consent of the Party providing such resources, that is the country of origin of such resources or a Party that has acquired the genetic resources in accordance with the Convention, unless otherwise determined by that Party.

Article 7 of the Nagoya Protocol also emphasises the importance of prior informed consent in the process of accessing and utilising any traditional knowledge associated with genetic resources. The article states that

In accordance with domestic law, each Party shall take measures, as appropriate, with the aim of ensuring that traditional knowledge associated with genetic resources that is held by indigenous and local communities is accessed with the prior and informed consent or approval and involvement of these indigenous and local communities, and that mutually agreed terms have been established.

The Nagoya Protocol also acknowledges the existence of community protocols to be used, the importance of setting up minimum requirements for mutually agreed term contracts to secure the benefit-sharing arrangements, the importance of composing a model of a contractual clause for benefit sharing, and finally the types of benefit sharing themselves. Benefit sharing can take the form of monetary or non-monetary benefits.

e   Protection of performers of the expressions of folklore in WPPT

Indonesia has ratified WIPO Performances and Phonograms Treaty 1996 (WPPT) by the endorsement of Presidential Decree Number 74 Year 2004. WPPT is the one in the conventional intellectual property international legal instruments which clearly extents its rights to the performers of expressions of folklore by defining the performers in Article 1 as

actors, singers, musicians, dancers, and other persons who act, sing, deliver, declaim, play in, interpret, or otherwise perform literary or artistic works or expressions of folklore.

Consequently, performers of traditional or folk musics, dances, plays, and other performances are entitled to enjoy many individual rights substantiated in this treaty; those are

- Economic rights on the performers' fixed performances, that include exclusive right on direct or indirect reproduction of their performances fixed in the phonograms in any manner or form, exclusive right on distribution of their performance fixed in phonograms, exclusive right of rental of their fixed performance, and exclusive right of making available to their fixed performances to the public;

- Economic rights of the performers in their unfixed performances or live repertoires; and
- Moral rights of the performers.

f   Indonesian intellectual property laws for intangible cultural resources

Although scattered, several laws regulating conventional intellectual property rights have been re-composed and amended to accommodate the need to protect intangible cultural resources.

Indonesian Patent Law Number 13 Year 2016 is unlike the old Patent Law Number 14 Year 2001, which lacked acknowledgement and administrative requirements to protect genetic resources as well as traditional knowledge associated with genetic resources in line with the Nagoya Protocol. Article 26 of the new Patent Law Number 13 Year 2016 now requires mandatory disclosure of origins for inventions which are based on genetic resources and/or traditional knowledge. Article 35 of the law also makes it possible to extend the term to complete administrative requirements of a patent application. This provision can be used in a case in which the submitted documents still lack the mandatory disclosure.

The other Indonesian laws on intellectual property rights which have inserted special clauses to protect the objects of intangible cultural resources are as follows:

1) Copyright Law Number 28 Year 2014 Article 38–39. These articles are concerned with regulating 'traditional cultural expressions'. The articles emphasise the state's responsibility to manage, safeguard, and maintain rights in respect to living cultures and the existence of the communities concerned and to exercise the copyright in cases where the community or custodians are unable to be found;

2) Trade Marks and Geographical Indications Law Number 20 Year 2016 and its implementing regulations, including the old Government Regulation Number 51 Year 2007 concerning Geographical Indications, which is still in force. The communal nature of geographical indications and indications of the ownership of sources allows this law to be used to protect certain final outputs or products from the utilisation of intangible cultural resources which are characterised by their place of origin;

3) Law Number 29 Year 2000 concerning the Protection of New Varieties of Plants. Article 7 of this law acknowledges and enhances the inscription of local varieties which are unable to be registered under this law because of the lack of newness but which have been cultivated

and maintained from generation to generation by traditional or local farmers.

g) Ideal Protection for Intangible Cultural Resources in the Indonesian Draft Law for the Protection of Traditional Knowledge and Traditional Cultural Expressions (Indonesian Draft Law on TKTCEs)

Considering the richness of the biodiversity and cultural diversity of Indonesia, there have been a number of means to protect the intangible cultural resources of Indonesia, namely:

1   negative protection: using the existing intellectual property regimes, including the legal system, against unfair competition practices;
2   positive protection: creating new legal regimes *(sui generis)* at national and international levels;
3   case-based protection: enhancing living culture, implementing prior informed consent and benefit-sharing provisions in any contracts related to the utilisation of genetic resources, traditional knowledge, and/or traditional cultural expressions;
4   defensive protection: establishing a national database for genetic resources, traditional knowledge, and traditional cultural expressions for the purpose of substantive examination and re-declaration of rights;
5   systemic protection: combining negative protection with case-based protection, together with accommodating defensive protection in institutional programs of related ministries, with the main objective of establishing positive protection at international and national levels.

Negative protection and case-based protection are the most efficient and effective ways of protecting genetic resources, traditional knowledge, and traditional cultural expressions, because the legal grounds are already available. Yet they don't provide comprehensive and maximum protection. Defensive protection is more easily afforded because it depends on political will at the national level. However, the common challenge to affording this protection is the difficulty in enhancing the institutional arrangements between ministries that should work together to establish an integrated database system. Positive protection is the ideal way. However, promulgating new laws, either at national or international levels, has never been easy. In this regard, the negotiations at WIPO have already been conducted since 2000, that is, for more than a decade. Nevertheless, since 2009, the Indonesian Ministry of Foreign Affairs, the Ministry of Law and Human Rights, and the Coordinator Ministry for Political, Legal, and Security Affairs have been enhancing systemic protection for intangible cultural resources by conducting a number of coordinative meetings between the ministries to accelerate the positive and defensive protection mechanisms for Indonesian genetic resources, traditional knowledge, and traditional cultural expressions.

Ideally, to protect the enormous potential of intangible cultural resources in Indonesia, the Indonesian legal system in the future should provide the most comprehensive protection in the form of a *sui generis* law or act. In this regard, the final draft of the Indonesian Draft Law on TKTCEs dated September 1, 2014, which was prepared by the House of the Senate, sets out that the minimum requirements for the legal utilisation of intangible cultural resources should consist of:

1   disclosure of geographical origin, which can be a specific area in the country of origin or the country of provider of the resources;
2   recognition of indigenous or local communities as the custodians or original right holders of the resources in the articles of the bill;
3   prior informed consent based on mutually agreed terms for traditional knowledge associated with genetic resources and silent prior informed consent for traditional cultural expressions and intangible cultural heritage objects. Silent prior informed consent is an implicit consent that can be assumed, although without any written contract, when custodians do not show any objection and clearly express their positive support to a certain utilisation program;
4   fair and equitable benefit sharing, including monetary, non-monetary, direct, or indirect benefit sharing.

The draft of the Indonesian Bill of Law on TKTCEs prepared by the Indonesian House of the Senate defines the intended rights associated with the intangible cultural resources based on the layers of rights, as follows:

1   rights of ownership rooted in traditional rights are to be held by indigenous and local communities, who are called the custodian/s. The custodian/s are to consist of local communities, customary law or *Adat* communities, and traditional communities;
2   right of ownership of the intangible cultural resources which are considered as strategic resources for the welfare of Indonesian society is to be a part of the state's responsibility;
3   sovereignty and the sovereign right to the strategic resources which are found in the territory of the Republic of Indonesia is to be exercised by the Indonesian government on behalf of the Indonesian nation. Strategic resources are to be determined by the relevant legislative and executive governmental bodies of Indonesia;
4   right of management is to be held by the government as the competent authority at the national level as well as by provincial or local governments, based on the attribution or delegation rights;
5   right of management on cross-border objects is to be held by a cross-border competent authority decided by agreement between related countries;
6   terms of protection for intangible cultural resources are to be perpetual as long as the objects remain eligible to fulfil the defined criteria and are still a part of the living culture.

In principle, the Draft Law on TKTCEs denotes no formality in the protection of intangible cultural resources. Administrative procedures are provided only to strengthen the burden of proof. This protection should then be implemented by the government in the form of defensive protection mechanisms by

1   conducting documentation of the resources by creating databases (open, half-restricted and restricted databases);
2   acknowledging sources based on self-identification or oral expressions of custodians of the sources. This acknowledgement is particularly to be used for sacred and secret traditional knowledge. The sacred and secret traditional knowledge should be respected to remain as it is, depending on the authorisation of the custodians.

h   Indonesian Law Number 5 Year 2017 concerning the Development of Culture

General, broad, and idealistic provisions about aspects of cultural developments are now substantiated in the Law Number 5 Year 2017 concerning the Development of Culture. This law claims a strong position as the only general law concerning culture by only referring to Articles 20, 21, and 34 of the 1945 Constitution of the Republic of Indonesia in its preamble. It means all existing laws should be in harmony with this law and not the other way around.

In fact, the law regulating culture had been drafted long before the amendments of the laws on copyrights, patents, trademarks, and TKTCEs were drafted. However, it was finally refined and endorsed later, with the intention to solidify a set of general rules for many existing yet scattered laws and regulations which have been dealing with different types of intangible cultural resources. The enactment of this law also answered the question why the bill on TKTCEs, regardless of the quality of its content, had not been prioritised for more than three years.

i   Environmental legal system associated with community-based intellectual property rights

Since the ratification of the UN-CBD and the Nagoya Protocol, there have been substantial changes at the implementation level. Firstly, the Ministry of Environment and Ministry of Forestry used to be the strong candidates to become a national focal point to protect most genetic resources and traditional knowledge associated with genetic resources in the lands of Indonesia. They are now merged into a single ministry called Ministry of Environment and Forestry. Secondly, several implementing regulations and guidelines have been endorsed by the ministry to implement the Nagoya Protocol.

Regarding the protection of intangible cultural resources, the most important regulation is the Environment and Forestry's Ministerial Regulation Number 34/ MEN/SETJEN/KUM.1/5/2017 concerning the Recognition and Protection of

Local Wisdom in the Management of Natural Resources and Environment. Several concepts in the Bill of Law on TKTCEs have been finely accommodated in this regulation, although they are all specified only for those associated with the preservation and management of environment and natural resources.

This ministerial regulation clarifies a number of debatable terms about the legal definitions of 'local wisdom' and 'traditional knowledge' in Article 1, including the communal right holders of the wisdom and knowledge, notably indigenous community (*Adat* people), local community, and the custodians.

Article 4 of the regulation is also interesting, as it states the scope of local wisdoms to include

1   Traditional knowledge on water, lands, and energy;
2   Traditional knowledge regarding sustainable livelihood, health and other aspects of life;
3   Traditional tools and traditional technology for the protection and management of sustainable environment and natural resources;
4   Traditional cultural expressions related to the protection and management of environment and natural resources, including traditional cultural expressions associated with genetic resources;
5   Traditional learning on the protection and management of environment; and
6   Intangible as well as tangible cultural heritage.

This regulation also meticulously recognises the importance to differentiate the protections for local wisdoms – those that are accessible by the public and those which are secret, sacred, and closely held ones. The latter category should be strictly disclosed or even unable to be published at all.

Example of affording comprehensive protection in Indonesia: masks of Sunda

West Java Province is the place of origin of Sunda communities. Nowadays the majority of Sundanese are Muslims. However, before the introduction of the foreign religions of Hinduism, Buddhism, Christianity, and Islam, the local beliefs of the Sundanese people had existed for hundreds and perhaps thousands of years. Today the local beliefs of the communities, such as Sunda Wiwitan and Sunda Buhun, still exist. The believers regularly conduct many rituals, which can be seen as major assets for the cultural reputation of the region as well as for eco-cultural tourism.

West Java Province is the first province in Indonesia to have successfully endorsed a provincial regulation relating to intellectual property, called the Provincial Regulation of West Java Number 5 Year 2012, concerning the Protection of Intellectual Property. Based on this provincial law, the West Java provincial government has been working on a number of intangible cultural resources to gain legal recognition and protection following the success story of the Indonesian angklung, Indonesian batik, and wayang puppet theatre, which have been inscripted as Intangible Heritage of Humanity elements by UNESCO. One of these resources is masks of Sunda.

Masks of Sunda consist of many variations, including the Cirebon, the Priangan, and the Bekasi mask styles. From the traditional point of view, a mask does not only represent a piece of artistic work or handicraft. Instead, the 'mask' also represents the maker, the story or legend of the mask, the dance, the musicians of the dance repertoire, the dancers, and even the act when they altogether dance with the mask. Some Sundanese masks are regarded as sacred in accordance with the Sundanese local beliefs and the influence of Hindu and Islamic traditions over hundreds of years.

The West Java provincial government differentiates the possibility of protecting the masks as individual works associated with traditional cultural expressions, traditional knowledge, and intangible cultural heritage, as well as being communal traditional cultural expressions, traditional knowledge, or intangible cultural heritage (Intellectual Property Committee of the Tourism and Cultural Agency of West Java 2013: 1). Protecting the masks as individual works has been developed more recently, because many artists are now using the Sundanese masks as the main source of their individual creative process.

The first phase of the protection process was commenced by conducting identification, collection, verification, and documentation and by composing the collected data as a source in open databases. This process was then followed by continuous updating of the databases and by dissemination programs.

The second phase of the protection process of masks from Sunda was conducted by

1   promotion programs to enhance masks as a living culture;
2   requesting written authorisation from the Directorate General of Intellectual Property, Ministry of Law and Human Rights to declare the existence of Sundanese masks as a traditional cultural expression;
3   requesting inscription from the Ministry of Education and Culture for the masks to be regarded as national intangible cultural resources and to be included in the ministry's programs of cultural mainstreaming, integrated cultural database system, stock taking of culture, safeguarding, maintenance, and publication of culture;
4   requesting inscription from UNESCO as an intangible cultural heritage of humanity;
5   requesting the possibility to acknowledge several Sundanese masks which are used in the context of curative or cleansing methods by using natural resources to be regarded as Traditional Cultural Resources associated with Genetic Resources by the Ministry of Environment and Forestry.

Example of possible comprehensive protection for the intangible cultural resources of Sumba Island

Sumba is an island in the East Nusa Tenggara archipelago.[4] Unlike Bali, Lombok, or Sumbawa Islands, where dense forests still can be found in many parts of the islands, Sumba Island is known as an exotic place of bush and savannah. It is well suited for dry rice fields, sandalwood plantations, and livestock. The most famous livestock of Sumba are horses, apart from buffaloes, pigs, and chickens. Poets love to portray Sumba Island as 'the island of sandalwood' or 'the island of a thousand horses'.[5]

Sumba has many intangible cultural expressions. Several notable ones are its traditional megalithic architecture, Sumba woven cloth, and the Sumbanese Marapu rituals. Several *adat* villages, such as Tarung Village in Waikabubak, West Sumba, have preserved the architecture of the houses and the layout of the house positions in the village since megalithic times. According to Tracey Kissoon and John Carrier, there are three different types of settlements in Sumba: ancestral villages or the original villages of a clan, major villages which are descended from the ancestral villages, and garden villages which are the offshoot of a major village. Many Sumbanese have left their ancestral villages to get closer to work-places, and they only regularly return to their villages for important ceremonies based on their local beliefs (Miranda Risang Ayu Palar 2009: 252); Kissoon and Carrier 1991: 14).

The basic religion of the people of Tarung Village is the local belief Marapu. Its safeguarding has been enhanced by the local community itself, especially by the head of the tribe, who also acts as the spiritual leader of Marapu: Rato Rumata. The Rato of Tarung Village is still called by his people Padiewa Rato, meaning 'the Rato, the honorable man'. He was elected by the custodians of the villages and should hold the position of Rato Rumata for life.

Sumba woven textiles are not merely fine fabrics. People can enjoy and learn Sumbanese tradition, legends, and local wisdom by contemplating the mean-ing behind the ornamentation in the textiles. The technique of weaving has been passed on from generation to generation by oral tradition. Woven cloths are a necessary part of the traditional clothes to be worn during the Marapu rituals and traditional ceremonies (Alit Djajasoebrata and Linda Hanssen 1999).

In order to establish the best comprehensive safeguarding and protection for the intangible cultural resources of Sumba Island, the protection should be conducted in a systematic way, as follows:

1   registering the land and plants of *adat* territories on Sumba Island, based on the borderlines determined by their custodians, with the relevant Indonesian ministries authorised in environmental and forestry affairs;
2   safeguarding the megalithic architecture and the sites of Sumba ancestral vil-lages according to UNESCO systems to safeguard the tangible and intangible cultural heritage of mankind;
3   requesting voluntary registration for various traditional handicrafts and orna-mentation of Sumba as traditional cultural expressions, based on Law Num-ber 28 Year 2014 Concerning Copyright Article 38, and uploading them in the Directorate General of Intellectual Property official database;
4   requesting formal inscription for selected intangible cultural resources, such as megalithic architecture, woven cloths and the Marapu rituals of Sumba

with the Indonesian ministry authorised in cultural affairs, and include them in a special comprehensive programs for Sumbanese culture which consists of Marapu local wisdom cultural mainstreaming in Sumba Island, uploading the intangible cultural resources in the integrated cultural database system, conducting stock taking of the culture, safeguarding the culture, maintaining the culture, and cultural conservation as well as publications;

5   protecting Sumba woven textiles, Sumba sandalwood, and Sumba coffee as geographical indications, or at least indication of sources;

6   Requesting formal recognition from the government through the Ministry of Environment and Culture regarding the existence of Sumbanese local wisdom, the custodians of the local wisdom and their traditional rights (*ulayat* rights).

Concluding remarks

The protection for intangible cultural resources should be afforded as comprehensive protection by using a systematic protection approach. it should use all possible protections available in the general and basic laws on culture as well as in the conventional intellectual property system, such as the clauses in copyright, patents, plant variety protection, trade marks, and, importantly, in geographical indications. It should also cover all objects, expressions and elements in the domain of local wisdom, traditional knowledge, traditional cultural expressions, and intangible cultural heritage.

Notes

1   *Nagoya Protocol on Access to Genetic Resources and the Fair and Equitable Sharing of Benefits Arising from Their Utilization to the Convention on Biological Diversity*, Article 6 & 7.

2   Rato Rumata Lado Regi Tera 2015, pers. comm., 30 June.

3   Ministry of Foreign Affairs of the Republic of Indonesia 2014, 'Reports of Academic Interventions from Delegation of the Republic of Indonesia in the Informal Session of Experts on the Cross Cutting Issues, WIPO Inter-Governmental Committee on Genetic Resources, Traditional Knowledge and Folklore, XXVIII Session, June 7–9, 2014', pp. 4–5: *"The 'publicly available traditional knowledge' was not the same as Intellectual Property objects which had entered public domain. In this regard, Intellectual Property's* sui generis *protection had to secure the economic rights, the direct or indirect monetary benefits, public safety and the community moral rights for the interest of the indigenous and local communities. . . . "*

4   Miranda Risang Ayu Palar, Rika Ratna Permata, Laina Rafianti 2014–2015, *Development Strategy to Establish a Territorial Asylum to Safeguard and Protect the Intangible Cultural Resources in Indonesia*, first mid-term report of the National Strategic Research of Indonesia, Ministry of Research and Higher Education & Universitas Padjadjaran; Miranda Risang Ayu 2009, *Geographical Indications Protection in Indonesia based on Cultural Rights Approach*, the Nagara Institute, Indonesia, pp. 245–255.

5 The famous Indonesian poet Taufik Ismail wrote one of his legendary poems in 1970 titled 'Give Me Sumba', "my longing for Sumba is my longing for a thousand of horses, freely running down from the hills. . . "

References

Ayu, M. (2009) *Geographical Indications Protection in Indonesia Based on a Cultural Rights Approach*, The Nagara Institute, Indonesia, *above*, 252.

Blakeney, M (1999) *Intellectual Property in the Dreamtime - Protecting the Cultural Creativity of Indigenous People*, Oxford Intellectual Property Research Centre, 1–9.

Djajasoebrata, A. and Hanssen, L. (1999) 'Sumbanese Textiles', in *Decorative Art of Sumba*, Peppin Press, 53–135.

Gervais, D. (2003) 'Spiritual But Not Intellectual? The Protection of Sacred Intangible Traditional Knowledge', in *Traditional Knowledge, Intellectual Property and Indigenous Culture Symposium*, Cardozo Journal of International and Comparative Law, 7.

Intellectual Property Committee of the Tourism and Cultural Agency of West Java Provincial Government of the Republic of Indonesia (2013) 'Minutes of Meeting for the Protection of Masks in Priangan and Cirebon', November 14, 1.

Kissoon, T. and Carrier, J. (1991) *Sumba, a Unique Culture*, Nafisa Production, 14.

Sampath, P. (2005) *Regulating Bioprospecting: Institutions for Drug Research, Access, and Benefit-Sharing*, United Nations University Press, Tokyo, 118.

UNESCO Convention for the Safeguarding of the Intangible Cultural Heritage (2003) Adopted in Paris, October 7, 2003; effective on April 20, 2006.

UNESCO Intergovernmental Committee for the Safeguarding of Intangible Cultural Heritage (2008) Third Session, Istanbul, Turkey, November 4–8, *UNESCO Document No.ITH/08/3.COM/CONF.203/1, Annex*.

UNESCO Intergovernmental Committee for the Safeguarding of Intangible Cultural Heritage (2009) Fourth Session, Abu Dhabi, United Arab Emirates, September 28 to October 2, *Nomination for Inscription on the Representative List in 2009 (Reference No. 00170)*.

UNESCO Intergovernmental Committee for the Safeguarding of Intangible Cultural Heritage (2010) Fifth session, Nairobi, Kenya, November 15–19, UNESCO Document No. ITH/10/5.COM/CONF.202/6.

UNESCO Intergovernmental Committee for the Safeguarding of Intangible Cultural Heritage (2011) Sixth Session, Bali, Indonesia, November, *Nomination File Number 00509 for Inscription on the List of Intangible Cultural Heritage in Need of Urgent Safeguarding in 2011*.

UNESCO Intergovernmental Committee for the Safeguarding of Intangible Cultural Heritage (2012) Seventh Session, Paris, France, *Nomination File Number 00619 for Inscription on the List of Intangible Cultural Heritage in Need of Urgent Safeguarding in 2012*.

UNESCO Intergovernmental Committee for the Safeguarding of Intangible Cultural Heritage (2015) Tenth Session, Windhoek, Namibia, *Nomination file no. 00617 for Inscription on the List of Intangible Cultural Heritage of Humanity* 2015.

WIPO Intergovernmental Committee on Intellectual Property and Genetic Resources, Traditional Knowledge and Folklore (2014a) XVIII Session, Geneva, July 7–9, The Protection of Traditional Knowledge Draft Article Rev. 2 (March 28, 2014, 8;00 p.m.), WIPO Document No. WIPO/GRTKf/IC/28/5 Annex, 5.

WIPO Intergovernmental Committee on Intellectual Property and Genetic Resources, Traditional Knowledge and Folklore (2014b)'Consolidated Document relating to Intellectual Property and Genetic Resources' Rev. 2, February 7, WIPO Document No. WIPO/GRTKF/IC/28/4Annex, 1.

WIPO Inter-Governmental Committee on Genetic Resources, Traditional Knowledge and Folklore (2014c) XXVIII Session, June 7–9, 'Draft of Articles of the Protection of Traditional Knowledge', WIPO Document No. WIPO/GRTKF/IC/28/6.

World Intellectual Property Organization (1980) *Glossary of Terms of the Law of Copyrights and Neighboring Rights*, 121.

Chapter 13

Local roles in the national scheme for intangible cultural heritage protection in China

The case of Yunnan

*Jianfu Chen**

Introduction

The term 'intangible cultural heritage' (ICH), despite being a foreign term imported into China only very recently,[1] became one of the top ten 'buzz' phrases in the Chinese media in 2006 (Gao n.d.). This development is remarkable, considering that the modern history of China is essentially a history that has rejected anything that is 'old' (or 'feudal' as it is more often referred to) ever since the May 4th Movement in 1919. Lu Xun, one of the best-known modern writers and a 'flag carrier' of the 'new' cultural movement in China, famously declared in 1925,

> [o]ur chief aims at present are: first, to exist; secondly, to find food and clothing; and thirdly, to advance. Any obstacle to these aims must be trampled down, whether it is ancient or modern, human or supernatural, ancient canon, rare text, sacred oracle, precious idol, traditional recipe or secret nostrum.
>
> (Lu 1980: 140)

This 'new' cultural movement reached its peak, or perhaps more precisely its lowest point, during the 'Cultural Revolution' (1966–1976), when the so-called 'four olds' (old thoughts, old cultures, old folklores, and old customs) were to be smashed and were indeed smashed throughout China.[2] Clearly, for the 'revolutionaries' cultural heritage has been a burden or a shackle on social development, not a value to be safeguarded.

Conceptually, the legal framework on ICH protection in China today is essentially based on the 2003 UNESCO Convention for the Safeguarding of the Intangible Cultural Heritage (Hereinafter referred to as the UNESCO ICH Convention). However, neither the UNESCO ICH Convention nor a national law is sufficient for the safeguarding of ICH in a country as large and diverse as China.

In addition to its dominant Han population China also has 55 ethnic minority groups (officially referred to as 'minority nationalities' or simply 'nationalities') whose cultural heritage is rich and, in some places, dying,[3] and which is, in many cases, radically different from the dominant Han culture and little understood by the Han population. A further obstacle is that more often than not, national laws in China only lay down principles and establish structures for administration, leaving the actual implementation to administrative regulations and local rules.

In this context, if any cultural heritage has been preserved and safeguarded, it has most likely been the result of local efforts – efforts by local governments and local communities and groups (and perhaps sometimes individuals). And if any cultural heritage is to be further safeguarded, the locals are the ones who will have a genuine interest in and understanding for such protection. Addressing the role of local players in the safeguarding of ICH is therefore essential in China and no doubt in other parts of the world.

This chapter first provides an overview of the national legal and policy framework on ICH protection and its development in China, with a focus on examining the central–local relations defined therein. Although not a comprehensive analysis of the national law on Intangible Cultural Heritage (2011), the examination highlights certain specific features of the national law that have direct implications for local implementation. Thereafter local regulations in Yunnan are analysed to ascertain whether Yunnan, as a pioneer in ICH protection in China, offers any better protection under its local regulations than under the national law.

ICH protection in China: national and local

Although national efforts to protect ICH only emerged a decade or so ago,[4] legal mechanisms for such protection have gone full circle: a national initiative – local experimentation – a national legal framework – local implementation.

The earliest consideration for legal protection of ICH emerged in 1998 when several members of the Culture and Education Committee of the 9th NPC took an interest in traditional cultures and folklore among the ethnic minorities in China (Kang 2012: 332). Concerned with the lack of legislative experience in this area and facing a pressing legislative agenda on economic and commercial laws, the NPC decided that local regulations should first be tried out, and thereafter national laws might follow. For this purpose Yunnan was suggested as an ideal place to undertake the first experiment in local legislation, for Yunnan has a large number of ethnic minorities, each with a rich cultural heritage. Under the supervision of the Culture and Education Committee of the NPC, Yunnan quickly enacted the first set of local regulations in China on ICH protection, the Yunnan Regulation on the Protection of Traditional Cultures and Folklore of Ethnic Minorities.[5] The regulation was soon promoted nationwide as the 'Yunnan Experience' and was followed by many other provinces, and so began local experiments on ICH protection in post-Mao China (Kang 2012: 332–333).[6]

The lengthy process to enact a national law on ICH protection also began not long after the successful adoption of the Yunnan Regulation. Without entering into details about the drafting process, suffice it to say that it took almost 10 years to enact the law. Initially a draft proposal was prepared by the Ministry of Culture, which was quickly submitted to the Culture and Education Committee of the NPC in August 2002. The latter then promptly established a legislative draft group within the committee. In line with the Yunnan approach, this draft law was designed to protect the traditional cultures and folklore of ethnic minorities. In August 2004 China ratified the 2003 UNESCO ICH Convention, prompting a re-drafting process. However, this time it was intended to draft a law on the protection of intangible cultural heritage generally, no longer limiting it to the traditional cultures and folklore of ethnic minorities. In September 2006 the Ministry of Culture formally submitted its draft law to the State Council. From this moment on the State Council took over the drafting process and submitted its final draft to the Standing Committee of the NPC in June 2010. Apparently the processes at the NPC were smooth, since it only took just a little over eight months for the NPC to complete its discussion and deliberation at three different sessions of the Standing Committee, and the Law of the PRC on Intangible Cultural Heritage was finally adopted in February 2011.[7] Whether it is considered a landmark or not,[8] the adoption of the ICH Law signalled the end of local experimentation and the beginning of a unified national approach to the protection of ICH in China.

The national ICH Law, in six chapters and containing 45 articles, is a reasonably comprehensive law by Chinese standards. It starts with general principles and the definition of ICH, as well as methods of and approaches to ICH safeguarding. Although it has been said that Chinese law follows the ICH definition as contained in the UNESCO ICH Convention (Wu 2011: 14), there are some subtle differences between the two. The Convention defines ICH as 'the practices, representations, expressions, knowledge, skills – as well as the instruments, objects, artefacts and cultural spaces associated therewith – that communities, groups and, in some cases, individuals recognise as part of their cultural heritage' (see Article 2(1) of the UNESCO ICH Convention). Following this abstract definition, the Convention identifies certain forms of ICH.[9] The Chinese ICH Law takes the same approach by first defining ICH in an abstract form and then following it with specific examples. While the examples given by the Chinese law are rather different from those in the Convention, they can be seen as a further elaboration of the Convention's example in accordance with Chinese traditional practices.[10] In its abstract definition the Chinese law defines ICH as the cultural representations or expressions – as well as tangible materials and venues associated therewith – of the various traditions that have been transmitted from generation to generation and have been recognised as components of their cultural heritage by the various ethnic groups (Article 2 of the ICH Law). Here, the conceptual difference between the Convention and Chinese law is not the absence of such words as 'practice', 'knowledge', and 'skills' from the Chinese law, since the Chinese list of examples has clearly included them. The difference, rather, is the emphasis in the Chinese law, in that ICH here refers to the heritage of the people of the various ethnic groups rather than to communities, groups, or individuals, as under the Convention. There has been no official explanation as to why China chose to define ICH this way, but it could be a result of the initial drafting of a law focusing on the traditional cultures and folklore of ethnic minorities, as well as the early local experimentation (Kang 2012: 332–333). One of the consequences of this definition is that the Chinese ICH is mostly classified according to ethnic origins, a classification that makes the owners of ICH abstract and thus allows government intervention.

More significantly different from the Convention is the imposition of a value judgement when it comes to protection. Article 3 of the Chinese ICH Law provides that

> [t]he State will preserve ICH by way of recognition, recording, archiving and other measures; and the State will protect, by way of transmission, dissemination and other measures, the ICH that has historical, literary, artistic, and scientific value and, hence, reflects the fine traditions of the Chinese peoples.

This approach to ICH protection deviates radically from that of the UNESCO ICH Convention, as the latter makes no value judgement on any ICH and leaves the recognition of ICH largely to communities, groups or individuals. Clearly China has no intention of allowing all kinds of ICH to be transmitted or disseminated, even if they all qualify for preservation under the ICH Law. Indeed, Article 1 of the ICH Law states '[t]his Law is enacted in order to strengthen the protection or preservation of intangible cultural heritage, to transmit and disseminate the fine cultural traditions of the Chinese people, and to promote the construction of socialist spiritual civilisation.' Article 4 of the ICH Law further provides that

> [t]he protection of intangible cultural heritage shall focus on authenticity, integrity and inheritability [of the heritage], which shall also be conducive to the strengthening of a common cultural identity of the Chinese peoples, beneficial to the national integrity and unity of ethnic groups, and beneficial to the promotion of social harmony and sustainable development.

Another strong feature of the Chinese ICH Law is its heavy emphasis on the responsibilities of governments at or above county level (see Articles 6–8 of the ICH Law), although the state would supposedly encourage and support the participation of citizens, legal persons, and other organisations in the protection of ICH (Article 9 of the ICH Law). This emphasis on the role of local governments has thus effectively established a multi-layered system of national and local protection.[11]

The bulk of the law addresses the responsibilities of governments at different levels in relation to ICH surveys, national and local lists, transmission and dissemination of ICH, and legal liabilities for violation of the law. All these matters are dealt with within a central–local framework, which also stipulates financial responsibilities to be borne by local government at or above county level, with an exception being made for ethnic minority areas, border areas, and economically underdeveloped areas, where the preservation and/or protection of ICH is to be financially assisted by the national government (see Article 6 of the ICH Law).

In summary, although the Chinese ICH Law is based on and meant to implement the UNESCO ICH Convention, it has certain features that deviate from the convention and hence make local implementation particularly important. In contrast to the convention, the Chinese ICH Law clearly requires some value judgements to be made before intangible cultural heritage is to be protected. Further, the UNESCO Convention does not mention unity/integrity and authenticity, while the Chinese law emphasises these, even though no criteria are set out in the Law. Thirdly, the UNESCO Convention requires a national inventory, while Chinese law establishes lists at different levels, thus giving more room for local protection and initiatives. And finally, like in other Chinese law, the approach to ICH is top down and its emphasis is on government leadership – an approach that is potentially in conflict with local initiatives from local communities. On the other hand, however, the multi-layered central–local protection scheme has the potential for a bottom-up approach to the preservation and protection of ICH in China.

Clearly, the seemingly restrictive and uniform national ICH Law has also left sufficient room for local initiatives. The realisation and actual implementation of any local initiatives therefore depends on how local authorities address the balance between the need for a community-led movement and the requirement for control by government, and it is particularly important for local rules to ensure that ICH is protected at the local levels if it fails to pass the national value judgement.

Yunnan and ICH protection

An overview

Yunnan Province, with 25 officially recognised ethnic groups besides the Han ('Beijing told Yunnan's cultural heritage "vanishing" '), has the largest number of ethnic minorities residing in one province. Yunnan is also a border province with a long history of interaction among people from Southeast Asian nations. It is sometimes referred to as a 'living museum of cultural diversity' (He 2008: 24). It is precisely for these reasons that Yunnan was chosen for initial experimentation in ICH protection.

The Yunnan Regulation on the Protection of the Traditional Cultures and Folklore of Ethnic Minorities 2000 was the first such regulation in China and, as noted, was later promoted as the 'Yunnan Experience' nationwide ('Yunnan speeding up the legislative mechanism: Yunnan Regulation to take effect in June'). It was under this Regulation that in March 2003 the Yunnan government established a large survey team led by government departments and participated in by cultural experts. Over two and a half years, this team, involving a total of 19,103 participants, surveyed 14,834 natural villages and interviewed 69,187 persons (Xiong 2007: 20; Cai and Yang 2013). As a result a four-level protection listing of ICH was established in Yunnan.[12] This early start on ICH protection also helped Yunnan gain its prominent national recognition. In May 2006 the State Council announced the first national list of national intangible cultural heritage, with a total of 518 items, and among these 34 came from Yunnan (the largest number for a single province).[13]

After the initial experiences and successes, Yunnan provincial government decided in 2008 to revise its 2000 regulation. However, partly because of the comprehensive scope of revision and partly because of the ongoing process of enacting a national law at the time, the provincial legislature then decided to abandon the revision effort and instead started a process of drafting a new set of regulations ('Yunnan speeding up the legislative mechanism: Yunnan Regulation to take effect in June').[14] The end result was the Yunnan Regulation on the Protection of Intangible Cultural Heritage (hereinafter referred to as Yunnan ICH Regulation), adopted by the Standing Committee of the Yunnan People's Congress on 28 March 2013. The new regulation took effect on 1 June 2013, and the 2000 regulation was simultaneously repealed.

As the title of the 2013 regulation indicates, it is now a set of regulations protecting ICH in general, not just that of the ethnic minorities. The regulation also makes clear that it is enacted to implement the national ICH Law in relation to the actual circumstances of the Province (See Article 1 of the Yunnan ICH Regulation). It is worth noting, however, that unlike the national ICH Law the Yunnan Regulation retains the word 'protection' in its title and makes no distinction between 'preservation' and 'protection,' as is the case in the national ICH Law. Further, while the Yunnan Regulation contains an abstract definition of ICH which is identical to that in the national ICH Law, the specific examples given by the Yunnan Regulation are more expansive. In addition to the examples listed in the national ICH Law, the Yunnan Regulation also singles out poetry, traditional architecture, costumes, and instruments that reflect the production and life of the various ethnic groups, as well as manuscripts, scrolls, classics, inscriptions on stone, and so forth that express traditional cultures (see Article 3 of the Yunnan ICH Regulation).

Between central and local authorities

While the UNESCO ICH Convention explicitly recognises the important role of communities, groups, and, in some cases, individuals 'in the production, safeguarding, maintenance and re-creation of the intangible cultural heritage' (see the Preamble of the UNESCO ICH Convention), by its nature as an international treaty the convention is, like all other international treaties, state centred. It is unclear what role the UNESCO ICH Convention intends for local communities, groups, or individuals in the actual safeguarding of ICH other than 'participating' in such efforts.[15] Article 1, which defines the purposes of the convention, makes things even more ambiguous. Article 1 states that the purposes of this Convention are:

1   *to safeguard* the intangible cultural heritage;
2   *to ensure respect* for the intangible cultural heritage of *the communities, groups and individuals* concerned;

3   *to raise awareness* at *the local, national and international levels* of the importance of the intangible cultural heritage, and of ensuring mutual appreciation
thereof;
4   to provide for international cooperation and assistance (emphasis added).

The objectives outlined here are ambiguous for practical purposes. It is unclear
whether the convention has ever had the intention of providing protection at three
levels – local, national, and international. It is clear, however, nomination for
UNESCO listing is undertaken by states. As such, it is unclear what roles 'communities and individuals' would have in the identification and nomination for
UNESCO listing and, hence, the safeguarding of ICH at an international level
and at national and local levels if such protection is to be provided at three levels.
These issues need to be addressed by national law and local regulations.

If the UNESCO ICH Convention is state centred, the Chinese national ICH Law
then goes a step further: the law makes it clear that the preservation and protection
of ICH will be led by the governments at different levels. As noted, the Chinese
national ICH Law is principally a law defining the powers and responsibilities of
the governments at different levels and provides little in the way of formal roles
for communities and individuals other than that their participation in safeguarding ICH is encouraged and supported (Article 9 of the ICH Law).[16] Although not
stipulated in the ICH Law, the working principles are defined by the State Council
as 'dominant government leadership with social participation; clear division of
powers and responsibility with all forces working together; long-term planning
with step-by-step implementation; and undertaking individual tasks in an overall
scheme with an emphasis on breakthrough [in achievement]' (政府主导、社会
参与，明确职责、形成合力；长远规划、分步实施，点面结合、讲求突破)
(Item II of the 2005 State Council Opinions on Strengthening the Protection of
Intangible Cultural Heritage in Our Country). Under these principles the real issue
then is a question of the division of powers and responsibilities between central
and local government authorities, not one between government and communities
(and certainly not one between government and individuals).[17]

While the national ICH Law clearly has a top-down approach, with the Ministry
of Culture taking a leadership role (see Article 7 of the ICH Law), there is nevertheless the potential for a bottom-up approach to ICH preservation and protection.
Essentially the ICH Law designates the governments at the county level as the
authorities in charge of the preservation and/or protection of ICH within their
administrative jurisdiction. While the county-level government is not necessarily
the same as the community that owns the heritage, it is an authority as close to the
community as possible.[18] More importantly, other than requiring the county-level
governments to have a specific budget item for ICH work, the national ICH Law
has largely left the specific functions of local governments to be determined by
local regulations and so allows maximum flexibility in the implementation of law.

The Yunnan ICH Regulation certainly has strong potential for a bottom-up
approach. The regulation defines the specific responsibilities of the governments

at county-level and above, which include the responsibility to organise surveys, identification, recording, and the establishment of archives for ICH located in their respective jurisdictions (see Article 5 of the Yunnan ICH Regulation). The regulation also specifically establishes a four-level listing system for protection at the national, provincial, prefectural, and county levels.[19] Under this system, it is the lower-level authority that recommends items to be included in a list at a higher level (see Article 8 of the Yunnan ICH Regulation). This arrangement means that initiatives for ICH protection are first to be undertaken at the county level, and such initiatives are to be first examined by an expert committee organised by the relevant county government. Though not strictly community led, this is as close to the community as is possible in light of the requirement for a dominating role for government leadership under the national law and policies.

Values and value judgement

The principal objectives of the UNESCO Convention are stated to be to safeguard and to ensure respect for intangible cultural heritage and to raise awareness in the communities of the importance of the intangible cultural heritage (see Article 1 of the UNESCO ICH Convention). To achieve these objectives, the convention avoids imposing any value judgement on intangible cultural heritage and insists that 'consideration will be given solely to such intangible cultural heritage as is compatible with existing international human rights instruments, as well as with the requirement of mutual respect among communities, groups and individuals, and of sustainable development' (see Article 2 of the UNESCO ICH Convention). Clearly, if the application of the Convention involves any value judgement it could only be a judgement based on notions of international human rights, community respect, and sustainable development, notions that have now been addressed by international treaties.

In a socialist country like China there is hardly any law that is free of value judgement. And with a history of almost a century of fighting against 'old' cultures it would be difficult for China to protect all forms of cultural heritage, some of which are clearly seen by Chinese and foreigners alike as 'bad habits,' such as foot binding. Not surprisingly, therefore, there was, during the drafting of the ICH Law, serious debate as to whether the national law should only protect cultural 'gems' (*jinghua*) (in contrast to cultural 'scum' or *caobo*) or 'positive' cultural heritage (Kang 2012: 341). The difficulty in practice for such an arrangement is clear – against what criteria are such value judgements to be made? As is so common in Chinese law making, a compromise was reached that ICH would either be safeguarded or preserved, depending on the nature and value of the cultural heritage concerned (see Article 3 of the ICH Law).[20] In this distinction preservation does not involve transmission and dissemination, but by implication safeguarding implies preservation as well (see Article 3 of the ICH Law).

However, the national ICH Law does not provide any criteria for the determination of the nature or value of an ICH item; Article 3 simply states that any ICH that has historical, literary, artistic, and scientific value and hence reflects the fine traditions of the Chinese peoples will be safeguarded by way of transmission, dissemination, and other measures. The problem is, however, that none of these 'criteria' seems to be specific enough for an objective assessment.

Article 1 of the Yunnan ICH Regulation essentially repeats Article 1 of the national ICH Law, stating that 'the Regulation is enacted in order to strengthen the protection of intangible cultural heritage, to transmit and disseminate the fine cultural traditions of the various ethnic groups, and to promote the construction of socialist spiritual civilisation.' However, the Yunnan Regulation does not make a distinction between preservation and protection and, as a result, does not impose a requirement for any value judgement other than upholding the rhetoric of promoting 'fine traditions' and 'socialist spiritual civilisation'. Theoretically the national ICH Law applies nationwide, and Yunnan should be no exception. In practice, however, county governments, the initial authorities to identify, nominate, and safeguard ICH, are more likely to follow the Yunnan Regulation closely than the national Law.

The absence of a direct requirement on any value judgement in the Yunnan Regulation could, however, also serve as a double-edged sword in view of the lack of expertise in the administration of ICH. It is no secret that there is a serious shortage of professional researchers and experts who are capable of fulfilling the ICH programs at both national and local levels (Liu 2010). The role of scholarly expertise is generally neglected, leaving government officials with little precise knowledge for making judgments about complex cultural phenomena (for detailed discussions, see McLaren 2010), so that they rely mainly on political judgement or economic utility. Further, local governments are often unduly influenced by powerful lobbyists and local interests (McLaren 2010), leading to a situation where governments develop intangible cultural heritage mainly for economic purposes rather than for the safeguarding or preservation of the ICH itself (Tan 2008: 86). This is particularly so where there are only very limited human and financial resources available, prompting governments to identify ICH items from a local economic perspective, thus undermining the official goal of protecting and transmitting ICH (Liu 2010).

Authenticity and integrity

The intangible cultural heritage identified under the UNESCO ICH Convention is one that is transmitted from generation to generation and 'is constantly recreated by communities and groups in response to their environment, their interaction with nature and their history, and provides them with a sense of identity and continuity, thus promoting respect for cultural diversity and human creativity.' This means that ICH can change (or be recreated) from time to time.

Chinese law, as noted, holds that

> [t]he protection of intangible cultural heritage shall focus on authenticity, integrity and inheritability [of the heritage], which shall also be conducive

to the strengthening of a common cultural identity of the Chinese peoples, beneficial to national integrity and the unity of ethnic groups, and beneficial to the promotion of social harmony and sustainable development.'

(see Article 4 of the Chinese ICH Law)

The requirement for a protected ICH item to be authentic, integral, and inheritable is also imposed by local regulations (see e.g. Article 4 of the Yunnan ICH Regulation). The last element is self-explanatory, and the second element means that the whole of an ICH item, in both its form and contents, shall be protected, rather than merely selected aspects, so as to prevent the misuse or degrading use of an ICH item (see Article 5 of the ICH Law and Article 4 of the Yunnan ICH Regulation). However, it is rather controversial as to whether an item must be 'authentic' to qualify as an ICH item (Kang 2012: 316).

Chinese scholars tend to treat an ICH item as a 'living fossil,' which implies that the nature and substance of an ICH item is fixed. With this understanding it is not surprising that such scholars also insist that an ICH item must be 'authentic' (Kang 2012: 316–317). However, neither Chinese scholars nor Chinese laws have explained the meaning of 'authenticity' or have provided any criteria for determining the 'authenticity' of an ICH item (Kang 2012: 317).

According to one authority on ICH protection in China, 'authenticity' is a notion directly adopted by the Chinese government and scholars from 'heritage' studies[21] into ICH studies, without any critical consideration (Kang 2012: 318–320). Even in 'heritage' studies, the notion of 'authenticity' does not have a fixed meaning but is one which incorporates and accommodates possibilities of change, especially when the notion is applied in the Asian context under the Nara Document on Authenticity (1994) (Kang 2012: 318–319). In other words, according to Kang, the Chinese central government and those in charge of ICH protection in China failed to understand the true meaning of 'authenticity' in 'heritage' studies when a rigid and 'dogmatic' notion was introduced into ICH law and policies, as well as into ICH studies (Kang 2012: 320–321). Kang insists that the ICH items that are recognised and listed on the official ICH Lists should not be seen as the only 'authentic' items (Kang 2012: 321).

The national ICH Law's requirement on authenticity, integrity, and inheritability is also adopted by the Yunnan ICH Regulation (see Article 4 of the Yunnan ICH Regulation). Again as in the national law, no criteria for such determination are provided by the Regulation. It seems that if the national ICH Law has blindly adopted a notion not strictly appropriate for ICH protection, the Yunnan Regulation has done the same. It can only be hoped that the requirement by the regulation to respect the customs and practices of all nationalities and ethnic groups in ICH protection work will ensure that the questions of 'authenticity' will be determined by the people concerned rather than by governments, which are often pre-occupied with economic development, social stability, and ethnic unity (on Respecting customs and practice, see Articles 6 & 27 of Yunnan ICH Regulation).

Between the Han majority and ethnic minorities

One of the fundamental principles in the preservation and protection of ICH in China is that such efforts must 'support the common cultural identity of the Chinese nation, the unity of the state and the solidarity of all nationalities, and the promotion of social harmony and sustainable development' (Article 4 of the ICH Law; Kang 2012: 343). Missing from Article 4 of the Law is a reference to cultural diversity and the importance of it. Thus, on the face of it, Chinese law on ICH does not seem to be particularly conducive to acknowledging the variety of the ICH of the different ethnic minorities.

However, the actual practice is much less Han centric, if only for economic purposes.[22] As noted, both Yunnan and national legislation on ICH started with a focus on protecting the ICH of ethnic minorities. Thus a 2005 Notice of the State Council specifically requires that special attention be given to the protection of ICH in areas where ethnic minorities reside,[23] even though such special attention is perhaps a response to the rapid 'disappearance' of ICH in these areas as noted by the notice (Para. 3 of Item 1 of the Notice). Article 6 (2) of the national ICH Law also singles out minority areas for special state financial support in ICH protection. On the basis of these legal and policy arrangements, some Chinese scholars assert that a relatively independent legal status of the ICH of ethnic minorities has been established under Chinese law.

National lists	Total ICH items	Those from ethnic groups	Percentage
First list (2006)	518	165	31.9%
Second list (2008)	510	248	48.6%
Third list (2011)	191	79	41.2%

(see Han & Sherab n.d.)

National practices seem to suggest that special attention has indeed been given to the protection of the ICH of ethnic groups. The percentage of ICH items from ethnic groups in the national ICH lists indicates both the rich cultural heritage of the ethnic minorities and the special priority being given to their protection (see Han & Sherab n.d.).

Some 25% of the national funds for ICH protection between 2002 and 2009 were spent in areas of ethnic minorities (see Han & Sherab n.d.). Additionally, most minority autonomous regions have special regulations on ICH protection (see Han & Sherab n.d.).

If the Chinese ICH Law has not explicitly made the ICH of ethnic minorities as having a relatively independent status in national law, the emphasis on this relative status under Yunnan Regulation is strong and clear.[24] As noted earlier, the Yunnan Regulation specifically adds traditional architecture, costumes, and instruments that reflect the production and life of the various ethnic groups to the definition of ICH (see Article 3 of the Yunnan ICH Regulation). The regulation specifically requires that the customs of the various ethnic groups must be respected. Perhaps most importantly, for practical purposes there is a mechanism to declare and establish Traditional Cultural and Ecological Zones of Ethnic Minorities, variously named as Ethnic Minority Traditional Cultural Protection Zones, Traditional Cultural Villages, Ethnic Folk Art Villages, Ethnic Ecological Museums, and so forth. These are comprehensive protection zones established under Chapter 4 of the Yunnan ICH Regulation.[25] They are established by local governments at county level, and their establishment is required to respect the will of the local people (Article 27 of Yunnan ICH Regulation). Once approved for establishment, they also receive preferential policy treatment and financial support by local governments and governments at a higher level (Article 27 of Yunnan ICH Regulation). Within the zones city planning must take ICH as its focus, and comprehensive protection measures must be established (Article 28 of the Yunnan ICH Regulation). There is of course no doubt that tourism development is an integral consideration for such establishment.[26] This is however not necessarily a bad thing, as tourism generates much-needed funds for ICH preservation and protection. The real question is the matter of balance between economic development and ICH protection.

Concluding remarks

Chinese national laws contain mostly general principles; few contain actual practical mechanisms or clear legal provisions capable of implementation. The usual practice is for the State Council to issue implementing regulations. As to the national ICH Law, there has been no indication that the State Council will be issuing such a set of implementing regulations. This effectively means that the Yunnan ICH Regulation is functioning as implementing rules for the national ICH Law.

On the whole the Yunnan Regulation does have the potential to overcome some of the problems found in the national ICH Law. This is particularly so in relation to the top-down, government-dominated process that also involves a value judgement. While government support is critical for ICH protection in China, active community involvement, especially in places like Yunnan where there are many people of ethnic minorities, must be said to be no less important. In this regard, the Yunnan Regulation has a much stronger mechanism than the national law.

While it has to be acknowledged that the genuine intention to protect ICH in China in general and in Yunnan in particular is not to be questioned,[27] the actual situation both in Yunnan and in China more generally is not a promising one. Fundamentally, the most serious threat to ICH protection comes from economic development, commercialisation, and, more recently, urbanisation. These problems are described in terms of 'constructive damage' and 'protective damage' (Cai and Yang 2013). The former refers to damage caused by urbanisation, urban migration, and even poverty-reduction projects, and the latter refers to commercial utilisation of ICH items once they are listed for protection. Both have caused some serious damage to or even the complete destruction of many ICH items (Cai and Yang 2013). Some have gone as far as to describe the damage as 'worse than [that caused by] the Cultural Revolution' (Johnson 2012). Others have asserted that ICH (in Yunnan) is 'vanishing' (see 'Beijing told Yunnan's cultural heritage "vanishing" ').

On the other hand, it should be acknowledged that commercialisation could also lead to the realisation of the value of ICH among the local people, and hence to local efforts and incentives to preserve and protect their own heritage. The bottom line remains: where the balance is and who decides on and who benefits from the commercialisation or utilisation of ICH. There are no easy answers to these questions, but, based on the efforts made so far in China, there are reasons to believe that ICH preservation and protection may not continue to be weakened any further if its protection is not strengthened in the future, particularly now that the Chinese government sees ICH as a 'soft power' (in contrast to 'hard powers – economic and military powers) in international politics and competition (see Kang 2012: 328–329).

Notes

* The author thanks Dr Enshen Li and Dr Difan Qu for their research assistance in the initial literature review. The views and errors herein are, however, those of the author.
1 It is said that the term is Japanese in origin and came to China in 2003 when the UNESCO Convention for the Safeguarding of the Intangible Cultural Heritage was adopted (see Johnson 2012; Kang 2012: 334).
2 See a partial but very depressing list of well-known cultural relics and heritage destroyed during the 'Cultural Revolution', see Ding (undated). For an academic analysis, see Gao (undated).
3 This is not to say that cultural heritage of the Han people is better protected in China.
4 In March 2005, the State Council issued its Opinions on Strengthening the Protection of Intangible Cultural Heritage in Our Country. These opinions are often seen as the initial national efforts (including the establishment of two practical mechanisms: the application and appraisal of national masterpieces of ICH and joint ministerial meetings for ICH protection) in post-Mao China to work out specific principles and mechanisms for ICH protection (see Kang 2012: 330). Thereafter, other national measures followed, including the State Council Notice on Strengthening the Protection of Cultural Heritage (2005); Temporary Measures on the Protection and Management of National Masterpieces of Intangible Culture Heritage (Ministry of Culture, 2006); the Provisional Measures on Management of Special Funds for National Intangible Cultural Heritage (Ministry of Culture and the Ministry of Finance, 2006); Notice on Improving the Protection of Intangible Cultural Heritage of Time-honoured Brands (Ministry of Commerce and the Ministry of Culture, 2007); and Management Measures on Marks of Chinese Intangible Cultural Heritage (Ministry of Culture, 2007).
5 The regulation was adopted by the 16th Meeting of the Standing Committee of the 9th People's Congress of Yunnan Province on 26 June 2000.
6 In addition to the Yunnan Regulation, major local regulations include Guizhou Regulation on the Protection of Traditional Cultures and Folklore of Ethnic Minorities (2003); the Fujian Regulation on the Protection of Traditional Cultures and Folklore of Ethnic

Minorities (2005); the Guangxi Regulation on the Protection of Traditional Cultures and Folklore of Ethnic Minorities (2006); the Regulation on the Protection of the Intangible Cultural Heritage of Hui Nationality Autonomous Region of Ningxia (2006); the Regulation on the Protection of the Intangible Cultural Heritage of Zhejiang Province (2007); and the Regulation on the Protection of the Intangible Cultural Heritage of Uighur Nationality Autonomous Region of Xinjiang (2008). Upon the promulgation of the national ICH Law in 2011, many of these regulations have now been replaced by local implementation rules for the national Law, such as the Regulation on the Protection of the Intangible Cultural Heritage of Yunnan Province (2013); and the Regulation on the Protection of the Intangible Cultural Heritage of Jiangsu Province (2013).

7   It is worth noting however that the word 'protection' was dropped at the stage of deliberation for adoption by the Standing Committee of NPC, and this will have some implications for the protection of intangible cultural heritage in China, which is further discussed in what follows. For further discussions on the drafting process, see Kang 2012: 332–333. The Law of the PRC on Intangible Cultural Heritage is hereinafter referred to as the (national) ICH Law.

8   The law is described by some Chinese scholars and officials as an 'extraordinary landmark' in ICH protection in China (see Kang 2012: 333; 'The ICH Law is a Landmark'; and Li 2011: 285).

9   These include oral traditions and expressions, performing arts, social practices, rituals and festive events, knowledge and practices concerning nature and the universe, and traditional craftsmanship. See Article 2(2) of the UNESCO ICH Convention.

10 Chinese Law lists the following: traditional oral literature and its language medium; traditional art, calligraphy, music, dance, drama, folk art, and acrobatics; traditional skills, medicine and calendar; traditional rituals, festivals and customs; traditional sports and games; and other forms of intangible cultural heritage (see Article 2 of the ICH Law).

11 Although the ICH Law only refers to national- and provincial-level lists of ICH, Article 43 allows the provincial governments to issue local rules for the establishment of local lists of ICH. In reality, a four-level scheme in China has been established: national, provincial, prefectural, and county levels.

12 Initially, 5,416 items of ICH were listed at the county level (announced in June 2005), 373 items at the prefectural level (announced September 2005), and 147 items at the provincial level (announced in May 2006) (Cai & Yang 2013). These lists then were expanded rather quickly. By September 2012, 8,590 items were listed at the various levels in Yunnan (See Zhou 2012).

13 By the time the third National List was published in 2011, Yunnan had 84 items included on the National List (based on my own calculation of national lists).

14 For a detailed explanation on the drafting process and objectives of the new Regulation, see Zhou 2012.

15 See Articles 11 (b) and 15 of the UNESCO ICH Convention, both of which refer to 'participation (or widest possible participation) of communities, groups and individuals'.

16 As such, Chinese scholars define the ICH Law as a piece of administrative law that defines government powers and their exercise (see Kang 2012: 336).

17 In fact, part of the State Council working principles is stipulated in the Yunnan ICH Regulation (see Article 4 of the Yunnan ICH Regulation).

18 Although in the Chinese bureaucratic hierarchy there are still lower-level governments, that is, the township and village governments, these lower-level governments simply have no financial resources to undertake any such projects as ICH preservation and protection.

19 The national ICH Law refers to only a two-level listing system (national and provincial), but the ambiguous language would allow lower-level lists as well, as indeed is the case in all provinces in China (see Article 18 of the ICH Law).

20 It is for this reason that the word 'protection' was dropped from the title of the law (see discussions in Kang 2012: 340–342).
21 Principally about the restoration of monuments and sites under the International Charter for the Conservation and Restoration of Monuments and Sites, 1964 (see Kang 2012: 318).
22 It is no secret that increasingly Chinese governments have discovered that special cultural features of ethnic minorities have a strong pulling power for tourism in China. Indeed, Article 37 specifically encourages the 'reasonable' utilisation of ICH to develop cultural products and cultural services that have the local and special features of ethnic minorities.
23 See Item 4(5) of Notice of the State Council on Strengthening the Protection of Cultural Heritage, *Guofa* (2005) No. 42, issued by the State Council on 22 December 2005.
24 According to the *People's Daily*, the strongest feature of the Yunnan ICH Regulation is its emphasis on the protection and transmission of the ICH of ethnic minorities (see 'Yunnan speeding up the legislative mechanism: Yunnan Regulation to take effect in June').
25 As of November 2013, 56 minority villages and towns had been declared by the provincial government as Ethnic Minority Cultural and Ecological Protection Zones (see 'Yunnan has its own experiences in ICH protection')
26 See Article 29 of the Yunnan ICH Regulation, which specifically encourages the development of tourism and other cultural projects.
27 On China's efforts on ICH preservation and protection, see the Annual Development Report on Chinese Intangible Cultural Heritage Safeguarding (*Zhongguo Fei Wuzhi Wenhua Yichange Baohu Fazhang Baogao*), published by the ICH Research Centre at Zhongshan (Sun Yatsen) University. On Yunnan efforts, see Cai and Yang 2013; Huang 2009; Xiong (n.d.); and 'A Record of the Protection of Ethnic ICH in Yunnan.'

References

A Record of the Protection of Ethnic ICH in Yunnan. Available: www.ihchina.cn/inc/detail. jsp?info_id=2239 (last accessed 7 May 2014).
Beijing Told Yunnan's Cultural Heritage "Vanishing". Available: www.gokunming.com/en/blog/item/3176/beijing_told_yunnans_cultural_heritage_vanishing (last accessed 10 April 2014).
Cai, Y. and Yang, J. (2013) *A Study on the Protection and Utilisation of Intangible Cultural Heritage in Yunnan.* Available: http://blog.sina.com.cn/s/blog_535f0a1801017zy4.html (last accessed 27 August 2014).
Ding, Y. *How Many Cultural Relics Were Burned? A Short Record of the Smashing of the "Four Olds" in 1966.* Available: www.edubridge.com/erxiantang/l2/posijiu.htm (last accessed 1 November 2013).
Gao, B. *The Protection of Intangible Cultural Heritage in China and the Termination of Cultural Revolutions.* Available: www.ihchina.cn/inc/detail.jsp?info_id=4298 (accessed 7 May 2014).
Han, X. and Sherab, N. *Legal Characteristics of China's Protection of Ethnic Intangible Cultural Heritage.* Available: www.ihchina.cn/inc/detail.jsp?info_id=4252 (last accessed 7 May 14).
He, Y. (2008/09) 'Characteristics of and Protection Strategies for Intangible Cultural Heritage of Ethnic Groups in Yunnan', *Journal of Yunnan Nationalities University* (*Yunnan Minzhu Daxue Xuebao*), 216, 24.
Huang, Q. (2009) 'A Report on the Protection and Utilisation of ICH in Our Province', delivered at the Standing Committee of the Yunnan People's Congress, July 28.

Available: www.360doc.com/content/12/0319/16/4891348_195683932.shtml (last accessed 27 August 2014).

'The ICH Law is a Landmark', National People's Congress, 28 February 2011. Available: www.npc.gov.cn/huiyi/cwh/1119/2011-02/28/content_1627361.htm (accessed 19 August 2014).

Johnson, I. *"Worse Than the Cultural Revolution": An Interview with Tian Qing.* Available: www.nybooks.com/blogs/nyrblog/2012/apr/07/worse-cultural-revolution-interview-tian-qing/ (last accessed 10 April 2014).

Kang, B. (ed.) (2012) *Annual Report on the Development of the Protection of China's Intangible Cultural Heritage (2012) (Zhongguo Fei Wuzhi Wenhua Yichange Baohu Fazhang Baogao 2012)*, Beijing: Social Sciences Academic Press (China).

Li, L. (2011) 'Extraordinary Landmark in the Protection of Intangible Cultural Heritage of China', *Queen Mary Journal of Intellectual Property*, 1(3), 285.

Liu, K. (2010) 'Several Issues on Protecting Intangible Cultural Heritage in China', a special seminar delivered at the Standing Committee of the National People's Congress, September 3. Available: www.npc.gov.cn/npc/xinwen/2010-09/03/content_1594663.htm (last accessed 29 December 13).

Lu, X. (1980) 'Sudden Notions (6)', in Y. Xianyi and G. Yang (trans.), *Lu Xun Selected Works*, Beijing: Foreign Languages Press, vol. 2, 140.

McLaren, A. (2010) 'Revitalisation of the Folk Epics of the Lower Yangzi Delta: An Example of China's Intangible Cultural Heritage', *International Journal of Intangible Heritage*, 5, 34.

Tan, H. (2008) 'The Existing Problems and Solutions of the Development of Economic Value of Intangible cultural Heritage in China', *Theoretical Discussion (Lilun Tantai)*, 2, 84.

Wu, B. (2011) 'Two Suggestions on Implementing the Intangible Culture Heritage Law', *Northwestern Journal of Ethnology (Xibei Minzhu Yanjiu)*, 2, 14.

Xiong, Z. (2007) 'The Practice of and Thoughts on Yunnan Intangible Cultural Heritage Protection', *Studies in Minority Arts (Minzhu Yishu Yanjiu)*, No. 2, 20.

Xiong, Z. *The Journal to the Protection of ICH in Yunnan.* Available: www.ihchina.cn/inc/detail.jsp?info_id=2086 (last accessed 7 May 2014).

'Yunnan Has Its Own Experiences in ICH Protection', November 21. Available: www.1698.cc/coucent_page.aspx?id=102070 (last accessed 10 April 2014).

'Yunnan Speeding up the legislative mechanism: Yunnan Regulation to take effect in June', *People's Website*, May 23. Available: www.mzb.com.cn/html/Home/node/405032-1.htm (last accessed 10 April 2014).

Zhou, Y. 'Explanations on the Draft Yunnan Regulation on the Protection of Intangible Cultural Heritage', delivered at the 34th Meeting of the 11th Yunnan People's Congress' Standing Committee, September 26. Available: www.srd.yn.gov.cn/ynrd-cwh/10130295492832133112/20130828/249414.html (27 August 2014).

Index